Undead in the West

Vampires, Zombies, Mummies, and
Ghosts on the Cinematic Frontier

Edited by
Cynthia J. Miller and
A. Bowdoin Van Riper

THE SCARECROW PRESS, INC.
Lanham • Toronto • Plymouth, UK
2012

Published by Scarecrow Press, Inc.
A wholly owned subsidiary of The Rowman & Littlefield Publishing Group, Inc.
4501 Forbes Boulevard, Suite 200, Lanham, Maryland 20706
www.rowman.com

10 Thornbury Road, Plymouth PL6 7PP, United Kingdom

British Library Cataloguing in Publication Information Available

Library of Congress Cataloging-in-Publication Data

Undead in the West : vampires, zombies, mummies, and ghosts on the cinematic frontier / edited by Cynthia J. Miller and A. Bowdoin Van Riper.
    p. cm.
  Includes bibliographical references.
  ISBN 978-0-8108-8544-8 (cloth : alk. paper) — ISBN 978-0-8108-8545-5 (ebook)
  1. Western films—United States. 2. Horror films—United States. 3. Western television programs—United States. 4. Horror television programs—United States. 5. Television programs—Social aspects—United States. 6. Popular culture—United States. I. Miller, Cynthia J., 1958- II. Van Riper, A. Bowdoin.
  PN1995.9.W4U53 2012
  791.43'6278—dc23   2012016352

∞™ The paper used in this publication meets the minimum requirements of American National Standard for Information Sciences—Permanence of Paper for Printed Library Materials, ANSI/NISO Z39.48-1992.

Printed in the United States of America

In honor of the

Gun-toting preachers
Cursed townspeople
Mystical medicine men
Unrepentant outlaws
and Pale riders

that brought the cinematic frontier to life.

Spirits of the West, all.

Contents

Acknowledgments

This collection owes its existence to the efforts and good will of many individuals, from colleagues whose work provided inspiration and encouragement to loved ones who graciously accepted less than our full attention and offered words of support during long days spent conquering the undead. To all of them, we give our thanks. Additionally, thanks to our seventeen fine contributors for their energy, scholarship, and creativity.

We would also like to extend a special "thank you" to John C. Tibbetts for his untiring work on our behalf, and to Helen Lewis, for providing us with the opportunity to begin thinking and talking about *Undead in the West* during the 2010 Popular Culture Association conference. Our thanks, also, to Peter Stanfield, Sari Stewart, and Scott Charles Stewart, Deborah Miller, Joey DePaolo, Billy Drago, Brendan Wayne, and Joe R. Lansdale for lending their help, thoughts, and inspiration to the project. A final thank-you goes to Stephen Ryan for his support, patience, and unfailing good humor.

Introduction

Cynthia J. Miller and A. Bowdoin Van Riper

The Western frontier—those "wide, open spaces" where civilization and savagery meet—often serves as the focal point for traditional national identity.[1] Brimming over with social and cultural meaning, the American West serves not only as the country's heartland but also as a setting for morality tales, a proving ground for mainstream values and ideals, and a point of encounter between order and chaos, progress and ruin, humanity and the "wild." From the silent era to the present, cinematic representations of the West have portrayed these multiple and intersecting roles in increasingly complex ways, and the portrayals have been complicated further still by the presence of the undead—entities that terrify the living and exist in tension with many of the traditional meanings and functions of the West, challenging the very forces and ideals that gave it form. At first glance, the undead present vicious, repugnant threats to humanity, terrorizing good and evil alike; on closer examination, however, their existence in the West, in relentless pursuit of the living, calls into question basic assumptions regarding the nature of humanity, the power of the moral order, and long-cherished notions of national identity.

While the undead first began to menace the West in the late 1950s, with Edward Dein's *Curse of the Undead* (1959), they did not truly begin to proliferate until the close of the twentieth century. Robert Rodriguez's *From Dusk Till Dawn* (1996) and John Carpenter's *Vampires* (1998) laid the groundwork for the undead's twenty-first-century invasion of the frontier. In the years that followed, films such as *Bubba Ho-Tep* (2002), *Western Zombie* (2006), *7 Mummies* (2006), *The Quick and the Undead* (2006), *Dead Noon* (2007), *Dead Walkers*

(2009), and *Devil's Crossing* (2011) created a convergence of twenty-first-century moral panics, situated in the heartland, in order to critique and comment on the Western tradition and the norms and values it promotes and maintains.

This careful positioning of the undead in the West is no accident. Technology, industry, and infrastructure are all absent, permitting the undead to attack humanity in one of its most elemental regions, at a time when rapid social change has called all fundamental elements of existence into question. The vampires, zombies, mummies, and ghosts of undead Westerns make our inner demons and social plagues visible, and they lay siege to a frontier tied to myths of freedom, independence, strength, and ingenuity that serve as building blocks of our identities, both individual and collective.

Putting the "Wild" Back in the West

The frontier, or more accurately the process by which it was conquered, is seen as one of the defining elements in American national identity—the catalyst and proving ground for the courage, individuality, and dynamism of the American character—the "dominant individualism" that Frederick Jackson Turner saw as a hallmark of that character.[2] The frontier was, for many, the "wellspring of the independent, indomitable American spirit."[3] It was the land of Manifest Destiny—of conquest—and the farmers, ranchers, schoolmarms, saloon girls, entrepreneurs, and adventurers who settled the West represented a progressive force that carried the beacon of change to the wilderness that existed, only temporarily, beyond civilization's reach.

Beginning with the silent film *The Great Train Robbery* (1903), Western films became a mainstay of entertainment in the United States and flourished for decades, achieving their Golden Age from the 1930s to the 1950s.[4] Classic Western films, with titles like *Rough Riders' Round-up* (1939), *Pals of the Silver Sage* (1940), and *Don't Fence Me In* (1945), were brought to life by characters that reinforced social norms, mainstream values, and conventional gender roles of the times.[5] These traditional Westerns emphasized the establishment of law and order and presented an essential and ritualistic conflict between civilization and savagery, with plot elements that were constructed into various oppositions—East versus West; light versus dark; social order versus anarchy; community versus individual; town versus wilderness; cowboy versus Indian; schoolmarm versus dancehall girl—and were manifested externally, in the landscape, and internally in the community.[6] The boundaries that existed between these positive and negative poles were clearly signposted for all to see, with symbolic markers displayed in characters' dress, speech, and morals. Heroes and villains played out familiar roles, according to well-established rules of engagement, and transgressions—of the laws of man or nature—were ultimately answered by similarly well-established consequences.

Heroes of the traditional West have long been recognized as guardians of civilization—positioned with one foot in the "wild" and one foot in the civilized world—bearing the responsibility for maintaining the boundaries between order and chaos, civilization and barbarism. Agents of right and reason, Western heroes balanced frontier independence with concern for the common good, and they tempered the need for violence with a mandate for restraint. They were champions of the moral order and icons of national identity, playing a leading role in not only the taming of the West but also in expanding and extending mainstream American values and lifeways across borders, boundaries, and ideologies. Gunslingers, cattle rustlers, warriors, and *bandidos* all ultimately succumbed to the hero's campaigns on behalf of bringing the frontier and its inhabitants under the control of civilized law.

In the late 1960s, a revisionist trend began to shape the genre, bringing a dark realism to the cinematic West. These revisionist Westerns, such as *The Wild Bunch* (1969) and *McCabe & Mrs. Miller* (1971) called the genre's taken-for-granted binary oppositions into question by challenging the use of violence, complicating interpersonal and intergroup relationships, providing a more sympathetic treatment of Native Americans and Mexicans, and creating disaffected heroes—"saviors" who battled their own demons and struggled against crises of conscience, checkered pasts, and resistance to civil authority's unreflexive notions of right and wrong. The relevance of the classic Western's uncomplicated moral messages also came into question, and from the revisionist era forward, frontier men on both sides of the moral divide evidenced a stronger identification with "the wild" than their more "civilized" counterparts, making them troubled embodiments of a vanishing way of life.

Frontier life, however, had begun to vanish much earlier. The first Westerns depicted a world that was already rapidly fading into myth and legend. The films that appeared in the Golden Age of Western films sustained and embellished those myths and, after the Golden Age itself faded, the new generation of revisionist Westerns reinterpreted them for a new era—they more cynical and less certain. Decades of dormancy followed, but the genre has been revitalized in the late twentieth and early twenty-first centuries as mainstream America has increasingly sought certainty in tradition. Through contemporary uses, appropriations, and adaptations of well-known icons, symbols, and tropes of the classic Western, its moral, ethical, and philosophical messages and meanings continue. Those messages and meanings take on new significance, however, as the undead put the "wild" back in the Wild West—gunslingers walk out of hell to once again besiege dusty towns; Native Americans rise from the grave to right ancient wrongs; vampires, mummies, and zombies ensure that human sins are, in fact, deadly; and ghostly cowboys guide the living from atop fire-breathing steeds. Often, the presence of the undead on the cinematic frontier creates a lens that allows tales with narrative roots in the nineteenth century to speak to and shed light on the complexities of the modern era.

The Code of the West

Beneath the protean surface of the Western lies an enduring core—a code—an unwritten doctrine that staked out moral guideposts for settlers, wanderers, and gunslingers alike, demanding courage, fair play, loyalty, respect, and honor. The Code of the West, as it came to be known, marked the boundaries of right and wrong, civilized and wild, and good and evil, and it safeguarded the frontier from chaos and abandon.

First chronicled by Western writer Zane Grey in his 1934 novel *Code of the West*, the Code has been handed down and adapted throughout popular culture for over three-quarters of a century, in the codes and creeds of cowboy philosophers and Western heroes such as Gene Autry, Hopalong Cassidy, Roy Rogers, Wild Bill Hickok, and the Texas Rangers. In 1969, cowboy historian Ramon F. Adams elaborated on the Code and its functions for individuals and the community in *The Cowman & His Code of Ethics* (1969), observing that:

> Though the cowman might break every law of the territory, state and federal government, he took pride in upholding his own unwritten code. His failure to abide by it did not bring formal punishment, but the man who broke it became, more or less, a social outcast . . . subject to the punishment of the very code he had broken.[7]

Even though the frontier has vanished, the Code persists as the defining ideology of the American West—with twenty-first-century lawmen in states such as Wyoming and Montana lobbying to adopt it as their state's official code of ethics.[8] The social and moral force of the Code thus continues in an era of compound film genres and hybrids, where it is simultaneously reinforced and violated by the undead, as they invade the cinematic West.

The rotting flesh and unsettled spirits of the undead are both products and embodiments of earthly transgressions; their presence and predations violate the laws of nature, mock the laws of man, and scorn the Code of the West. An increasingly broad range of scholarly work has focused on undead critiques of consumerism, capitalism, religion, racism, nationalism, and other contemporary ideological concerns in relation to the frontier, but it is the Cowboy Code and the traditional dualism of good and evil—the moral foundation of the heartland—that are the focus of the undead threat.[9] Unlike the characters of revisionist Westerns, who simply challenge and interrogate the Code and its assumptions, the living dead render them obsolete. There is no fair play, no honorable death, in the West of the undead—only cannibalism, evisceration, and mutation. Whether lying in wait, like the denizens of the borderlands bars in From Dusk Till Dawn and 7 Mummies, or laying siege, like the shambling masses in It Came from the West (2007) and Dead Walkers, the undead defile the living in intimate, yet impersonal ways. They even threaten—in the nightmare world of the postapocalyptic Western Priest (2011)—to dissolve the very fabric of what remains of civilization, reducing all human activity into the mindless pursuit of the most basic animal needs. Their presence thus engenders chaos and moral panic, as lawmen and outlaws alike find the framework of their shared existence rent apart and scattered in the dirt.

At the same time, the relevance of that shared framework is also underscored by the undead, as traditional heroes and villains become unlikely partners in the battle against these entities that defy death. Ranging from the calculating vampire figures in films such as Curse of the Undead, Billy the Kid vs. Dracula (1966), and BloodRayne II: Deliverance (2007) to the mindless, shambling zombies of The Quick and the Undead, Dead Walkers, and Devil's Crossing, the undead present a horrific, incomprehensible Otherness that terrifies even the bravest and boldest. While the hero and his villainous counterpart traditionally make visible the dual nature of the Old West—the rugged wildness and unbridled freedom of the frontier, on one hand, and the moral order of civilization, on the other—the menace presented by the undead complicates this duality and threatens the very context in which earthly good and evil exist.[10] As Max Brooks notes, "When the living dead triumph, the world degenerates into utter chaos. All social order evaporates."[11]

All undead in the West are not created equal, however, and while many embody earthly transgressions of the Cowboy Code—delivering grisly messages about the consequences of greed, lust, and injustice—others have an even more direct link to earthly morality. They are not merely symbolic reminders of the Code of the West; they also serve as its tutors. "Seek not the plunder that's buried in the evil earth," the eerie sheriff Drake (Billy Drago) warns six convicts who have just arrived at his ghost town's saloon in search of hidden gold in *7 Mummies*. The ghostly cowboy Carter Slade (Sam El-liott) serves as a moral compass for stuntman Johnny Blaze (Nicolas Cage) after the headstrong motorcyclist sells his soul to the devil (Peter Fonda) in *Ghost Rider* (2007), while the deceased-and-awaiting-judgment Wild Bill Hickok (Sam Shepard) upholds the Code on behalf of the wayward Sonny Dillard (Brad Rowe) at the risk of his own eternal damnation, in *Purgatory* (1999). In *Dead Noon*, a fearful and troubled lawman (Scott Phillips) seeks refuge in the local church after learning that a bloodthirsty outlaw named Frank (Robert Bear) has walked out of hell in search of him. As his unseen nemesis appears in the pew behind him, he struggles over a course of action, and the undead gunslinger literally plays "devil's advocate." He could run, long and far, he reckons:

> Frank: "Is that what a hero does?"
>
> Sheriff: "I'm no hero."
>
> Frank: "Are you a man? How do you think you're going to feel a year from now? Ten years from now? Will you be proud of that decision—that you abandoned this town, your destiny? You chose to be sheriff of this town. You took an oath to protect these people . . . A man honors his word."

Similarly, in the animated *Rango* (2011), the golf-cart-riding Spirit of the West sagely advises the tenderfoot chameleon hero: "It doesn't matter what they call you. It's the deeds make the man." And occasionally, the undead provide less intentional moral tutelage, as in *From Dusk Till Dawn*, where bank robber Seth Gecko (George Clooney) attempts to shore up the faith of a preacher (Harvey Keitel) who was formerly his captive, as they flee from vampires:

> I always said that God could kiss my ass. But I just changed my lifetime tune about thirty minutes ago. Because I know that whatever is out there trying to get in is pure evil straight from hell. And if there is a hell and those sons of bitches are from it, then there has *got* to be a heaven.

In each of these cases, regardless of the fate of the flesh, the Spirit of the West is upheld: Faith, honor, and civilization are championed, the moral force of the Cowboy Code lives on, and the living dead are put to rest. In each, the undead actively engage with the living in ways that reinforce the Code—cautioning and converting the weak and wayward—acting as complex figures that frequently work to practically or symbolically emphasize the very moral order their presence seeks to undermine.

Retaliation and Redemption

Tales of the Old West and its Code routinely turn on themes of retaliation and redemption. Those who honor the Code by their own actions are implicitly charged with calling to account those who transgress it. Enforcement of the Code—by an officer of the law in *High Noon* (1952), by a mysterious stranger in *Shane* (1953), by a courageous citizen in *3:10 to Yuma* (1957)—is the central drama of the classic Western. Redemption of a flawed hero, who transgresses the Code by action or inaction, fulfills a similar dramatic role in revisionist Westerns such as *Unforgiven* (1992). The introduction of the undead into the cinematic West broadens and deepens these themes while raising the possibility that the punishments meted out to violators of the Code are not merely temporal, but eternal.

The liminal nature of the undead—capable of fully participating in the world of the living but imbued with the powers of the world beyond—makes them avengers of unmatched tenacity and ferocity. Those who, in life, lose sight of their moral compass and willfully flout the Code encounter the full force of both. The title character of Clint Eastwood's *Pale Rider* (1985) is, seemingly, just another Man with No Name—laconic, unshaven, and lethal. Like his unnamed counterpart in *High Plains Drifter* (1973), however, he is implied to be something more: an emissary from beyond the grave, bearing the scars of seemingly fatal wounds and resembling a man known to be dead. Defying the limits placed upon the living by time and space, he metes out punishment to the wicked and corrupt with the implacable grace of a warrior-angel.[12] His first appearance is juxtaposed with a girl's prayer for deliverance and his arrival outside her family's home with her reading the Book of Revelations: "And behold a pale horse, and his name that sat on him was death. And Hell followed with him."

The undead are, as supernatural beings, capable of inflicting punishments on the guilty far worse than that exacted by any lawman's gun or hangman's rope. The escaped convicts in *7 Mummies*, enacting a familiar Western story by fleeing the law-bound West for the safety of lawless Mexico, are drawn by their greed toward a swifter and more brutal reckoning than the one they fled.[13] Diverted by a lone Indian's tales of a legendary treasure assembled and hidden by the conquistadors, they encounter the mummies of the title— undead Jesuit priests sworn to guard the gold—and are bitten, stabbed, and torn apart by the mummies' zombie minions. The zombies themselves are also victims of greed: earlier gold-seekers slaughtered by the mummies and trapped in the twilight between life and death. Told by the Indian that the border and the gold lie in opposite directions, convicts declare their greed (and seal their fate) by choosing riches over freedom.

The role of the undead in maintaining the Code, however, is not always discriminating and exact. The indiscriminate brutality of some white settlers toward the Indians is, in films such as *It Came from the West*, *Dead Walkers*, and *Undead or Alive* (2007), inflicted in turn upon *all* white settlers, by hordes of zombies created by Indian magic. The undead in such films devour the just and unjust alike, and they act as an extension of the indiscriminate and (nearly) unstoppable forces of Nature itself.[14] Resistance to their attacks—where they fall upon the just and the innocent—is thus the pursuit rather than the avoidance of justice and a possible road to redemption for those brave (or desperate) enough to undertake it.

Virgil, the sensitive young man at the center of *It Came from the West*, is bullied by his brutish saloonkeeper father and mocked as a "weak pisser" by the cowboys who frequent the saloon. When zombies overrun the town and invade the saloon, however, Virgil displays courage and a capacity for righteous violence that mark him as a true man of the West and—combined with his quick wits—vanquish the zombies. Virgil's battle with the zombies saves the town but also redeems him in the eyes of the townspeople, revealing him to be a classic Western hero, fully capable of mastering the unruly frontier.[15] The elderly heroes of *Bubba Ho-Tep*, robbed of their masculinity by the effects of aging and the rhythms of life in their Texas nursing home, similarly redeem it in combat with the undead. Their defense of the nursing home and its residents against a marauding mummy dressed in boots, spurs, and Stetson—no less than Virgil's of the saloon—brings about a personalized form of the "regeneration through violence" that, Richard Slotkin has argued, is the defining myth of the American frontier.[16]

The undead themselves, however, are not exempt from punishment for their transgressions or from the desire to find, in death, the redemption that escaped them in life. In *Purgatory*, Wild Bill Hickok and three other recently dead gunfighters live under assumed names in a town that straddles the border between the worlds of the living and the dead, waiting for God to pass final judgment on their souls, aware that any misstep that will send them to hell rather than heaven. Carter Slade, the undead cowboy in *Ghost Rider*, is a former Texas Ranger who fell from grace in the 1850s when he broke the law and was hanged for his crimes. He spends a century and a half as the devil's undead messenger—racing through the night on a fiery horse and collecting the souls of those who, in moments of weakness, were foolish enough to sign them away—but he constantly strives to atone for his own moments of weakness. Slade's search for God's mercy even leads him, in an act redolent of Western legend, to defy the devil himself.[17] The stakes, for Slade as for all characters in undead Westerns, are high, for they live in a world where death is only a beginning.

Undead in the West

Each of this volume's three segments explores a key point of articulation between classic Westerns and tales of the undead. We see that while the vampires, zombies, mummies, and ghosts brought to "life" in these narratives sometimes subvert the traditional symbols, motifs, and moral messages that comprise the archetypal Western, at other times, they serve to reinforce them. Of perhaps greater significance, however, is the ability of the undead to provide a new lens through which to view the too often taken-for-granted cultural work of the Western.

The first section of chapters, "Reanimating Classic Western Tropes," examines the ways in which the undead breathe life into the traditional elements of Western film and television. In a genre that relies heavily on audiences' immediate familiarity with icons and archetypes, the presence of the undead can make the familiar strange—and, perhaps, terrifying. Cynthia J. Miller's chapter, "So This Zombie Walks into a Bar . . ." begins the section with a look at one of the Old West's most time-honored locations, the saloon. She examines the ways in which the frontier barroom—traditionally a meeting place for gunslingers and lawmen, travelers and adventurers, shady ladies and gambling men—continues to fulfill that function, serving as a point of encounter, and often, a battleground between the living and the undead, drawing together heroes and villains in standoffs against an even greater evil.

The next chapter, "'Hey Sammy, We're Not in Kansas Anymore': The Frontier Motif in *Supernatural*," Michael J. Klein and Kristi L. Shackelford explore the impact of the undead on the notion of the frontier itself. They argue that as the frontier—the meeting point between civilization and the untamed wilderness—has been drawn into the realm of speculative fiction, it has become a shifting construct, no longer fixed in either time or space. In the case of *Supernatural*, it serves as a boundary between the mysterious and the familiar, the worlds of the undead and the living.

Foremost among Western archetypal characters is the whore with a heart of gold. This figure takes on an added dimension in Lindsay Krishna Coleman's chapter, "The Whore with the Vampire Heart: Frontier Romanticism in John Carpenter's *Vampires*." Through his exploration of the character Katrina, the vampire whore of John Carpenter's *Vampires*, Coleman sheds light on the ways in which the presence of the undead may work to subvert gender norms and expectations on the frontier, illustrating how Katrina's vampirism rescues her from the narrative periphery, endowing her with a power, centrality, and agency only dreamed of by traditional "soiled doves," while at the same time, connecting her more closely with the wildness of the Wild West.

This exploration of vampires on the frontier continues with "*Billy the Kid vs. Dracula*: The Old World Meets the Old West," by Rachel E. Page, Robert G. Weiner, and Cynthia J. Miller. While this early film was not the first to introduce the undead to the West, the chapter examines the ways in which its unique confluence of Western and horror genres, and the exploitation-film promotional strategies of the 1960s, led it to become a cult classic, tracing the evolution of Billy the Kid from outlaw to Western icon to camp icon.

In the next chapter, Sue Matheson crafts a discussion of the redemptive power of the Old West in "The West—Reanimated and Regenerated: Hollywood Horror and Western Iconography in Gore Verbinski's *Rango* (2011)." Here, we not only find a parody of classic Western ideals but also their unequivocal reinforcement, as city slicker Rango finds his inner hero with the help of the undead. Matheson focuses on the ways in which Rango—the reluctant champion of Dirt, Nevada—and his guide, the Spirit of the West—a stoic, serape-draped parody/homage to Clint Eastwood's iconic Man with No Name—evoke the regenerative impulse of the American character.

This notion of redemption is put to the test, however, in the section's concluding chapter: Shelley Rees's "Frontier Values Meet Big-City Zombies: The Old West in AMC's *The Walking Dead*." Through a close reading of the televised series, Rees examines the ways in which this grotesque "changeling Western" subverts the range of traditional frontier characters: disempowering heroes, making monsters of the innocent, and transforming peacekeepers into grim executioners. Rees demonstrates that in the series postapocalyptic story world overrun by zombies, even the most pure-hearted of lawmen is unable to fulfill his tradition-bound duty to bring order and justice to chaos.

The second section of the book, "The Moral Order under Siege," explores the ways in which the undead—and the desperate attempts of the living to defeat them—threaten to unravel the fabric of frontier society. The classic Western focuses on attempts to create a space for civilization to flourish on the margins of the wilderness, but the undead—relentless, implacable, and immune to the weapons that vanquish other foes—put that civilization (perhaps even the *possibility* of civilization) in jeopardy. They do not merely kill but corrupt and defile their victims, and their attacks tear at the institutions on which frontier society rests: the church, the law, and even the saloon. Defeating them means casting aside the carefully maintained limits on violence that define civilization and inflicting savage violence on marauding Others and "turned" loved ones alike.

The possibilities for such unraveling are suggested in the section's opening chapter. A. Bowdoin Van Riper's "Savage, Scoundrel, Seducer: The Moral Order under Siege in the *From Dusk Till Dawn* Trilogy" argues that—

although the undead Western classic and its two direct-to-video sequels all present the vampire denizens of a certain Mexican bar as threats to the moral order—they frame that threat in distinct ways. The three films present the vampires as, respectively, mindless savages, wily outlaws, and silken-voiced tempters of the weak willed, offering viewers a choice of moral apocalypses.

The next three chapters in the section take a wider view, focusing on films that chronicle the threatened (or actual) breakdown of entire societies under the onslaught of the undead. Thomas Prasch explores a struggle for control of the southwestern United States in "Blood on the Border: The Mexican Frontier in *Vampires* (1998) and *Vampires: Los Muertos* (2002)." Treating the films' vampires and slayers as rival border-dwelling subcultures—lightly disguised stand-ins for illegal immigrants, the *coyotes* who lead them across the border, and the citizen-vigilante groups that hunt them—he shows how border crossing by both sides kindles fears of erasure of one subculture by another, provoking anxiety, anger, and ultimately violence. The borders discussed in Outi J. Hakola's "Colliding Modalities and Receding Frontier in George Romero's *Land of the Dead*" are more circumscribed, but no less fraught, than the one separating the United States and Mexico. They define—geographically, economically, and socially—the film's fractured, barely functioning postapocalyptic society, dividing the living from the undead but also the ground-dwelling poor from the tower-dwelling rich. Hakola contends that, in Romero's bleak, post-9/11 vision of the zombie apocalypse, the true threat to civilization comes not from the undead beyond the walls but from injustice and inequality within.

Robert Rodriguez's *Planet Terror* (2007) takes the story a step further, depicting civilization—a small Texas town—already crumbling under a zombie onslaught. Christopher Gonzalez's chapter "Zombie Nationalism: Robert Rodriguez's *Planet Terror* as Immigration Satire" explores the social and political subtexts layered beneath the film's lurid exploitation-horror surface. It traces the director's use of zombie film conventions to build viewers' sympathy for the Texan protagonists and render comprehensible their decision to flee their homeland for the relative safety of Mexico. The film, Gonzalez argues, is constructed to show American audiences immigration from the unfamiliar (to them) perspective of the often-desperate immigrants and to undermine too-easy American assumptions about those who seek refuge in the United States.

The final two chapters in the section also aim to undermine their audiences' assumptions, but they focus not on political issues but on the conventions of the classic Western itself. In "Undead and Un-American: The Zombified Other in Weird Western Films," James Hewitson uses the traditional concept of the zombie—an individual held in magical thrall by a master and forced to do his bidding—to explore the stock Western character of the villain's henchman. Considering depictions of zombie figures across multiple films, Hewitson argues that they highlight the henchman's inability to act or even think independently and so serve to deconstruct the glorification of independence and individual initiative that lies at the heart of the classic Western. Finally, in "Hungry Lands: Conquest, Cannibalism, and the Wendigo Spirit," Robert A. Saunders considers the Cree and Ojibwa spirit-being that drives the characters in Adriana Bird's *Ravenous* (1999) to cannibalism. The wendigo, Saunders contends, plays a multilayered role in the film: It is a straightforward, supernatural avenger of the wrongs committed against native peoples by conquering white settlers, but it is also a means of commenting on the white man's perceived *need* to conquer. When the wendigo turns members of a frontier army garrison into mindless cannibals, Saunders argues, it makes their obsessive drive to consume into a grotesque parody of the ideology of Manifest Destiny that underlay westward expansion.

The final section of this volume, "And Hell Followed with Him," explores the themes of retribution and redemption in undead Westerns, and the complex, often interwoven roles assigned to the undead. Whether redeemers or seekers of redemption, agents of retribution or objects of righteous violence, the undead remind audiences that the consequences of inhumanity are . . . eternal. The section begins with Matthias Stork's chapter, "The Ghost from the Past: The Undead Avenger in Sergio Leone's *Once Upon a Time in the West*." Here, Stork suggests that Leone's film serves as an opera of death, acted out on the frontier, as it, too, begins to die. He argues that the director plays with the statuses of "living" and "dead" as malleable concepts far broader than our usual conceptualizations, allowing his characters to "resurrect," confront agents of earlier trauma, exact revenge in order to find peace, and ultimately, move on.

Just as retaliation and revenge are strongly bound up with Western specters, notions of redemption find their place, as well, for both the living and the undead. In "Moving West and Beyond: Life in the Midst of Death in *Purgatory*," Hugh H. Davis examines a classic tale of Wild West gunfighters who are drawn into a final showdown where the fate of their souls hangs in the balance. Here, Western legends become symbols of Dante's quest for personal justice, as they band together on the streets of Refuge to defend the common good. Davis demonstrates how, through their ultimate adherence to the Code of the West, the town's champions find both purpose and salvation. Similarly, in "'You Nasty Thing from Beyond the Dead': Elvis and JFK versus the Mummy in *Bubba Ho-Tep*," Hannah Thompson traces the trail to redemption for a pair of unlikely Western heroes—elderly residents of an

East Texas rest home, who claim to be Elvis and John F. Kennedy. Thompson's chapter examines how the pair's battle against a predatory mummy, clad in a Stetson and spurs, breathes an unanticipated spark of life into their "walking dead" existences, allowing them to reclaim their masculinity and die as true champions of the West.

The section's next chapter is "The Subversive *Jonah Hex*: Jimmy Hayward's Revision and Reconfiguration of a Genre," Michael C. Reiff's study of the 2010 film that brought the scarred, embittered, revenge-driven bounty hunter from the pages of comics and graphic novels to movie screens. Implicitly rejecting criticism of *Jonah Hex* as an empty exercise in special-effects-driven filmmaking, Reiff shows how Hex—a man with one foot in the world of the living and one in the world of the dead—undermines audience expectations of how Western heroes think and act. *Jonah Hex*'s most profound subversion of genre convention comes, Reiff argues, in the moral status of its protagonist. Alone among Western heroes, Hex *knows* that he is beyond redemption, for he has seen what awaits him when he crosses, permanently, to "the other side."

The volume closes with an extended exploration of the undead as a catalyst for justice, in Fernando Gabriel Pagnoni Berns's "Queer Justice: Supernatural Strangers and Different Conceptions of Law and Punishment in Two Horror Westerns." Arguing against a static notion of Western justice, Pagnoni Berns examines two classic Western horror films, *Curse of the Undead* and the "spaghetti Western" *Se sei vivo spara* (1967; *Django Kill . . . If You Live, Shoot!*). His essay traces shifts in the concept and its enactment, from Old West notions of retribution to more contemporary frameworks of restorative justice, guided by the otherworldly perspective of the films' undead protagonists.

Conclusion

The central myths of the frontier are myths of transformation: the weak become strong; the defiant are conquered; the wild is tamed. Fueled by tenets of honor, morality, and virtue—the Code of the West—these myths are the stuff of song and story and the building blocks of closely held notions of rugged American individualism and national identity.

The intrusion of the undead onto the Western frontier challenges the core ideas of the Code, blurring the once-sharp lines separating the wild from the civilized, the righteous from the wicked. It brings the crimes of the past to light and gives human form to their dark legacy, and it confronts lawmen and gunslingers alike with forces beyond their comprehension: guardians and guides who bring an otherworldly wisdom to the realm of the living and enemies who know no honor, defy order and reason, and relentlessly pursue the destruction of all in their path. Undead advisors to the living reinforce the centrality of the Code as forcefully as the mute, ravenous, undead hordes transgress it. Both, however, exist to articulate its importance and—by their example—remind the living that the cost of violating the Code may be higher than they had ever imagined.

On a larger scale, the presence of the undead in the West simultaneously complicates and reinforces the myth that the taming of the West is inevitable. Their appearance brings chaos—moral as well as physical—that threatens to sweep away the still-tenuous order that the living have painstakingly imposed on the once-wild land. Their insatiable appetites mock the decorum of the church, school, and café, and they make the wildness of the saloon seem tame. Their numbers and inhuman resilience make them, collectively, a match for the quickest-drawing, straightest-shooting gunfighters. The triumphs of civilization over wildness, and the righteousness of those triumphs, are articles of faith in traditional Westerns, only recently (and, even then, only rarely) interrogated. With the arrival of the undead, those comforting certainties are up for grabs.

Ultimately, however, despite the magnitude of the challenge they pose, even the undead cannot stop the (re)imposition of civilization on the West. The struggle against them ends as struggles for control of the frontier have always ended on screen: with peace restored, the Code of the West intact, and the townsfolk filtering cautiously back onto the dusty street to carry on their orderly, civilized lives.

Notes

1. Frederick Jackson Turner, *The Frontier in American History* (New York: Henry Holt and Company, 1923), 199.

2. Turner, *Frontier in American History*, 199.

3. Robert J. Higgs and Ralph L. Turner, *The Cowboy Way: The Western Leader in Film, 1945–1995* (Santa Barbara, CA: Praeger, 1999), xix.

4. Jack Nachbar, *Focus on the Western* (Englewood Cliffs, NJ: Prentice Hall, 1974).

5. Peter Stanfield, *Horse Opera: The Strange History of the 1930s Singing Cowboy* (Urbana and Chicago: University of Illinois Press, 2002).

6. Elise M. Marubbio, *Killing the Indian Maiden: Images of Native American Women in Film* (Lexington, KY: University Press of Kentucky, 2006), 113; Christopher Sharrett, "The Western Rides Again," *USA Today*, July 12, 1991, 91.

7. Ramon Adams, *The Cowman & His Code of Ethics* (Encino, CA: Encino Press, 1969), 13.

8. David S. Lewis, "The Code of the West: Some Things Never Go out of Style," *The Montana Pioneer*, March 2011. http://www.mtpioneer.com/2011-Mar-cover-code-west.html

9. See Shawn McIntosh and Marc Leverette, *Zombie Culture: Autopsies of the Living Dead* (Lanham, MD: Scarecrow Press, 2008); Mary Y. Hallab, *Vampire God: The Allure of the Undead in Western Culture* (Albany: State University of New York Press, 2009); David Flint, *Zombie Holocaust: How the Living Dead Devoured Pop Culture* (London: Plexus, 2009); Kyle Bishop, *American Zombie Gothic: The Rise and Fall (and Rise) of the Walking Dead in Popular Culture* (Jefferson, NC: McFarland, 2010).

10. Marubbio, *Killing the Indian Maiden*, 113.

11. Max Brooks, *The Zombie Survival Guide: Complete Protection from the Living Dead* (New York: Three Rivers Press, 2003), 155.

12. David McNaron, "From Dollars to Iron: The Currency of Clint Eastwood's Westerns," in *The Philosophy of the Western*, ed. Jennifer L. McMahon and B. Steve Csaki (Lexington: University Press of Kentucky, 2010), 157–58.

13. Camilla Fojas, *Border Bandits: Hollywood on the Southern Frontier* (Austin: University of Texas Press, 2008), 27–28.

14. Sean Moreland, "Shambling towards Mount Improbable to Be Born: American Evolutionary Anxiety and the Hopeful Monsters of Matheson's *I Am Legend* and Romero's *Dead* Films," in *Generation Zombie: Essays on the Living Dead in Modern Culture*, ed. Stephanie Boluk and Wylie Lenz (Jefferson, NC: McFarland, 2011), 77–81.

15. Barry Keith Grant, *Shadows of a Doubt: Negotiations of Masculinity in American Genre Films* (Detroit: Wayne State University Press, 2010), 51–53.

16. Richard Slotkin, *Regeneration through Violence: The Mythology of the American Frontier, 1600–1860* (Norman: University of Oklahoma Press, 2000), 5.

17. Grant, *Shadows of a Doubt*, 38.

Bibliography

Adams, Ramon. *The Cowman & His Code of Ethics*. Encino, CA: Encino Press, 1969.

Bishop, Kyle. *American Zombie Gothic: The Rise and Fall (and Rise) of the Walking Dead in Popular Culture*. Jefferson, NC: McFarland, 2010.

Brooks, Max. *The Zombie Survival Guide: Complete Protection from the Living Dead*. New York: Three Rivers Press, 2003.

Flint, David. *Zombie Holocaust: How the Living Dead Devoured Pop Culture*. London: Plexus, 2009.

Fojas, Camilla. *Border Bandits: Hollywood on the Southern Frontier*. Austin: University of Texas Press, 2008.

Grant, Barry Keith. *Shadows of Doubt: Negotiations of Masculinity in American Genre Films*. Detroit: Wayne State University Press, 2010.

Grey, Zane. *The Code of the West*. New York: Grossett and Dunlap, 1934.

Hallab, Mary Y. *Vampire God: The Allure of the Undead in Western Culture*. Albany: State University of New York Press, 2009.

Higgs, Robert J., and Ralph L. Turner. *The Cowboy Way: The Western Leader in Film, 1945–1995*. Santa Barbara, CA: Praeger, 1999.

Lewis, David S. "The Code of the West: Some Things Never Go out of Style," *Montana Pioneer*, March 2011. http://www.mtpioneer.com/2011-Mar-cover-code-west.html

Marubbio, M. Elise. *Killing the Indian Maiden: Images of Native American Women in Film*. Lexington, KY: University Press of Kentucky, 2006.

McIntosh, Shawn, and Marc Leverette. *Zombie Culture: Autopsies of the Living Dead*. Lanham, MD: Scarecrow Press, 2008.

McNaron, David. "From Dollars to Iron: The Currency of Clint Eastwood's Westerns." In *The Philosophy of the Western*, edited by Jennifer L. McMahon and B. Steve Csaki, 149–69. Lexington: University Press of Kentucky, 2010.

Moreland, Sean. "Shambling towards Mount Improbable to Be Born: American Evolutionary Anxiety and the Hopeful Monsters of Matheson's *I Am Legend* and Romero's *Dead* Films." In *Generation Zombie: Essays on the Living Dead in Modern Culture*, edited by Stephanie Boluk and Wylie Lenz, 77–89. Jefferson, NC: McFarland, 2011.

Nachbar, Jack. *Focus on the Western*. Englewood Cliffs, NJ: Prentice Hall, 1974.

Sharrett, Christopher. "The Western Rides Again," *USA Today*, July 12, 1991, 91.

Slotkin, Richard. *Regeneration through Violence: The Mythology of the American Frontier, 1600–1860*. Norman: University of Oklahoma Press, 2000.

Stanfield, Peter. *Horse Opera: The Strange History of the 1930s Singing Cowboy*. Urbana and Chicago: University of Illinois Press, 2002.

Turner, Frederick Jackson. *The Frontier in American History*. New York: Henry Holt and Company, 1921.

PART I

REANIMATING CLASSIC WESTERN TROPES

CHAPTER ONE

"So This Zombie Walks into a Bar . . ."

The Living, the Undead, and the Western Saloon

Cynthia J. Miller

From the swinging doors to the dust-covered bottles of bourbon lining the shelves behind its paneled bar, the saloon stands as a quintessential icon of the Old West. Situated in the heart of every Western town, but morally, on its margins, the saloon served as a site of refuge and release. It was a gambling den, a meetinghouse, and the place where a man could drink in the company of men; where social convention and morality were loosened, and both bravado and indifference had their place.

First featured in the Edison Company's plotless and brief *Cripple Creek Bar-room*, an 1899 movie tableau, the Western saloon is featured in most of the genre's cinematic tales.[1] From the silent era onward, the saloon's ethos has lent itself equally well to melodrama, musical, adventure, and parody, with cinematic bartenders serving their stock to characters ranging from Clint Eastwood's Josey Wales to Karel Fiala's Lemonade Joe. Many of Western film and television's most iconic figures have risen, or fallen, within the confines of the saloon: John Wayne and Kirk Douglas brawled their way across the silver screen in *The War Wagon* (1967); James Stewart drank milk to the strains of "See What the Boys in the Back Room Will Have" in *Destry Rides Again* (1939); a grief-stricken Henry Fonda gave his saddle pal Anthony Quinn a "Viking funeral" in *Warlock* (1959); Clint Eastwood confronted Gene Hackman with the business end of his rifle in *Unforgiven* (1992); and of course, Amanda Blake's Miss Kitty charmed the patrons of the Long Branch Saloon in the long-running series *Gunsmoke* (1955–1975). But beyond merely serving as a stage from which Western stars shined, the saloon was a catalyst for action, a place of encounter. Shady ladies and cowboys, gamblers and miners, outlaws and bounty hunters, writers and adventurers all stepped through its doors to work, drink, tell tales, hear news, even scores, and satisfy longings.

When horror was introduced to the Western, however, the saloon also became the stage for encounters of a different kind—between the living and the undead. In films like *From Dusk Till Dawn* (1996), *7 Mummies* (2006), *It Came from the West* (2007), and others, zombies, vampires, mummies, and ghosts added a new dimension to the wild side of the Wild West, forcing lawmen and bandits to forge alliances, as traditional Western narratives of good versus evil were replaced by those of the living versus the undead, all played out with the saloon at the center.

Here, then, is a long, sober look at the role of the Western saloon as a site of encounter between the living and the undead. Drawing on the saloon's historical notoriety as a locus of transgression and transformation, where violence, risk taking, and sexuality asserted their dominance in the everyday business of the community, along with its mythic adaptations throughout decades of Western films, this chapter considers the world inside the swinging doors as liminal space, where order and chaos, strange and familiar, good and evil collide. While in the classic Western, the moral order emerges from the saloon, triumphant, the revisionist tension introduced by the undead blurs boundaries and conflates categories, leaving few of the West's iconic figures unchanged. Thus, while it may not be a surprise that one of the quintessentially transgressive institutions of the Old West—a place known as a home to a constellation of earthly excesses such as drunkenness, lust, and greed—would be a fitting battleground for men's souls, the ways in which that occurs in undead Westerns bears examination.

The saloon—icon of the Old West.

Troops of Lewd Women and Bullwhackers

Iconic as it is, the saloon of the Western frontier was a complicated place. As Richard Slatta observes, it stood as "a principal theater where Western and Eastern ideas and practices met, melded, and clashed."[2] While other mainstays of Western towns, like the schoolhouse and the church, were artifacts of a West that had already been tamed, the saloon was there first to witness and aid in the taming; with its roots in a West that was still wild, it often needed a little taming itself. Towns carried names like "Gintown" and "Fortification Creek" in testimony to the widespread influence of local drinking establishments, which sprung up in great numbers.[3] As Jay Robert Nash notes, saloons and bordellos were usually found in greater number than churches or schools in frontier towns, and their reputation for mayhem was well deserved, leading travelers like the Reverend Joseph Cook to observe, "This is the great center for gamblers of all shades, and roughs, and troops of lewd women, and bullwhackers. Almost every other house is a drinking saloon, gambling house or bawdy house."[4]

Playwright Oscar Wilde's well-known quip about a piano in a Colorado saloon carrying a notice that said, "Please don't shoot the pianist. He's doing his best" was but one of a long line of recitations on the wilds of the Wild West.[5] Tales of violence and bloodshed were commonplace throughout the late nineteenth century. One of the most graphic relates how, in October of 1870, inebriated gunfighter Robert Allison led a lynch mob that battered down the door of the jail holding convicted murderer Charles Kennedy in Elizabethtown, New Mexico, and—having lynched him, decapitated the body and "jammed the head on a pole"—"riding with this gory trophy all the way to Henry Lambert's saloon in Cimarron, where Allison put the head on display."[6]

Similarly, reporting on his sojourn through Kansas's notorious Hays City, a newspaper columnist for the *Junction City Union* described at length a similar air of lawlessness in one of the town's many saloons, observing that "on entering one you are astonished at the warlike appearance of the place, as it looks more like an arsenal than a bar room."[7] He went on, casting the barkeepers more as ironic gunslingers than as docile characters whose chief function was to pour and clean up:

> The adroitness with which the skilled barkeepers there handle their weapons is a marvel. When a noisy crowd enters, the keeper of the arsenal retreats gracefully behind his fortifications . . . he is surrounded with a halo of knives and pistols, and strikes an attitude of defiance among the spigots. Immediately upon the least sign of hostile demonstrations, he displays his skill as a marks-

man upon some unfortunate victim, and taking a piece of chalk in his hand, turns lithely to the French plate mirror at his back, and writes in large letters, "to be continued."[8]

Railheads and wagon train outfitting stations like Hays City—one of the deadliest cities in the West—drew throngs of notorious characters, and local saloons flourished.[9] The saloons served as a port of entry for these newcomers and a gathering place for those who had already laid their various claims to the West. It was a place where the conflicts between heroes and villains, laborers and owners, farmers and ranchers, young guns and old dogs, simmered just below the surface—and sometimes bubbled over and spilled out into the streets. As Nash relates, violence and disorder in Western towns typically had its roots in the local watering holes, noting that gunslingers "seldom, unless drunk in a saloon, fought it out with opponents in head-to-head combat."[10]

On the surface, these saloons, with their bright lights, music, and pretty women, appear to be outposts of civilization, each board and nail testifying to human triumph over the wildness of the frontier.[11] The sounds of laughter and clinking glasses that emanate from within give the illusion of safety, like a child whistling in the dark. But in reality, the saloon can be seen as a container for the same struggle between civilization and barbarity that was taking place on a grand scale, just outside its swinging doors. A microcosm of the frontier, the space of the saloon calls the control of civilization into question, mixing the promise of law and order with the risky business of the West. Alcohol and easy women lower inhibitions and erode the veneer of morality suggested by settlement, while drunkenness, illicit sex, gambling, and the fistfights that usually ensue give testimony to the dangers of giving way to man's (and woman's) more basic nature.

This weakening, and potential trampling, of Eastern morality and social control—the ongoing threat of unbridled lawlessness and barbarity in the midst of an oasis of civilization—make the saloon a kind of liminal space, a space of transition and transformation, bracketed apart from the moral order of the everyday. This liminal status unhinges the saloon from an easily defined position in cultural space and from many of the unproblematic narrative classifications that are generally used to describe social space.[12] Neither fish nor fowl, betwixt and between, it affords chaos roots in the frontier town, just as it provides civilization with a foothold in the midst of frontier wildness. It is a space where characters, values, and symbols from the margins challenge those of the mainstream, and unbalance the status quo.[13] Good and evil in the West—civilization and the "wild"—are always locked in an unstable relationship, which becomes even less stable, and often reverses, within the confines of the saloon.

In the historical West, that instability defined the social worlds of many a mining town, rail stop, and outfitting station. In the *cinematic* West, however, social and moral instability is more easily resolved: the watchful eye of the cowboy hero, a mainstay of the genre's classic era, guards against the complete inversion of the moral order as the struggle between social progress and savagery continues.

Encountering the Undead

Cast within this framework, the West of the undead is not a very different place, and the saloon, as the morally ambiguous space where good and evil meet, assumes a position of even greater significance. Indeed, the saloon's status as liminal space creates the ideal location for encounters that blur the boundaries between the living and the dead and exploit the tension that exists between those two categories in tales of the fantastic—just as the destabilization of moral power that historically exists within the saloon creates the ideal environment for supernatural challenges to the control unreflexively assumed by the living.

Moving beyond its usual role as a setting for conflicts spurred by gunfighters, shady ladies, and lawmen, the saloon of undead Westerns is a site for the clash between barbarity and law of a different kind—natural law—with villains (and sometimes, heroes) who challenge not merely social norms but the very definition of life, as well as the continuation of human existence. The undead violate temporal and existential norms, along with some of civilization's deepest taboos—flesh eating, blood drinking, corpse mutilating—presenting vicious, repugnant threats to humanity and the moral order. They shamble, lunge, fly, "flit," and sometimes just reach up from beneath the ground to make victims of earthly good and evil alike—often, for all of eternity—causing one-time human foes to forge previously unthinkable alliances in defense of humanity at large. Vampires, zombies, and other undead creatures lie in wait for the wayward among the living to pass through the saloon's swinging doors in Western-horror hybrid films such as *7 Mummies* and *Vampires: Los Muertos* (2002), while in films such as *It Came from the West* and *The Quick and the Undead* (2006), the saloon marks the site of a "last stand" for the living under siege. And here, in this site where transgression has historically thrived in the midst of civilization—where knowledge and power are destabilized and overturned—the undead often have the upper hand. As one hero of the living warns, "Never go inside. In there, they can outlast you. Never go inside."[14]

Santanico Pandemonium dances for the patrons of the Titty Twister.

In one of the best-known—and most often considered "classic"—undead Westerns, Quentin Tarantino's *From Dusk Till Dawn*, the saloon takes on the character of a true "den of iniquity" under the influence of the undead, where sensual excesses abound as the crowd gathers for the night. Chet Pussy (Cheech Marin) beckons passersby with a come-on that casts him as one part sideshow talker, one part used car salesman: "All right! Pussy! Pussy! Pussy! Come on in pussy lovers!" Inside as the stage show begins, vampire princess Santanico Pandemonium (Salma Hayek) weaves a spell of seduction through her audience with her raven hair and undulating hips. Seemingly mesmerized, outlaws and innocents alike shed the bonds of civilization as the crowd descends into an orgy of earthly transgressions—only to realize, far too late, that they, too, are about to be devoured by the all-consuming frenzy and must battle for their lives and souls. Pastor Jacob Fuller (Harvey Keitel) teams up with the Gecko brothers (George Clooney and Quentin Tarantino) to battle the vampire denizens of the isolated Mexican roadhouse known as the Titty Twister. Three years later, an even more complex alliance is formed in the film's prequel, *From Dusk Till Dawn 3: The Hangman's Daughter* (1999), when outlaw Johnny Madrid (Marco Leonardi) escapes the hangman's noose but then must join forces with the hangman who tried to execute him (Temuera Morrison), along with a drunken Civil War hero Ambrose Bierce (Michael Parks) and a prim missionary couple (Rebecca Gayheart and Lennie Loftin), if all are to survive a night in La Tetilla del Diable, an isolated inn run by the vampire priestess, Quixtla (Sonia Braga).

In the course of these battles, undead Westerns play with the symbols, tropes, and icons of the traditional Western film in ways that are often simultaneously reinforcing and subversive, with the difference between heroes and villains often best measured in degrees of darkness. In this, their hybrid state carries with it varying degrees of revisionism, calling into question the genre's taken-for-granted notions about masculinity and heroism, justice, and the moral order.

Even as the undead first began to menace the West in the late 1950s, with Edward Dein's *Curse of the Undead* (1959), the first confrontation with the living was set in the saloon. A tale of lost love and the brutal fight for water rights in the Old West, the film features vampire Drake Robey (played by Michael Pate) as the lone gunfighter who comes to the aid of a murdered rancher's daughter (while secretly drawing his strength from her as she sleeps). After the daughter, Dolores, nails up posters offering "$100 for the Death of a Murderer"—referring to the water-thieving Buffer, who killed her father—a dark rider, clad in black, arrives in town and strides into the saloon, poster in hand. When one of the villain's lackeys draws down on the newcomer, Robey shoots the Peacemaker revolver right out of his hand, although the gunslinger is certain he got off the first shot. The vampire, having established his prowess, calmly walks from the saloon, warning Buffer that they'll be seeing each other later.

The film firmly situates the saloon in classic Western tropes—as the town's (and the narrative's) port of entry, as the site of confrontation between honesty and corruption, and as the stage on which true manhood is established, where the hero single-handedly faces the forces of evil. And yet, the introduction of a traditionally evil vampire plucked straight from Spanish folklore, functioning as an instrument of Western honesty and justice, plays with those tropes, complicating them in ways that would continue throughout the next fifty years of undead Westerns. Robey, in life, was a fundamentally good man who strayed from the moral order and as a result, was forced to do evil for all eternity. Yet, as the undead embodiment of darkness and malevolence, he also becomes heroic within the saloon's complex constellation of humanity and barbarity, perhaps giving example to Diana Reep's observation that "the western saloon also provides the stage on which we can discern subtle degrees of savagery and civilized behavior that are not readily apparent in the wilderness."[15] It quickly becomes visible here, in the first unabashedly undead Western, that good and evil, morality and manhood, crime and punishment are no longer the unproblematic categories they seem in the traditional Western but are a matter of subtle—and sometimes, not so subtle—degrees.

Chaotic Categories

The saloon of the undead Western, then, creates "chaotic categories"—not merely subverting traditional understandings of the roles and moral messages of the genre but revealing the illusions of order that form the fundamental basis for those understandings. Masculinity, so central to the cinematic Western and its notions of heroism, is chief among these. As Jeff Hearn and Antonio Melechi observe, the classic Western "brings together a number of elements of masculinity, sometimes in contradiction," and as a result, it is a construct that has received a great deal of scholarly consideration.[16] Elise Marubbio views this contradiction as resulting from the Western hero's dual allegiance—to the rugged independence of the frontier, on one hand, and to the moral order of civilization, on the other. In attempting to account for that duality, she suggests, the genre offers a continuum of masculinity that privileges physical over intellectual prowess, self-control over hotheadness, independence over domestication, rancher over farmer, and gunslinger over peacemaker.[17]

In other interpretations of the genre's masculine narratives, Richard Dyer focuses on "the male (hetero) sexual narrative" of pursuit, while Robin Wood explores the homosocial subtext of posses, saddle pals, and others.[18] "The meeting point of [all] these . . . subtexts," Hearn and Melechi suggest, is often the saloon, where men "lose themselves in drink and . . . triumph over each other at the gambling tables."[19] Often, it is the site of advancement, or attempted advancement, along—or around—a constellation of masculine identities, as those lacking in masculine cache shore up their courage or loosen their inhibitions and stake their claims to manhood . . . the weak venture through the swinging doors to confront the strong, the lawman, to confront the outlaw. In one such classic cinematic confrontation—found in George Stevens's 1953 film *Shane*—the world-weary gunfighter (played by Alan Ladd) enters the local saloon and orders a bottle of soda pop. He is ridiculed for his lack of masculine indulgence by one of the local cattle baron's henchmen, who douses his new shirt with a shot of whiskey, chiding him to "smell like a man." Not rising to the challenge, Shane leaves the saloon, but the insults begin anew when he returns the empty bottle to the barman. When told that he can't "drink with the men," Shane has had enough. All of his efforts to relinquish the violence of his past comes undone, and the brawl begins.

These negotiations—and renegotiations—of masculinity become even more complex in the presence of the undead—a fact that did not go unnoticed by Marvin Chomsky, director of the televised series *The Wild Wild*

West. When the undead Western first made its way to television in the series's third season, in an episode titled "Night of the Undead" (1968), Chomsky observed that a key element in the episode's suitability for television was the framing of lead character James West as "solid" and "secure"—a traditional masculine defender who would, without question, restore order and normalcy, even in the face of zombies.[20]

In the saloon of the undead Western, however, vampires, zombies, mummies, ghosts, and others challenge constructions of masculinity from outside the moral order—as fantastic representations of an existence beyond the laws of man or nature. Their undead status serves as "the great equalizer," besting even the most feared or revered of masculine Western figures. However, such equalization can sometimes result in the emergence of unlikely heroes, as well. In the 2007 Danish animated zombie Western, *It Came from the West*, young Virgil, who lives above the saloon, is a character at the low end of the continuum of traditional Western masculinity, denied both Dyer's theme of "pursuit" and Wood's opportunities for homosocial bonding. Sensitive and intelligent, Virgil openly questions the values of the Wild West, yet aspires to embody them as well. He is mocked by the more masculine cowboys, bullied by his brute of a father, and derided as a "weak pisser" by all who enter the saloon. However, when local Indians, terrorized by a figure known only as "The Dark Butcher," bring the dead back to life as their defenders, the resulting barroom battle between the townsmen and the zombies ignites a spark that unleashes Virgil's Western manhood. He throws off the constraints of civilization and becomes its savior, embracing the wildness of the West as his own. Here, the space of the saloon functions as an overt site of transformation. When the conflict between cowboys and zombies begins, Virgil's father tosses him away in the saloon's safe so that

Zombies attack in *It Came from the West* (2007).

Every saloon has its "regulars."

the town's "real men" can act out their traditional roles, unhampered by the young man's weakness. However, in the film's deus ex machina, Virgil seizes his destiny: he bursts forth from the safe, wielding his father's chainsaw, slides down the banister into the barroom, and fearlessly hacks away at the invading horde of undead avengers. Virgil saves, then ultimately dispatches, his father—the film's icon of rough, frontier masculinity—when the latter is bitten and transformed into a zombie himself. Through the confrontation with the shambling masses, Virgil develops valued masculine qualities that combine with his existing intellectual prowess to not only redefine his masculinity but also comparatively (negatively) redefine the masculinities of those around him. Through his transformation, he becomes both a defender of civilization *and* a heroic figure embodying the undomesticated masculinity of the West—merging passion and intellect, bloodlust and sensitivity, youth and experience, rejection and salvation—that simultaneously uproots and preserves tradition. Virgil literally exterminates the Old West (and the main obstacle to his masculinity) in the figure of his father, yet in so doing, he does not merely invert Western tropes but reconfigures them.

A Coincidence of Opposites

At first glance, the moral coding of the saloon of the undead Western appears unproblematic—much like that of its historical counterpart, with its whiskey, loose women, and reputation for violence—a fitting location from which to illustrate the consequences of lives gone wrong. Such morality tales are traditionally the mainstays of B Western films of the Golden Age, where heroes such as Gene Autry, Fred Scott, Tex Ritter, and others embody the values of "civilized" society, and they unquestioningly restore and reinforce the moral order with a smile and a song.[21] These champions of civilization promote a framework for morality motivated by the conformity to law for its own sake and the equation of duty with morality—thus, those who resist, or who lack respect for the Code, are unambiguously cast as immoral and villainous.[22] In countless mainstream Westerns such as these, as Rosa observes, the local saloon is the site where "the villain—a rustler, outlaw or other undesirable whose hold on the town threatens its existence—holds court."[23] However, even this certainty is lost as vampires, zombies, and other supernatural creatures inhabit the West, and the pathos of distance between those who are considered good and evil, moral and transgressive, is confounded by the presence of the undead.[24] These are, as Mary Hallab notes, "bringers of death" which, at the same time, confound death; they are embodiments of evil, which, at the same time, warn of its consequences—once again, not merely inverting the moral order or subverting Western themes but utterly confounding the categories through which those are constructed.[25]

Greed, lust, and other excesses, for which saloons are iconic homes, lure the living, yet frontier tales of the undead often present dualist portrayals of the undead as both violators and guardians of earthly morality. "Seek not the plunder that's buried in the evil Earth," the eerie sheriff Drake (Billy Drago) warns the six convicts who've just arrived at the ghost town's saloon in search of gold in *7 Mummies*. The town is the ancient hiding place for a fortune in Spanish gold, now protected by the title characters (former Jesuit priests who vowed to guard the treasure) and by the entire population of the town, who were transformed by the mummies into walking dead as revenge for disturbing the gold. Once he has recognized the convicts' intentions, however—perceiving, perhaps, dark hearts that will not be swayed—Drake abandons his warnings and preaches to them, amid saloon girls and beer, to indulge their uncivilized desires:

> I say to you "*Drink* all of these cold libations that you can! I say to you to just simply *take* anything that you desire, because the darkness will be upon us soon enough."

And with the darkness, the sheriff knows, comes chaos—the overthrow of knowledge, reason, and human authority—and with it, transformation and death. Urging them on, Drake informs the group that "first and last [drink] is always free," and one by one, the convicts succumb to the temptations of drink and whores. As the moon rises and the denizens of the saloon are transformed, the convicts—brutal killers all—are hunted and torn apart for their greed, as they attempt to unearth the gold and unwittingly awaken the

Temptations abound in the frontier saloon of *7 Mummies* (2006).

mummies. The sole survivors—each a revision (and hence, complication) of the classic "outlaw" and "lawman" figure—are those who did not yield to Drake's seduction.

The tension within and around the moral order shifts yet again in *Purgatory* (1999), as the saloon is shunned as a territory of damnation, not by the living righteous, but by the souls trapped in the town of Refuge—a final proving ground before receiving passage on a stagecoach to heaven or a wagon ride to hell. Here, we find outlaws, gamblers, gunslingers, and shady ladies—historical figures whose exploits animated the pages of pulp Westerns—making common cause for the redemption of their souls. Familiar names, commonly linked to the wildness of the frontier, populate the town: Wild Bill Hickok, Jesse James, and Billy the Kid all walk a narrow path in the hope of salvation. "One drink, and it's all over," a sadder-but-wiser Doc Holliday warns a newcomer. The saloon—which, for him, no longer represents his life, but rather, his eternal death—is now a site with decidedly *fixed* meaning here in the realm between worlds. Ascribed morality, in this liminal space between life and the hereafter, becomes inextricably linked with the struggle for "survival" of the soul—with the moral worth of the characters' actions determined solely by its redemptive value.[26] Only when the undead residents of Refuge abandon their quest for prescribed "goodness" and morality and return to their transgressive ways do they truly achieve redemption.

Thus, the undead complicate the moral certainty of the West in a constellation of ways, highlighting what may be thought of as the "coincidence of opposites"—*coincidentia oppositorium*—inherent in its characters, tropes, and morality tales.[27] Heroes prevail when they loosen the shackles of duty and codified righteousness; villains deliver and embody messages of righteousness and restitution. Often, only when the two are joined—as seen in undead Westerns from *Curse of the Undead* to *Jonah Hex* (2010)—can the living overcome the threat posed by the undead. This intricate interweaving of lawlessness and morality, hope and despair, darkness and light—the interconnectedness of contrary states—is not only made apparent, in ways similar to those found in revisionist Western narratives, but also is demonstrated to be an essential quality of the Western's very context and nature. And the saloon, as a complex space where all of these elements collide, is often at the center of these illustrations.

Conclusion

Taking advantage of the betwixt-and-between nature of the saloon—as a civilizer of the frontier, and the least civilized site in the frontier town—undead Westerns grant inhumanity, in the form of zombies, vampires, and others, a foothold, compelling the living beings who enter to defend their existence and champion the natural (and with it, the moral) order. At the same time, these fantastic narratives use the presence of the undead to dislocate and reconfigure the Western genre's taken-for-granted notions of the most fundamental building blocks of civilization: archetypes of heroism and villainy; values and ideals such as justice, transgression, redemption, and morality; and certainty about the boundaries of time, space, and existential worlds. In this way, undead Westerns may be thought of as the most recent representatives of the genre's revisionist urge, designed to address a new generation.

Monsters, as Judith Halberstam notes, are "meaning machines," invoked purposefully to comment, critique, and question the narrative context into which they are drawn.[28] The creatures conjured in undead Westerns—vampires, zombies, mummies, and ghosts—are no different. They wander, menace, and sometimes defend the frontier, speaking to the civilized world from a place of wildness. Morality tales are commonplace in classic undead films across genres—horror, comedy, fantasy, romance—where otherworldly villains such as zombies, vampires, and mummies unquestioningly reinforce the moral order, with fangs and a snarl. Warnings of human excesses—greed, lust, violence, cruelty—and their consequences (usually a hideous, painful death) are inherent in *all* these films, offering lessons about both the nature of humanity and the importance of the moral codes of civilization. The presence of the undead in the West, however, complicates what, in traditional Westerns, had been a simple moral equation, highlighting degrees of savagery in all characters—heroes *and* villains—while at the same time mitigating their moral differences through their shared opposition to the undead.

As a morally ambiguous venue of the Old West, the saloon provides an ideal setting for the workings out of these tales. From its historical framework as a container for the uncertainty and risk of encounters with the unknown, to its contemporary role as a venue for encounters with the supernatural, the saloon persists as an icon of the frontier—adapting to the challenges brought about by the presence of the undead while retaining its centrality in the life of the community, welcoming all comers. Its significance as a site for these encounters—where tensions, passions, hierarchies, and wills collide—lies in its own duality, as it merges wilderness and civilization behind a single set of swinging doors.

Notes

1. Richard Aquila, *Wanted Dead or Alive: The American West in Popular Culture* (Champaign: University of Illinois Press, 1998).

2. Richard W. Slatta, "Comparative Frontier Social Life: Western Saloons and Argentine Pulperias," *Great Plains Quarterly* 7.3 (1987): 156.

3. Elliott West, *The Saloon on the Rocky Mountain Mining Frontier* (Lincoln: University of Nebraska Press, 1979), 3.

4. Reverend Joseph Cook, *Diary and Letters of the Reverend Joseph W. Cook: Missionary to Cheyenne* (Laramie, WY: Laramie Republican, 1919), 12.

5. Jeff Nunokawa and Amy Sickels, *Oscar Wilde* (New York: Chelsea House, 2005), 35.

6. Jay Robert Nash, *The Encyclopedia of Western Lawmen & Outlaws* (Cambridge, MA: Da Capo Press, 1994), 3.

7. Joseph G. Rosa, *The Gunfighter: Man or Myth* (Norman: University of Oklahoma Press, 1979), 82.

8. Rosa, *Gunfighter*, 82.

9. Hays City, for example, granted thirty-seven licenses to sell liquor in two days during the first meeting of the Board of County Comissioners. See www.legends ofkansas.com.

10. Nash, *Encyclopedia of Western Lawmen & Outlaws*, 3.

11. See Diana C. Reep, "See What the Boys in the Back Room Will Have: The Saloon in Western Films," in *Beyond the Stars: Locales in American Popular Film, volume 4*, ed. Paul Loukides and Linda K. Fuller (Bowling Green, KY: Bowling Green State University Popular Press, 1993), 204–20.

12. Victor W. Turner, *The Ritual Process: Structure and Anti-Structure* (Piscataway, NJ: Aldine Transactions, 1995).

13. For a more theoretical discussion of this process, see Jacques Derrida's theses on the margins of rational discourse in *The Margins of Philosophy* (Brighton, UK: Harvester, 1982).

14. *The Quick and the Undead* (2006).

15. Reep, "See What the Boys in the Back Room Will Have," 205.

16. Quoted in Steve Craig, *Men, Masculinity, and the Media* (Newbury Park and London: Sage Publications, 1992), 223.

17. M. Elise Marubbio, *Killing the Indian Maiden: Images of Native American Women on Film* (Lexington: University Press of Kentucky, 2009), 113.

18. Richard Dyer, "Male Sexuality in the Media," in *The Sexuality of Men*, ed. Andy Metcalf and Martin Humphries (London: Pluto, 1985), 28–43; Robin Wood, "Raging Bull: The Homosexual Subtext in Film," in *Beyond Patriarchy: Essays by Men on Pleasure, Power, and Change*, ed. Michael Kaufman (Toronto: Oxford University Press, 1987), 266–76.

19. Eric Rhode, *A History of the Cinema from its Origins to 1970* (London: Allen Lane, 1976), 217–18.

20. Susan E. Kesler, *The Wild Wild West: The Series* (Downey, CA: Arnett Press, 1988), 112.

21. For a thorough and engaging discussion of these iconic figures, see Peter Stanfield, *Horse Opera: The Strange History of the 1930s Singing Cowboy* (Urbana and Chicago: University of Illinois Press, 2002).

22. See Bruce Aune, *Kant's Theory of Morals* (Princeton, NJ: Princeton University Press, 1979), especially with respect to Immanuel Kant's theories on duty and respect for moral law.

23. Rosa, *Gunfighter*, 6.

24. See Friedrich Nietzsche's *Beyond Good and Evil: Prelude to a Philosophy of the Future* (New York: Vintage Books, 1966).

25. Mary Y. Hallab, *Vampire God: The Allure of the Undead in Western Culture* (Albany: State University of New York, 2009), 6.

26. See John Stuart Mill, *Utilitarianism* (New York: Penguin Classics, 1987).

27. See C. J. Emlyn-Jones, "Heraclitus and the Identity of Opposites," *Phronesis* 21.2 (1976): 89–114.

28. Judith Halberstam, *Skin Shows: Gothic Horror and the Technology of Monsters* (Durham, NC: Duke University Press, 1995), 21.

Bibliography

Aquila, Richard. *Wanted Dead or Alive: The American West in Popular Culture*. Champaign: University of Illinois Press, 1998.

Aune, Bruce. *Kant's Theory of Morals*. Princeton, NJ: Princeton University Press, 1979.

Cook, Reverend Joseph. *Diary and Letters of the Reverend Joseph W. Cook: Missionary to Cheyenne*. Laramie, WY: Laramie Republican, 1919.

Derrida, Jacques. *The Margins of Philosophy*. Brighton, UK: Harvester, 1982.

Dyer, Richard. "Male Sexuality in the Media." In *The Sexuality of Men*, edited by Andy Metcalf and Martin Humphries, 28–43. London: Pluto, 1985.

Emlyn-Jones, C. J. "Heraclitus and the Identity of Opposites." *Phronesis* 21.2 (1976): 89–114.

Halberstam, Judith. *Skin Shows: Gothic Horror and the Technology of Monsters*. Durham, NC: Duke University Press, 1995.

Hallab, Mary Y. *Vampire God: The Allure of the Undead in Western Culture*. Albany: State University of New York, 2009.

Hearn, Jeff, and Antonio Melechi. "The Transatlantic Gaze: Masculinities, Youth, and the American Imaginary." In *Men, Masculinity, and the Media*, edited by Steve Craig, 215–32. Newbury Park and London: Sage Publications, 1992.

Kesler, Susan E. *The Wild Wild West: The Series*. Downey, CA: Arnett Press, 1988.

"Legends of Kansas." www.legendsofkansas.com.

Marubbio, M. Elise. *Killing the Indian Maiden: Images of Native American Women on Film*. Lexington: University Press of Kentucky, 2009.

Mill, John Stuart. *Utilitarianism*. New York: Penguin Classics, 1987.

Nash, Jay Robert. *The Encyclopedia of Western Lawmen & Outlaws*. Cambridge, MA: Da Capo Press, 1994.

Nietzsche, Friedrich. *Beyond Good and Evil: Prelude to a Philosophy of the Future*. New York: Vintage Books, 1966.

Nunokawa, Jeff, and Amy Sickels. *Oscar Wilde*. New York: Chelsea House, 2005.

Reep, Diana. "See What the Boys in the Back Room Will Have: The Saloon in Western Films." In *Beyond the Stars: Locales in American Popular Film, volume 4*, edited by Paul Loukides and Linda K. Fuller, 204–20. Bowling Green, KY: Bowling Green State University Popular Press, 1993.

Rhode, Eric. *A History of the Cinema from Its Origins to 1970*. London: Allen Lane, 1976.

Rosa, Joseph G. *The Gunfighter: Man or Myth*. Norman: University of Oklahoma Press, 1979.

Slatta, Richard W. "Comparative Frontier Social Life: Western Saloons and Argentine Pulperias." *Great Plains Quarterly* 7.3 (1987): 155–65.

Turner, Victor W. *The Ritual Process: Structure and Anti-Structure*. Piscataway, NJ: Aldine Transactions, 1995.

West, Elliott. *The Saloon on the Rocky Mountain Mining Frontier*. Lincoln: University of Nebraska Press, 1979.

Wood, Robin. "Raging Bull: The Homosexual Subtext in Film." In *Beyond Patriarchy: Essays by Men on Pleasure, Power, and Change*, edited by Michael Kaufman, 266–76. Toronto: Oxford University Press, 1987.

CHAPTER TWO

"Hey Sammy,
We're Not in Kansas Anymore"

The Frontier Motif in Supernatural

Michael J. Klein and Kristi L. Shackelford

Vast. Empty. Untamed. When one thinks of the frontier in American film history, these are the images that come to mind. In films such as *High Noon* (1952) and *Once Upon a Time in the West* (1968), the frontier is tied to a specific time and place: the American West of the late nineteenth century. As the epic Western faded from view, futuristic films such as *Outland* (1981) and *Blade Runner* (1982) seized upon the familiar ethos of these wild, untamed regions and reimagined the frontier, disengaging it from the traditional West in both space and time.

In this chapter, we demonstrate how the creators of the television series *Supernatural* (2005–) have relocated the frontier once again, expanding this imaginative territory to encompass the borders between the living and the dead. The series follows Sam and Dean Winchester, two brothers from Lawrence, Kansas, who hunt things that go bump in the night: vampires, demons, shape-shifters, and other assorted mythical creatures. As hunters, the two travel the country following news reports related to legends and urban myths, riding into town on their black steed: a 1967 Chevy Impala. Their most powerful weapon is a classic six-shooter made by renowned munitions maker Samuel Colt in Sunrise, Wyoming, in 1835. Colt has crafted a gun that can kill supernatural beings, making it an invaluable tool in the brothers' quest to avenge the death of their mother, who was killed by a demon. The pair learn the power of this tool firsthand when they save their father from a similar fate. The mythology of this extraordinary Colt revolver becomes a key component of the larger mythology of the series, and the gun functions as a deus ex machina for the brothers as they pursue justice for their family.

While the series makes use of classic Western genre motifs, from characters such as Colt and the brothers Winchester to the use of an iconic trusty steed, the frontier of *Supernatural* is not located in a specific geographic location. Rather, the frontier becomes dislocated, becoming a state of mind in which the viewer accepts the reality of undead creatures such as vampires, ghouls, ghosts, and zombies roaming the world. Rather than simply representing a boundary between society and untamed nature, as it did in the Western and science fiction genres, the frontier now functions as a borderland between the natural and the supernatural.

This redefinition of the frontier makes even the settled, "civilized" world seem untamed and vulnerable to the supernatural creatures that— taking the place of native peoples and outlaws in traditional Westerns— challenge the protagonists. The series evokes the uncanny by superimposing the familiar world we live in with an unfamiliar, and seemingly unreal, world we are usually exposed to only through folklore and stories. Despite this reimagining, however, the frontier in *Supernatural* remains a boundary between the civilized and uncivilized, and thus the series strongest tie to traditional Westerns.

The Frontier and the American Imagination

In his considerations of westward expansion, Frederick Jackson Turner observed that "the frontier is the outer edge of the wave—the meeting point between savagery and civilization."[1] Long before it assumed a significant role in Western fiction and film, the concept of the frontier enjoyed a special place in American national identity. Partially a manifestation of nineteenth-century America's fascination with the concept of Manifest Destiny, partly a representation of an original American myth, images of the frontier shaped Americans' conceptualization of the natural world. Individuals' witness of the vast scale of the continent's natural features—from the Delaware Water Gap and Mammoth Cave in the East to Pike's Peak and Yosemite Valley in the West—reinforced their sense of their own insignificance. Similarly, glimpses of the untamed wilderness beyond the limits of civilization—the Appalachians, the Mississippi, the Rockies, and the Sierra Nevada— reminded them of their tenuous place within the natural order and the power of the unrestrained forces of nature.

The frontier is intrinsically linked to Manifest Destiny: the idea that the United States was destined to expand across the North American continent to the Pacific Ocean. Even at the end of the nineteenth century—when the Pacific Coast had been reached and settled and attention had turned to the Hawaiian islands and beyond—the concept of the frontier remained a vital element in American consciousness. Writing in 1893, historian Frederick Jackson Turner linked the drive for westward expansion to the biological concept of evolution:

> Limiting our attention to the Atlantic coast, we have the familiar phenomenon of the evolution of institutions in a limited area, such as the rise of representative government; the differentiation of simple colonial governments into complex organs; the progress from primitive industrial society, without division of labor, up to manufacturing civilization. But we have in addition to this a *recurrence of the process of evolution in each western area reached in the process of expansion* [emphasis original].[2]

For Turner, westward expansion along the frontier was a natural—indeed, nation-defining—theme in the history of the United States. His use of the term *evolution*, which in late-nineteenth-century America connoted steady progress along a clearly defined path toward a predetermined goal, would have evoked in his listeners a sense of inevitability for the move westward and the taken-for-granted right of domination held by European settlers as representatives of "civilization."[3] Despite the presence of indigenous populations, the frontier is viewed as "empty" space that inevitably needs to be settled and tamed. This conceptualization of the frontier as empty does double duty: providing a space for expansion for Americans while at the same time marginalizing the native peoples who live there, who are either used in the service of conquering the land or viewed as an obstacle to progress.

Even as it was being settled, the frontier had already begun to take on mythical dimensions, in dime novels, Wild West shows, and other stylized depictions of it. Its "closing" in 1890—the occasion of Turner's famous commentary—accelerated the process. The frontier became the centerpiece of the Western genre, and the story of its settlement—the "winning" or "taming" of the West—became "the most enduring and characteristic American myth."[4] The mythical frontier flourished—first in fiction, then on film, and finally on radio and television—even as, over the course of the twentieth century, the real frontier faded further and further from popular memory. The visions of the mythical West created by directors such as John Ford, Howard Hawks, and Anthony Mann had, by midcentury, long since become inseparable from those in the minds of most Americans: "Just as the cinema marks the culmination point in the tradition of American mythmaking, the myths of the American West are forged most effectively in the Western film, particularly in the works of some of the masters of American cinema."[5]

As the Western moved from its celebratory Golden Age, brimming over with possibility and promise, into a darker and more critical "revisionist" period, the wonder of unexplored and unconquered territory shifted to more speculative and spectacular tales found in science fiction and fantasy. As Janice Rushing observes:

> America has constantly sought new frontiers as the old are tamed, and as long as it has found them, has preserved the backdrop of its identity even as the drama has evolved. The frontier narrative, as we now know, has not remained static, but has changed with its scenes.[6]

In the real world, President John F. Kennedy's call to put a man on the moon captured the public imagination, and the frontier fantasies shifted from the American West to outer space.[7] Film and television reinforced these fantastic notions, as space became "the final frontier," explored by a new generation of pioneers riding "wagon train[s] to the stars." New tales of wondrous frontiers sprang up across screens big and small, each offering the opportunity to explore and conquer—or at least tame—the uncharted lands and exotic characters they depicted.

The human imagination, ever seeking new territory for expansion, stretched not only upward and outward in space but also forward and backward through time, and as it did, fantastic new renderings of frontiers came into being, unyoked from both the temporal and geographic moorings of the Old West. Tales of the fantastic, with their ability to transcend not only space but also time, offered the notion of the frontier more rhetorical flexibility than did the Western, opening up borders and boundaries that the genre's traditional fixed time and place would not allow. Through the literature and cinema of the fantastic, romanticized pasts interweave with hopes and fears of the present and fantasies of the future to engage with complex challenges, conquests, and commentary that the highly bounded West could not contain.

Eric Kripke, creator of the series *Supernatural*, has adapted these possibilities to his own reappropriation of the frontier and its myths to construct tales that merge the Old West, the horrific, and the fantastic. Throughout the series, Kripke exploits the dual nature of the frontier as a space both mysterious and familiar, using it as a means of separating the supernatural world apparent to the protagonists from the mundane world of everyday life.

The Tale of Two Winchesters and a Colt

Supernatural follows Sam and Dean Winchester as they travel the country and hunt down supernatural creatures. Though they are members of a family of hunters—those who know about the evils that inhabit the earth and the danger these monsters present to those who are unaware—they embody the characteristics of heroes traditionally found in Westerns: individual ruggedness, a willingness to flout traditional rules, and a determination to keep civilized society safe from unseen dangers. In this way, they fit the traditional mold of the Western hero, being of "rather dubious, even criminal nature in real life."[8] The Winchesters follow their own moral code, which is often in conflict with actual law. They gather information by lying and sometimes by impersonating law enforcement or other officials, and they support themselves with stolen credit cards and fake IDs. Yet they are guided by a moralistic code of protection, with the ends—dispatching monsters and saving lives—justifying the less-than-legal means.

Told retrospectively, in bits and pieces over the course of the first season, the backstory of the two characters explains their growth as hunters and their subsequent involvement with the "family business." When Sam is a baby, a

Western heroes Dean Winchester (left) and Sam Winchester (right) patrol the frontier separating the world of the everyday from that of the fantastic in *Supernatural*. *Courtesy of Photofest*

creature attacks the family home and kills the boys' mother, Mary, in Sam's nursery. The attack by this yellow-eyed demon, later identified as Azazel, motivates John, the boys' father, to become a hunter. The Winchesters hunt otherworldly beings, not other humans or animals like the heroes in Westerns, but their call to hunt is equally strong and—like those of Western heroes from Ethan Edwards in *The Searchers* (1956) to Dan Evans in *3:10 to Yuma* (2007)—is driven by a desire to avenge lost loved ones and ensure the safety of those still living.

Dean and Sam grow up on the road with their father, tracking reports of supernatural happenings as they hunt the demon that killed Mary. The boys are shown the supernatural world as small children and grow up understanding that they know a truth about the world that most people don't. John exposes Sam and Dean to the horrors of both this world and the supernatural one, dragging them along on his quest to fight evil spirits and find Azazel. The boys grow up living a secret life, moving frequently as John hunts, never able to share what they know with anyone else. Along the way, the Winchesters save many lives, but that is almost beside the point. John's ultimate goal is to destroy the demon that killed Mary; others may be saved in the process but that is not his main purpose. In this, his role more closely resembles the damaged, disaffected antiheroes of revisionist or "counterculture" Westerns—more avenging angel than stalwart champion.

The two boys react differently to their common upbringing. Older brother Dean follows his father's lead without hesitation and embraces what he considers as his lot in life. A loner in many ways, he is fiercely loyal to his family and his role as a hunter. Despite his faith in his father and blind trust in what John has taught him, he tries to protect his younger brother from the harsh life of a hunter and the unintended neglect of their father. Younger brother Sam struggles with his role as a hunter as well as his place in the family. Somewhat protected—both from foes and from his father's zeal for the hunt—by Dean, he is more ambivalent toward the family business and his role in it. When given the opportunity, he chooses to leave his family and secret life behind and instead head west to attend college at Stanford University. Like the commonalities that unite them, the differences between them—the hardened frontiersman versus the quiet, college-educated city dweller, the rootless life of violence and the settled life of the mind—reflects one of the classic Western's most fundamental themes. Like Tom Doniphon and Ransom Stoddard in *The Man Who Shot Liberty Valance* (1962), one belongs to the untamed world that adjoins the frontier and the other to the orderly, civilized world that is slowly displacing it.

The pilot episode opens as Dean contacts Sam and asks for his help when John disappears. While they search for their father, the brothers quickly fall into their old habits, fighting the supernatural creatures they find along the way. While their father is driven primarily by his need for revenge for his wife's death, the Winchester brothers are motivated by their role as protectors. Like the heroes of classic Westerns, they constantly are on the move, putting themselves in harm's way to protect those around them, individuals who aren't even aware of the danger they are in. Their journey continues after they have located John and even after they defeat Azazel.

Sam and Dean are united in their desire to fight the forces of evil, but they have differing opinions of what that means. Dean takes a direct approach, literally taking no prisoners and seeing no distinction among the supernatural beings they come across. Sam is more conflicted and looks at the actions of those creatures rather than just what they are. When the brothers encounter a group of vampires who don't kill humans in "Bloodlust," these differences come to a head:

> Dean: "What part of 'vampires' don't you understand, Sam? If it's supernatural, we kill it, end of story. That's our job."
>
> Sam: "No, Dean, that is not our job. Our job is hunting evil. And if these things aren't killing people, they're not evil!"
>
> Dean: "Of course they're killing people, that's what they do. They're all the same, Sam. They're not human, okay? We have to exterminate every last one of them."[9]

This exchange showcases Dean's black-and-white view of good and evil, contrasting it with Sam's more nuanced and contextualized view. Dean's worldview functions according to the binary oppositions that structure the classic Western: hero versus villain; order versus chaos; civilization versus wilderness.[10] The absolute equation of the undead with evil that needs to be "exterminated" reminds the viewer of the way the "other" in a different genre—such as indigenous peoples in the Western—was also portrayed as something that must be destroyed.

Much as the cinematic Western grew through its adaptations of frontier mythology, the series also appropriates and adapts specific details from classic Westerns. The family name (Winchester) and hometown—Lawrence, Kansas, which was burned to the ground by William Quantrill's Confederate guerillas in 1863—evoke a sense of the nineteenth-century frontier. The Winchesters act as guns for hire, guided by stories of supernatural events—dispatching one villainous creature, then moving on to where they are needed next. They choose elemental weapons—guns and knives—over more advanced technology, calling to mind folk stories of "cold iron" having the power to dissipate magic and ward off, or even destroy, supernatural beings.

The greatest weapon in the Winchester's arsenal is the Colt, the legendary six-shooter forged by gun maker Samuel Colt in 1835 that has been passed down through generations of hunters. John Winchester tells his sons the history of the Colt in the episode "Dead Man's Blood":

> Back in 1835, when Halley's comet was overhead, the same night those men died at the Alamo. They say Samuel Colt made a gun. A special gun. He made it for a hunter, a man like us only on horseback. Story goes he made thirteen bullets, and this hunter used the gun half a dozen times before he disappeared, the gun along with him.[11]

The Colt is inscribed *non timebo mala* or "I will fear no evil," in reference to Psalm 23:4. In addition to the gun, Colt made thirteen sterling silver bullets, engraved one through thirteen.

Legend has it that the gun can kill any creature. The gun thus brings together, in a single powerful object, magic both sacred and secular and folklore both ancient and modern. The inscription evokes the Old Testament, and the number of bullets evokes a number that—according to folklore—was made unlucky because it was the number of guests at the Last Supper. Silver bullets kill werewolves and—in one of the fairy tales collected by the Brothers Grimm—witches, but they were also the calling card of the Lone Ranger. The date of the gun's manufacture fuses the legend of the Alamo and its defenders—arguably the most "sacred" of all the stories in the secular mythology of the West—with much older folklore about the talismanic significance of comets, Halley's in particular. The gun, like the series's version of the frontier, is thus a nexus where the natural world of the Western and the supernatural world of horror meet.

The Winchesters first encounter the gun when they investigate the death of a fellow hunter. John uses the seventh bullet to shoot a vampire, killing him immediately. Creatures struck by one of the Colt's bullets suffer from more than a physical wound: light pours out of the bullet hole, symbolizing an essential as well as a physical death. Over the course of the next few seasons, the brothers use the gun sparingly. Kripke's decision to limit the usefulness of the weapon in this way helps balance out the incredible powers it possesses, including the slaying of Azazel with the thirteenth bullet.

As his injured brother Dean (left) looks on, Sam Winchester (right)—holding the brothers'
magical Colt revolver—frees their father, John (center), from demonic possession in
"Devil Trap," the second-season finale of *Supernatural. Courtesy of Photofest*

The influence of Samuel Colt is shown repeatedly throughout the series, culminating with the brothers' research uncovering that Colt was, like them, a hunter. In "Frontierland," the brothers fight an adversary that can only be defeated with the ashes of a phoenix.[12] Dean and Sam discover Colt's journal, in which he describes killing a phoenix. The pair, with the assistance of an angel, travel back in time to 1835 and meet Colt, who aids them in their quest. Acquiring the gun, they kill the creature, but they are transported back to the present before they can secure the ashes. Later, however, they receive a package from Colt containing them, delivered through time and space, with help from Federal Express. With this episode, Kripke openly acknowledges within the series itself that *Supernatural* is, at heart, a modernized Western.[13] The characters are taken back in time to the nineteenth century to participate in a gunfight. However, by featuring an angel as the means of transport, and a mythical creature—the phoenix—as the opponent in the fight, Kripke uses the frontier as the means of uniting, yet keeping distinct, the two genres.

Reimagining the Frontier

Western themes notwithstanding, it is readily apparent that *Supernatural* is a product of the fantastic, owing debts to both horror and fantasy for the supernatural, mythical, and spiritual creatures that drive many of the episodes' plots.[14] The most interesting aspect of the series, however, is its reimagining of the frontier as related not to a specific time or place but to a boundary between what we perceive in the natural world and what lies beyond: a world of ghosts, demons, ghouls, and zombies. For Sam and Dean, the frontier is a semipermeable membrane. They can pass into and out of the supernatural world, but they are never completely free of the spirits they encounter.

This is most apparent in the beginning of the sixth season, after Sam's apparent death in the fifth season's finale. Dean has settled down with his old flame, Lisa, and her son, Ben.[15] Lisa has known of Dean's profession for a number of years, but she only allowed him to move in after he promised to give up being a hunter. Dean tries to lead a normal life but is pulled back into hunting after people go missing, with only strange scratches on walls and small piles of sulfur (the marks of a demon) left behind. Dean's return to the life of a hunter damages his relationship with Lisa, who is unable to reconcile Dean's role as a hunter with his role as a provider/protector for the family, so Lisa separates herself from Dean. But as long as she is aware of Dean and the realm of the supernatural, her life is in jeopardy. In "Let It Bleed," a group of demons kidnap Lisa and Ben.[16] Dean realizes that Lisa and Ben must be completely separated from his life so that they are no longer targets for the demons. Dean has an angel erase their memories of him so they can move on with their lives.

Lisa's relationship with Dean highlights the permeable nature of the frontier, the barrier between the mundane and the unknown, by showcasing Dean's ability to maneuver between the two worlds. Lisa moves beyond the barrier once, but she must completely retreat back to her own world, back across the supernatural frontier, in order to be safe and to protect Ben. The savagery of a world full of demons and vampires must literally be erased from their consciousness so they can go on living a normal life—happiness, for them, depends on not just abandoning all contact with the frontier but all memory that it even existed: that there *is* a place where the wild and the civilized collide. Conversely, Dean knows that he can never fully go back to the ordinary world; thus, the frontier acts as a barrier for him, as his memories cannot so easily be erased as those of Lisa and Ben. His quest to rid the world of supernatural creatures keeps him from returning to a "normal" life, just as the heroes of many traditional Westerns—from *Stagecoach* (1939) and *Shane* (1953) to *The Wild Bunch* (1969) and *Unforgiven* (1992)—find that their life on the frontier has left them unable to function, much less be happy, in the civilized world.

However, the frontier affects not only the living but also the undead. In "Dead Men Don't Wear Plaid," the dead in Sioux Falls, South Dakota, rise from their graves.[17] Seemingly normal, the dead return to their previous lives, reuniting with family and loved ones. Their families are aware that they have risen, but they simply accept the fact that the dead have returned. One of the dead is Karen, the wife of fellow hunter Bobby Singer, who died at his hands five years earlier when she was possessed by a demon. Bobby tries to dissuade Sam and Dean from investigating too deeply the reason for the dead individuals' return. He fears the brothers will take it upon themselves to dispatch those that came back from the dead, including Karen, whom he still deeply loves. When the dead start to change after five days, becoming true mindless zombies hungry for flesh, the brothers, and eventually Bobby, kill them in the traditional fashion: with a gunshot to the head. Mirroring Sam and Dean's inability to escape the world of the supernatural, the zombies are unable to return to their old lives. Having crossed the frontier, the boundary between life and death, the zombies exist in an animated state rather than a living one. Like the brothers, they are the victims of fate, tossed to and fro between the two worlds separated by the frontier, pawns in a battle between the sacred and profane.

Conclusion

Supernatural showcases the struggle between the natural and supernatural worlds in a manner that is reminiscent of the way Westerns' tales of the traditional frontier chronicle the tension between the civilized world of society and the uncivilized world of nature. The series can be viewed as a television Western disguised as a horror story and embellished with classic Western motifs transported from the Wild West to the present day. Its story of two brothers who fight against the forces of evil and rescue those caught in its path could be that of countless classic Westerns. The Winchesters ride into town in their Impala—complete with an arsenal of pistols, shotguns, and knives in the trunk—and fight to protect the people of that town from the supernatural intruders in their midst. They follow their own moral code and are not bound by laws.

The most significant link between this modern-day tale and original Westerns, however, is in the role of the frontier. It functions, in both genres, as a barrier between the civilized and uncivilized worlds, but in *Supernatural* it is removed from its traditional time and place of the Old West and reimagined as a divide between the natural world we live in and the realm of the supernatural. Rather than expanding west, the frontier expands across the realms of existence, and the native people beyond the frontier are demons and monsters. Most people are—and choose to remain—ignorant of the world beyond this one, just as most of those in the world of traditional Westerns have no comprehension of what the frontier is like or what it takes to survive there. It is not that they choose not to cross the frontier but that they simply don't know that the other side exists. That option is not available to the Winchesters, who are raised all too aware of the mythical creatures that inhabit the world beyond ours and consider it their job and moral obligation to fight them. Shaped by the frontier since birth, they serve as heroic archetypes, defending the world of the living from an otherworldly "wildness," but their role as supernatural gunfighters derives from an inherent wildness of their own. The price they pay for living on the border between the two worlds is to be fully comfortable, and fully at home, in neither. By expanding the definition of the frontier, *Supernatural* tells a story that spans genres while joining classic with modern storytelling.

Notes

1. Frederick Jackson Turner, "The Significance of the Frontier in American History," in *Frederick Jackson Turner: Wisconsin's Historian of the Frontier*, ed. Martin Ridge (Madison: State Historical Society of Wisconsin, 1986), 1.

2. Turner, "Significance of the Frontier," 1.

3. The idea of progress through a series of ever-more-complex, ever-more-sophisticated stages toward a definable climax was applied to biology (where it meshed

readily with folk wisdom and Christian doctrine), anthropology (where it reinforced existing ideas about racial hierarchy), and history (where it rendered the spread of European-derived cultures at the expense of native ones "natural" and "inevitable").

4. Janice H. Rushing, "The Rhetoric of the American Western Myth," *Communication Monographs* 50.1 (1983): 15.

5. Martin M. Winkler, "Classical Mythology and the Western Film," *Comparative Literature Studies* 22.4 (Winter 1985): 519.

6. Janice H. Rushing, "Mythic Evolution of 'The New Frontier' in Mass Mediated Rhetoric," *Critical Studies in Media Communication* 3.3 (1986): 265–66.

7. Rushing, "Mythic Evolution," 266.

8. Winkler, "Classical Mythology," 517.

9. Season 2, episode 3.

10. M. Elise Marubbio, *Killing the Indian Maiden: Images of Native American Women in Film* (Lexington: University Press of Kentucky, 2006), 113.

11. Season 1, episode 20.

12. Season 6, episode 17.

13. Previously, Kripke stated in an interview that he "consider[s] *Supernatural* a kind of modern-day western." See Angie Rentmeester and Noelle Talmon, "A 'Supernatural' Spin-Off? Death by Bad Taco? Series Creator Eric Kripke Explains," Starpulse. com. http://www.starpulse.com/news/index.php/2008/02/14/a_supernatural_spin_off_death_by_bad_taco

14. Kripke has stated that the show draws its inspiration from urban legends and ghosts stories, ranging from academic studies to information he finds on Wikipedia. See Angie Rentmeester and Noelle Talmon, "A 'Supernatural' Spin-Off?"

15. "Exile on Main Street," Season 6, episode 1.

16. Season 6, episode 21.

17. Season 5, episode 15.

Bibliography

Marubbio, M. Elise. *Killing the Indian Maiden: Images of Native American Women in Film*. Lexington: University Press of Kentucky, 2006.

Rentmeester, Angie, and Noelle Talmon. "A 'Supernatural' Spin-Off? Death by Bad Taco? Series Creator Eric Kripke Explains." Starpulse.com, February 14, 2008.

Rushing, Janice H. "The Rhetoric of the American Western Myth." *Communication Monographs* 50.1 (1983): 14–32.

———. "Mythic Evolution of 'The New Frontier' in Mass Mediated Rhetoric." *Critical Studies in Media Communication* 3.3 (1986): 265–96.

Turner, Frederick Jackson. "The Significance of the Frontier in American History." In *Frederick Jackson Turner: Wisconsin's Historian of the Frontier*, edited by Martin Ridge, 1–19. Madison: State Historical Society of Wisconsin, 1986.

Winkler, Martin M. "Classical Mythology and the Western Film." *Comparative Literature Studies* 22.4 (Winter 1985): 516–40.

CHAPTER THREE

The Whore with the Vampire Heart

Frontier Romanticism in John Carpenter's Vampires

Lindsay Krishna Coleman

Cinematic depictions of the Wild West would not be complete without the "soiled doves," "shady ladies," and "sporting women" of saloons, dancehalls, and bordellos. Such women are complex figures—part of the wildness and "risky business" of the frontier, yet peripheral to its central conflicts—provocative of mainstream norms and values, yet silenced in realms ordered by hierarchy and power. They are "civilians," if you will—minor players in the conflict between good and evil. How are these roles and relationships reordered, though, when the "whore with a heart of gold" so familiar to audiences becomes something different—a "whore with a heart of a vampire"—and when a "lady of the evening" not only represents the dark side of early frontier civilization but also the very Heart of Darkness?

Noted horror master John Carpenter offers a look at this dark, lusty side of undead Westerns—embodied in the whore Katrina (Sheryl Lee)—in his 1998 film *Vampires*. This chapter explores the unexpected inversions and subversions of Katrina's "civilian" status when a vampire's bite makes her something more than the archetypal Western harlot. Through Katrina, the film reinterprets the narrative, thematic, and emotional importance of the peripheral civilian in the Western, as she begins the film in a state of passivity, is empowered by the vampire's bite, then returns to a conventional role at the film's end, restoring the traditional Western narrative status quo.

While technically a vampire film, its dependence on Western visual and character tropes and its effective fusion of vampire horror with Western-style heroism constitutes *Vampires* as generically a Western. The mythical frontier of the West is a realm noted for the limited breadth of its characterizations. The sole figures of narrative force are men in their prime, or—in the case of John Wayne in *The Searchers* (1956) and the cast of *The Wild Bunch* (1969)—coming to the end of a magnificent prime. These characterizations are tailored to simple realities, in which tests of manhood and male friend-ship take place amid a landscape as raw and powerful as the central conflicts that drive classic Westerns. The genre demands a clean narrative line and characters who—with noted exceptions—embrace a version of humanity devoid of complex psychology.

At the margins of most great Western tales are the civilians, the non-combatants—the schoolmarms, bartenders, preachers, blacksmiths, and shopkeepers who round out the narrative and social landscape of the West-ern town. The common folk exist to be protected, not indulged. These civilian figures are, in films of the genre's Golden Age, typically hamstrung, irrelevant, or merely charming distractions, and in the revisionist period that dominated the 1960s, they receive little to no protection from the new breed of disaffected protagonists and antiheroes, their "characters" distilled to quick flashes of pain and panic on anonymous faces. The common folk of the cinematic West are at best a distraction, at worst a hindrance.

Key among these Western civilians are female characters, ranging from nameless extras to featured players. Women are the Western hero's inspi-ration and moderating force, but rarely his focus. Strong female figures who transgress normative gender roles on the frontier—*bandidas*, cowgirls, ranchers, and women of ill repute—hold a degree of social power, but all suffer fates that serve as cautionary tales to others, in the interest of preserving the "civilized" status quo.[1] Similarly, Western women in tra-ditional, positively coded roles are seldom depicted as figures of power or agency. Gary Heba and Robin Murphy observe that "compared to their male counterparts," even representations of women in starring roles "have not had the same iconic immediacy and value."[2] Jane Tompkins is likewise dismissive of the power of women in the Western, arguing that regardless of their resourcefulness, they falter and revert to normative gender roles rather than successfully display heroic (masculine) traits.[3] The school-teacher played by Carroll Baker in John Ford's *Cheyenne Autumn* (1964) provokes love in the heart of Captain Archer (Richard Widmark), but her probity precludes her narrative agency. Her honorable conduct and desire to care for and protect the Indian population prevent her from pursuing a liaison with the captain and also prevent her from taking a more active role in the volatile social conflict in which she finds herself. Philadelphia Thursday (Shirley Temple) in Ford's earlier work, *Fort Apache* (1948), is flirty and very much appropriate to the actress's star persona, yet Ford's decision to cast Temple seems inappropriate and damaging to the film's integrity in this grim film. Even bold, transgressive female characters, such as Linda Darnell's Chihuahua in Ford's *My Darling Clementine* (1946) or Paulette Goddard's Louvette in Cecil B. DeMille's *North West Mounted Police* (1940), fall victim to the narrative dictates governing heroic romance.

Women in Westerns become more peripheral as the action advances and are rejected if, like Debbie (Natalie Wood) in Ford's *The Searchers*, they have contact with the enemy. In Carpenter's vampire Western, however, Katrina becomes *more* central to the action as it advances and enjoys greater agency and power precisely *because* of her contact with the principal villain. Sullen and possessed, Katrina is essential to the plot of *Vampires*. Likewise she is the film's sole emotional focus, her predicament provoking sympathy and affection from Montoya. In this way, Woman becomes the silent center and heart of Carpenter's picture.

Adapting the Wild West

A student of the Western, Carpenter's affinity for the genre is strong, and *Vampires* is not his first project with frontier overtones. In his urban thriller *Assault on Precinct 13* (1976), Carpenter adapts the story line and characters of Howard Hawks's *Rio Bravo* (1959) to a more contemporary law-and-order setting. The film features a stripped-down Western narrative: a simple tale of survival pitting the urban lawmen against a gang of streetwise killers—a thinly veiled rendition of Hawks's original gang of outlaws. The heroes of *Assault* luxuriate in their comradeship. Their mutual admiration, as in the traditional Western, is the force that binds them together during the film's narrative crisis. Carpenter maintains the morality, the tempo, and the tough-guy fantasy of Hawks's original, and he creates an urban Western in a vein similar to Walter Hill's *The Warriors* (1979).

Carpenter's *Vampires*, released over a decade later, is instructive in its equally deliberate deconstruction of numerous Western tropes. Set in the modern-day West, the film follows a team of Catholic-Church-sanctioned vampire hunters known as Slayers, led by Jack Crow (James Woods), as they attempt to prevent Master Vampire Jan Valek (Thomas Ian Griffith) from gaining control of an artifact that would render him unstoppable: the centuries-old Bersier Cross. Early in the film, the prostitute Katrina is bitten by Valek, which both transforms her and creates a telepathic link between the pair. The Slayers use Katrina's connection with the vampire in their attempt to hunt him down before he gains access to the cross.

Set in the Southwest, the film is very much a Western, using numerous classic tropes and familiar characters.[4] The film, though, is a hybrid right from the start. The mean streets of *Assault on Precinct 13* are now replaced with sagebrush, deserted mining towns, and farmyards. The film opens on Crow and his team "cleaning out" a vampire nest, but Carpenter soon upends the narrative when the group of mercenary scoundrels, caught indulging in the great pastimes of the Western antihero—drink and whores—are caught off guard and summarily are dispatched by Valek. Tim Guinee's Father Adam becomes the second action lead in the film when Daniel Baldwin's Anthony Montoya, Crow's trusted second-in-command, is rendered suspect after being bitten by Katrina. While representatives of the Church are often portrayed as ineffectual in cinematic Westerns, such as the preacher gunned down in the opening scene of *Tombstone* (1993), Father Adam proves courageous and resourceful, becoming a classic Hawksian sidekick. In *The Cinema of John Carpenter*, Ian Conrich and David Woods note numerous Hawksian gestures of respect, including Adam's tossing of a knife to hero Crow in a melee with vampires, much as Walter Brennan tosses a gun to John Wayne during a brawl in *Red River*.[5] Like Brennan before him, Father Adam is a sidekick respected and esteemed for his competence, even to the point of Crow engaging in homoerotic banter with him.

The route to the romantic, vampiric heart of this picture—to a story line full of literal and figurative darkness so ably embodied by the victim and victimizing Katrina—is rooted, first, in Carpenter's conviction that the Western and the vampire story may coexist in the same narrative. He perceives how the narrative's central thread may be transplanted:

> One of the offshoots of the vampire myth from *Dracula* is the death of the aristocracy in Europe. You see, as the aristocracy decayed and its rule became decadent, well guess what—that's what Dracula was. He was an aristocrat, and he was trying to drink the blood of his people. So that's what that was about. Well, mine wasn't so European Gothic. Mine was Southwestern. So we just changed it a little bit. It's the same f— story.[6]

What doubtless aids in the success of such a wild combination—one genre firmly rooted in daybreak and sunsets, the others in moonlight—is in fact this change in location, and an assimilation of the particular local flavor of horror film. Mexican horror, known for its colorful and bizarre hybrids and decontextualizations, demonstrates a creativity and reflexiveness seldom seen in films made north of the border, outside of the exploitation genre. Carpenter confessed his fascination with over-the-top Mexican horror mashups in a Starz television network documentary exploring the vampire picture:

Oh God, they are fabulous. They do insane things. For instance, there'll be a professional wrestling match with masked wrestlers, and one wrestler will pull off the mask and there's a werewolf underneath. It's unbelievably crazy s— with blood and naked women—aw, it's the greatest. It's crazy.[7]

The image below illustrates the degree to which this assimilation achieves a wild fusion of genres. The tale echoes back as far as the original book of *Dracula*, yet Carpenter cannot help but appropriate the wildness associated with Mexican vampire films. Katrina, a contemporary working girl of the Southwest, hooker boots and all, is menaced by a figure true to the traditional aspect of Dracula: tall and dark, immaculately tailored, the continental gentleman of yore.

Carpenter positions Katrina as a multiple hybrid character. She is victimized within both genres: as the silent, objectified whore of the traditional Western and as the vampire's prey of the gothic horror tale. Once bitten,

Katrina, a jaded New Mexico prostitute, prepares to begin her night's work, unaware that Jan Valek is about to transform her into a vampire—and a vastly more significant player in the ongoing battle between the living and the undead.

however, the combination of her vampirism and her profession place her at an unexpected juncture of the two canons, embodying both vampiric and sexual power and acquiring agency over the course of the narrative. This alignment of the vampiric and the erotic is, perhaps, a "natural" mingling of traits for the daughters of darkness. The "terrible women" in Bram Stoker's *Dracula*—the vampiresses who torment Jonathan Harker—would have reminded Stoker's contemporaries of prostitutes with their rough, aggressively predatory manner.[8] Katrina's embodiment of the tropes of both genres makes her a fulfillment—both fascinating and essential—of *Vampires'* generic prerequisites as a vampire Western.

The coupling of the two genres is a paradoxical notion. Westerns are spectacles set in daylight—taking full advantage of the expansive landscape so critical to the myth of the frontier—with the odd scene set at night, under cover of darkness. Traditional vampire films are set primarily at night.[9] One genre favors expansiveness, the other claustrophobia. In the vampire picture the creature itself is the spectacle, often set against some gloomy gothic background. In the Western, the hero is dwarfed by the physical wonders of the Arizona deserts or Monument Valley. Carpenter's *Vampires* consciously combines these binary oppositions, containing and using the spectacles of both the environment *and* the vampire. Katrina serves as a portal between genres and worlds, darkness and light. To follow Valek, Crow and his allies must enter the literal and metaphorical dark with Katrina leading the way. This whore, this "terrible woman," serves as a generic gateway, close enough to both harridan and harlot to transport audiences across genres and draw them into the mystery of her dance with the master vampire.

Vampire Sensuality

Women are, by narrative and genre necessity, at the center of the classic vampire tale—as essential to the vampire saga as they are generally inessential to the masculine world of the Western. The heteronormative perspective typical of the vampire picture places the vulnerable female as the prey of the male vampire, the sexual frisson of his attack responsible for the genre's potent subtext. The vampire preys on women in their beds and penetrates them with his fangs, to the frequent accompaniment of orgasmic moans. This eroticism has always accompanied the vampire tale, persisting and becoming more fully elaborated over time, from Mina Harker (Helen Chandler) in the original *Dracula* (1931) to Sookie Stackhouse (Anna Paquin) in the television series *True Blood* (2008—).[10] Women in vampire tales are not simply acted upon, however: they (with occasional lesbian exceptions) inspire the vampire's lust—sexual as well as sanguinary—or even his romanticism, tempting him out of his lair and into the metaphorical daylight of domesticity and the complex emotional and social interactions of everyday life. Women elaborate the genre's emotional palette, bringing depth and complexity to a scenario that is, at its core, merely threat and apprehension in its simplest form. Mina Harker and Lucy Weston, the Count's innocent victims in *Dracula*, establish vampirism as a metaphor for emotional violence and are the human vectors of the genre's capacity to inflict heartbreak. As victims, they are the focus of audience sympathy; their suffering (and, in Lucy's case, death) demonstrate the toll of the vampire's bite.

Katrina, in contrast, is both the victim and the victimizer. Bitten by Valek, then held captive by Crow for use against him, she enters—and bites—her protector, Montoya. Enacting her role as gothic predator, she upends the Western narrative conventions regarding female passivity and victimhood, but she reinforces—and, indeed, powerfully amplifies—those that establish heartbreak, ruin, and (potentially) death as the consequences of loving a spirited, transgressive woman willing to seize control of her own destiny.

For Carpenter the vampire is inherently sensual, and the interaction between the creatures and their prey cannot avoid sexual overtones. This sensuality, however, morphs and changes from age to age. Historically the sensuality of the vampire, as revealed through the nuances of his relationship to his prey, has been ever changing. Carpenter notes:

> It became more sensual as the culture changed. The vampire myth as it's reflected in the movies reflects the culture around it, the people who are living. When you look at *Nosferatu*, that's the time in which it was made. Pretty stunning back then. But we look at it now and we say . . . "Look at that gnomy guy [*laughs*] with the long fingernails." Then Bela Lugosi comes along, and he looks like Rudolph Valentino . . . his slicked back hair, the come-hither look. At the time, that was some pretty steamy stuff. You cut down the road to 1958, England, Hammer Films. Christopher Lee, he has a different take on the sensuality in that film. It's because the culture has changed.[11]

The presentation of vampiric sensuality in *Vampires* reflects—indeed, calls attention to—the changes. Katrina's pose and attitude as she is bitten—legs parted, back arched, head thrown back—pointedly reminds the viewer of her status as a whore interrupted in the course of an evening's work. Valek's piercing of her upper thigh, rather than her neck, underscores just how wide a gulf separates her from the newly betrothed female victims in *Dracula*: sensible schoolmistress Mina and her achingly virginal friend, Lucy. Valek, for his part, resides on a continuum somewhere between the pallid vampires of the contemporary *Twilight* series and the tall, dark, elegant Count played by Christopher Lee in the Dracula films produced by Hammer Studios in the 1950s and 1960s. He could be a glam rocker, with his fusion of suave romance and animal magnetism, spiced with hints of bloody decadence. Vampires are so polymorphous because, as Carpenter suggests, they reflect the elements of the "monstrous" found in the wider culture—the horrors of the everyday:

> Because we know people in real life who are sort of mental or emotional vampires. We sense that there's a truth to it, somebody using someone else, using their blood to refresh themselves. That kind of feels familiar to us as a people. It's an expansion on the truth. Monsters in movies are us, always us, one way or the other. They're us with hats on. The zombies in George Romero's movies are us. They're hungry. Monsters are us, the dangerous parts of us. The part that wants to destroy. The part of us with the reptile brain. The part of us that's vicious and cruel. We express these in our stories as these monsters out there.[12]

Monstrous Love

The effective hybridization of the Western with the vampire film is, therefore, prone to a greater complexity in characterization and emotional amplitude. The vampire picture allows for the exploration of sadism, desire, and the loss of humanity. Katrina, in being the vampire's prey, inevitably introduces the themes of emotional cruelty, desire, and eroticism. Whereas those impulses are denied or sanctioned in the traditional Western, and their object—the whore—is relegated to the margins, the more central role played by the Woman in the vampire film allows these themes to be explored exhaustively by Carpenter's vampire-Western hybrid.

The interplay is not only between Katrina and Valek, however. Katrina is half-vampire, and she seduces the vulnerable Montoya in spite of herself. Responding to her beauty and her need as a victim, he succumbs to her charms and then to her bite. Smitten from the inception, he is drawn like a moth to the flame. Linda Williams succinctly explains such a phenomenon, arguing that in fact there is little difference between the gaze of desire and that of horror. The "freakishness" and difference of the monster is akin to the difference of the woman to the man. In desiring a woman, a man's rapt gaze is akin to the dazed look of horror that any monster might provoke. Williams writes: "For she too has been constituted as an exhibitionist-object by the desiring look of the male. There is not that much difference between an object of desire and an object of horror as far as the male look is concerned."[13]

This blurring of the gaze is apparent as the film's narrative progresses. In the scene below, Katrina has already been bitten by Valek and captured by the Slayers. She is stripped, objectified, gagged, and silent—in short, an erotic body without a voice. Her status as a whore makes using her as a tool, and keeping her bound despite her protests, acceptable. She exists, in the film's [Western] universe, as an object and commodity, to be used by men as they see fit. The genre's conventions also make it acceptable for Carpenter, Montoya, and the audience to let their gazes linger on her body. In the context of Katrina's biting, however, the question becomes: Is this gaze that of the admiring male, or the horrified male?

In her dual status as a monster and a woman worthy of desire, Katrina complicates the stereotypical gender relations of the Western genre. She remains, in the basic details of her characterization, the marginal and easily dismissed figure of the frontier whore. She first appears in what is essentially an orgy of paid sex—Crow's posse enjoying the favors of various women of the night—in a scene reminiscent of Pat Garrett's carousing with multiple Mexican whores in Sam Peckinpah's *Pat Garrett and Billy the Kid* (1973). Even as the narrative unfolds, Katrina remains, to a significant extent, anonymous—a woman

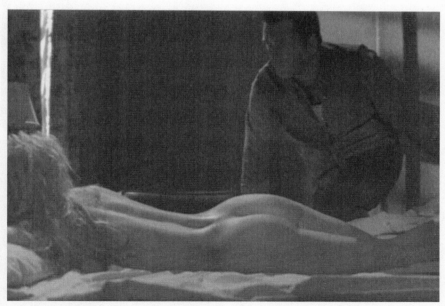

Stripped and bound to prevent her escape, Katrina's body becomes a focal point for the gaze of her captor-users (Crow and Montoya), for director John Carpenter's camera, and—through it—for the audience.

without history or context. She remains a sexual object throughout the film, even appearing in the gratuitous nude bondage scene. If it were not for her initial victimization—Valek's bite—she would remain a marginal, powerless character, a figure of gendered spectacle. Carpenter thus does not reinvent the characterization of the frontier whore. Instead, through his careful merging of genres, he gifts her with the power of a vampire, and, with it, narrative agency. Katrina maintains her passivity for much of the picture, but as her otherworldly qualities—her psychic connection to Valek and her aggressive bloodlust as a vampire—grow, she transforms, albeit temporarily, into a figure of power, with enough agency to affect the narrative outcome.

In a West where women are most closely associated with civilization and domestication—the taming of the frontier wilderness and the wildness of the men who have made it their home—Katrina's character arc is particularly provocative. Through her, Carpenter complicates the tension between control and chaos, civilization and the wild, female and male, weakness and power inherent in traditional frontier narratives. Katrina not only blurs the boundaries of those binary oppositions but also demonstrates their fluidity, as well.

In "Go West Young Woman!," Heba and Murphy suggest that Western women are often cast as having "emerging identities"—formed through a contrast with the identities of others.[14] This dialectical approach is particularly useful in considering the arc of Katrina's character and its implications as an artifact of the Western-horror hybrid. At the film's outset, Katrina holds a role sharply limited by generic convention. Already peripheral to the traditional narrative structure of the Western by virtue of her gender, she is further defined and marginalized in the social hierarchy by her relationship to men, through her status as a whore. As a transgressive woman who threatens the moral order, she stands as an icon of "wildness" in the otherwise civilized sphere of the frontier town—alternately feared, reviled, and objectified—the antithesis of her gender's civilizing function.

Katrina's identity as a traditional Western archetype—the "soiled dove"—deepens, strengthens, and crosses genre boundaries through contact with the film's supernatural elements. Valek's bite functions not only to transform her from woman to vampire, and Western character to hybrid character—an embodiment of the dialectic between Western and horror genres—it also allows the wildness of the frontier to reassert itself through her. She no longer holds claim even to the margins of civilization, she has emerged as "wild"—a creature of the night, embodying all the tensions of the Western genre's binary opposites. As the film's narrative resolves, however, and Valek, the master vampire, is killed, the wildness he represents is conquered and Katrina is "tamed" as her connection shifts from villain to hero (Montoya). Viewers, aware that she is destined to revert to her vampiric state—and, in good "transgressive woman" fashion is taking Montoya with her—are also positioned to recognize that the struggle between order and chaos, civilization and wildness, is eternal. Wildness will reassert itself in the pair, and the battle will begin anew, on some other frontier.

The destruction of Valek, the progenitor of film's supernatural elements, is key to a larger generic transition, as well; the master vampire's eradication allows the conventions of the Western to reassert itself. The emotional dynamic of the picture has altered, affecting a sudden reversal in the film's generic polarity as the emotional tone shifts from thriller to Western. The hybridized tone of the film is gone, and the paradigm now is that of three heroes in a quintessential final stand in a deserted Southwestern mining town, with Crow, Montoya, and the priest, battered and bitten, debating what comes next. The men's homosocial bond returns to the fore, and Katrina's role recedes to the periphery. As she and Montoya set out for the border—Mexico—Crow allows his friend, infected with vampirism, to depart unharmed, for the present. Echoing countless cinematic lawmen who have uttered, "The next time we meet . . ." and looked the other way as their friend-turned-outlaw rode out of town, he swears he will hunt them down.

This conclusion demonstrates Carpenter's urge to evoke the classic Western resolution, typified in films such as Howard Hawks's *Red River* (1948). He affirms: "You can't kill John Wayne. You can't kill him. You've got to let him go."[15] In the spirit of the battling Thomas Dunson (John Wayne) and Matt Garth (Montgomery Clift) of *Red River*, the men show one another compassion as they part company.

The film's hybridity, however, continues in the conclusion's ambiguity. A vampire future, and vampire tropes, will effectively return as the drama continues off screen. Katrina and Montoya will transform; the Slayer will hunt them as prey. In the world of the film, both genres will persist, in uneasy tension. Carpenter's choice to end the film with this element of ambiguity highlights his abiding faith in the Western form. The director's refusal to resolve the film's hybridity—allowing his vampires to roam the frontier—is a reminder that the undead need know no generic boundaries, that "monsters are us, the dangerous parts of us."[16]

Notes

1. See M. Elise Marubbio, *Killing the Indian Maiden: Images of Native American Women in Film* (Lexington: University Press of Kentucky, 2009).

2. Gary Heba and Robin Murphy, "Go West Young Woman!: Hegel's Dialectic and Women's Identities in Western Films," in *The Philosophy of the Western*, ed. Jennifer L. McMahon and B. Steve Csaki (Lexington: University Press of Kentucky, 2010), 309.

3. Jane Tompkins, *West of Everything: The Inner Life of Westerns* (New York and Toronto: Oxford University Press, 1992), 61.

4. Including an active evocation of Hawks—a small group of competent men efficiently doing their jobs, found in all of the director's Westerns.

5. Ian Conrich and David Woods, *The Cinema of John Carpenter: The Technique of Terror* (New York: Wallflower Press, 2005), 18.

6. Mike Bruno, "John Carpenter: The Sultan of Scare," *Entertainment Weekly*, October 23, 2007, 1. http://www.ew.com/ew/article/0,,20153543,00.html

7. Bruno, "John Carpenter," 2.

8. Bram Stoker, *Bram Stoker's Notes for Dracula: A Facsimile Edition*, ed. Robert Eighteen-Bisang and Elizabeth Miller (Jefferson, NC: McFarland, 2008), 270.

9. This rule is frequently broken, however, by the twenty-first-century vampire film.

10. Stackhouse was created by author Charlaine Harris in the 2001 novel *Dead until Dark*, the first volume in the Southern Vampire Mysteries series.

11. Bruno, "John Carpenter," 1.

12. Bruno, "John Carpenter," 2.

13. Linda Williams, "When the Woman Looks," in *Horror: The Film Reader*, ed. Mark Jancovich (New York: Routledge, 2002), 63.

14. Heba and Murphy, "Go West Young Woman!," 310.

15. Anthony C. Ferrante, "Carpenter King," *Dreamwatch*, November 1997. http://www.theofficialjohncarpenter.com/pages/press/dreamwatch9711.html

16. Bruno, "John Carpenter," 2.

Bibliography

Bruno, Mike. "John Carpenter: The Sultan of Scare," *Entertainment Weekly*, October 23, 2007. http://www.ew.com/ew/article/0,,20153543,00.html

Conrich, Ian, and David Woods. *The Cinema of John Carpenter: The Technique of Terror*. New York: Wallflower Press, 2005.

Ferrante, Anthony C. "Carpenter King," *Dreamwatch*, November 1997. http://www.theofficialjohncarpenter.com/pages/press/dreamwatch9711.html

Heba, Gary, and Robin Murphy. "Go West, Young Woman! Hegel's Dialectic and Women's Identities in Western Films." In *The Philosophy of the Western*, edited by Jennifer McMahon and Steve Csaki, 309–28. Lexington: University Press of Kentucky, 2010.

Marubbio, M. Elise. *Killing the Indian Maiden: Images of Native American Women in Film*. Lexington: University Press of Kentucky, 2009.

Stoker, Bram. *Bram Stoker's Notes for Dracula: A Facsimile Edition*. Edited by Robert Eighteen-Bisang and Elizabeth Miller. Jefferson, NC: McFarland, 2008.

Tompkins, Jane. *West of Everything: The Inner Life of Westerns*. New York and London: Oxford University Press, 1992.

Williams, Linda. "When the Woman Looks." In *Horror: The Film Reader*, edited by Mark Jancovich, 61–66. New York and London: Routledge, 2002.

CHAPTER FOUR

Billy the Kid vs. Dracula

The Old World Meets the Old West

Rachel E. Page, Robert G. Weiner, and Cynthia J. Miller

"*Billy the Kid vs. Dracula*, about the strangest Western ever made without a pornographic subplot."

—Sean Macaulay

Billy the Kid . . . one of the most evocative figures of the Old West, and one of its most historically ambiguous. The mention of his name conjures images of bank heists, train robberies, gunfights, and desperate escapes across the prairie—romantic images associated with a daring antihero rather than a murdering outlaw. History tells us that in his short life, his unrepentant villainy led him to become one of the most wanted men in the West, eventually meeting his end at the hand of lawman Pat Garrett. Embassy Pictures' *Billy the Kid vs. Dracula* (1966), however, tells a different tale. Here, Billy is a hero through and through. None of his historical predecessor's misdeeds cling to the fictional Kid, as he pits his wits and guns against the king of the undead, Dracula, in a hybrid Western film that was bizarre for its genre, but not for its day. This chapter will trace the remarkable shift in the image of the outlaw Billy the Kid, as he is transformed—through his portrayal as an Old West gunfighter battling an Old World vampire—from Western icon to camp icon, at a time like no other in the history of American film.

Billy the Kid vs. Dracula was not the undead's first foray into the West. Seven years earlier, another vampire, gunslinger Drake Robey, brought a new kind of bloodlust to the frontier in Edward Dein's *Curse of the Undead* (1959). But all undead are not created equal, and the two films, like their undead characters, could not have been more different. The earlier, produced by Universal Studios, featured production values only made possible by big studio budgets; its successor, shot on a compromised budget similar to that of most Poverty Row B movies, owes its persistence in popular consciousness to marketing strategies that rivaled P. T. Barnum's in their ability to lure and exploit the consumer. Directed by William Beaudine, *Billy the Kid vs. Dracula* was released to the grindhouse and drive-in movie circuits in 1966, on a double bill alongside *Jesse James Meets Frankenstein's Daughter*. Billed as the "4 greatest names in Terror history . . . in One Big Show" the double bill promised eager patrons all the gunslinging excitement of Jesse James and Billy the Kid, combined with the "undead" monster thrills of Dracula and Frankenstein's creation (or his daughter's creation, as the case may be).

The Old World Meets the Old West

The film begins as a typical horror tale, set on the prairie, importing and interweaving conventions of traditional European horror tales with elements of frontier saga. The Oster family, German immigrants, are camped under the stars in the Old West, but they are plagued by Old World fears. The mother's apprehension for the safety of her beautiful daughter is focused not on earthly predators but on the supernatural. She nestles a cross in the palm of her daughter's hand as a safeguard, and only minutes later it fulfills its duty, warding off John Carradine's Dracula as he begins to drain the young woman's life. This decontextualized predation prefigures struggles yet to come, against forces of evil seldom seen in the West.

What follows is a tale all too familiar to fans of gothic horror. Dracula books passage on a carriage and encounters a pair of siblings—Mary Bentley and James Underhill—en route to visit the former's daughter Betty (Melinda Plowman). Although her brother tries to cut her conversation short, Bentley prattles on about the visit, and she reveals that her daughter has never seen her uncle, James. She shares a picture of the girl with Dracula, who is instantly transfixed by her beauty. He decides that he must have her, and as the action unfolds, fate provides the opportunity. When all aboard the carriage are massacred by Indians, avenging the death of one of their own, Dracula assumes Underhill's identity and travels on to meet his "niece."

The narrative threads converge when both Dracula and the Osters arrive in town. The immigrants attempt to alert the townspeople to the presence of supernatural evil, but they are ultimately won over by the vampire's charade and Old World charm. Their guard down, he is free to victimize their daughter, finishing what he began that night on the plains. The tale then

The poster for *Billy the Kid vs. Dracula* reveals its basic premise—a traditional European horror story combined with a traditional Western—but it does not reveal the degree to which the two are interwoven. *"Exhibitors' Shockmanship Manual," courtesy of Robert G. Weiner*

shifts to the Double Bar B Ranch, where the struggle between good and evil is played out, with Betty Bentley—desired by both Dracula and Billy the Kid—at the center.

The Osters (Walter Janovitz, Virginia Christine) continue to warn of the vampire, but try as they might to protect the young ranch owner, their wisdom is quickly shunted aside in favor of the protection of traditional Western heroism. Too late, Billy the Kid (Chuck Courtney), the gunslinger whose past is littered with evil deeds, becomes suspicious of Bentley's "uncle" and accepts the Osters' claims about the existence of an evil beyond even *his* experience. Dracula kidnaps Bentley and takes her to his lair in the ranch's abandoned silver mine, where he plans to transform her into his undead mate. In good Western fashion, however, the Kid gives chase, armed only with his passion and a gun. He ignores warnings that his gun is powerless against a vampire, insisting that he hasn't "met a man yet that a bullet couldn't stop." When his gunslinging ways prove useless against this new Western evil, the quintessential Western outlaw—known far and wide for his violent instincts and transgressions of the moral order—must join forces with Doc (Olive Carey), an icon of science and intellect, and the sheriff (Roy Barcroft), an icon of law and order, in order to overcome the undead predator.

Imagining Billy the Kid

The character of Billy the Kid has long served as a staple of tales of the American West, featured in television programs, film series, radio shows, and literature. The short life of frontier outlaw William H. Bonney[1] (1859–1881) was catapulted into legend after he was gunned down by Lincoln County sheriff Pat Garrett, in one of the most famous (and still contested) confrontations in the history of the Wild West.[2] The product of a time when right and wrong, lawman and outlaw, were sometimes shifting categories, Bonney was a man with a price on his head, known for his cunning and skill with a gun. The ambiguities of his status led to his immortalization as both notorious outlaw and celebrated folk hero. As historian George Turner relates, the Kid is either framed as a "moronic sadistic delinquent" or "avenging angel," a kind of "Robin Hood of the Wild West."[3] His story and the frontier ethos it represents has inspired work across the genres, from historical novels to science fiction, ballads to ballets, radio plays to stage shows, and, of course, countless film and television renditions and references. His tale has been the subject of renewed interest and investigation with each passing decade, including a 2004 televised inquiry that linked Bonney's legend to the twenty-first century's popular culture fascination with forensic science.

Some of the better-known cinematic portrayals of Billy the Kid and his legend across the decades include a 1940s low-budget Poverty Row movie series featuring Buster Crabbe as the Kid, and its contemporary, Howard Hughes's *The Outlaw* (1943), starring Jane Russell; the 1950s delivered Arthur Penn's *The Left-Handed Gun* (1958), with Paul Newman in the outlaw's role; in 1961, *One-Eyed Jacks* featured Marlon Brando as "Rio"—a thinly veiled rendition of the Kid; and Westerns in the next quarter-century included Sam Peckinpah's *Pat Garrett and Billy the Kid* (1973), featuring James Coburn and Kris Kristofferson in the title roles, and Christopher Cain's 1988 *Young Guns*, with Emilio Estevez as the notorious gunfighter. Fascination with the life and legend of the Kid has continued into the present, through TV dramas and films such as the undead Western *Purgatory* (1999), the docudrama *Billy the Kid, Unmasked* (2004), and *Birth of a Legend: Billy the Kid & The Lincoln County War* (2011), directed by Andrew A. Wilkinson and featuring Robert Shrimplin as Billy.

These moving-image texts are not only products of a range of understandings of history but also of the eras in which they were brought into being. The figure of Billy the Kid transitions, accordingly, throughout their narratives—transformed from brazen enemy of civilized order, to romantic hero, to disaffected gunslinger, to nostalgic archetype—reflecting, in each film, the desires, fantasies, needs, fears, and conventions of the historical moments in which it was produced and initially consumed.[4] From this perspective, Beaudine's rendition of the Kid as sadder-but-wiser reformed gunfighter, acting out the role of "avenging angel" (following Turner) in a genre mash-up contextualized by carnivalesque ballyhoo is particularly significant. Far from being easily dismissed low-budget "trash," the film—along with its usage of and impact on the image of Billy the Kid—bears closer examination as a historically situated cultural artifact of the American mid-1960s.

An era of questioning values, traditions, and boundaries, marked by creativity and experimentation in both the arts and society at large, the 1960s gave rise to a broad spectrum of new cultural products, particularly in film. The freewheeling fun and angry turbulence of the decade were felt in both Western and horror genres alike. Revisionist Westerns such as *The Magnificent Seven* (1960), *The Man Who Shot Liberty Valance* (1962), *The Professionals* (1966), and *The Wild Bunch* (1969), along with "spaghetti Westerns" such as Sergio Leone's "Dollars Triology," including *A Fistful of Dollars* (1964) and

BILLY THE KID vs. DRACULA

3 Cols. x 100 Lines—300 Lines (20 Inches)   Mat 301

Mat 101
1 Col. x 14 Lines—14 Lines (1 Inch)

2 Cols. x 75 Lines—150 Lines (11 Inches)   Mat 202

ACCESSORIES AVAILABLE FOR
INDIVIDUAL SHOWING
(not illustrated)
1 SHEET · 22 x 28 · 40 x 60
SET OF EIGHT 11 x 14's and BLACK
& WHITE STILLS · COLOR TRAILER
ORDER FROM NATIONAL SCREEN SERVICE

Marketing materials for *Billy the Kid vs. Dracula* and *Jesse James Meets Frankenstein's Daughter,* presented as a double bill, used the four iconic title characters to appeal, on multiple levels, to the young viewers the distributors sought to attract. *"Exhibitors' Shockmanship Manual," courtesy of Robert G. Weiner*

JESSE JAMES MEETS
FRANKENSTEIN'S DAUGHTER

3 Cols. x 100 Lines—300 Lines (20 Inches)   Mat 301

1 Col. x 56 Lines—56 Lines (4 inches)
Mat 102

2 Cols. x 50 Lines—100 Lines (7 Inches)   Mat 202

ACCESSORIES AVAILABLE FOR
INDIVIDUAL SHOWING
(not illustrated)
1 SHEET · 22 x 28 · 40 x 60
SET OF EIGHT 11 x 14's and BLACK
& WHITE STILLS · COLOR TRAILER
ORDER FROM NATIONAL SCREEN SERVICE

The Good, the Bad, and the Ugly (1966), offered critical commentary on long-cherished assumptions about gender, race, power and authority, and American expansionism. At the same time, studios large and small were attempting to capitalize on the youth market and the rising popularity of the cult film, resulting in a wide range of horror and horror-tinged films—such as *Teenage Zombies* (1959), *Eegah!* (1962), and *The Horror of Party Beach* (1964)—that offered their own challenges to authority, convention, and the taken-for-granted aspects of cinematic productions.

Beaudine's *Billy the Kid vs. Dracula*, along with its double-feature co-bill *Jesse James Meets Frankenstein's Daughter*, brought their revisioned classic Western heroes to life in ways that drew upon many of these sources and urges in the contemporary cinema of the day. Their genre mash-ups brought together not only frontier action and gothic menaces but also elements of the sensationalism, resistance to definition, youth appeal, and cultural creativity that thrived in this era. Together, these forces propelled an already ambiguously interpreted Billy the Kid from Western icon to cult icon, using cinematic and promotional codes from each that were already highly recognizable to audiences of the day, providing ready points of reference for this new heroic, vampire-vanquishing rendition of a familiar frontier character.

Cycles and Trends

Billy the Kid vs. Dracula was thus the product of a time of change in American film as an industry—a time when the nature of on-screen images was being renegotiated and the frontiers of the bold and shocking were being explored. The Production Code governing the content of motion pictures had been partially rewritten in the mid-1950s to allow the treatment of such formerly taboo topics as graphic violence, drug addiction, and prostitution, so long as they were "treated within the careful limits of good taste."[5] By 1967, even that less restrictive Code would be ignored, and in 1968 it was eliminated entirely, replaced by the Motion Picture Association of America (MPAA) rating system. In the meantime, independent filmmakers were often on the front lines of censorship battles, as they stepped into spaces created by content regulation—taking advantage of opportunities and pushing boundaries where major studios did not dare (or care) to tread—and helped pave the way for widespread change throughout the film industry.

While cinema's association with exploitation began with early moving picture shorts in the first decade of the twentieth century, by midcentury it had truly come into its own.[6] The 1950s and 1960s witnessed the rise of several cycles of exploitation films and the sensational promotion that propelled them into popular consciousness. Spearheaded by larger-than-life entrepreneurs such as Kroger Babb, Joe Solomon, Dwain Esper, and others, these film cycles attempted to cash in on target audiences, particularly the growing teen market, with fare not found among major studios' offerings. Their promotional tactics promised theater owners "a hypodermic for boxoffice [sic] grosses that any Dr. Exhibitor can inject into his own community and create an epidemic of S.R.O."[7]

The formula was simple: take a low-budget, independently produced film on a sensational topic, release just a few prints to grindhouse theaters and drive-ins, and create an array of captivating extrafilmic events to accompany the show, luring audiences with the promise of a true "one of a kind" cinematic experience.[8] As Eric Schaefer relates: "Lectures, slide presentations, the sale of pamphlets or books on the picture's topic, and the presence of uniformed 'nurses' to attend to those who might faint due to the 'shocking' sights became a major part of the exploitation experience."[9] Exploitation techniques adapted well to any genre: the press kit for the 1939 *Hitler, Beast of Berlin* advised theater owners to use "Teutonic-looking strapping young men" dressed in SS uniforms to open movie house doors for female patrons and to commission the construction of "torture boxes" for audiences to try out in the safety of the theater's lobby; while David Friedman promoted the distribution of "vomit bags" printed with the warning "You May Need This When You See *Blood Feast*" for screenings of his 1963 film, one of the campiest and most repulsive productions of its era. Friedman credits the carnival as the birthplace of 1960s cinematic exploitation: "You know, it's the old razzle-dazzle—sell the sizzle not the steak—and uh, that's what it was all about. It worked for me, it worked for Babb, it worked for Barnum, and it worked for Bailey, so why change it?"[10] Beaudine himself was no stranger to exploitation film, having directed the infamous *Mom and Dad* (1945), along with other sensationalist fare.

The prolific director's Western-horror hybrid double bill emerged from midst of this cinematic era, along with countless other low-budget films that laid claim to the status of "Bold! Daring! Shocking! True!"[11] These ranged from *She Shoulda Said "No!"* (1949)—a cautionary tale that asked, "How bad can a good girl get?"—to the playfully sexual *My Tale Is Hot* (produced in 1964, by Dan Sonney under the alias "Seymour Tokus"), and from the over-the-top horror of *Blood Feast* (1963) to the rock-and-roll monster camp of *The Beach Girls and the Monster* (1965). Exploitation films, regardless of the "payoff" on their sensational come-ons, were promoted in a style that ushered prospective audience members back and forth between the world of carnival sideshows and low-budget celluloid spectacle, using colorful promises of the fantastic. And so, surrounded by carnivalesque promotional ballyhoo, *Billy the Kid vs. Dracula* and *Jesse James Meets Frankenstein's Daughter* offered up a double bill unlike any other. The promotional strategies that proved so successful in drawing crowds to other offbeat films on the margins of American cinema were perfectly suited to Beaudine's hybrids, capitalizing on their novelty rather than relying on their conformation to generic conventions. In the company of Western films, the pair is a dismal failure, and when compared to the body of horror films of the decade, the result is similar. But when processed through the imaginative lens of exploitation—rough edges highlighted and lack of convention celebrated—the films become something more—unique cultural products—and their lead characters transform from Western icons into camp icons.

The Newest in Terror-tainment!

The official press kit ("Exhibitor's Shockmanship Manual") promoting these Embassy Pictures films presents a fascinating picture of how the genre mash-ups were marketed. Both films were hyped with the same fervor and sensationalism as the films of exploitation pioneers like William Castle, Dwain Esper, and Dave Friedman. Although acknowledging the Western component of both films, Embassy marketed them as horror films. The slogan for both was the "Newest in Terror-tainment! Shockorama . . . See the greatest names in Terror History in One Big Show."[12] The film company recommended that exhibitors hire bodyguards and have first aid stations and ambulances waiting to help those who were too faint of heart to handle the excitement of the features. Other suggestions included having a "nervous service" offering "free coffee to steady your nerves" with a "Blood-chilling display" featuring a heater to warm those who were "chilled" by the films before they left the theater. Embassy even urged theater managers to offer a "shock warranty," guaranteeing that the bearer attending the "shockorama" features would have "palpitations, goose pimples, spine tingles, perspirations, (and) suspirations."[13]

This ballyhoo and hyperbole was present in other marketing media, as well, with "blood curdling trailers, terrorizing TV spots, (and) electrifying radio spots."[14] This type of sensationalism, which revived the sense of playful

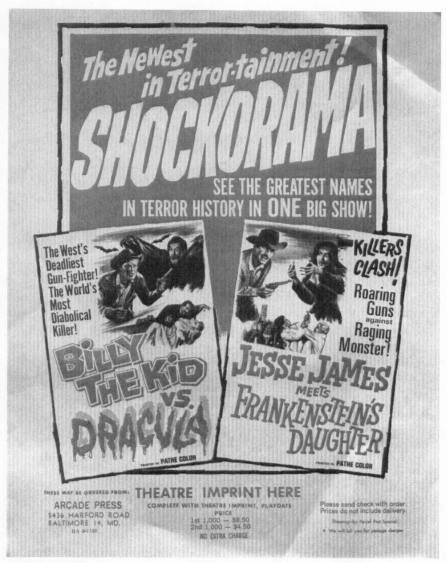

Designed and produced to play as a double bill on the grindhouse and drive-in circuit, *Billy the Kid vs. Dracula* and *Jesse James Meets Frankenstein's Daughter* were marketed using the techniques of exploitation films, including extravagant promises about what they offered. *"Exhibitors' Shockmanship Manual," courtesy of Robert G. Weiner*

Barnumesque larceny of earlier exploitation films, illustrated the creativity of small independent film companies in their efforts to entice moviegoers to see their low-budget features. Interestingly, while Carradine's Dracula is prominently featured on promotional materials for *Billy the Kid vs. Dracula*, promotions for the *Jesse James* feature resort to sexualized marketing to draw audiences to the film. Press materials do not depict Frankenstein's monster, but rather a sexualized female vampire.

Acknowledgment of both films' status as Westerns was limited to the narrative text of promotional materials:

> The last of the wide open spaces of the far west provide the dramatic settings for the film. Key scenes were shot at Red Rock Canyon California, famed site of many Western movies, where even today conditions are so primitive [sic] that an unskilled traveler could meet danger or death if lost there.[15]

> The setting for the picture is the dramatic early West where for ages man fought an endless struggle against the forces of nature. The wide-open spaces again become a battleground for good versus evil in the film, but the battle is one of a far different nature from those in the normal cowboy tales.[16]

The two films were made specifically for release to the drive-in theaters. "They were 'midnight movie' fare fraught with campy characters and nonsensical [sic] situations never meant to be taken seriously."[17] At the Waldorf drive-in theatre, in Washington, D.C., both films were screened along with four cartoons and the Cold War John Wayne vehicle *Jet Pilot* (1957) in a very odd triple feature.[18] Both *Billy the Kid* and *Jesse James* were also among the earliest "pay as you watch" (think pay-per-view) films offered on television as an "experiment in subscription TV."[19]

Both actor Carradine and director Beaudine were in familiar territory with *Billy the Kid vs. Dracula*. The pair had previously worked together on several other low-budget films, including *Voodoo Man* (1944) and *Face of Marble* (1946), and each had a long and varied history in motion pictures. Beaudine (1892–1970) was one of the industry's most prolific directors. Known as "one-shot" for his single-take filming, he completed both *Billy the Kid vs. Dracula* and *Jesse James Meets Frankenstein's Daughter* in a sixteen-day period.[20] No stranger to low-budget horror mash-ups, his films include *Bela Lugosi Meets a Brooklyn Gorilla* (1952) and *Spook Busters* (1946) with the Bowery Boys.

John Carradine (1906–1988), for his part, performed in nearly five hundred films and television shows during his career. His credits ranged from award-winning A-list films, such as John Ford's *Grapes of Wrath* (1940) and *Stagecoach* (1939), to horror films such as Pete Walker's *House of Long Shadows* (1983), alongside horror film royalty Sir Christopher Lee, Peter Cushing, and Vincent Price, and the early zombie/science fiction alien hybrid *Invisible Invaders* (1959). He had already brought the vampire count to life in several films prior to *Billy the Kid vs. Dracula*, such as Universal's *House of Frankenstein*

The exhibitors' guide not only suggested ways of using carnivalesque hype and ballyhoo to promote the low-budget double feature but also modeled such techniques, billing itself as a "Shockmanship Manual." *"Exhibitors' Shockmanship Manual," courtesy of Robert G. Weiner*

(1944) and *House of Dracula* (1945), and went on to play him in *Blood of Dracula's Castle* (1969), *Doctor Dracula* (1978), and the comedic *Nocturna* (1979), as well as on television, in series such as *Matinee Theatre* (1955) and *McCloud* (1977). While the press materials claim that Carradine "eagerly accepted the role [of Dracula] as fascinating challenge," Carradine himself commented to numerous sources that the film was his worst.[21]

From Western Icon to Cult Icon

Far from receiving the scholarly and critical attention afforded contemporary compound genre films, this pair of undead Westerns has proven problematic in terms of both reception and analysis. Both films were dismissed for their low B movie production values—earning spots on various lists of the worst Westerns ever made—with *Billy the Kid vs. Dracula* decried as "The Genre's Worst Movie!" and "not much to sink your teeth into," and Beaudine's Frankenstein character derided for a stitched head "resembling a broken-down albino bowling ball."[22] Of greater interest is the criticism received by both films specifically for their hybridity. As late as the 1980s, the pair was dismissed as a "mind boggling fuse" of the "Western and horror genres," with little additional consideration.[23]

If, following Adam Knee, we view *Billy the Kid vs. Dracula* (and, similarly, *Jesse James Meets Frankenstein's Daughter*) as a compound genre film, that status signals that it will "concurrently engage multiple distinct and relatively autonomous horizons of generic expectations."[24] With the introduction of the undead, a staple of the horror genre, into the midst of conventional Western tropes and characters, the two "quite distinct sets of generic conventions have been pulled together and forced into a showdown."[25] Dracula dressed as a gunslinger, sleeping in a cave-turned-silver mine, positions the undead creature firmly in the Western tradition, while German immigrants, the Osters—"old-world peasants bearing what turn out to be well-grounded fears and superstitions in the horror films"—maintain the film's connection to the horror genre.[26] Knee argues that the compounding of genre conventions exists even within characters, evidenced by the key role played by a "tough drinking frontier doctor (Olive Carey)" who "by virtue of her knowledge of vampirism is crucial to the destruction of Dracula."[27] Doc's "specialized knowledge" as a woman of science is as reminiscent of Bram Stoker's Dutch vampire hunter, Dr. Abraham Van Helsing, as it is of traditional frontier physicians. As an opponent of the undead, she, like the Old World peasant, the lawman, and the young hero, directly map the conventions of classic European supernatural horror onto this updated Western saga, while traditional elements of both genres, such as the damsel in distress, provide points of coarticulation.

However, the notion of the compound genre, while useful, also implies that the generic elements coexist unchanged—in tension, perhaps, but nonetheless intact. *Billy the Kid vs. Dracula* moves beyond this format, with both the characters and the narrative suggesting a degree of hybridity, as well. While the narrative follows a traditional genre template, this collision of characters is far from ordinary, as elements of both horror and the Western are adapted for the encounter. We see this most significantly, perhaps, in the characters of hero and villain. The classic vampire trope is significantly altered in order to function on the frontier: while retaining his Old World demeanor, Dracula moves about under the Western sun, and he trades his traditional coffin for a bed. In contrast to the vampire's eternal evil, the outlaw Billy the Kid takes on an uncharacteristically heroic sheen, and, in sharp contrast to his historical and legendary counterpart, he also moves about freely without fear. In one of the film's most telling bits of adaptive commentary, however, the Old World vampire is ultimately a victim of modernity, done in with a metal spike rather than the traditional wooden stake, in an era that conquered the wildness of the frontier with railroads and barbed wire.

It is this element of hybridization that captured the imaginations of promoters and audiences alike. When the genre magazine *Monster World* featured articles on the *Dracula/Frankenstein* double bill in 1966, it was the hybridization as monster Westerns that the magazine found most fascinating. The feature taglines described how the "Count goes West" and how the "monster wore spurs . . . (where) the badmen of the Old West never had it so bad as when they met this lad" (referring to Igor, Madame Frankenstein's monster).[28] The films' status as hybrids granted them entrée into a world of novelty and spectacle previously reserved for more risqué, taboo, or sensationalized subject matter.

Knee argues that *Billy the Kid vs. Dracula* was a simple reminder that the Western film genre was dying by 1966 and that production on Westerns had dropped considerably, and indeed, considerations of the timing of the film within the life of the genre are critical, as are discussions of their historical situatedness. At the time of the release of the first vampire Western, *Curse of the Undead*, in 1959, production of low-budget Westerns had dropped by 75 percent.[29] While major studios continued their production of high-budget Westerns and Western epics, this ebb in low-end production created a space where cultural creativity, such as hybrid genre forms, could occur. During the Golden Age of the B Western, low-budget films enjoyed significant box

Beaudine's films featured in the short-lived magazine *Monster World* (1964–1966). *Courtesy of Robert G. Weiner*

office success by adhering to mainstream genre conventions and audience expectations. In a waning market, however, Poverty Row studios had little to risk and everything to gain through genre innovation—and that choice, made within the larger context of film cycles and promotional trends, proved both economically and culturally successful. The imaginative hybrid elements featured in the film were ideally suited to the industry's youth market thrust, along with that other artifact of the 1960s—exploitation marketing— and promotion of the film. Its double-bill companion, as a chilling combination of undead monsters and gunslingers, was expected to give Embassy Pictures surefire hits. At the time of the pair's release, producer Joe Levine anticipated that the studio would "clear more than $5 million on each film."[30] From an economic standpoint, then, the impact of these hybrid films was not expected to be trivial. Culturally, the films' shared impact has been felt, as well. Although critically dismissed and derided ("too bad the actors and director didn't turn [it] into a comedy rather than playing it straight"[31]), *Billy the Kid vs. Dracula*—along with *Jesse James Meets Frankenstein's Daughter*—have persisted as icons of cult films and camp.[32]

The interest generated by *Billy the Kid vs. Dracula* at the time of its release, and the attention that the film (and its double-bill companion) have continued to draw in the nearly half-century since, confirm what William Beaudine, John Carradine, and the Poverty Row showmen of the 1960s instinctively knew: that Billy the Kid, like Dracula himself, was a protean figure capable of transcending period, setting, and even genre. The Billy who faced off against the king of the vampires in Beaudine's film was, like the film itself, a collision of seemingly disparate elements: traditional Western gunslinger, morally pure scourge of the undead, and misunderstood youth hero. It was the particular genius of the exploitation film industry to realize that those elements could, if brought together, not merely coexist, but sell tickets.

Notes

1. Born William Henry McCarty.

2. See Jon Tuska, *Billy the Kid: His Life and Legend* (Westport, CT: Greenwood Press, 1994); Mark L. Gardner, *To Hell on a Fast Horse: Billy the Kid, Pat Garrett, and the Epic Chase to Justice in the Old West* (New York: HarperLuxe, 2010).

3. George Turner, *George Turner's Book of Gunfighters* (Amarillo, TX: Baxter Lane, 1972), 2; Michael H. Price and George E. Turner, *Forgotten Horrors 2: Beyond the Horror Ban* (Baltimore: Midnight Marquee, 2001), 125.

4. For an extended discussion of this, see John E. O'Connor, *Image as Artifact: The Historical Analysis of Film and Television* (Malabar, FL: Robert E. Krieger Publishing, 1990).

5. Cynthia Miller, "The 'B' Movie Goes to War in *Hitler, Beast of Berlin* (1939)," *Film & History: An Interdisciplinary Journal of Film and Television Studies* 36.1 (2006): 58–64.

6. For more, see Alan Betrock, *The I Was a Teenage Juvenile Delinquent Rock 'n' Roll Horror Beach Party Movie Book* (New York: St. Martin's Press, 1986).

7. Betrock, *I Was a Teenage Juvenile Delinquent Rock 'n' Roll Horror Beach Party Movie Book*, 18. See also Robert G. Weiner, "Dwain Esper: Prince of Exploitation Films," in *From the Arthouse to the Grindhouse: Highbrow and Lowbrow Transgression in Cinema's First Century*, ed. John Cline and Robert G. Weiner (Lanham, MD: Scarecrow Press, 2010), 41–54.

8. Eric Schaefer, *Bold! Daring! Shocking! True!: A History of Exploitation Films, 1919–1959* (Durham, NC: Duke University Press, 1999), 6.

9. Schaefer, *Bold! Daring! Shocking! True!*, 6.

10. David Friedman, *A Youth in Babylon: Confessions of a Trash-Film King* (New York: Prometheus Books, 1990).

11. A note of gratitude here to Eric Schaefer for the loan of the title of his 1999 volume on exploitation film.

12. Embassy Pictures, "Exhibitors' Shockmanship Manual" (Arcade Press, 1965), 4.

13. "Shockmanship Manual," 3.

14. "Shockmanship Manual," 2–3.

15. "Shockmanship Manual."

16. "Shockmanship Manual," 9.

17. Wendy L. Marshall, *William Beaudine: From Silents to Television* (Lanham, MD: Scarecrow Press, 2005), 280.

18. "Classified Ad #6," *Washington Post and Times-Herald*, April 15, 1966, B15.

19. Clay Gowran, "Forrest Tucker Plans to Be 2 Places at Once," *Chicago Tribune*, August 1, 1967, A8.

20. Bob Thomas, "Lassie's Best Friend Is Director Beaudine," *Dallas Morning News*, April 27, 1967, 7.

21. "Exhibitors' Shockmanship Manual," 12; John Carradine, quoted in Tom Weaver, *John Carradine: The Films* (Jefferson, NC: McFarland & Company, 1999), 262.

22. Marke Andrews, "The Return of the B-Movie: B-Movies Feature Awful Acting, Bad Dialogue and Cheap Special Effects. So, What's Not to Like?" *Vancouver Sun*, March 13, 2004, D1; and Ed Naha, *Horrors: From Screen to Scream* (New York: Avon Books, 1975), 21, 158.

23. Dennis Hunt, "Video Log," *Los Angeles Times*, August 22, 1986, D23.

24. Adam Knee, "The Compound Genre: *Billy the Kid versus Dracula* meets *The Harvey Girls*," in *Intertextuality in Literature and Film: Selected Papers from the Thirteenth Annual Florida State University Conference on Literature and Film*, ed. Elaine D. Cancalon and Antoine Spacagna (Gainesville: University Press of Florida, 1994), 141.

25. Knee, "Compound Genre," 143.

26. Knee, "Compound Genre," 145.

27. Knee, "Compound Genre," 145.

28. James Warren, ed., "*Jesse James Meets Frankenstein's Daughter*: First Pics of Frankie's Daughter & Jesse James," *Monster World* 8 (May 1966): 19–20.

29. Knee, "Compound Genre," 149.

30. Marshall, *William Beaudine*, 280.

31. Johnny D. Boggs, *Jesse James and the Movies* (Jefferson, NC: McFarland and Company, 2011), 188.

32. Chris Hicks, "Movies So Bad They're Actually Good," *Deseret Morning News* [Salt Lake City], October 27, 2011, n.p.

Bibliography

Andrews, Marke. "The Return of the B-Movie: B-Movies Feature Awful Acting, Bad Dialogue and Cheap Special Effects. So, What's Not to Like?" *Vancouver Sun*, March 13, 2004, D1.

Betrock, Alan. *The I Was a Teenage Juvenile Delinquent Rock 'n' Roll Horror Beach Party Movie Book*. New York: St. Martin's Press, 1986.

Billy the Kid vs. Dracula. Directed by William Beaudine. 1966. Portland, OR: Cheezy Flicks Entertainment, 2003. DVD.

Boggs, Johnny D. *Jesse James and the Movies*. Jefferson, NC: McFarland, 2011.

Embassy Pictures. "Exhibitors' Shockmanship Manual." Arcade Press, 1965.

Friedman, David. *A Youth in Babylon: Confessions of a Trash-Film King*. New York: Prometheus Books, 1990.

Gardner, Mark L. *To Hell on a Fast Horse: Billy the Kid, Pat Garrett, and the Epic Chase to Justice in the Old West*. New York: HarperLuxe, 2010.

Gowran, Clay. "Forrest Tucker Plans to Be 2 Places at Once." *Chicago Tribune*, August 1, 1967.

Hicks, Chris. "Movies So Bad They're Actually Good." *Deseret Morning News* [Salt Lake City], October 27, 2011, n.p.

Hunt, Dennis. "Video Log." *Los Angeles Times*, August 22, 1986.

Jesse James Meets Frankenstein's Daughter. Directed by William Beaudine. 1966. Portland, OR: Cheezy Flicks Entertainment, 2003. DVD.

Knee, Adam. "The Compound Genre: *Billy the Kid versus Dracula* meets *The Harvey Girls*." In *Intertextuality in Literature and Film: Selected Papers from the Thirteenth Annual Florida State University Conference on Literature and Film*, edited by Elaine D. Cancalon and Antoine Spacagna, 141–56. Gainesville: University Press of Florida, 1994.

Marshall, Wendy L. *William Beaudine: From Silents to Television*. Lanham, MD: Scarecrow Press, 2005.

Miller, Cynthia. "The 'B' Movie Goes to War in *Hitler, Beast of Berlin* (1939)." *Film & History: An Interdisciplinary Journal of Film and Television Studies* 36.1 (2006): 58–64.

Naha, Ed. *Horrors: From Screen to Scream*. New York: Avon Books, 1975.

O'Connor, John E. *Image as Artifact: The Historical Analysis of Film and Television*. Malabar, FL: Robert E. Krieger Publishing, 1990.

Price, Michael H., and George E. Turner. *Forgotten Horrors 2: Beyond the Horror Ban*. Baltimore: Midnight Marquee, 2001.

Schaefer, Eric. *Bold! Daring! Shocking! True!: A History of Exploitation Films, 1919–1959*. Durham, NC: Duke University Press, 1999.

Thomas, Bob. "Lassie's Best Friend Is Director Beaudine." *Dallas Morning News*, April 27, 1967.

Turner, George. *George Turner's Book of Gunfighters*. Amarillo, TX: Baxter Lane, 1972.

Tuska, Jon. *Billy the Kid: His Life and Legend*. Westport, CT: Greenwood Press, 1994.

Warren James, ed. "*Billy the Kid vs. Dracula*: Can Billy Outdraw Drac? . . . See Our Exclusive Preview." *Monster World* 8 (May 1966): 20–23.

———, ed. "*Jesse James Meets Frankenstein's Daughter*: First Pics of Frankie's Daughter & Jesse James." *Monster World* 8 (May 1966): 14–19.

Weaver, Tom. *John Carradine: The Films*. Jefferson, NC: McFarland, 1999.

Weiner, Robert G. "Dwain Esper: Prince of Exploitation Films." In *From the Arthouse to the Grindhouse: Highbrow and Lowbrow Transgression in Cinema's First Century*, edited by John Cline and Robert G. Weiner, 41–54. Lanham, MD: Scarecrow Press, 2010.

CHAPTER FIVE

The West—
Reanimated and Regenerated

Hollywood Horror and Western Iconography in Gore Verbinski's Rango *(2011)*

Sue Matheson

In *Regeneration through Violence: The Mythology of the American Frontier 1600–1860*, Richard Slotkin notes that Americans "have continually felt the need for the sense of coherence and direction in history that myths give to those who believe in them."[1] America's concerns, its hopes, its terrors, its violence, and its justification of itself, are the foundation stones of its mythology, which informs American history and is expressed in its literature.[2] Among the complex of narratives that express America's mythic paradigms, the frontier narrative (in general) and Western film (in particular) offer their audiences opportunities to revisit, remember, reaffirm, and reexperience the regenerative impulse underlying America's frontier psychology. As Slotkin points out, the means to that material and spiritual regeneration that the West embodied (and arguably still embodies) became the means of violence, and "the myth of regeneration through violence became the structuring metaphor of the American experience."[3] When one considers the development of Western film, it is evident that, even though the details of the American frontier narrative have changed somewhat since *The Great Train Robbery* (1903), the paradigm continues to rely on aggression and bloodshed to drive the narrative forward. Disputes and conflicts that create plots, complicate the action, and produce tension in these stories are resolved brutally: as one bad man after another bites the dust, American civilization is protected and preserved, and the use of violence as a means of individual and social regeneration is sanctioned and reinforced. Tellingly, the later spaghetti Westerns are generally distinguished from traditional and Cold War Westerns because of the level of their violence, which is not only much higher but also much more stylized. Given the importance of violence to the genre, it is not surprising, then, that parodies of the Western, such as *Cat Ballou* (1965) and *Blazing Saddles* (1974), satirize the use of violence in the Western and that the runaway popularity of these parodies at the box office (*Cat Ballou* grossed $20 million in 1965; overall, *Blazing Saddles* has grossed $119.5 million) demonstrates how deeply embedded the mythos of the frontier was, and still is, in the American psyche.

In 2011, then, it was not surprising that a computer-animated comedy about a lizard in search of self, directed by Gore Verbinski and produced by Graham King, received favorable, even enthusiastic, reviews from viewers who appreciated and understood it to be a genre parody: Roger Ebert of the *Chicago Sun-Times* judged *Rango* as an "animated comedy for smart moviegoers, wonderfully made, great to look at, wickedly satirical"; Robert Mondello of National Public Radio considered "*Rango* . . . a real movie lover's movie, conceived as a *Blazing Saddles*–like comic commentary that's as back-lot savvy as it is light in the saddle"; and Frank Lovece of *Film Journal International* noted that "with healthy doses of Carlos Castaneda, Sergio Leone, Chuck Jones and *Chinatown* . . . [*Rango* is] the kid-movie equivalent of a Quentin Tarantino picture . . . a film buff's parade of great movie moments." From a troupe of singing owls in its opening credits (a nod to *Cat Ballou*'s troubadours who fulfill the same choral function) to its satisfying conclusion when the cowboy falls off his horse after riding even further West off into the sunset, *Rango* is a meta-romp for the initiated, sending up and spoofing the icons, conventions, and codes of Hollywood's celluloid and America's mythic frontier. No Western convention is spared in *Rango*, and neither are directors and actors: John Ford, Sergio Leone, Clint Eastwood, Lee Van Cleef, and Pat Buttram, to name a few well-known personalities connected with Western films, are all vigorously roasted. But unlike *Cat Ballou* and *Blazing Saddles*, *Rango* is much more than a clever genre and ingenious industry parody involving a very lonely lizard, a town named Dirt, and the Spirit of the West. Gore Verbinski's complex and sophisticated conflation of stylized screen treatments gleaned from Hollywood horror movies with the conventions of the Hollywood West sends lizard and viewer alike on a quest to meet the spirit figure of the Wild West—oddly, a journey that supports *and* critiques the American Character.

The Significance of Dirt

As Slotkin would point out, myth-making is simultaneously a psychological and a social activity in literature or film.[4] Rango himself establishes the relationship that exists between the character and myth as the movie's central issue, when, as he points out (in the opening scene) that he is "the guy, the protagonist, the hero" but his character is "undefined"—that is, uninvolved in conflict. "The stage is waiting. The audience thirsts for adventure. Who am I?" Rango asks his audience. "I could be anyone . . . the sea captain returning from a mighty voyage . . . the rogue anthropologist battling pythons down in the Congo . . . the greatest lover the world has ever known." Faced with a plethora of generic possibilities, Rango, an ordinary lizard, decides that the nature of his character will have to be determined by "an ironic, unexpected event that will propel the hero into conflict."

Propelled from his aquarium into the American Southwest, it quickly becomes apparent that Rango's character is drawn from the Western. In 1893, Frederick Jackson Turner identified the West as the birthplace of the American Character. His groundbreaking and highly popular address, "The Significance of the Frontier in American History," notes that every American generation returned "to primitive conditions on a continually advancing frontier line" until the closing of the frontier in 1890. According to Turner, the frontier experience was a crucible that produced a social and psychological phenomenon characterized by the qualities of strength and inventiveness that settlers acquired after jettisoning colonial institutions and ideas to solve problems created by their harsh new environment. Turner argued that the hardships involved in settling the wilderness also produced in Americans distinctive qualities of individualism, materialism, and egalitarianism and ensured their resistance to centralized political power. For Turner, the West was the quintessentially American place, a land of freedom and opportunity. Rango, like Turner's early American settler, reinvents himself in the West. However, unlike the settler, Rango is sent on a journey of self-discovery, a vision quest in the wilderness. Following Roadkill's advice, he begins looking for the Spirit of the West in Dirt, a frontier community populated with type characters from Hollywood Westerns: among the Dirtonians, one finds a rancher's daughter, a corrupt businessman, a gunslinger, a number of honest townsfolk, a floozy, a number of hillbillies, and a handful of outlaws.

As Slotkin points out in *Gunfighter Nation: The Myth of the Frontier in Twentieth-Century America*, the frontier has always been seen through "a distorting-lens of mythic illusion"; as "a mythic space," the West is comprised of "a set of symbols" representing its own "peculiar geography, politics, and cultures."[5] Located in the middle of the desert, Dirt itself is easily recognizable as a Western icon. Rising up out of the desert dunes and lacking suburbs, Dirt's peculiar geography is the iconic Main Street of the frontier town of classic Western films. Even at a distance, Dirt is unmistakably Western, modeled after Tucumcari, the archetypal frontier town found in *For a Few Dollars More* (1965), boasting a ramshackle tower and single street along which one finds a two-story saloon, bank, and other businesses. Stepping back into the past, Rango discovers that, unlike Tucumcari, Dirt also shows signs of the passage of time. Lacking paint, its sagging, patched, run-down, monochromatic buildings record the effects of the harsh, desert conditions.

Soon, it becomes apparent that Rango has not merely stepped back in time. Verbinski's playful presentation of a frontier town is purposely disturbing. One expects a frontier town named Dirt to be dirty, and, historically, such places most likely were. However, it should be noted that the semiotics of cleanliness in the Western film are firmly rooted in Victorian social norms and mores. Because the Victorians associated filth with poverty and disease, dirt was deemed to be not only physically unpleasant but also morally and ethically questionable. Those deemed socially undesirable during the second half of the nineteenth century were called "the great unwashed" because they were physically and *morally* unclean. "Dirt" meant excrement in the vernacular of that era—as it still does sometimes—but it is noteworthy that horse manure does not litter the Main Streets and well-used thoroughfares of Western towns, in spite of the large, healthy, well-fed horses that are always picturesquely tied to hitching posts. Indeed, when considering the immaculate streets that this genre boasts, it seems that every horse in a Western must relieve itself offset or magically have no need to relieve itself at all.

Raised by Victorian parents, John Ford understood the importance of these semiotics when presenting the American myth to the average American. When approached by his assistant, Wingate Smith, with the concern that the set of *The Man Who Shot Liberty Valance* (1962) would not be accepted by audiences as "real" because it didn't look lived-in, he snapped, "If they notice it, then we'll give 'em their nickel back."[6] John Ford, like hero Ransom Stoddard, knew that what his audiences wanted was the myth of the West, not its reality. Accordingly, the town of Shinbone in *Liberty Valance* transmitted the legend of the West via its recognizable buildings and their cleanliness. Generally, the celluloid outposts of civilization found in the Wild West are characterized by the absence of dirt and the presence of law and order. As outposts of civilization, Western towns promote clean living, and it is the duty of every sheriff and public-minded citizen is to clean up the town. In *Stagecoach* (1939), for example, cleanliness—in both senses—is next to godliness. The buildings in the town of Tonto are so white and its wooden sidewalks so well kept that they appear to have been built the day before the action of the film occurs. As the prostitute Dallas and alcoholic Doc Boone discover, however, Tonto is also no place for those socially and morally debased. They are expelled into the wilderness, at the beginning of the film, by Tonto's League of Decency.

Thus, even in spaghetti Westerns, dust that swirls through the streets of towns like Tucumcari does not adhere to the walls of its buildings or inhabitants. Built in studios and studio back lots, towns of the Wild West are unrealistically clean places because they are meant to be. Paint does not peel in these places, and their inhabitants' clothes are pressed, their teeth are brushed and sparkling, and their boots are polished; in such places, cowboys and even the gunslingers are usually clean shaven and always well dressed. Even on cattle drives, the cowboys' horses are always curried, and the leather of their saddles glints in the sunshine. Supporting the Yankee Protestant work ethic and what Slotkin identifies as the frontier's promise of the renewal of American's material fortunes, spirits, and the power of the church as well as the nation,[7] the squeaky-clean appearance of towns in Western films reassured viewers that America remained unsullied by the dirty environment and the equally filthy lucre that produced it.

It is no surprise then that Verbinski's iconic Western town is a tidy, orderly place. True to the precedents set by places like Shinbone and Tucumcari, Dirt's sandy streets are clean and its sidewalks are swept bare. As in Shinbone and Tucumcari, no one really seems to live in Dirt, and there is far too little traffic, human and equine, in its empty streets. Dirt, however, is aptly named. In this place, the desert does stick to what it touches. Dust thickly coats its buildings, creating a sepia effect, encouraging audiences to recognize that this is nineteenth-century America and that, as such, the frontier of which it is a part is a place of social and moral contagion. Verbinski reinforces this perception with a subcategory of filth so dirty that it, too, cannot be overlooked—grime.

The jarring note that Verbinski strikes with his representation of Dirt is due in part to the fact that Dirt's buildings and inhabitants are incredibly grimy (though its streets are still strangely devoid of horse manure). Verbinski's playful use of grime parodies one of the genre's most central, yet often unnoticed, conventions central to the mythology of the West. Like cleanliness, dirt, too, is an essential signifier in the Western. As Martin Pumphrey points out in "Why Do Cowboys Wear Hats in the Bath?: Style Politics for the Older Man," over the years washing, bathing, and shaving have provided Westerns with a familiar set of narrative moments, and cleanliness (or the lack of it) has played a crucial part in their coding of character.[8] Heroes, Pumphrey says, are not "stained, grimy, or disheveled in the style of the rough, unmannered villains. Heroes may be dusty but not dirty. Their clothes may be worn but not greasy. They seldom sweat. Above all, they have always just shaved."[9] In short, everyone in Dirt (with the exception of Rango) is just too filthy to be a hero. The Dirtonians' dismal and grimy color palette of grays, brown, and blacks disqualifies them as Western protagonists—as does their lack of personal hygiene. Rango, the only colorful character in the film, sporting brilliant green skin and a loud red-and-white Hawaiian print shirt, attempts to blend in but fails. The children of Dirt immediately recognize him as a stranger. Tubbed and scrubbed, he discovers that he may be able to walk and talk like a Westerner, but he cannot be mistaken for a Dirtonian because he does not have their dirty habits. Morally and ethically clean, he cannot even spit on the street, and accordingly he becomes the town's sheriff.

American Gothics and the Supernatural Frontier

Verbinski also uses dirt and grime to marry his movie's Western iconography with Hollywood horror conventions. Without water, Dirt's townsfolk do not seem to have bathed in years. Grotesquely unclean, they look like they have just been dug from the ground. Outside the town, the association between characters and dirt is even closer: Balthazar's hillbillies literally emerge from the floor of their canyon hideout like reanimated corpses clawing their way out of their graves. Throughout, Verbinski's use of the grotesque insists that the imbalance that the townsfolk's filthiness indicates is not just a matter of social appearance. Verbinski's critique of the American Character runs much deeper. Even socially desirable hieroglyphs in Dirt, characters like Beans— the spinster daughter, dressed in her Victorian collar and high-buttoned

Rango's Hawaiian shirt—white flowers on a bright red background— initially sets him apart from the citizens of Dirt, who (in defiance of genre conventions) are conspicuously grimy.

boots—and Willy, the feed man, in his blue-jean overalls, need only be furnished with a pitchfork to complete Verbinski's nod to *American Gothic*, that popular and often parodied expression of the pioneer spirit. Painted by twentieth-century American artist Grant Wood, *American Gothic* shows a gaunt, middle-aged famer and a severe-looking woman in front of a farmhouse. The man holds a pitchfork. Symbolizing thrift, work, and faith, *American Gothic* became a cultural icon during the Dirty Thirties by transmitting the qualities of strength and endurance thought typical of the American Character. Like the Iowa farmers in Wood's painting, Beans and Willy are themselves thrifty, hardworking Americans who believe that "things will get better." But unlike the couple, they are grotesques—caricatures of the settler in the American heartland. Computer animation allows Verbinski an enormous amount of scope in this regard, for expressionism's highly stylized screen realities found in horror movies, traditionally created by extreme uses of makeup, lighting effects, and camera angles that suggest emotional, social, or psychological abnormalities, are all supported by characters that are already dehumanized. Most of the characters in *Rango* are abhuman—literally nonhuman beings fashioned after the animal inhabitants of the Mojave Desert. Dirt is a place in which the predators are for the most part unmistakable: being birds of prey, snakes, and foxes, the outlaws are depicted as desert carnivores, while the hapless, law-abiding citizens who are preyed upon are portrayed as herbivores, residing on lower rungs of the food chain. Aptly, when Rango arrives in Dirt, it is a family of rabbits who have lost their land and are giving up and traveling further West in the hope of finding greener pastures.

Verbinski's treatment of Dirt's architecture is also expressionistic. While Dirt's Main Street is modeled after that of Tucumcari, there are no rectilinear buildings gracing it. Dirt's buildings sag and lean alarmingly. Of all the disturbing diagonal lines displayed by the buildings in Dirt, the saloon best illustrates the absence of right angles, suggesting social disorder and the unstable nature of the community itself. Because Dirt is a pioneer town, Verbinski includes it in the tradition expressed in Grant Wood's picture. Notably, the Gothic-style church window that appears on the second floor of the Carpenter Gothic style house in *American Gothic* is first placed ironically in the Town Hall over the door to the mayor's office and then appears behind his desk to frame his figure. The Christian charity of the figures suggested by the church window in *American Gothic* is certainly not an element of any predator's psyche—and it is certainly not a salient characteristic of the town's secretary, a vixen, and certainly not of Dirt's mayor, a character who bankrupts and robs his citizens.

Verbinski's use of *American Gothic* is only one of the many elements of the Gothic tradition found in Rango's story. Set in a location isolated in time and space from contemporary life, *Rango* houses what at first appears to be a single narrative. True to the Gothic, the sheriff and his posse's discovery of the town's aquifer reveal that there is a hidden reality lurking beneath its surface. Combined with what have become standard compositional riffs found in Hollywood horror, Dirt is a place in which the perverse and the nightmarish exist in the most literal fashion beneath its ordered and orderly surface. Under its streets, one finds subterranean passages, tunnels, and caverns. As Verbinski's acknowledgement of *Godzilla* (1998) beneath Dirt's grubby surface suggests, in this town there lies, hidden within its interior, the malevolent life of a monster. Only one of Rango's intrepid band of explorers notices the huge eye of a gigantic reptile that watches them as they search the empty aquifer for the source of Dirt's water problem. His comment, "that was a big one," clearly indicates that there are more monsters. Witnessing sensational and supernatural occurrences of the eyes and mouths of Spanish daggers glowing fiendishly in the dark and cacti walking across the sand in search of water, Rango, like the viewer, also discovers that the order of things usually separate has become disturbed: boundaries between the supernatural and the natural, dream life and reality, the spirit life and the living, good and evil, rationality and madness have become disturbed and unnatural. Even the physical condition of the town signals the conditions of psychic imbalance and social alienation found in Gothic narrative via the shadowy and drafty interior of the saloon and its twisting, narrow alleyways that Rango discovers much to his despair as he is being chased through them.

Explicit or implicit, Verbinski's use of Gothic and expressionistic conventions not only reveals the unbalanced social and psychological conditions of the American Frontier but also simultaneously supports and critiques the regenerative impulse of the American Character itself. Throughout *Rango*, these references revive and comment on the West's iconography, producing a self-reflexive, generic metaromp with the supernatural that showcases classic cinematic moments from the Wild West and its seminal stars. Rango's quest for his character (and the Spirit of the West) begins with references to the supernatural: directed by Roadkill, a dying armadillo flattened by traffic and lying on the edge of the Road, to seek the Spirit of the West, the hapless lizard walks into the desert on a quest for his identity that involves him crossing over to the "Other Side." His conversation with the dying armadillo prepares the audience for the supernatural tropes that follow. The most explicit horror movie reference to the supernatural occurs when Rango and his posse attempt to recover the town's stolen water at Balthazar's canyon hideout.

Balthazar's kinfolk literally emerge from the ground like reanimated corpses to help their relative: their hands burst out of the earth as if they were emerging from the grave, as at the end of Brian de Palma's *Carrie* (1976). Reanimated, the mob of hillbillies, having emerged from their underworld, chases the posse down the canyon to the score of Wagner's *Ride of the Valkyries* (played on the banjo). Less direct references to the supernatural are found in Verbinski's expressionistic camera angles—for example, the extreme high angle in the saloon when Rango enters the room clearly transmits psychological abnormality to the viewer by borrowing the same camera angle in the American Gothic movie, *Psycho* (1960), which was used by Hitchcock at the top of the landing in the Bates' house when the private investigator, Milton Arbogast, enters Norman's home and "Mother" rushes down the stairs with a butcher knife to murder him.

Surely what may be considered the most stylized and humorous moment provided by the supernatural in *Rango* occurs when the townsfolk of Dirt gather at high noon and perform a folk dance prior to the town's hydration ceremony. When the clock strikes noon, the Dirtonians, except the mayor and his henchmen, as if compelled by the bell, ritualistically gather on the street in silence. Every Wednesday, they do this, shuffling into place like zombies to await the sound of Bob Nolan's "Cool Water," performed by Hank Williams. Reminiscent of the elaborate dances found in John Ford's Westerns, during which the community gathers for a hoedown or even an Officers' Ball, this dance, which extends most of the length of Main Street, transmits the social code and beliefs of Dirt's citizens. Social and psychological hieroglyphs of the frontier, these dancers, whose motions resemble those of the walking dead, reanimate their belief that life in Dirt is going to improve. Explaining the workings of the American Character to Rango, the mayor says, "The citizens of Dirt believe that the water will come. They believe against all odds and evidence that tomorrow will be better than today. People have to believe in something."

In Westerns, participation in rituals express the individual's and the community's need for belief. Religious rituals such as funerals are integral parts of the plot structures of movies such as John Ford's *The Searchers* (1956) and *The Man Who Shot Liberty Valance*. Secular rituals also develop character, regenerate community, and drive the action of Westerns. In *Fort Apache* (1948), for example, the yearly ritual of the Non-Commissioned Officers' Ball symbolizes and recreates the communal bond of those living and working together in the isolated post. As Slotkin points out, the believer's response to his myth, be it sacred or secular, is essentially nonrational and religious.[10] Thus, in *Rango*, Verbinski's expressionistic treatment of the Grand

March transforms this same activity, first into a scene of mass hypnosis, then into one of group psychosis, rather than the realistic celebration of communal order found in *Fort Apache*. As the clock strikes high noon, the Dirtonians compulsively leave their activities and congregate silently, forming a single column of two long lines. After the citizens have assembled, a voice establishes the nature of the ceremony, singing over a loudspeaker, "All the land is a barren waste without the taste of water . . . ooooooh waaaaater." The dancers begin their promenade through the Main Street, mechanically bobbing up and down together, ludicrously stepping in unison from side to side and awkwardly hopping from heel to toe while carrying their empty glass jars and bottles to collect water at the dance's conclusion. Rango joins this ritualized attempt to reproduce the act of sharing the community's water supply, but he is unable to blend into the group or dance the steps successfully in time to the song. Finally finding a spot in line, he gabbles, "This is a heck of hoedown you've got going. So I'll work on those steps. So is this considered normal here?" Priscilla responds affirmatively, "Uh-huh. Every Wednesday just like clockwork." Reanimating moments of the past is a type of regeneration even if those reanimated act like those hypnotized. At the end of the dance, the Dirtonians' participation in Dirt's ritual regenerates their ability to create a community for another week, even though the ritual itself does not produce any of the desired water and a large glob of dirt comes out of the faucet when it is opened.

(Re)Animated Western Heroes

The power of parody to evoke its original object is another equally effective means by which the regenerative power of the Western is expressed in *Rango*. That which is not extant in this movie is called into being, reanimated if you will, by its parody. As a result, Dirt and its environs are not only populated by its townsfolk but also by the cinematic undead—the ghostly, ancestral models on which their characters are based. How many reanimated apparitions are apparent at any time depend entirely on an audience member's familiarity with the genre. For example, in the Other Side, characters and plot lines are called into being from spaghetti Westerns. After leaving Dirt and before crossing the Road himself, Rango discovers that he is "Nobody." A nobody, of course, is an insignificant person, but, to the fan of spaghetti Westerns, the name "Nobody" evokes Terrence Hill's character in Tonino Valerii's *My Name Is Nobody* (1973) and Damiano Damiani's *Nobody's the Greatest* (1975).

Waking the next morning on the Other Side, Rango finally completes his quest and understands his character. He encounters the most prominent spirit-figure in the film: the "Spirit of the West," whom he identifies as "The Man with No Name." As Roadkill has prophesied, the "Spirit of the West" is accompanied by his alabaster carriage—a white golf cart that carries five Academy Awards in its back compartment. Aptly, this Man with No Name looks and sounds like Clint Eastwood, who received five Oscars, including the Irving G. Thalberg Award, and he is wearing that character's serape from *A Fistful of Dollars* (1964) while prospecting for fishhooks in the desert with a metal detector. Imparting the cultural secrets of the American Character to Rango, The Man with No Name says, "It doesn't matter what they call you, it's the deeds make the man." When Rango protests that he is no hero, the figure tells him that he is exactly right. "You came a long way to find something that isn't out here," he says, reminding Rango that in chasing a myth he is chasing something that does not actually exist. "Don't you see, it isn't about you," he says, reminding Rango that being a Western hero is a figment of the Dirtonians' need to believe in something, "It's about them." As the mayor pointed out earlier before the weekly commencement of Dirt's Grand March, the actuality of the thing is not important. What is important is one's belief in its existence. Appropriately, when The Man with No Name drives off into the desert, he, his golf cart, and his Oscars dissolve into the landscape, which in turn dissolves into the desert sky. Appropriately, Rango turns to find a reanimated Roadkill standing behind him. "We each see what we need to see," Roadkill states, reminding the lizard and the audience that the frontier has always been seen through "a distorting lens of mythic illusion"; that the West is "a mythic space."[11] Roadkill then asks, "Beautiful, isn't it?" Once more Verbinski emphasizes that it is the individual's belief that awards the myth—that which is believed in, beauty and credibility. Ironically, in the next shot, Rango and Roadkill are seen to be gazing at nothing: the audience is confronted with only the baked, cracked floor of the desert itself.

Other spirit figures from spaghetti Westerns also appear in *Rango*. Tuco (Eli Wallach) from *The Good, The Bad and the Ugly* (1966) is recalled when Rango escapes from the hawk that takes Rock-Eye. As the hawk flies off with him, Rock-Eye, a caricature of Tuco's burly frame and bulging eyes, yells at Rango, "You son of a . . ." Rock-Eye's furious scream cut off by the hawk's screech parallels Tuco's howl that is also cut off: *The Good, the Bad and the Ugly* ends as Tuco, left on foot, screeches at Blondie (Clint Eastwood): "You know what you are? Just a dirty son-of-a b——!" As well, Rattlesnake Jake's Zorro-style hat, thin moustache, and steely manner parodies and, in doing so evokes, Lee Van Cleef's "Angel Eyes" from *The Good, the Bad and the Ugly* and Colonel Douglas Mortimer from *For a Few Dollars More*.

Other staple Western actors are also reanimated in *Rango*. The banker Merrimack's voice, for instance, mimics that of Pat Buttram from *The Gene Autry Show* (1950) and *Green Acres* (1965–1971). In his greasy, red long johns, cowboy boots, and dirty Stetson, Rango is accompanied on his nightly rounds in Dirt by Robert Mitchum's Sheriff J. P. Harrah, the drunken and loveable lawman of *El Dorado* (1966). Other examples of the undead from Western cinema can also be found in moments borrowed from *Cat Ballou*, regenerated via the silver nose on the hawk, which evokes the silver nose that Lee Marvin wore as the villain, Tim Strawn. *Rango*'s singing, guitar-playing owls also reanimate *Cat Ballou*'s balladeer Shouters (Nat King Cole and Stubby Kaye) for audiences. Both sets of troubadours fulfill the same choral function in their movies, providing expository material for the audience and commenting on the action at hand. As well, like *Cat Ballou*, Rango begins with electric guitar music.

Iconic treatments of landscape—in particular, *Rango*'s many treatments of Monument Valley—bring classic cinematic moments from John Ford's Westerns out of the Hollywood vaults, in particular, high-angle shots of the panoramic sweep of the open desert and imposing buttes of the valley and breathtaking tableau of man and nature created by the Apaches before their pursuit of the stagecoach begins in *Stagecoach*. Verbinski's treatment of this tableau also brings the John Ford stock company from *The Searchers* back to life on the screen. Instead of the Apache chief, his medicine man, and his warriors, Rango and Wounded Bird survey the vista spread before them. Where a band of Apache warriors should be stands the posse, who—sporting a top hat, Stetson, and cavalry cap—are parodies of Ward Bond (as the Reverend Captain Samuel Johnston Clayton), Harry Carey Jr. (as Brad Jorgenson), and Hank Worden (as Mose Harper). Clearly Dirt is a place populated with the undead: as American gothics walk its streets, the ghosts of stars from Hollywood's Western past that they parody accompany them. Dirt itself could be considered a ghost town, conjuring up the specters of other frontier communities. Its squeaking windmill, including the specific sound of the squeaking, reanimates the creaking windmill found at the beginning of *Once Upon a Time in the West* (1968). The most elaborate reference to the spaghetti Western mise-en-scène in Dirt is found in its saloon, the interior of which is modeled after, and decorated like, the inside of the bar in Tucumcari in *For a Few Dollars More*.

Conclusion

A hybrid horror/Western that resurrects cinematic conventions and is populated with spirit figures not forgotten, *Rango* regenerates, reanimates, and

Rango and members of his posse—evocations of characters from classic and revisionist Westerns—confront the theft of the town's water.

critiques the American Character. Earlier Westerns often investigate and resolve a conflict expressed as a social and economic imbalance, but Verbinski's hybrid expressionism also establishes the locus of frontier psychology to be found within the individual haunted by spirit figures from America's celluloid frontier. *Rango* is a film that engages its protagonist *and* its viewers in a vision quest, because, at its end, they discover what the Spirit of the West is and recognize who they are when the source of Dirt's water problem is discovered to be a golf course situated just outside of what appears to be Las Vegas. As the sprinklers drench the grass greens, it is obvious that corporate greed and capitalism have won in this struggle between small businessmen and large corporations, the conflict that underpins so much of the action of the Western. One cannot help but cheer when the water is finally turned off and returned to its rightful owners. As Rango and his friends decide to take a dip and wash the dirt of their adventures away, it seems that the problem posed by centralized political power in the movie has been dissolved and the mythological West of the American Frontier has been restored: because the water has been restored, Dirt will no longer be a dirty place in which to live.

The American Character, regenerated by the violence that purged Dirt of its crooked mayor and his gunslingers, also seems to have been cleansed and regenerated; at the end of this movie, it is still possible to be a hero. However, to end here would be to ignore the important warning of the undead in this movie that those individuals who identify themselves with the American Character do so because they themselves are seeking social and psychological balance—by believing their material fortunes and spirits will be renewed despite the fact that there is no evidence that such a renewal can or will take place. In final analysis, *Rango* expresses what Richard Slotkin would recognize as the foundation stones of America's mythology: "its concerns, its hopes, its terrors, its violence, *and its justification of itself.*"[12] At the last, *Rango* reveals that America is truly what it imagined itself to have been. The maxim of the duster still holds true: as the mayor would say, "He who controls the water controls everything." And anyone who wishes to challenge the truth of that slogan will find himself, like the Dirtonians, fighting City Hall.

Notes

1. Richard Slotkin, *Regeneration through Violence: The Mythology of the American Frontier 1600–1860* (Norman: University of Oklahoma Press, 2000), 3.
2. Slotkin, *Regeneration*, 4.
3. Slotkin, *Regeneration*, 5.
4. Slotkin, *Regeneration*, 8.
5. Richard Slotkin, *Gunfighter Nation: The Myth of the Frontier in Twentieth-Century America* (Norman: University of Oklahoma Press, 1998), 61.
6. Lindsay Anderson, *About John Ford* (London: Plexus Publishing, 1999), 180.
7. Slotkin, *Regeneration*, 5.
8. Martin Pumphrey, "Why Do Cowboys Wear Hats in the Bath?: Style Politics for the Older Man," in *The Book of Westerns*, ed. Ian Cameron and Douglas Pye (New York: Continuum, 1996), 50–62.
9. Pumphrey, "Why Do Cowboys Wear Hats in the Bath?," 53.
10. Slotkin, *Regeneration*, 7–8.
11. Slotkin, *Gunfighter*, 61.
12. Slotkin, *Regeneration*, 4 (emphasis added).

Bibliography

Anderson, Lindsay. *About John Ford*. London: Plexus Publishing, 1999.
Ebert, Robert. "Rango." *Chicago Sun-Times*, March 2, 2011. http://rogerebert.suntimes .com/ apps/pbcs.dll/article?AID=/20110302/REVIEWS/110309997
Lovece, Frank. "Film Review: Rango." *Film Journal International.* http://www.film journal.com/filmjournal/content_display/reviews/major-releases/e3i968f4bb3029 b32a67cd0024a62e4e73d
Mondello, Robert. "Ride 'Em Chameleon! *Rango* a Wild, Wacky Western." National Public Radio, March 4, 2011. http://www.npr.org/2011/03/04/134055109/ride-em-chameleon-rango-a-wild-wacky-western

Pumphrey, Martin. "Why Do Cowboys Wear Hats in the Bath?: Style Politics for the Older Man." In *The Book of Westerns*, edited by Ian Cameron and Douglas Pye, 50–62. New York: Continuum, 1996.

Rango. Directed by Gore Verbinski. Hollywood, CA: Paramount Home Entertainment, 2011. DVD.

Slotkin, Richard. *Gunfighter Nation: The Myth of the Frontier in Twentieth-Century America*. Norman: University of Oklahoma Press, 1998.

———. *Regeneration through Violence: The Mythology of the American Frontier 1600–1860*. Norman: University of Oklahoma Press, 2000.

Turner, Fredrick Jackson. "The Frontier in American History." University of Virginia, XRoadsVirginia.edu. http://xroads.virginia.edu/~hyper/turner/

CHAPTER SIX

Frontier Values
Meet Big-City Zombies

The Old West in AMC's The Walking Dead

Shelley S. Rees

Graham Greene, in his 1939 *Spectator* review of the film *Dodge City*, outlines "the Western formula," a prominent element of which is "straight-shooting cowboy is asked to become sheriff, refuses, sees child killed, accepts, cleans up."[1] The "straight-shooting" protagonist of A&E's zombie apocalypse series, *The Walking Dead* (2010–), embodies the show's troubled use of Western tropes from its opening scene, in which Deputy Sheriff Rick Grimes (Andrew Lincoln), wearing full uniform, invokes the Western lawman's protective orientation toward children with his first line of the series—"Little girl, I'm a policeman"—and then shoots said "little girl" through the forehead. The scene is drawn for maximum pathos, as the waif shuffles through the wasteland of abandoned vehicles in her nightgown, the camera lingering on her tattered bunny slippers and the stuffed toy dangling from her listless hand. The camera spares the viewer no details of Grimes's shot; we watch in slow-motion horror as blood and gore spew from beneath her tangled blond locks and her fragile body drops to the pavement, and the scene ends on a close-up of Rick's face, mirroring devastation and shock that the viewer is presumed to share.

Through scenes like this, in which Rick's dedication to his work as an officer conflicts with the grisly necessities of a mutated world, *The Walking Dead* uses the traditions of the Western genre to construct Rick as a pure-hearted lawman who brings an outdated value system of order and justice into the realm of the new, the postapocalyptic city, overrun with blind appetite and a noncommunicative mass of individuals and dramatizing a collapse of order so profound that its chaotic taint spreads to the surrounding rural retreats and the nuclear family embodied by the Grimeses. By conflating the traditional Western with the more modern zombie narrative, *The Walking Dead* produces a grotesque hybrid, a changeling Western, animated yet altered, infected with a strain of postideological nihilism that disempowers its heroes, creates child monsters from its child victims, and turns sheriffs bound to protect children and avenge harm done to them into their grim killers.

The Postapocalyptic West

Connections between the Old Western, empowered by nostalgia for an idyllic past and the zombie apocalypse genre, which drives its audience forward into a ghastly future, may seem counterintuitive. However, the established myth of the frontier, its threatening landscape steeped in potential for individual triumph, contributes to the popularity of postapocalyptic fantasy, since such texts generally offer a representative group of survivors the challenge of rebuilding a new world from the ashes, even as they confront the horror of the previous world's devastation. As Peter Dendle explains:

> In twenty-first century America—where the bold wilderness frontier that informed American mythic consciousness for four centuries has given way to increasingly centralized government amidst a suburban landscape now quilted with strip malls and Walmarts—there is ample room to romanticize a fresh world purged of ornament and vanity, in which the strong survive, and in which society must be rebuilt anew. Post-apocalyptic zombie worlds are fantasies of liberation: the intrepid pioneers of a new world trek through the shattered remains of the old, trudging through shells of building and the husks of people.[2]

The show often frames Rick visually in classic Western poses to invoke the sense of movement toward this decontextualized future, such as in his lone, straight-backed walk away from the technologically advanced and morally ordered civilization represented by the dead police car and toward the camera, so that whatever Rick is walking toward remains behind the viewer and thus unknown. The image invites hope for success in the off-camera future, as Rick's unwavering stare, the forward-pointed orientation of the car, and the lines of the road appear to propel him toward a goal. Even his stride projects confidence, his forward foot in such perfect alignment with the one behind as to obscure it from view.

Rick's insistence upon maintaining his sheriff's deputy uniform in this lawless world emphasizes his function as the text's threshold between the ordered past and a (re)ordered future; his visual signification projects law and justice standing tall among the rubble of a devastated civilization. He persists in constructing himself, sartorially and otherwise, as the mythical lawman who will rescue the beleaguered town that has fallen into lawlessness and anarchy. Rick's choice to ride a horse into the city again represents his status as a bridge from mechanized civilization back to a more primitive frontier existence; once he has no more fuel for an automobile, he adapts by reverting to an older method of transportation. In one of the episode's light moments, Rick asks the horse to go easy because he "hasn't done this in years," revealing that he has ridden a horse at some point in the past—he does manage to saddle and bridle the horse, after all, which takes specialized knowledge—another instance of Rick's function as ambassador from and to the past that underscores the text's association of the apocalyptic landscape with older Western social contexts and values.

Complicating the gunslinger stereotype, though, Rick is a mere small-town Georgia deputy, no high-falutin' sheriff. In addition, the text undercuts Rick's heroism on multiple fronts: in this first episode he is immobilized by a coma while the world devolves into a zombie apocalypse, lying inert and then blundering across the shattered landscape in a hospital gown; he is supplanted in his position as husband and father to his family as his wife, Lori (Sarah Wayne Callies), begins a sexual relationship with Rick's partner and best friend, Shane (Jon Bernthal), who has ushered Lori and her son, Carl (Chandler

A classic Western hero emerges into the postapocalyptic near future: Deputy Rick Grimes, mounted and armed, investigates the ruins of Atlanta in the pilot episode of *The Walking Dead*.

Riggs), to relative safety in his absence; and, immediately after repurposing his masculinity with rifles and a horse, Rick is divested of them by a horde of city zombies, his guns lost and his horse slaughtered. Indeed, the Western trope of the "new sheriff in town" informs a central irony in the text of *The Walking Dead*, particularly through the familiar Western plot elements that surround Rick. AMC's first advertising poster for the show features an image of Rick on the horse, shot long and from above and behind the figures as they head away from the viewer toward a distant and menacing version of Atlanta. Rick's iconic cowboy/deputy hat and the rifles slung across his back contribute to an image of the lone gunslinger riding into an unknown ghost town. Inside the city, long shots of empty streets reinforce the ghost-town effect, with blowing papers replacing the ubiquitous tumbleweeds of the Western film and reflecting the wasted human effort that was expended in creating messages that will no longer be received and that are now mere decontextualized garbage.

The promotional poster also reinforces the show's integration of the cowboy-hero figure into its undead apocalypse narrative and the resulting disempowerment of that figure. Rick, along with his borrowed horse, represents the only "walking" occurring in this image, meaning the title head "The Walking Dead" implies that Rick (again, perhaps along with the horse) is himself dead or at least walking toward his death, foreshadowing the humiliating failure of this venture into the city, where our hero is divested of horse and weapons by a horde of walkers and then called a "dumbass" by a stranger's voice over the radio as he cowers in an abandoned military tank. This opening episode of the series ends with a view looking down on the street from high above, so that viewers must watch as walkers stream through the city to feast on the remains of Rick's poor dead horse while the upbeat "Space Junk," by Wang Chung, with its prominent lyric "welcome to my world," plays to the credits. The ironic music and the physical distance of the audience perspective relieve the viewer of some of the tension of sympathizing with a protagonist whose ability to succeed appears so embarrassingly compromised, while also inviting us to participate in the text's ambivalent attitude toward the ideals Rick stands for. Indeed, ending with a detached (and thus framed as realistic and objective) view on Rick's loss suggests that his stubborn commitment to the ideology of the old world likewise will be consumed by these creatures of pure, mindless hunger, as the endearing speech with which Rick cajoled the horse out of its paddock with promises of safety and companionship in the city is exposed as terrible, naive lies. This final image also highlights the connection between the dead horse and the dead tank and the focal points of the zombie swarm, signifying the collapse of the frontier past and the technological present, as well as Rick's occupation of liminal space as he moves from one to the other.

Cathartic Violence

Another way that *The Walking Dead* writers incorporate Rick's character into this generic complexity is through his relationship to violence. The unequivocal categories upheld by the Old Western invite us to identify with the "good" characters against the "bad" ones and to take voyeuristic—and guiltless—pleasure in the violence that ends all question of whose position merits ultimate approval. The mythos of the original Western narrative depends upon a clear distinction between good and evil, providing audiences with the pleasure of what Ed Minus calls "intensely satisfying unsurprised."[3] Or, as William McClain argues, "the Western is, and should be, a historical morality play based on the questions of the frontier, the role of the individual in society, the (dis)continuity of contemporary American society with its mythological past, and of course the morals, meaning, and consequences of just versus unjust violence."[4] The escapism provided to consumers of the traditional Western includes satisfying, justified violence and a glimpse of the freedom of the frontier, where possibilities beckon beyond the horizon and justice is swift and confident. As Stephen Weathers explains, "In the Old Western, bad men are thoroughly bad, irremediably bad."[5] In addition, they allow us to imagine ourselves tested like the hero, by the elements of nature, by confrontation with evil, by challenges that force self-defining acts: "If Westerns seem to long for the out-of-doors, for a simplified social existence, for blizzards and shoot-outs and fabulous exploits, it isn't because their readers want to give up TV and computers and fast foods and go back to life on the frontier. It's that life on the frontier is a way of imagining the self in a boundary situation—a place that will put you to some kind of ultimate test."[6] In effect, the Western affirms trial by combat as a legitimate indicator of moral superiority for individuals (and national and ethnic identities), a generic convention so appealing to Americans that "the Western, for American audiences, was not only one more genre; it was a—perhaps *the*—national genre."[7]

Postapocalyptic narratives like *The Walking Dead* replicate the Western's appeal to liberation from the discontents of civilization through sanctioned violence. According to Richard Slotkin:

> The organizing principle at the heart of each subdivision of Western genre-space is the myth of regeneration through violence; the cavalry Western has its Indian massacre or charge into battle, the gunfighter or town-tamer movie its climactic shoot-out in the street, the outlaw movie its disastrous last robbery or assassination, the romantic Western its bullet-ridden rescue scene. Each has its own special ways of explaining or rationalizing the culminating shoot-out. But in general, when we are told that a certain film is a Western, we confidently expect that it will find its moral and emotional resolution in a singular act of violence.[8]

The Walking Dead adopts this aspect of the Western seamlessly, substituting dehumanized human bodies for the Western's soulless bad guys. As Dendle notes, "Since the audience knows that the zombies are usually not sentient and in most cases do not feel pain, it is free to enjoy the spectacle of wanton destruction of human bodies rather than human beings."[9] Authors and filmmakers of zombie texts are, because of the exaggerated Otherness of the zombie creature, even freer to explore violent images than Western cinematographers, and so the violence in these texts has become infamous for its enthusiastic goriness. Indeed, the producers of *The Walking Dead* have encouraged fan interest in the various ways that characters "kill" walkers, so that the official AMC website for the show includes a page titled "How to Kill a Walker,"[10] with a video compilation of zombie deaths from Season 1, and a cursory Google search will locate dozens of fan montages, such as the one titled "Every Zombie Death in *The Walking Dead*."[11]

The Othering of villains that allows consumers of Westerns to orient themselves so easily in their relationships to characters is intensified by *The Walking Dead*, as the undead walkers provide targets of violence even more uncomplicated than villainous gunslingers. As Gerry Canavan argues, "The audience for zombie narrative, after all, never imagines *itself* to be zombified; zombies are always other people, which is to say they are Other people, which is to say they are people who are not quite people at all."[12] Further, "because zombies mark the demarcation between life (that is worth living) and unlife (that needs killing), the evocation of the zombie conjures not solidarity but

Shorn of their humanity and their individuality by the zombie plague, "walkers" are reduced to ambulatory targets, whose deaths audiences are encouraged to celebrate.

racial panic."[13] Many Westerns do characterize racial Others—usually Native Americans—as a threat to their (white) protagonists, their construction as savages outside of the laws of civilized society making them fair game for legitimized violence. Those racial markers that separate "savages" from civilized folk in the Old West reappear in *The Walking Dead* in the form of grotesque unpeople who retain human features but no humanity. The show makes deliberate use of the motif of the wagon-train migration as the group of survivors makes its perilous trek across the hostile landscape in search of a homestead, their fear and watchfulness affirmed by frequent encounters with walkers, just as denizens of the Old West circled their wagons against Indian attacks. In fact, the show characterizes the zombie walkers as animals in the first episode of Season 2, titled "What Lies Ahead," labeling a mass of them traveling together a "herd," further deferring their humanity while maintaining the connection to images of the West, in which stampedes of cattle sometimes threaten settlers.

The Walking Dead uses this tradition of sanctioned violence against foes constructed as soulless through their dark hearts (or dark skin) to further associate Rick's character with the transitional space between Old West past and apocalyptic future. In the episodes that have aired at the point of this writing, up to Season 2's midseason break, Rick's story is framed by shootouts: He is shot by criminals in the first episode's preapocalyptic flashback and, in Season 2's midseason finale, he watches as his people line up with guns and massacre dozens of walkers that pour out of Hershel Greene's (Scott Wilson) barn. The first incident establishes Rick's professional relationship to the violence necessitated by his job as a sheriff's deputy; he refuses to romanticize violence, admonishing Officer Leon Basset for wondering if they will "get on one of them video shows, like *World's Craziest Police Chases*" while they position themselves to intercept a fleeing suspect, reminiscent of heading off outlaws at the pass. Moreover, Rick's executions of walkers tend to be framed as acts of mercy; in fact, though he realizes the shot will draw more walkers, he later "kills" the walking revenant of Leon Basset because, even though he "didn't think much of him" when he was alive, Rick "can't leave him like this." Before leaving town to search for his family, Rick also returns to a park to find a zombie half-woman he encountered earlier; upon locating her, a ragged torso dragging a path through the wet grass with emaciated arms, he bends down to look her in the eyes, tears gathering in his own, and intones, "I'm sorry this happened to you" before shooting her. Though Western fiction encourages viewers to exult in legitimized violence, an Old West hero must exercise his right to kill only when unavoidable, and not with pleasure, so while other characters come to enjoy executing walkers, Rick never does.

Conflict of Ideologies

Through Rick's correspondence to the Western hero, *The Walking Dead* engages the stylized familiarity of the Western genre as a narrative embodiment of stabilizing ideology, and then troubles it by disempowering its Western-infused protagonist and the values associated with him every time he appears to have achieved a goal through his adherence to those values. In this context, the voracious yet mindless zombies represent the collapse of ideologies propagated by Westerns, including their investment in ideals of community, justice, family, and individuality. Joshua Gunn and Shaun Treat identify the emergence of the zombie creature as a symptom of the collapse of ideological pressures in a community: "Like the infant of pre-interpellation, the living dead is a post-interpellated subject, a being of pure drives, an id in need of a superego, which ideology provides. Ideology marks the emergence of self-consciousness in a being of needs and desires."[14] Without self-consciousness, there is no chance of morality, coding the walkers as inhuman on yet another level.

Ironically, the apocalypse that erases people and turns them into walkers also, in a sense, effaces the selves of those who technically survive. In this world bereft of ideology, disinterpellated individuals in *The Walking Dead* are responsible for constructing new selves. Law is gone, so they have nothing against which to define themselves and no expectations to fail to measure up to. Under this new paradigm, Alan Ladd's virtuous Shane, from the 1953 film of the same name, a mysterious gunslinger who silently leaves town rather than insinuate himself between a husband and wife and their son, has become a postideological Shane who in Season 2 shoots an innocent man and leaves him to be eaten by walkers, in part due to his desire to poach his best friend's family. Lingering close-ups of Otis's slow, grisly death force viewers to experience the horror of Shane's choice to save himself and the medical supplies he carries by shooting Otis in the leg as they run from a horde of walkers, underscoring the grotesque nature of a parallel universe Western hero who saves Carl, the child victim, by sacrificing another innocent. *The Walking Dead*'s version of Shane argues that "nostalgia [for the old world] is like a drug [that] keeps you from seeing things the way they are." Even Rick, who holds the collective conscience for the group, wonders if "maybe [he is] holding on to a way of thinking that doesn't make sense anymore," and the narrative declines to refute this as it verifies Shane's cynicism more often than not, so while viewers are encouraged to prefer Rick's hope, we are never allowed to confirm it.

Indeed, the characters who vigorously question Rick's dedication to the old ways, down to the ancient rules of guest-host behavior to which he insists everyone adhere to while staying at Hershel's farm in Season 2, are ex–police officer Shane and ex-attorney Andrea (Laurie Holden), who loses her sister in Season 1 and is thwarted later from committing suicide. They represent versions of law and order modified for the postapocalyptic paradigm, and they see Rick's refusal to revise his morality for the altered context as foolish, weak, and irresponsible. By the final episode of Season 2, "Pretty Much Dead Already," Shane and Andrea travel together to a town overrun by walkers, where Andrea learns to enjoy killing them, so much so that she and Shane stop their car on the way back to camp and have sex, in a scene that constructs them as Bonnie-and-Clyde-style outlaws. Indeed, Season 2 deepens the separation between Shane and Rick, who begin the series as partners and best friends, move through Shane's usurpation of Rick's place with his wife and son, and finally split to embody dichotomous ideals. Shane claims that Rick does not belong in "this world"; Dale (Jeffrey DeMunn), an older man who ineffectively attempts to mitigate Shane's anarchic influence, counters that Shane *does* belong there. When Lori Grimes discovers herself pregnant, the fact that she cannot know whether the biological father is Rick or Shane emphasizes the double-sidedness of the men and their divergent paths toward the future: a child of Shane's will be a child of the new world, while a child of Rick's might carry his ideals forward, though the question of which view will prevail remains unanswered. As Colette Balmain explains, "The traditional function of the child within bourgeois mythology is the perpetuation of the past into the future, the propagation of the same rather than the embodiment of difference, and a promise of the continuation of the dominant ideological order."[15] *The Walking Dead* uses Lori's pregnancy to ask which ideology will emerge dominant in this group and by extension in humanity's future: Shane's survivalist self-interest or Rick's altruism.

The Children Are Our Future

The signifying function of children in Westerns provides another trope for *The Walking Dead* to adapt. Season 2's battleground for the characters' conflicting values is Rick's insistence upon searching for lost ten-year-old Sophia Peletier (Madison Lintz), a quest that Shane considers pointless and dangerous. The Sophia plot line recalls the Western sheriff's protective impulses toward children and invokes the motif of the Western captivity narrative. When walkers chase Sophia into the woods, Rick runs after her. He gives her instructions on how to find her way back to the highway and then acts as a decoy to draw the pursuing walkers away so that she can escape, but she never returns. The captured and/or missing woman provides Western heroes a cause or quest to establish their masculine and ideological heroism. As Slotkin explains:

> In the various historical narratives associated with [Daniel] Boone, the narrative formulas and ideological themes of the captivity tale (redemption through suffering) are integrated with the triumphalist scenario of the Indian-war story to make a single unified Myth of the Frontier in which the triumph of civilization over savagery is symbolized by the hunter/warrior's rescue of the White woman held captive by savages.[16]

Thus, though some fans became impatient with the lost Sophia plot, its significance to the narrative cannot be overstated, for Rick believes that the triumph of regaining Sophia would not only redeem his own connection to law and traditional values but also stabilize the group's wavering ideological orientations by reminding them of their differentiation from the savage Others. As Rick begs Shane to understand, "This means something, finding her."

While Rick seeks redemption through saving Sophia, Shane argues that prolonging the search endangers the rest of the group. In a particularly brutal instance of the show's cynical undermining of Rick's optimism, Rick's son, Carl, is shot in the midst of what the narrative, camera work, and musical score construct as an epiphanic moment. Searching for Sophia, the group is drawn by the sound of church bells and, in the church, characters take turns approaching a statue of the crucified Christ. Sophia's mother, Carol Peletier (Melissa Suzanne McBride), begs for the return of her daughter, and Rick, returning to the statue alone after the others have left, delivers an earnest, frustrated prayer recognizable as the dramatic setup for an archetypal scene of spiritual significance. He confesses to having placed his faith in other things besides religion, including family, friends, and his job, but he pleads for guidance, "a sign—any sign'll do, some kinda acknowledgement, some indication I'm doin' the right thing." Rick, Shane, and Carl head into the woods to continue searching for Sophia and encounter a buck deer, framed in a clearing like a magic spirit animal; the music swells, and Carl's face lights with wonder as he approaches the deer and it does not run from him. Rick watches enraptured, clearly beginning to believe he has received the sign he sought, when a shot fires from off camera and deer and Carl both fall to the ground. If this is a sign, it does not point Rick's way, and Shane, who urged Rick to return with the others instead of continuing the search, is proved correct, not for the last time.

Though Rick considers himself responsible for rescuing Sophia, the text does not appoint him her champion. Interestingly, that role is deferred to secondary character Daryl Dixon (Norman Reedus), a gruff Georgia "redneck" whose racist, drug-addled older brother, Merle, is left behind in Atlanta in Season 1. Daryl occupies a tenuous position within the group, as his economy of speech and self-conscious defensiveness about his lower-class status keep him on the periphery. He is an expert tracker and hunter, and Rick takes advantage of those skills often, placing Daryl in the role of Indian sidekick to Rick's Lone Ranger persona, an image reinforced visually by Daryl's crossbow and arrows. Daryl's muscular body, like Shane's, contrasts with Rick's more slender, compact frame, and his accomplished woodsmanship further asserts his masculinity; in fact, when Rick and Daryl discover a zombie with flesh in its teeth in the woods near Sophia's disappearance, Rick prepares to eviscerate the body to see if it has fed on Sophia and Daryl stops him, saying, "I'll do it. How many kills you skinned and gutted in your life anyway?" He then pulls out a larger knife than the one Rick holds and deadpans, "Mine's sharper."

In the Season 2 episode "Chupacabra," however, Daryl's character rises to archetypal significance. He takes a horse from Hershel's stable and separates from the group to look for Sophia from the top of a ridge, his native status accentuated by demonstrations of skill with the horse and the bow. Indeed, Daryl's connection to nature and his outsider status in relation to the more middle-class members of Rick's group recall the Western genre's fraught portrayals of Native Americans. Slotkin explains the function of Indian enemy/hero duality in Westerns, claiming:

Daryl's skills as a hunter, tracker, and woodsman—marks of a low-status "redneck" in the preapocalyptic city—become vital to the survivors of the zombie apocalypse.

Although the Indian and the Wilderness are the settler's enemy, they also provide him with the new consciousness through which he will transform the world. The heroes of this myth-historical quest must therefore be "men (or women) who know Indians"—characters whose experiences, sympathies, and even allegiances fall on both sides of the Frontier. Because the border between savagery and civilization runs through their moral center, the Indian wars are, for these heroes, a spiritual or psychological struggle which they win by learning to discipline or suppress the savage or "dark" side of their own human nature. Thus they are mediators of a double kind who can teach civilized men how to defeat savagery on its native grounds—the natural wilderness, and the wilderness of the human soul.[17]

Significantly, the episodes "Cherokee Rose" and "Chupacabra" both take their titles from supernatural beliefs expressed by Daryl. In the former, Daryl relays a story of Indian mothers whose weeping for their lost children created a certain species of flower along the Trail of Tears, and in the latter he claims to have seen a chupacabra—a cryptozoological creature most often associated with Mexico—in the woods near his home years before. These stories extend the characterization of Daryl as uneducated and unsophisticated, as well as racially different, but they also suggest a susceptibility to mystical experiences that associates him with the "magical Other" stereotype and foreshadows the vision quest he undertakes in the "Chupacabra" episode.

Daryl's commitment to finding Sophia signifies a subconscious desire to align himself with innocence and empathy, to restore the group, and to resolve the ambivalence he suffers over his unwanted role as mediator between Shane's darkness and Rick's optimism. When Daryl's borrowed horse shies away from a snake—a mythical figure of both trickery and wisdom—and throws him off the ridge into the creek bed below, he begins the classical hero's descent into the underworld, the world of death. During his journey he confronts his divided loyalties and insecurities through sustained hallucinations of his brother, Merle, who sneers that Rick's people will "scrape him off their shoes" before long and exhorts Daryl to rejoin the savagery of his "kin" and go back to camp and "shoot your buddy Rick in the face for me." During one of these hallucinations, Daryl revives to find that a walker, not Merle, is tugging at his leg, and in the ensuing fight, he manages to kill two walkers, literal embodiments of the symbolic death the hero submits to in the underworld vision quest. The arrow wound in Daryl's side mimics Christ's wound, identifying Daryl as a martyr, and when he does manage to climb out of the pit, the camera shifts from the interior view to the exterior so that the viewer sees Daryl's hands emerge over the edge before the rest of him, reinforcing the resurrection imagery of his ascent. Traditionally, the hero returns from this experience changed, restored, and in possession of a token object or crucial piece of knowledge. Daryl staggers from the woods near camp carrying Sophia's doll, and he is so changed by his ordeal, covered in blood and wearing a necklace of zombie ears that associates him with Western settlers' fears of being scalped by Indians, that the others think he is a walker and Andrea shoots him in the head.

Daryl's descent and return takes place in the center of the episode in which the Rick/Shane split appears irreconcilable. The wrenching apart of Shane from Rick leaves Shane with the masculine characteristics of violence, dominance, and anger, and Rick with the more nurturing, peace-seeking feminine qualities, partly represented by his retention of the woman both men desire: Rick's wife, Lori. With Rick functioning as the superego and Shane performing the id, Daryl emerges as the unlikely ego, the mediating Other identified by Slotkin above, a concept reinforced visually by the image of Daryl's ravaged body suspended between Rick and Shane as they carry him back to camp. Indeed, after his trials, Daryl appears to be moving toward a productive integration of his own identities, merging the primal native self with the one blessed by bereft mother Carol as "every bit as good as [Rick and Shane]." If we consider this psychological interpretation of the scene and characters, Rick, Shane, and Daryl must integrate their separate identities into a harmonious healthy whole, or the resultant group-self will remain fragmented and neurotic. The group's increasingly desperate search for Sophia supports this reading, for as mentioned above, reclaiming her could heal this fragmentation and reinvigorate everyone's hope for a future that children can survive to embody, including the child of the Rick/Lori/Shane triangle.

Alas, hopeful Western ideals of a future repopulated by determined frontier-conquering settlers do not survive long in *The Walking Dead*, a text in which every occurrence that evinces a trajectory of heroic victory ends in bitter disappointment. Thus the first half of Season 2 ends where Season 1 begins, with tragic, virtuous Rick Grimes, now bereft of his deputy's uniform, gunning down a zombie child he wished to protect. Belmain claims that "monstrous-children" in fiction "function as signifiers of instability and uncertainty from within,"[18] and for this text Sophia's death appears to signify the imminent collapse of Rick's community. The discovery that she has become a walker intensifies that grim foreshadowing for, again, in cases of possessed or changeling children, "the threat moves from outside to the inside, from the external to the internal, and projection becomes introjection."[19] The child-victim the group strove so hard to rescue has mutated into a child-monster, along with everything she represented to them, and the fact that it is Shane who breaks into the barn and forces Rick and the others to confront this reality reasserts the primacy of his bleak new world over Rick's outdated value system. So, as the massacre of the walkers housed in Hershel's barn ends, the entire group stills, staring in horror at the twice-dead corpses of loved ones, including Sophia, and the series pauses for its midseason break, leaving Deputy Grimes standing, perhaps, over the now unresurrectable corpse of his hope that the future could redeem the present by reclaiming the past.

Notes

1. David Parkinson, *The Graham Greene Film Reader: Reviews, Essays, Interviews & Film Stories* (New York: Applause Press, 2000), 326.

2. Peter Dendle, "The Zombie as Barometer of Cultural Anxiety," in *Monsters and the Monstrous: Myths and Metaphors of Enduring Evil*, ed. Niall Scott (New York: Rodopi, 2007), 54.

3. Ed Minus, "Westerns," *Sewanee Review* 118.1 (2010): 83.

4. William McClain, "Western, Go Home! Sergio Leone and the 'Death of the Western' in American Film Criticism," *Journal of Film and Video* 62.1–2 (2010): 61.

5. Stephen Weathers, "Death with Dignity: Comitatus in Sam Peckinpah's 'New Western,'" in *Westerns: Paperback Novels and Movies from Hollywood*, ed. Paul Varner, (Newcastle: Cambridge Scholars, 2007), 104.

6. Jane Tompkins, *West of Everything: The Inner Life of Westerns* (New York: Oxford UP, 1992), 14.

7. McClain, "Western Go Home!," 57.

8. Richard Slotkin, *Gunfighter Nation: The Myth of the Frontier in Twentieth-Century America* (New York: Atheneum, 1992), 352.

9. Dendle, "The Zombie as Barometer of Cultural Anxiety," 52.

10. AMCTV.com, "How to Kill a Walker," 2011. http://www.amctv.com/the-walking-dead/videos/the-walking-dead-how-to-kill-a-walker

11. Landstrider, "Every Zombie Death in The Walking Dead," 2010. http://www.youtube.com/watch?v=afcWyJhsBXo

12. Gerry Canavan, "'We *Are* the Walking Dead': Race, Time, and Survival in Zombie Narrative," *Extrapolation* 51.3 (2010): 432.

13. Canavan, "'We *Are* the Walking Dead," 433.

14. Joshua Gunn and Shaun Treat, "Zombie Trouble: A Propaedeutic on Ideological Subjectification and the Unconscious," *Quarterly Journal of Speech* 91.2 (2005): 155.

15. Colette Balmain, "The Enemy Within: The Child as Terrorist in the Contemporary American Horror Film," in *Monsters and the Monstrous: Myths and Metaphors of Enduring Evil*, ed. Niall Scott (New York: Rodopi, 2007), 137.

16. Slotkin, *Gunfighter Nation*, 15.
17. Slotkin, *Gunfighter Nation*, 14.
18. Balmain, "The Enemy Within," 137.
19. Balmain, "The Enemy Within," 140.

Bibliography

AMCTV.com. "How To Kill a Walker." http://www.amctv.com/the-walking-dead/videos/the-walking-dead-how-to-kill-a-walker

Balmain, Colette. "The Enemy Within: The Child as Terrorist in the Contemporary American Horror Film." In *Monsters and the Monstrous: Myths and Metaphors of Enduring Evil*, edited by Niall Scott, 133–47. New York: Rodopi, 2007.

Canavan, Gerry. "'We *Are* the Walking Dead': Race, Time, and Survival in Zombie Narrative." *Extrapolation* 51.3 (2010): 431–53.

Dendle, Peter. "The Zombie as Barometer of Cultural Anxiety." In *Monsters and the Monstrous: Myths and Metaphors of Enduring Evil*, edited by Niall Scott, 45–57. New York: Rodopi, 2007.

Gunn, Joshua, and Shaun Treat. "Zombie Trouble: A Propaedeutic on Ideological Subjectification and the Unconscious." *Quarterly Journal of Speech* 91.2 (2005): 144–74.

Landstrider. "Every Zombie Death in *The Walking Dead*." YouTube, 2010. http://www.youtube.com/watch?v=afcWyJhsBXo

McClain, William. "Western, Go Home! Sergio Leone and the 'Death of the Western' in American Film Criticism." *Journal of Film and Video* 62.1–2 (2010): 52–66.

Minus, Ed. "Westerns." *Ssewanee Review* 118.1 (2010): 82–90.

Parkinson, David. *The Graham Greene Film Reader: Reviews, Essays, Interviews & Film Stories*. New York: Applause Press, 2000.

Slotkin, Richard. *Gunfighter Nation: The Myth of the Frontier in Twentieth-Century America*. New York: Atheneum, 1992.

Tompkins, Jane. *West of Everything: The Inner Life of Westerns*. New York: Oxford University Press, 1992.

The Walking Dead. Developed by Frank Darabont. 2010. New York: AMC Studios, 2010–.

Weathers, Stephen. 2007. "Death with Dignity: Comitatus in Sam Peckinpah's 'New Western.'" In *Westerns: Paperback Novels and Movies from Hollywood*, edited by Paul Varner, 103–11. Newcastle: Cambridge Scholars, 2007.

PART II

THE MORAL ORDER
UNDER SIEGE

CHAPTER SEVEN

Savage, Scoundrel, Seducer

The Moral Order under Siege in the From Dusk Till Dawn Trilogy

A. Bowdoin Van Riper

The cinematic West is full of exotic ways to die. The landscape teems with grizzly bears and mountain lions, scorpions and rattlesnakes, hostile Indians and murderous bandits. The next person who rides through your front gate could be a claim jumper who'd kill you for your land, a rustler who'd kill you for your herd, or a cattle baron who'd kill you for your water rights. Death even—or, perhaps, especially—lurks in the saloon, where hundred-proof lubricants erase good judgment and worldly cares. Accuse the wrong card player of cheating, spill the wrong man's drink at the bar, or make time with the wrong dancing girl, and yours could be the body that, when it hits the floor, startles the patrons into an impromptu moment of silence that ends when the piano player finds his place again.

These dangers function, in classic and revisionist Westerns alike, both as plot tropes and as a means of framing the frontier as a space for dramatic action. They define the frontier and establish the qualities that are required to survive there: alertness, resourcefulness, and toughness both physical and mental. The Westerner is set apart from the Easterner, on screen, by their ability to recognize dangers and respond to them quickly and decisively, even if that means taking a human life. The classic Western's stock heroes—the stalwart sheriff, the noble cowboy, the wandering stranger—place themselves between the dangers of the West and those who are too weak, sheltered, or inexperienced to deal with them. The classic Western's central theme—the "taming" of the West and the establishment of civilization on the frontier—is about creating a world from which the old dangers have been permanently banished.

Robert Rodriguez's modern-day Western *From Dusk Till Dawn* (1996) opens with talk of a bank robbery that left seven law officers and a civilian dead, and it descends—as the thieves flee toward Mexico—into arson, kidnapping, and murder. Its two direct-to-video sequels, the first set in the present and the second a century in the past, begin with similar images of a lawless frontier where violent death waits around every corner. In *From Dusk Till Dawn 2: Texas Blood Money* (1999) a crew of bank robbers from the squalid, sun-baked border towns of South Texas plot to break into a Mexican bank and steal a fortune in cash from a drug cartel. The opening scenes of *From Dusk Till Dawn 3: The Hangman's Daughter* (1999) include the execution of an American expatriate, author Ambrose Bierce, by firing squad and the attempted execution of a Mexican outlaw by hanging. The latter is first delayed by the hangman's impromptu public whipping of his willful nineteen-year-old daughter and then thwarted when a well-aimed rifle shot severs the rope, allowing the prisoner to escape amid a hail of gunfire. Past or present, the films suggest, the Western frontier is fraught with danger.

Roughly halfway through its running time, however, each of the films leads its principal characters into a seedy bar just south of the Mexican border. The bar links all three films, and functions, in all three films, like an island universe. Outside lies the familiar visual furniture of the cinematic West: sagebrush and cattle skulls, windswept highways and dust-streaked cars, the trackless desert and the blistering sun. Inside, the rooms are dark, the ceilings are high, and the atmosphere is a disorienting fusion of Old West saloon and modern strip club, overlaid with a thick layer of Western Gothic and studded with statues of Aztec serpent-gods. When the characters walk through its doors, they enter not just a different space but a different genre: the world outside the bar belongs in a Western, the world inside in a horror movie. The majority of undead Westerns—from *Billy the Kid vs. Dracula* (1966) to *Jonah Hex* (2010)—have interwoven horror and Western tropes in a single setting. The *Dusk Till Dawn* trilogy embeds one within the other, but keeps each distinct.

Each film in the trilogy unfolds in essentially the same way: it carefully establishes its Western setting, then allows the main characters to walk (unwittingly) out of that world and into the horror-world inside the bar. The first film begins as a road movie, the second as a heist film, and the third as a romantic-outlaw tale . . . but all three become, in their final acts, full-on horror films in which—literally—all hell breaks loose inside the bar and the main characters must scramble to survive. The pivotal moment in each film comes when blood is spilled and the denizens of the bar reveal themselves as vampires and—hungry for more blood—begin to prey on the living. The vampires, unnatural and undead, are a more potent threat than any living being or force of nature that Western heroes traditionally face. Killing them requires attention to the genre rules of horror—they are capable of "turning" victims with a single bite, but they are vulnerable to crosses, stakes, and sunlight—but also to the traditional virtues of the Western hero: alertness, toughness, and self-reliance.

The vampires, and the horror world of the bar they inhabit, are the point at which the three *From Dusk Till Dawn* films visibly intersect. Lost amid the Western Gothic décor, the dripping fangs, and the flying body parts, however, is a less obvious connection between them. Each of the three parts of the trilogy is very much a Western, and like most classic Westerns they are concerned with threats to civilization and the heroes' struggle to overcome them. The vampires are, in each film, a threat not just to the heroes' physical well-being but to the moral order of which they are a part. The nature of the vampires' threat to the moral order is different in each film, but in each case threat is familiar to any fan of classic Westerns. The vampires are unreasoning savages in the first film, calculating outlaws in the second, and seductive agents of moral dissolution in the third.

Savages: *From Dusk Till Dawn* and the Vampire as Indian

The Steven Seagal thriller *Under Siege* (1992) was, famously, pitched to studio executives as "*Die Hard* on a boat."[1] The third act of Rodriguez's original *From Dusk Till Dawn* is, in the same sense, "*Stagecoach* in a bar." It traps an unlikely crew of travelers in a confined space from which they cannot escape, surrounds them with enemies determined to destroy them, and sets them the challenge of staying alive long enough for help to arrive.

Like the travelers in John Ford's 1939 classic *Stagecoach*, the travelers in *From Dusk Till Dawn* are a motley crew thrown together by circumstance rather than by choice. Their ranks include Jacob Fuller (Harvey Keitel), a preacher who has lost his faith; his son, Scott (Ernest Liu), a boy who longs to become a man; his daughter, Kate (Juliette Lewis), a girl on the uncertain verge of womanhood; a tough loner nicknamed "Sex Machine" (Tom Savini); an even tougher ex-soldier named Frost (Fred Williamson); and the two outlaws who unleashed mayhem in the opening moments of the film, Seth Gecko (George Clooney) and his psychotic brother Richard (Quentin

Tarantino). Looking at them, even a casual fan of Westerns can plot their character arcs. Under the vampire onslaught, the preacher will regain his faith, the outlaw will reveal his humanity, and the boy will learn that being a man means making hard—sometimes heartbreaking—choices. The psychotic brother will expiate his sins by dying horribly, at least one of the tough guys will find purpose in life by dying gallantly, and the girl will walk away at the end older, wiser, and physically unscathed. Mapping Rodriguez's characters one-to-one onto Ford's, however, is neither possible nor necessary. The pattern that makes the story: civilized people, trapped in an isolated outpost, fighting for their lives against hordes of savages howling for their blood.

Ford's savages, of course, were the Apache. Rodriguez's savages are vampires, but like the Indians in early Westerns they are, functionally, animals in human form. They attack with relentless, berserker-like ferocity, driven by instinct rather than reason. Driven by the dual coercions of instinct and need, impervious to reason and indifferent to pain, they continuously press their attack until they or their prey are dead.[2] Ford's Apaches were barbarians who merely *acted* like animals, but in *From Dusk Till Dawn* Rodriguez underscores the vampires' savagery by making them *look* conspicuously animal. Frost, after he is bitten and turned, has a boarlike quality to his head and facial features, and vampire queen Santanico Pandemonium (Salma Hayek) morphs from a beautiful woman into a scaly snake creature. A vampire beheaded by Sex Machine instantly sprouts a wormlike appendage (with its own small, wrinkled face) from its empty neck, and other unnamed vampires crouch and leap like wolves.

Death inflicted by the claws and teeth of wild beasts carries a particular horror, because it implies the defilement of the body: dismemberment, evisceration, and consumption.[3] Death at the hands of "savage" humans carries with it intimations of even worse defilement, carried out slowly and deliberately and driven by sadism or lust rather than animal hunger. Bound by the limits of the Production Code and the conventions of the genre, classic Westerns merely hinted at the possibilities, euphemizing it with phrases like "a fate worse than death." In *Stagecoach*, the gentleman-gambler Hatfield (John Carradine) saves his last bullets to ensure that army wife Lucy Mallory (Louise Platt) will not fall into Apache hands alive. Civil War veteran Ethan Edwards (John Wayne), having buried his niece, Lucy, after her abduction and murder by the Comanche in *The Searchers* (1956), answers her fiancé's halting questions with anger: "What do you want me to do? Draw you a picture? Spell it out? Don't ever ask me! Long as you live, don't ever ask me more!"[4] Combined with Edwards's determination to kill Lucy's younger sister, Debbie (Natalie Wood), if he finds her alive among the Comanche, it underscores the assumption—always present, never discussed openly—that, for women, a "fate worse than death" would include miscegenation and, if they resisted, rape.

The vampires in *From Dusk Till Dawn* make manifest the defilement of the body that classic Western films—and even the lurid covers of pulp magazines, with bound captives threatened by knife-wielding savages—merely suggest. They rip and tear at throats rather than delicately puncturing jugular veins, and their victims writhe and scream in agony rather than gasping and fainting. They see their victims not as companions, lovers, or even slaves, but purely and simply as food; having fed, they toss the limp body aside like a discarded husk. The bodily pollution of miscegenation, threatened in so many classic Westerns, becomes the bodily pollution of being "turned," and it is visited on men and women equally. The vampire's bite brings not the final release of death, and not even the subtle transformation of the classic vampire film (signaled by fangs and a hunger for blood), but wholesale rebirth as one of the animalistic undead: inhumanly savage and forever hungry.

Life-or-death struggles between the living and the undead, Gerry Canavan argues, "repackage the violence of colonial race war in a form that is ideologically safer" by depicting—and inviting viewers to cheer—"total, unrestrained violence against absolute Others whose very existence is seen as anathema to our own, Others who are in essence living death."[5] The inhumanness of the vampires in *From Dusk Till Dawn* functions in precisely this way, wiping away ethical nuances and justifying extreme, even genocidal, levels of violence. Seth Gecko screams at the assembled vampires who turned his brother: "I'm gonna kill every one of you godless, motherfucking pieces of shit!" and later declares that "I don't care about living or dying anymore. I just want to send as many of those devils back to Hell as I can." Seth is established, in the first half of the film, as a man capable of ferocious violence; the attack of the vampires gives that violence a higher purpose: not merely self-defense, but righteous extermination.

The Fullers, initially meek, are similarly transformed. Jacob, who lost his faith watching his wife die of cancer, finds it again in the bar, becoming a "mean, motherfucking servant of God" who wields cross, shotgun, and wooden stake with deadly efficiency against the legions of the undead. Kate—a quiet, withdrawn teenager who fades into the background of any room she's in—is transformed into a latter-day Joan of Arc who wears her own unswerving faith like armor as she wades into the melee with a pump-action crossbow held confidently before her. Scott, younger than Kate and exposed to violence only in video games, equips himself with weapons of mass destruction: a Super Soaker squirt rifle and a belt hung with condoms, both filled with tap water turned to vampire-dissolving holy water by Jacob's blessing. The film's "fetishization" of their improvised weapons and their skill in using them contrasts sharply, as Elizabeth McCarthy notes, with its reduction of vampires to an undifferentiated horde.[6] Like the shambling undead in a George Romero zombie apocalypse film, or the Apaches in *Stagecoach*, the vampires in *From Dusk Till Dawn* are merely targets.

The utter alienness of inhumanness of the enemy raises the stakes of the battle, making suicide, fratricide, and even patricide preferable to capture. Jacob, bitten by a vampire before the final battle, declares himself "already dead," and he tells his companions: "When I turn into one of them, I won't be Jacob anymore—I'll be a lapdog of Satan. I want you three to take me down, no different from the rest." His children offer only half-hearted assent, leading him to put a pistol to his temple and threaten to take his own life immediately if they do not "swear, to God, that when I become one of the undead, you'll kill me." Seth, who has already driven a stake through his own brother's heart, already understands and readily agrees. Ultimately, both Scott and Kate are obliged to follow in his footsteps, committing acts more horrible than any ever hinted at in Westerns—"gruesome, barbarous acts of mutilation and desecration"—in order to grant loved ones "a merciful, human, 'true' death" and spare them the horror of joining the undead.[7]

The Fuller family (left to right: Scott, Jacob, and Kate) brandish their improvised weapons as they prepare for a last stand against the vampire hordes lurking in a Mexican roadhouse in *From Dusk Till Dawn*.

The battle ends in a narrow victory for the living. Jacob and Scott die, but Seth and Kate hold off the vampires long enough for the sun to drive them back into their lairs. The film ends with them returning to their own world—the bright, familiar world of the Western—having played out what Richard Slotkin describes as "the structuring metaphor of the American experience"—regeneration through violence.[8]

Scoundrels: *From Dusk Till Dawn 2* and the Vampire as Outlaw

The regeneration that concludes the second film in the trilogy, *From Dusk Till Dawn 2: Texas Blood Money*, is also achieved through epic violence, but it is societal rather than—as with Seth and Kate—personal. Its vampires are, initially, members of a modern-day outlaw gang, quickly assembled to steal $5 million in drug-trafficking money from a poorly defended Mexican bank. Before they can rendezvous at the bank, however, the leader's car breaks down, and his search for help brings him unwittingly to the vampire bar, where he is bitten and turned. Luther (Duane Whitaker), the leader, bites and turns three of the other four members of his crew in the course of the job—leaving only Buck (Robert Patrick), his second-in-command, fully human. The vampire-outlaws retain their rationality, their skills, their ability to plan, and (perhaps most important) their ability to delay gratification, but they acquire superhuman strength and near immunity to conventional weapons. Once a threat only to the bank, they are now capable of destabilizing the entire town of Bravos.

The first half of the film establishes the crew as classic Western outlaw-heroes, struggling to retain their independence even as the trappings of civilization wipe away the last traces of the frontier and constantly threaten to smother them. It contrasts the grim details of their lives—cheap rented rooms, soul-deadening jobs, worn-out Texas border towns—with the appeal of the outlaw life: easy money, freedom, and excitement. At the same time, however, the early scenes constantly undercut their outlaw bravado with scenes underscoring what small-time operators they really are.[9] The result is both an homage to and a deconstruction of the big-budget Westerns of the 1960s. The gang is a road-company version of the Magnificent Seven, risking their lives in Mexico because they have no better offer; a bargain-basement Butch and Sundance, knowing that "one more job" probably isn't a good idea but doing it because they don't know how not to. Most of all, perhaps, they're a half-baked version of the Wild Bunch: arguing about the aesthetics of pornographic movies in a run-down motel room rather than about the outlaw code in a saloon.[10]

The gang of five small-time thieves that enters the Banco Bravos would be no match for the dozens of lawmen—local police, *federales*, and Texas sheriff Otis Lawson (Bo Hopkins), who is tracking Luther and Buck along with his deputy—that surround the building when the heist goes awry. The gang of four vampires that emerges (Buck, appalled by their transformation, has already fled and been apprehended by Lawson) is infinitely more formidable. Unlike the slavering mob in the first film, they are capable of thinking tactically, and they use their now superhuman strength, reflexes, and regenerative ability—coupled with fists, fangs, and scavenged guns—to wipe out a police assault team sent in to apprehend them. Emerging from the bank, armed with the assault team's automatic rifles and seemingly impervious to gunfire, they slaughter the assembled police with ease, leaving only Otis, his deputy, and Buck—their captive-turned-ally—standing.

The hail-of-bullets shootout in front of the bank evokes a long tradition of similar scenes in the revisionist Westerns of the 1960s and 1970s: the decimation of the James-Younger gang in *The Great Northfield Minnesota Raid* (1972) and *The Long Riders* (1980), the massacre of the Bunch by the Mexican army in *The Wild Bunch* (1969), and the deaths of Butch and Sundance at the hands of the Bolivian army in *Butch Cassidy and the Sundance Kid* (1969). In all those films, however, it is the outlaws (and by extension the Wild West itself) that die and the forces of order and conformity that prevail. The deaths of the outlaws and the gradual erasure of their wild and

A gang of vampire outlaws—combining the guile and lawlessness of their living selves with the strength and near invulnerability of the undead—threaten the rule of law in the Mexican town of Bravos in *From Dusk Till Dawn 2: Texas Blood Money*.

independent spirit are presented as a lamentable, but necessary. The mythology of the West hinges on the eventual triumph of civilization and the
displacement of the free-spirited loners who paved the way for it. The shift
from a Wild West, where outlaws must be faced down by lone sheriffs or
wandering strangers, to a more civilized West where they are held in check
by the laws, courts, and armed force of the state is an unambiguous sign of
progress. Outlaws able to defy the full power of the state, to "challenge the
fundamental values of America" and "bring the institutions of our modern
society to a halt," call that progress into question.[11]

The easy triumph of the vampire outlaws over the *federales* in *From Dusk
Till Dawn 2* is thus, on multiple levels, a threat not just to law and order in
one Mexican town but to the moral order of the West itself. Vampirism allows the outlaws to steal and kill—and, though the film does not pursue the
idea, presumably commit any other crime—with impunity. It sets the stage
not just for a wave of vampirism but a wave of violent felonies to sweep across
the West, tearing at the fabric of society. Their ability to flout the rule of law
and defy those who would enforce it undoes the defining quality that separates wilderness from civilization in the West: personal safety. It threatens
to turn every street, every town, to the wildness of the rawest mining camp.
That *From Dusk Till Dawn 2* clearly frames this as a threat, declining to
participate in what Majid Yar sees as the original *From Dusk Till Dawn's* self-
consciously postmodern view of crime-as-play,[12] reflects its close connection
to classic Western tales of outlaws and lawmen.

That connection is evident in the self-conscious throwback that initiates
the film's climax: a classic showdown. Buck and the two Texas lawmen face
off against the four vampire outlaws on the street in front of the bank, lined
up shoulder-to-shoulder like the Earp brothers meeting the Clantons and
McLowerys at the O.K. Corral. Holstered pistols hang from their belts, and a
pump-action shotgun rests against each man's hip, muzzle pointed skyward.
The outlaw gang, similarly shoulder-to-shoulder, faces them with fangs
bared and hands open, ready to grapple. They have, significantly, discarded
their modern, automatic weapons—symbolically leaving the late twentieth
century and returning to the world of the Wild West. Musical cues, terse
dialogue—"Looks like it's just about over, Otis" . . . "Looks like you might
be right, Luther"—and tight close-ups of faces and trigger fingers heighten
the Wild West atmosphere. At the moment battle is joined, however, the
heroes reach even further into the past for their weapons. Using their shotgun barrels and nightsticks drawn from their belts, they form large crosses
from which the vampires shrink back, cowering. The gang scatters, allowing
the heroes to—in classic Western fashion—defeat them in single combat

and vanquish the threat they pose to civilization. The scene—staged as a self-aware, if not overtly comic, commentary on the traditional Hollywood showdown—fulfills what Matthew Turner has argued is the central function of such deconstructions by reaffirming the generic conventions it calls attention to.[13]

The final act of the film—from the annihilation of the *federales* to the death of the last vampire—thus takes place in a West where, in Bravos at least, the clock has been turned back and all trace of law and order wiped away. The two lawmen, out of their jurisdiction and no longer under Mexican authority, cease to be agents of any recognized authority. Buck, released from his handcuffs so he can join the fight against the vampires, ceases to be a prisoner. All three become simply, men—defending the moral order against evil forces that would overturn it because, according to the mythical Code of the West, that is what honorable men do.

Seducer: *From Dusk Till Dawn 3,*
Vampires, and Moral Dissolution

The third film of the trilogy takes place nearly a century in the past, during the Mexican Revolution. It is, at first glance, a period remake of the first: innocent bystanders and outlaws on the run, besieged by vampires, join forces to defeat them. The vampires in the third film—like those in the second—have more than blood hunger on their mind, however, and the threat they pose to the moral order is more subtle than the frontal assault undertaken by those in the first. Nearly all the living characters that find their way to the bar in the third film harbor dark secrets and hidden desires that they carefully conceal from the rest of the world. Once inside—lulled perhaps by the seductive, otherworldly atmosphere—they let their carefully composed masks slip and expose their true selves. Having done so, they have broken (and thus fatally undermined) the compact on which frontier civilization rests.

Reece (Jordana Spiro), the sharpshooter who saved outlaw-hero Johnny Madrid (Marco Leonardi) from the gallows in the opening scene, presents herself to the world as a wide-eyed innocent who wants to learn the outlaw life from her idol Madrid. Once inside the bar, however, she is revealed as a cold-blooded psychopath who murdered her entire family in a two-state killing spree. Esmeralda (Ara Celi), the hangman's daughter of the title, appears at first to be a cloistered-but-rebellious nineteen-year-old, but the vampires greet her ecstatically as their long-awaited "chosen one." Her father (Temuera Morrison) seems at first to be a stern and unbending enforcer of society's laws and moral codes. His first interaction with his daughter—ordering her dragged onto the gallows and, as punishment for her disobedience, whipping her until her bare back bleeds—underscores his seeming rigidity. In the bar, however, it is revealed that his transgressions far exceed hers, for he fathered Esmeralda in an illicit relationship with the vampire priestess Quixtla (Sonia Braga) and then tried, multiple times, to murder her while she was still an infant. Mary Newlie (Rebecca Gayheart), an apparently pious missionary who travels with a stack of Bibles destined for a school in the village of Tierra Negra, presents herself to the world—even to her new husband, John (Lennie Loftin)—as innocent and virginal, uninterested in sex, but she becomes gleefully wanton when a total stranger asks her to dance in the bar. John himself falls the furthest. He enters the bar appearing to be a soft-spoken, happily married, milk-drinking man of God, but has, before the night is over, become well acquainted with four or five of the seven deadly sins.

Crucially, none of these "fallen" are—at least at the moment of their fall—physically corrupted (and thus morally weakened) by the vampires. Their sins are their own, already committed or at least contemplated, but carefully hidden under the masks that they wear in public. As long as they are outside the bar, their masks remain in place, their sins remain hidden, and the desires that led them to sin remain under control. To do so, Robin Wood suggests, is prerequisite for being counted as a well-adjusted member of society:

> What, then, is repressed in our culture? First, sexual energy itself, together with its possible sublimation into non-sexual creativity—sexuality being the source of creative energy in general. The "ideal" inhabitant of our culture will be an individual whose sexuality is sufficiently fulfilled by the monogamous heterosexual union of future ideal inhabitants . . . The "ideal," in other words, is as close as possible as an automaton in whom both sexual and intellectual energy have been reduced to a minimum.[14]

The abandonment of that repression and the rejection of that ideal is, Wood argues, central to the drama of the horror film, and so it is in *From Dusk Till Dawn 3: The Hangman's Daughter*. The presence of the vampires alters reality inside the bar, encouraging the living to drop their masks and embrace, in full, their sexual and creative energy.

Once inside, the travelers find themselves comfortable, even happy, with behavior they would recoil from—or at least be shamed by—in the outside world, where the eyes of the living are on them. Esmeralda, her back still bleeding from the wounds inflicted by her father's whip, meets an elegant, middle-aged woman (her mother, though she does not yet know it), who solicitously inquires, "Who did this to you, child?" Within moments, the woman has begun to slowly, lovingly lick the fresh blood from her skin—an act of shocking intimacy that Esmeralda freely accepts, with a rapturous expression on her face. The hangman, facing Esmeralda after she has rejected him and openly embraced her vampire heritage, does not flinch or pull away when she presses her body against his and delivers a gleefully lascivious, open-mouthed kiss. John Newlie guzzles tequila and takes brutal revenge—unleashing a premeditated, choreographed explosion of violence—on a man who insulted him: assailing him with fists, feet, and a heavy wooden club before drawing a Bowie knife and pinning his head to the bar.

Mary Newlie's embrace of her inner sybarite is particularly extravagant, and uniquely public. Descending from her upstairs room to the bar, still wearing the long, demure, white nightgown that served to deflect John's sexual advances, she encounters Ezra Traylor, an African American traveling salesman already turned to a vampire by the bar's "regulars." Jacket and vest discarded, white shirt unbuttoned to the waist, he asks her, "Care to dance?" and she willingly, though silently, accepts. The house band strikes up a smoldering tango, and she freely allows Traylor to strip the ribbon from her hair and split the skirts of her nightgown nearly to her hip, allowing her legs freedom to move. Settling into his arms she follows him step for step through the passionate dance, her expression leaving no doubt that she is experiencing a sexual awakening. The dance ends, predictably, with Traylor biting Mary and turning her, but the bite—by the standards of the trilogy—is restrained, even delicate. It could almost be the "vampire's kiss" of older, more conventional films: orgasm by another name, and thus the climax—in both senses—of her awakening.

Mary—gleefully embracing fornication, miscegenation, and vampirism in the space of a single dance—is the architect of her own moral downfall. So is John, who calmly discusses his plans for tequila-fueled mayhem with bartender Razor Charlie (Danny Trejo) before carrying them out. The vampires in the bar do not push them, or even lead them, down the road to moral dissolution. Esmeralda and her parents freely enter into their brief, disturbingly sexual encounters, and—viewers are invited to conclude—the Hangman entered into his affair with Quixtla, and conceived Esmeralda, with his eyes open. The master plot of all horror films, Robin Wood argues, is simply this: "Monster threatens normality."[15] The vampires in *From Dusk Till Dawn 3* threaten the moral order not by frontal assault but by subtle sabotage. Their presence is like a constant, seductive voice undermining the will to be good, whispering: "Do it . . . it's okay . . . you know you want to."

Her sense of moral restraint and social propriety eroded by the seductive presence of vampires, Mary Newlie—once a prim, virginal missionary—discovers the joys of passion and physicality in a tango with vampire traveling salesman Ezra Traylor.

Conclusion

The heroes of classic Westerns face a narrow, well-defined range of threats to the moral order of the frontier: savages, outlaws, and purveyors of temptation. The techniques available for combating them are equally well defined. Indians can be wiped out by armed force, negotiated into peaceful coexistence, or assimilated into society. Outlaws can be shot down in the streets, handed over to lawful authorities, or occasionally co-opted into becoming lawmen themselves. Those who offer cards and dice, liquor and loose women to the weak-willed can—if not driven out of business—be confined to well-known, clearly labeled establishments to which "decent folk" can give a wide berth. Over the genre as a whole, repetition brings reassurance. Each new threat confronted and successfully met reinforces faith in the durability and rightness of the moral order and in the ability of Westerners to triumph over the dangers of the frontier.

The introduction of the undead wipes away the familiarity, confronting the heroes with enemies they have never encountered or (very likely) even imagined. It overturns the easy certainties, raising the disquieting possibility that the way the world is is very different than they had assumed. "I always said God could kiss my ass," Seth tells Jacob after the first vampire attack in *From Dusk Till Dawn*. "But I just changed my lifetime tune about thirty minutes ago. Because what's out there is pure evil, straight from Hell. And if there's a Hell, and those bastards are from it, there has *got* to be a Heaven." The mingling of the Western and horror genres—the intrusion of the supernatural into the dangerous but seemingly stable world of the frontier—confronts the heroes with threats to the moral order that they do not fully comprehend, and may not (at least initially) understand how to defeat. Compounding those challenges is the very real possibility that their enemies may be not just inhuman, but more-than-human: stronger, tougher, or driven by some dark, mysterious magic.[16]

All this raises the possibility that the heroes will be defeated and the moral order undermined. The same possibility exists in revisionist Westerns such as *The Wild Bunch* and *McCabe & Mrs. Miller* (1971) but there, typically, it can be traced to the flawed nature of the hero's character. In undead Westerns, the heroes are not so much flawed as—potentially—out of their depth, overwhelmed by forces beyond their comprehension or control. The nature of the vampires' threat varies from film to film, but the nature of those who survive it, and finally defeat it, does not: they are characters who know exactly who they are and what matters to them, who say exactly what they mean, and do exactly what they say they will do. They preserve the moral order of the classic Western not just by defending it but by embodying it—with a conviction and an intensity that not even the undead can tear down.

Notes

1. Stephen Keane, *Disaster Movies: The Cinema of Catastrophe* (Wallflower Press, 2006), 60.

2. Gregory A. Waller, *The Living and the Undead: From Stoker's* Dracula *to Romero's* Dawn of the Dead (Urbana and Chicago: University of Illinois Press, 1986), 276–78; Stacey Abbott, *Celluloid Vampires: Life After Death in the Modern World* (Austin: University of Texas Press, 2007), 172.

3. David Quammen, *Monster of God: The Man-Eating Predator in the Jungles of History and the Mind* (New York: Norton, 2003), 10–15.

4. Edwards is, admittedly, an extreme—even monstrous—figure, presented as such (as are, to a lesser extent, the other settlers) in order to render such views troubling. See Christopher Sharrett, "Through a Door Darkly: A Reappraisal of John Ford's *The Searchers*," *Cineaste* 31.4 (2006): 4–8; and J. David Alvis and John E. Alvis, "Heroic Virtue and the Limits of Democracy in John Ford's *The Searchers*," *Perspective on Political Science* 38.2 (2009): 69–70.

5. Gerry Canavan, "We Are the Walking Dead: Race, Time, and Survival in Zombie Narrative," *Extrapolation* 51.3 (2010): 439.

6. Elizabeth McCarthy, "Death to Vampires! The Vampire Body and the Meaning of Mutilation," in *Vampires: Myths and Metaphors of Enduring Evil*, ed. Peter Day (Amsterdam: Rodopi, 2006), 203–4.

7. Waller, *The Living and the Undead*, 46.

8. Richard Slotkin, *Regeneration through Violence: The Mythology of the American Frontier 1600–1860* (Norman: University of Oklahoma Press, 2000), 5.

9. They are, for starters, either so overconfident that they believe they can steal from the drug traffickers and escape retribution, or so stupid that the possibility of retribution never occurred to them in the first place.

10. John Sturges's *The Magnificent Seven* (1960) is the story of seven American gunfighters who agree to defend a Mexican village against bandits. George Roy Hill's *Butch Cassidy and the Sundance Kid* (1969) follows an amiable pair of bank and train robbers, first in the United States and then in South America. Sam Peckinpah's *The Wild Bunch* (1969) follows a gang of aging outlaws as they search for one last big score in 1913 Mexico.

11. Waller, *The Living and the Undead*, 260.

12. Majid Yar, "Screening Crime: Cultural Criminology Goes to the Movies," in *Framing Crime: Cultural Criminology and the Image*, ed. Keith J. Hayward and Mike Presdee (New York: Routledge, 2010), 74–76.

13. Matthew R. Turner, "Cowboys and Comedy: The Simultaneous Deconstruction and Reinforcement of Generic Conventions in the Western Parody," in *Hollywood's West: The American Frontier in Film, Television & History*, ed. Peter C. Rollins and John E. O'Connor (Lexington: University Press of Kentucky, 2005), 231–32.

14. Robin Wood, "An Introduction to the American Horror Film," in *Movies and Methods: An Anthology, volume II*, ed. Bill Nichols (Berkeley and Los Angeles: University of California Press, 1985), 214.

15. Wood, "Introduction to the American Horror Film," 203–4.

16. The final shot of *From Dusk Till Dawn* teases the audience with that last possibility, showing that—like the nine-tenths of an iceberg that lies below the ocean's surface—a vast Aztec temple lies below and behind the Titty Twister.

Bibliography

Abbott, Stacey. *Celluloid Vampires: Life after Death in the Modern World*. Austin: University of Texas Press, 2007.

Alvis, J. David, and John E. Alvis. "Heroic Virtue and the Limits of Democracy in John Ford's *The Searchers*." *Perspective on Political Science* 38.2 (2009): 69–78.

Canavan, Gerry. "We Are the Walking Dead: Race, Time, and Survival in Zombie Narrative." *Extrapolation* 51.3 (2010): 431–53.

From Dusk Till Dawn. Directed by Robert Rodriguez. 1996. LaCrosse, WI: Echo Bridge Home Entertainment, 2011. DVD.

From Dusk Till Dawn 2: Texas Blood Money. Directed by Scott Spiegel. Burbank, CA: Dimension Home Video, 1999. DVD.

From Dusk Till Dawn 3: The Hangman's Daughter. Directed by P. J. Pesce. Burbank, CA: Dimension Home Video, 1999. DVD.

Keane, Stephen. *Disaster Movies: The Cinema of Catastrophe*. Wallflower Press, 2006.

McCarthy, Elizabeth. "Death to Vampires! The Vampire Body and the Meaning of Mutilation." In *Vampires: Myths and Metaphors of Enduring Evil*, edited by Peter Day, 189–208. Amsterdam: Rodopi, 2006.

Quammen, David. *Monster of God: The Man-Eating Predator in the Jungles of History and the Mind*. New York: Norton, 2003.

Sharrett, Christopher. "Through a Door Darkly: A Reappraisal of John Ford's *The Searchers*." *Cineaste* 31.4 (2006): 4–8.

Slotkin, Richard. *Regeneration through Violence: The Mythology of the American Frontier 1600–1860*. Norman: University of Oklahoma Press, 2000.

Turner, Matthew R. "Cowboys and Comedy: The Simultaneous Deconstruction and Reinforcement of Generic Conventions in the Western Parody." In *Hollywood's West: The American Frontier in Film, Television & History*, edited by Peter C. Rollins and John E. O'Connor, 218–35. Lexington: University Press of Kentucky, 2005.

Waller, Gregory A. *The Living and the Undead: From Stoker's* Dracula *to Romero's* Dawn of the Dead. Urbana and Chicago: University of Illinois Press, 1986.

Wood, Robin. "An Introduction to the American Horror Film," in *Movies and Methods: An Anthology, volume II*, edited by Bill Nichols, 195–220. Berkeley and Los Angeles: University of California Press, 1985.

Yar, Majid. "Screening Crime: Cultural Criminology Goes to the Movies." In *Framing Crime: Cultural Criminology and the Image*, edited by Keith J. Hayward and Mike Presdee, 68–82. New York: Routledge, 2010.

CHAPTER EIGHT

Blood on the Border

The Mexican Frontier in Vampires (1998) and Vampires: Los Muertos (2002)

Thomas Prasch

Early in *Vampires: Los Muertos* (2002), Tommy Lee Wallace's sequel to John Carpenter's *Vampires* (1998), surfboard-toting vampire slayer Derek Bliss (played by Jon Bon Jovi) gets his new assignment from the Van Helsing Group, for whom he does his vampire exterminating: "North Mexico. Sucker count's way up. Client wants a preemptive strike so they don't move up to San Diego or Tucson." The job is just a trick, staged by a sexy vampire master to lure the vampire hunters south for ends of her own, having to do with the quest (continued from the earlier movie) for the Bersier Cross, the early Christian artifact that will give the vampires the power to live in daylight and tip the balance in their favor in the centuries-long contest with humans for control of the world. But that the job is not what it seems to be does nothing to change the inflection of the Van Helsing Group's message. The terms of the instructions emphasize that the vampire hunting aims to prevent a threat crossing the border north, and thus underline the ways in which these two films use the tropes of the vampire Western to explore the issues of illegal aliens and the policing of boundaries along the frontier between the United States and Mexico. Vampires thus stand in for illegal immigrants, who, if allowed to continue to cross the border unimpeded, will sap the lifeblood of the northern nation, and secondarily, they will bring illegal drugs from Mexico into the United States. The project of stopping them thus dovetails with immigration concerns and the "War on Drugs" in contemporary America. At the same time, the vampires' own deeper roots in the terrain of the once-Mexican American Southwest complicates the simple vision of the problem being a matter of policing the borders between nation-states. The Van Helsing Group does not quite understand the full depth of the situation, although the vampire hunters remain the key to a solution.

Using the vampire Western—the hybrid genre of both *Vampires* and *Vampires: Los Muertos*[1]—as a vehicle to explore the problem of the porous border between the United States and Mexico might seem a natural leap. On the one hand, intrinsic characteristics of the vampire genre, in particular the constant tendency of vampires to migrate away from their distant homelands and the attendant threats they pose to the social order in the metropole, map conveniently well onto the anxieties in contemporary American society about an immigrant "threat." As Teresa Goddu has suggested, "traveling vampires remind us of the gothic's mobility. It is precisely the fear that the vampire might relocate" that charges the genre, while at the same time in any given instance the same logic insists that "gothic horror is articulated through particular locations. If the gothic is the repository for cultural anxieties, then the specific form and site of its conventions have much to say about its cultural effects."[2] It would seem to follow that the relocation of the vampiric Gothic to the American West should provide a simple formula for inscribing frontier anxieties—such as the porous border and the presumptive problem of illegal immigration from the south—onto the vampire genre. And, on the other hand, the Western's borderlands have always been complexly multicultural territories, in which the preexisting presence of a Mexican population, dating to before the United States' Manifest Destiny expansion westward, would seem to guarantee a subtext of tension over Mexican presence and prior claims. Given that history, the notion of firm national borders and simply homogenous nation-state populations (more mythical than actual in the American record in any case) are undermined by the more complicated facts on the ground, where American settlement is layered atop previous indigenous and Mexican populations and where the vestiges of those earlier settlements remain at least partially in place. The record of the Western genre for grappling with such issues may not stretch quite as far back as it could, and certainly not back to Tom Mix days. In *Gunfighter Nation*, Richard Slotkin convincingly argues that the cinematic Western only begins to engage with the issue of Mexico in a Cold-War context, in the "Mexico Westerns" that engage with the history of the Mexican Revolution as an early example of the problem of counterinsurgency in the early 1950s, and that the Mexican's place in the Western develops further, in more complex and nuanced ways, in the border-crossing Westerns of the later 1960s.[3] Still, by the time of the appearance of the first vampire Western, *Curse of the Undead*, in 1959, the Mexican's place in the representation of the borderlands was firmly established.

The particular inheritances of the vampire tradition, however, going back to its Byronic roots (and massively reinforced by Bram Stoker's *Dracula* [1897]), negate the possibility of the early hybrids effectively engaging the existence and potential problematics of a Mexican subculture on the frontier. In its earlier incarnations, the focus of the vampire film on the individual exotic outsider penetrating the territory of the metropole left the genre ill equipped to deal with larger population movements and broader cultural structures. It would take the fundamental reorienting of the genre in the late 1980s and early 1990s—toward an understanding of the vampire as part of a subculture, rather than as an isolated outsider—to give the vampire film the proper dynamics to deal with the Mexican border issue, with the subculture of illegal immigration and its ramifications. In this reshaping of the genre, interestingly, a vampire Western—Kathryn Bigelow's *Near Dark* (1987)—has a central place. A steady stream of vampire Westerns has followed in *Near Dark*'s wake, sometimes (as with the *From Dusk Till Dawn* trilogy) involving Mexican characters and locations in significant ways, but *Vampires* and its sequel remain unusual for the direct ways in which the films use the new subcultural possibilities of the genre to address border issues. We can gain a fuller understanding of the narrative strategies of the two films, however, if we first glance back at the inception of the vampire Western and then examine the repercussions of the generic shift of the vampire film, both generally and in relation to the Western.

Jack Crow, a mercenary vampire slayer backed by the resources of the Catholic Church, patrols the southwestern United States, maintaining a constant watch for vampires trying to cross the border and infiltrate the country, in *Vampires*.

The Vampire Moves West

Edward Dein's *Curse of the Undead,* a Universal release penned by Dein and his wife Mildred, is widely recognized as the first vampire Western, although it has received little critical evaluation.[4] Its generic hybridity has less to do with self-conscious rethinking of genre than with an exhaustion of possibilities, as Andrew Tudor argues: "Most of the other vampire films of this period [late 1950s] are amalgams or extensions of other prevailing themes. Thus, *Curse of the Undead* finds a vampire in a Western township; *The Fantastic Disappearing Man* (1958) places him in the body of a fugitive from behind the Iron Curtain; while *Blood Is My Heritage* (1958) gives us a schoolgirl vampire magically created by her chemistry mistress."[5] Self-conscious genre revisioning, Tudor suggests, would have to wait another decade; the full reorientation of the vampire genre, I argue, would need another three decades or so.

Without that sort of fundamental reordering, the possibilities of genre hybridity were limited; in *Curse of the Undead,* neither Western nor vampire conventions are seriously challenged or undermined. As Peter Day points out, "Despite . . . unlikely plot twists, the general theme of the vampire movie remained fairly constant,"[6] and the same could be said about the film's Western conventions. Gunfights in front of the saloon end up working out differently when one of the two gunslingers is immune to ordinary bullets (he can be killed, it turns out, by bullets with crosses etched into them), but in other respects, the rules are the same. The long-established conventions of vampire films and literature—that the vampire is an exotic Other (usually Orientalized to a greater or lesser degree), sexually charged (as the exchange of bodily fluids pretty much necessitates), turned into threat when he or she appears in the promiscuous urban space of the metropole (which, granted, the average cowtown might only aspire to be, but the principle still holds)—require no major reordering when imposed on the Western. In turn, the Western hardly needs to be reorganized to make room for a lone outsider with possibly evil intent.[7] *Billy the Kid vs. Dracula* (1966) did little to shake up either genre, either.

But in the late 1980s and early 1990s, the foundations of the vampire genre shifts: instead of the lone vampire (or at most a small party, a count and his three wives, say), we see the emergence of full-fledged vampire subcultures, existing alongside and in competition with human cultures over long spans of time. This shift in orientation produces a range of effects: it creates the grounds for a continuous battle over the eons between vampires and variously designated slayers (think *Buffy* [1992 for the film version]);

it encourages the development of vampire-exclusive subcultural spaces, especially those vampire bars that figure so much like gay bars (the one in *Modern Vampires* [1998] or *True Blood*'s Fangtasia, say [2008]); it seems to connect with the emergence of the chaste vampire (who can be tracked from television's *Forever Knight* [1989] forward to the *Twilight* series [beginning in 2008]); and it establishes the grounds for subcultural competition, the vampiric counterparts to gang warfare (as in the vampire versus werewolf wars in the *Underworld* series [beginning in 2003] or, again, in *Twilight*'s Team Jacob/Team Edward divide).[8] And, for the vampire Western, the shift to vampirism as subculture functions to destabilize both genres in the hybridized form.

The effects are already evident in the first vampire Western to take on vampire subcultures (and the most deeply analyzed of all vampire Westerns): Kathryn Bigelow's *Near Dark*.[9] In Bigelow's film, a road movie as well as a vampire Western, a nomadic troupe of vampires stalk the highways of the Southwest, savagely slaking their thirst for blood. Caleb, the central character, turned in his encounter with Mae, one of the crew, struggles throughout the film between his attraction to the vampires, his longing for family and home, and his inability to kill for himself. Pam Cook, placing the film in the context of other Western movies of the era, has noted how the film constitutes "an extreme statement of this preoccupation with subversive subcultural groups."[10] Stacey Abbott, grouping *Near Dark* with Robert Rodriguez's *From Dusk Till Dawn* (1996) and *Vampires*, underlines the destabilizing impact of Bigelow's treatment:

> By setting the film on the roads crossing desert landscapes of the old west, Bigelow, who has stated that it was her intention to make a "vampire western," merges both the modern and historical meanings of the setting. . . . The highway is the perfect location as it leads away from the urban landscape by moving through the vast expanse of the American rural landscape. . . . The characters, in effect, bring the danger and dehumanizing qualities of the city with them. . . . The highway upon which the vampires travel is itself technologically produced and reminds the audience that the western frontier no longer exists.[11]

The echoes here of *In Cold Blood* depend on the terms of the Western—what Nina Auerbach terms "its rigid polarization of good vs. bad, settlers vs. aliens, the family home vs. the open spaces"[12]—while at the same time undermining them by collapsing an alternative genre, as Sara Gwenllian Jones argues: "Where the western celebrates America's confident, striving, and glorious dream of itself . . . the gothic horror is Europe's sepulchral vision of decay, chaos, madness and death. . . . The diurnal world of the western is consumed by monster-populated night."[13] Jones also contrasts the rooted features of the Western domestic territory, where "blood, sociocultural belonging and lifestyle are inextricably linked," with the nomadic, Indian-like character of the vampires: "Repeatedly, the film represents their characteristics in ways that recall cinema's traditional constructions of hostile Indians as uncivilized savages and white settlers as rational, peaceable, and decent."[14] That that order is restored in the film's happy ending seems altogether too convenient in the wake of such undermining, equivalent to Euripedes' use of deus ex machina as a too-easy solution to intractable problems.

The terms of the new vampire Western—vampires placed among competing subcultures and destabilizing both genres, while generally wreaking havoc—were thus well established by the time Rodriguez and his screenwriter, Quentin Tarantino, offered up their own mash-up of outlaw road movie and vampire film: *From Dusk Till Dawn*. But, with the sensitivity toward the Mexican presence in American borderlands that Rodriguez had already showcased in *El Mariachi* (1992) and its sequel *Desperado* (1995), *From Dusk Till Dawn* incorporates border crossing and a vampire-filled Mexican destination. What the film's bloodlusty gang of armed robbers hope for when crossing the border with their kidnap victims is haven, and the Titty Twister roadhouse seems to offer both that and low entertainment, in the erotic snakedancing of Santanico Pandemonium (played by Salma Hayek). But haven proves elusive in what turns out to be, yes, another vampire bar; much mayhem ensues. The mayhem (and perhaps the sheer fun of genre mash-up, looking forward to their collaboration on *Grindhouse* [2007]) preoccupies Tarantino and Rodriguez far more, however, than any politically resonant issues cross-border vampirism might present. The film's two sequels—*From Dusk Till Dawn 2: Texas Blood Money* (1999), which sends another group of marauders into Mexico with essentially similar results, and *From Dusk Till Dawn 3: The Hangman's Daughter* (1999), a prequel that seeks to explain the origins of Santanico Pandemonium (finding it in an earlier vampire bar in turn-of-the-century Mexico, where yet another outlaw will confront unexpected bloodsucking evil)—keep the action south of the border, but do nothing to broaden the material thematically.

Subsequent vampire Westerns have hewed to the subcultural vein. Some, like *The Forsaken: Desert Vampires* (2001), retread the path taken by Bigelow to rather less interesting effect, playing with vampire gangs on Western highways. Others take the genre in new directions (if often with rather disastrous results in terms of box office and critical reception). Anthony Hickox's *Sundown: The Vampire in Retreat* (1990) posits a whole town of would-be peaceful vampires (led by David Carradine) trying to live off artificial blood until a rebellion by some who want to return to more fully sanguinary ways;[15] until everything breaks down into routine, possibly comic battle, the set-up suggests a sort of vampire Exoduster tale, with vampirism substituting for racial difference. *BloodRayne II: Deliverance* (2007) revisits, with a reverse twist, Billy the Kid's vampire encounter: here, Billy leads an outlaw vampire band, until the central European woman vampire slayer joins up with Pat Garrett to defeat them.[16] *Priest* (2011) jumbles vampire Western with postapocalyptic, alternative-universe dystopianism, to rather bizarre effect. But none of these films offer much border crossing.

Policing the Border

Critics who have taken note of John Carpenter's *Vampires* have tended to read it against *From Dusk Till Dawn* without attending to the differences between the two. Kim Newman writes of both that they "counter-programme Rice's posy Gothicism with feral, vicious bloodsuckers who attack in packs, preying on disposable transients in a modern-day West,"[17] which, while true enough of their shared un-Lestat-ness, does not go far enough in noticing what they are as well as what they are not. Newman misses the boundary issues, the parallels between Carpenter's vigilantes and anti-immigrant vigilante groups in contemporary America, and the vampires' links to an earlier Mexican incarnation of Western spaces. Stacey Abbott similarly plays Carpenter against Rodriguez, using the two films to argue for the postmodernity of the contemporary vampire Western. Thus, of *From Dusk Till Dawn*, she argues that "the road brings the food to the vampire's den as they feed off the truck drivers, outlaws and travelers who stop in their roadside bar. . . . the vampires are defined by movement while staying the same, therefore undermining the transformative experience of the road movie," while of the locations in *Vampires* she writes: "Both the vampire nest and the Sun God Motel [where the hunters hole up] are presented as yet another in a long line of interchangeable locations through which the vampires and their slayers travel, feed and hide. . . . On the road, the vampire and the slayer have become interchangeable."[18] Again, true enough as far as it goes, but Abbott's paralleled argument also misses the difference, the way the border and border crossing have become the business that defines the relationship between the vampires (as illegal immigrants) and the slayers (as vigilante protectors of the border) in Carpenter's film.

This dynamic is abundantly evident in *Vampires'* opening sequence. The imagery—sunset-red skies, mesa Southwestern landscapes, a sherifflike figure (hardened looks, sunglasses, cigar-chomping—James Wood plays the role), a ragtag band of vigilantes (ethnically mixed, tending toward long hair a decade after it qualified as fashion, seedy and rough around the edges), an isolated weathered house (in need of a paint job several decades back, broken windows, questionable roof)—is all familiarly the territory of the Western.

But the business that brings Jack Crow's slayer gang to the territories is tracking down clusters of immigrant vampires, led by "masters" instead of coyotes, who constitute a problem that needs to be purged. As Jack Crow puts it, when asked, "How's it look?": "Like another New Mexican shithole. Perfect spot for a nest." The instructions he delivers clarify the parallels even further: "OK, we think we have a nest in this place. Figure at least six goons, maybe more, and chances are we'll find the master in here somewhere. Rule number 8: if you find the nest, you'll find the master, usually won't leave it on its own. So it's strictly by the book today, gentlemen." The ethnic slur—vampires are routinely called "goons" in the film, echoing Vietnam-era usage—combined with the location and form of the nest, firmly establish the context of the film's vampire slaying: the threat of the illegal immigrant crossing the border. It does complicate the story in ways that will become important later, however, that those illegals have earlier roots in these territories; the place is called New Mexico for a reason, after all. And the particular version of the Western on which Carpenter riffs quickly becomes clear. First, Carpenter offers the brutal, long passage of the clearing of the vampire nest (vampires are blasted full of bullets, skewered with pikes, and shot with arrows connected to a winch on the truck so they can be hauled from their sanctuary into the sunlight, where they burst into slightly explosive flame, and then their charred corpses are staked through the heart and beheaded to complete the job). Then he presents the parallel mayhem of the postslaying

Equipped with an eclectic mixture of medieval and modern gear, Jack Crow and his team prepare for a ruthless attack on a vampire nest located in a dilapidated house—"another New Mexican shithole."

party at the Sun God Motel (in a Route 66-ish classic motel, the men party down with too much liquor, skimpily dressed whores, a paid-off local sheriff, much whooping and room trashing, a broken window). And thus we know: this is the post-Peckinpah West, another wild bunch at work.

Things do, of course, get complicated. They never find the master (he was self-buried nearby the whole time, his tactic for protection from the sun), but the master finds them, pausing for some oral play with one of the prostitutes, Katrina, before making a bloody mess of their party. Although Jack escapes with one of his men, Montoya, and the vampire-bitten whore, the rest of his crew and all of their guests are slain. Jack hangs onto Katrina as a means back to the master, since she has a "telepathic link" to him. Against Montoya's arguments to kill her and move on, since "she'll start screening his thoughts, seeing what he sees," Jack insists: "Exactly. Like a surveillance camera. So we can find him. And shove a stick right up his ass." But that telepathic link works both ways, it turns out; so the master finds them as well, holed up in a fleabag of a once-prosperous-now-downtrodden hotel in an anonymous Western town, and meanwhile she has bitten Montoya as well.

Meanwhile as well, Jack has dealt with the carnage at the Sun God (not very well, since news reports Montoya sees on the hotel room's TV tell of the police finding not only the burnt bodies at the motel but also the separately buried heads) and has checked in with the Catholic hierarchy, a Cardinal Alba who pays for his slaying services. There he gets the rest of the exposition we need to understand what is going on. When Jack fills in the cardinal and another priest, Father Guiteau, on his encounter ("No master was ever like this one. Superhuman strength. Unkillable. Like a machine. We didn't

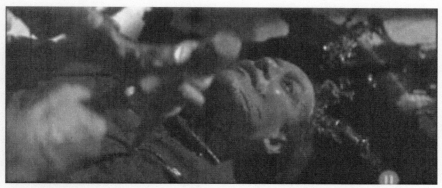

After the massacre at the Sun God Motel, Crow prepares to release one of his team— Father Giovanni—from the effects of the vampire curse by driving a stake through his heart and cutting off his head.

stand a chance. So tell me if I'm wrong, Cardinal, but couldn't he be the one we always talked about, the one we knew would come along one day?"), Guiteau explains the deep background. The master is Jan Valek; Guiteau shows a portrait of him from 1311 and recounts: "He was a priest who turned against the church and the led the Bohemian peasants in an uprising, actually captured several small towns. Valek was captured, tried for heresy and burned at the stake. But after his death there were reports that he was seen walking at night. They opened his grave and it was found empty. It was the first known case of vampirism." So forget all that Vlad the Impaler talk: this is the ur-vampire on the loose.

The revelation complicates the story in multiple ways. This is, for one, now a Czech Mexican Jack is dealing with, the central European traditional roots of the vampire preserved in the process (even if moved a few countries north). Further, the referencing of Bohemian peasant revolts mixes up the theology considerably: that puts Valek on the proto-Protestant side of pre-Reformation heretical challenges to the Catholic Church—he becomes, in essence, a stand-in for Jan Hus—which, mapped onto the West as locus, means that Valek is more closely aligned with the forces of Manifest Destiny—the dominantly Protestant United States in its expansionist city-on-the-hill discursive range—than with the Catholics, who held sway earlier, when it was all still Mexico.

And speaking of maps, Crow explains to Adam what distinguishes the patterns of vampire nomadism from the chasing of the slayers: showing the priest a map of "all the vampire encounters in the United States back to the 1800s," he points out: "See this spiral pattern? If you time-sequence all the encounters, you get a logarithmic pattern, ever widening. It's a search pattern, padre. They're looking for something." And Father Guiteau knows what, although it is only later that he reveals it: "Valek is looking for an ancient relic, the Cross of Bersier. After his trial, the Church declared that Valek was possessed by demons. He was taken to a small town in the south of France called Bersier. An exorcism was performed using an ancient forbidden form of the ceremony. It was long and very brutal. And then something went wrong. . . . The exorcism turned Valek into a creature whose body is dead but who lives on." Meanwhile, Guiteau further explicates: "The stories you heard about the black cross are true. It was used in Valek's exorcism and then sent back to Rome. It's known as the Bersier Cross. The cross was then shipped to the New World. It was moved over the years from one Spanish mission to another. Its exact location was kept secret even from the Vatican. For hundreds of years it was lost." The cross matters to Valek because completing the aborted rites of exorcism would give him the one power he lacks, the one thing that has limited his ability to work in the world: the ability to face sunlight. As the preacher tells the slayer: "Valek wants to complete his transformation. . . . For six hundred years, Valek has wanted to find a way to live in the daylight. With the Bersier Cross he will. A master vampire, able to walk in the sun, unstoppable, unless we stop him." To complete the ceremony, Valek just needs that hidden cross and the blood of a crusader, who will be crucified in the ritual. You can guess whose blood Valek has in mind for that. In the race that follows—Valek working to assemble what he needs for the ritual, Jack and Father Guiteau trying to stop him—Valek seems consistently a step ahead. For example, Cardinal Alba had just learned of the last priest who knew its location, but by the time Jack and Father Guiteau reach him, he has been beheaded by Valek. It will take Jack far longer than the audience to realize that Alba has betrayed them.

All the explication fills viewers in on what they need to know about these vampires and their quest, but it has several additional effects. First, it shifts the terrain of the Western back to its Mexican colonial days: it had been part of the aim of Mexican mission churches to keep the location of the cross a secret, and it is thus through a series of Mexican-named, adobe-styled mission towns—San Miguel, Santiago—that Jack and Montoya track the master. Simultaneously, the information dislocates our understanding of the vampires as well: it is they who have the clear, organized mission in the West, and their chasers seem disorderly and disorganized in comparison. Meanwhile, the sympathetic figure of vampire-turning Katrina mixes our emotional investment; by comparison to the routinely crude and brutal slayer crew, she seems the one with whom we should identify.

By movie's end—one bloodily pillaged monastery, one yet-again-aborted exorcism/crucifixion ritual, a host of dead priests and vampires, one climactic battle, one convenient sunrise, and one crisped master later—everything will be resolved. But one loose end will point forward toward a sequel: Montoya had been bitten by Katrina (twice, in fact: once lightly, on the arm in the hotel; once deeply, after she turned, on the night of the rite). At movie's end, Jack addresses his partner: "You look like shit, Montoya. Where are you going?" "South," Montoya answers, and Jack lets him drive away, although with a sinister promise: "Wherever you go, I will find you, I will hunt you down, and I will kill you." After the threat, the two hug (but, given the genre conventions, not for too long). But Montoya's stated destination, and Crow's promised pursuit, open the door to the obvious potential sequel: taking the fight against vampires south, across the border, to the source (at least currently) of the vampire threat.

Crossing the Border

Jack hunting Montoya down will not, in fact, propel the sequel into being. Indeed, none of the actors from the first movie will return for the second (since most, whether slayer or vampire, had been killed off, that is perhaps no surprise; new slayer Derek Bliss will find Father Guiteau lately deceased as well). And, although Carpenter kept a hand in as producer, *Vampires: Los Muertos* was written and directed by someone else: Tommy Lee Wallace, who already had sequels to *Halloween, Fright Night,* and *Amityville Horror* to his credit before he took on the project. What is preserved from the earlier film is the expositional logic: there are slayers and vampires, of course, although neither seem quite as brutal here (the sexily diaphanous drapery of the new female master softens her look considerably, and Bliss's crew—one local boy, one fresh priest, and one expat young American woman—hardly matches Carpenter's earlier marauders), and once again the vampires seek to reclaim daylight through a ritual involving the Bersier Cross and the crucifixion, with sipped chalices of the blood of some slayer. But what is different is also significant: the sequel moves the action firmly south of the border, where—despite the feint of the false mission—the emphasis is on preemptive prevention of vampire immigration.

The tone is set in the opening sequence. The film begins, before any credits roll, with flashing bilingual warnings: "Welcome to Mexico. Be Careful. *Bienvendos a Mexico. Tenga Cuidado.*" And then we are on the nighttime streets of Tijuana (handheld camera and low-light pixilation underlining the effects): neon signs, milling people, street food, hookers, bars. A razor-wielding would-be rapist corners a hooker in an alley until Bliss intervenes, seeming to save the woman, until he destroys her: staking her as a vampire, letting her separated head burst into flames in the next day's dawn. The territory of the sequel is thus rooted in Mexico itself, by a logic that is made clear in those instructions, already quoted, from the Van Helsing Group: "Client wants a preemptive strike so they don't move up to San Diego or Tucson." By implication, with vampires as much as with, say, Pancho Villa's raiders, the real solution to the problem lies not just in border patrols but in militarized intervention at the source. And *Vampires: Los Muertos* underlines its commitment to explore border issues by abandoning entirely the Central European roots of the vampire. These vampires are ethnically and culturally identified with the Mexican geographies they inhabit.

The Mexican locations play into the story in multiple, if seldom fully explicated, ways. Zoey, the girl in the slayer group, has actually been bitten by a vampire, but she staves off full-scale turning with drugs: "When I got bit, I

Masked revelers celebrating the Day of the Dead remind vampire slayer Derek Bliss and his crew that, in crossing the Mexican border, they have entered a different world.

went to Mexico City," where a doctor "slipped me some sort of experimental drug and it worked. I take it every day and the infection is in check," despite the persistence of a few symptoms. "I crave red meat. I get cranky in sunshine. Sometimes I see stuff," usually visions of her master. The plot strand alludes to the easy access to pharmaceuticals in Mexico and cross-border visitors' recourse to such drugs (among others). Later, the motif of Mexico as a site for experimental, not-FDA-approved alternative cures is reinforced when Zoey tries a transfusion cure to deal with her vampirism.

Meanwhile, the vampires have holed up, as the boy Sancho (echoes of *Don Quixote* in his sidekick role to the slayer) explains, in "an old sugar mill built on top of Toltec ruins." The mill is by now a ruin as well, and as the slayers stalk their prey through its unlit cavernous spaces, Toltec stelae mark the site's ancient purpose. Nothing too clear is done with the significance of a Toltec foundation for the vampire lair, but it corresponds to the sequel's generalized abandonment of the central European tropes of its predecessor: these vampires are firmly fixed in Mexican space, in ethnicity as well as in location. The town near the sugar mill is celebrating the Day of the Dead when the slayers arrive. An older villager, who has dreamt that "the Nortenos have come to kill the devils of the night," tells them: "Today is *Dio los Muertes*, Day of the Dead. Your timing is very good." As Derek and his team set to work, skeletons dance in the streets to mariachi brass tunes. By implication, the celebration suggests

Derek Bliss, seated on the hood of a car, considers how best to protect the Old Man and other citizens of a Mexican town from the vampires who have killed their priest, burned their church, and begun to prey on them in the night.

deep rather than recent roots for vampirism in Mexican cultural forms; it is rooted enough to have shaped their forms of popular culture.

At the same time, the conventions of the Western are preserved as well. The echoes are clearest in the development of a classic sidekick relationship between Derek and the young local boy, Sancho. When Derek travels to a local church to follow up on a reported infestation of vampires, Sancho follows, hoping for work. "Who are you?" Sancho demands, and Derek tells him, "I'm the Lone Ranger." "Then I'm Tonto," Sancho insists. Derek catches his first vampire by lassoing her; Sancho will follow his example when they confront the master at the end. Elsewhere, the film's language repeatedly hearkens to the Western genre. Derek's initial instructions, for example, insist, "It has to be a team. They don't want cowboys." Derek, however, is cowboy through and through, from his lasso to his hard-bitten fatalism: "The only choice left is how to die," he proclaims as the final conflict looms. And, through the film's course, it follows generic conventions, staging a sequence of gunfight-style confrontations between the two sides, much as its predecessor had. What it means that the generic territory of the West has been broadened to include Mexico itself is something the film itself does not much explore—after all, it scarcely even bothers to explain cross-border presences like expat Zoey—but the implication is, at the very least, that the Western constitutes less a matter of specific territories than of conceptual frameworks, modes of existing and interaction defined by stylized confrontation and repeatedly restored forms of order. In the context of *Vampires: Los Muertos*, the clear analog to the vampire plague that besets the small town near the sugar mill is the lethal impact of narcotics gangs on northern Mexico. The parallels become clear when the village's old man recounts the town's history to Derek: "This was once a thriving place. Now people cower in bed while devils walk the streets. Two days ago our priest disappeared. Last night our church was burned." The connection of vampirism and narcotics trade is underlined by the comparisons Zoey makes about her vampire-bit state: "You can see why people get hooked on drugs." But, in the context of the film's central struggle, the implication is clear: vampires pose a threat on both sides of the border, and a comprehensive solution must target both sides as well. For the range of analogs the film makes to vampirism—whether it be illegal immigrants, pushed by economic circumstances as well as pulled by economic opportunities, or the drug traffic, again as much about demand on one side as supply on the other—the film's argument for a solution that

Ancient Toltec ruins beneath an abandoned sugar mill—the latter a symbol of the modern drug trade—form the site for the final confrontation between vampires and slayers in *Vampires: Los Muertos*.

essentially erases the border, that makes Mexico a part of the territory of the West, remains the same.

The solution to the vampire problem proves easier than that for the narcotics trade. To face the vampire threat, Derek has to become like them; just as Zoey, near film's end, gets blood transfusions to keep her human after the vampire master steals her drugs, so Derek gets transfusions of her vampire blood to make him more like them (and less visible to them). And then it all gets simple: again, one aborted ritual, one extended final shoot-out, one more rising sun. But, as in the first film, a loose strand keeps the horror film's generic never-quite-finished promise of more: at film's close, as he puts on sunglasses because—as Zoey asks rhetorically, "The sunlight bothering you?"—he is becoming one of them.

What can we conclude about these border-crossing and genre-crossing experiments? Neither John Carpenter's *Vampires* nor *Vampires: Los Muertos* constitutes, by any stretch of the imagination, a masterpiece of the vampire genre. They are crude, low-budget, definitely B-picture material; they lack full development of the themes they raise, and they routinely sacrifice depth for cheap thrills. But what they nevertheless make clear is the rich possibilities opened up by the reformulation of the vampire into subcultural phenomenon. If vampires constitute subcultures, the parallels between them and existing subcultures can be mapped out in ways that have resonance for our political and cultural identity. And for that set of possibilities, the Mexican border, such a fraught terrain for American contemporary politics, provides the perfect space for the vampire Western to take on deeper meanings, exploring the meaning of the border, the problem it presents politically, and its deeper history in interesting ways. If neither film quite lives up to this promise, both still show where the promise lies. Look south to find that answer.

Notes

1. Kim Newman identifies *Vampires: The Turning* (2005) as a third film in the series—see *Nightmare Movies: Horror on the Screen since the 1960s* (rev. ed. London: Bloomsbury, 2011), 343—but this seems clearly wrong, given that the later film shares neither locale (it is set in Thailand) nor any personnel with the earlier works.

2. Teresa A. Goddu, "Vampire Gothic," *American Literary History* 11:1 (1999), 126.

3. Richard Slotkin, *Gunfighter Nation: The Myth of the Frontier in Twentieth-Century America* (Norman: Oklahoma University Press, 1998), 405–40, 560–77. Negative stereotypes of Mexicans, of course, have a longer history in the Hollywood film—see, for example, Joanne Herschfield, *The Invention of Dolores Del Rio* (St. Paul: University of Minnesota Press, 2000), 40–41—but simple negative stereotyping largely negates significant engagement with issues. But for an alternative view to Slotkin's, anchoring the deeper history of Hollywood's cinematic engagement with the border in an understanding of Mexican representations in Westerns going back to the silent era, see Camilla Fojas, *Border Bandits: Hollywood on the Southern Frontier* (Austin: University of Texas Press, 2008), especially chapters 1–2.

4. See, for example, Wheeler Winston Dixon, *A History of Horror* (New Brunswick: Rutgers University Press, 2010), 69; John L. Flynn, *Cinematic Vampires: The Living Dead in Film and Television* (Jefferson, NC: McFarland, 1992), 107; Raymond McNally and Radu Florescu, *In Search of Dracula: The History of Dracula and Vampires*, revised edition (New York: Mariner Books, 1994), 263.

5. Andrew Tudor, *Monsters and Mad Scientists: A Cultural History of the Horror Movie* (London: Basil Blackwell, 1989), 46. Similarly, Christopher Golden, Stephen R. Bissette, and Thomas E. Sniegoski refer to "the inevitable hybrid, the first gunslinger vampire," in *Buffy the Vampire Slayer: The Monster Book* (New York: Simon and Schuster, 2002).

6. Peter Day, "Introduction," in *Vampires: Myths and Metaphors of Enduring Evil*, ed. Peter Day (Amsterdam: Editions Rodopi, 1994), xi.

7. See, for example, Joanna Hearne, "'The Ache for Home': Assimilation and Separatism in Anthony Mann's *Devil's Doorway*," in *Hollywood's West: The American Frontier in Film, Television and History*, ed. Peter C. Rollins and John E. Connor (Lexington: University of Kentucky Press, 2005), 146; Mary P. Nichols, "Heroes and Political Communities in John Ford's Westerns: The Role of Wyatt Earp in *My Darling Clementine*," in *Print the Legend: Politics, Culture, and Civic Virtue in the Films of John Ford*, ed. Sidney A. Pearson (New York: Lexington Books, 2009), 85–86; Anneli S. Rufus, *Party of One: The Loners' Manifesto* (New York: Marlowe, 2003), 47–48.

8. I deal with this genre shift more fully in "Vampirism as Subculture: Trends in Bloodsucking," *Ryder Magazine* (Bloomington, IN), October–November 2010, 22–26.

9. The combination of feminist interest in Bigelow's engagement with traditionally male film genres and the interest of students of genre in what amounts to the reinvention of the vampire Western has ensured extensive critical attention to *Near Dark*. See, for example, Stacey Abbott, *Celluloid Vampires: Life after Death in the Modern World* (Austin: University of Texas Press, 2007), 171–73; Nina Auerbach, *Our Vampires, Ourselves* (Chicago: University of Chicago Press, 1995), 186–92; Sara Gwenllian Jones, "Vampires, Indians, and the Queer Fantastic: Kathryn Bigelow's *Near Dark*," in *The Cinema of Kathryn Bigelow: Hollywood Transgressor*, ed. Deborah Jermyn and Sean Redmond (London: Wallflower Press, 2003), 57–71; Yvonne Tusker, *Spectacular Bodies: Gender, Genre, and the Action Cinema* (New York:

Routledge, 1997), 156–57; Wheeler Winston Dixon, *The Transparency of Spectacle: Meditations on the Moving Image* (Albany: State University Press of New York, 1998), 129–32; Needeya Islam, "'I Wanted to Shoot People': Genre, Gender, and Action in the Films of Kathryn Bigelow," in *Kiss Me Deadly: Feminism and Cinema for the Moment*, ed. Laleen Jayamanne (Sydney: Power Institute of Art, 1995), 102–03; William Patrick Day, *Vampire Legends in Contemporary American Culture: What Becomes a Legend Most* (Lexington: University of Kentucky Press, 2002), 140–45; Christina Lane, *Feminist Hollywood: From* Born in Flames *to* Point Break (Detroit: Wayne State University Press, 2000), 109–13, and "The *Loveless* to *Point Break*: Bigelow's Trajectory in Action," *Cinema Journal* 37.4 (1998): 68–69; Ken Gelder, *Reading the Vampire* (New York: Routledge, 1994).

10. Pam Cook, *Screening the Past: Memory and Nostalgia in Cinema* (New York: Routledge, 2005), 194.

11. Abbott, *Celluloid Vampires*, 171.

12. Auerbach, *Our Vampires*, 187–88.

13. Jones, "Vampires, Indians, and the Queer Fantastic," 60.

14. Jones, "Vampires, Indians, and the Queer Fantastic," 63, 64.

15. See Newman, *Nightmare Movies*, 334; John Kenneth Muir, *Horror Films of the 1990s* (Jefferson, NC: McFarland, 2011), 188.

16. Paul Green, *Encyclopedia of Weird Westerns: Supernatural and Science Fiction Elements in Novels, Pulps, Comics, Films, Television, and Games* (Jefferson, NC: McFarland, 2009), 41.

17. Newman, *Nightmare Movies*, 343.

18. Abbott, *Celluloid Vampires*, 172, 173.

Bibliography

Abbott, Stacey. *Celluloid Vampires: Life after Death in the Modern World*. Austin: University of Texas Press, 2007.

Auerbach, Nina. *Our Vampires, Ourselves*. Chicago: University of Chicago Press, 1995.

Cook, Pam. *Screening the Past: Memory and Nostalgia in Cinema*. New York: Routledge, 2005.

Day, Peter. "Introduction." In *Vampires: Myths and Metaphors of Enduring Evil*, edited by Peter Day. Amsterdam: Editions Rodopi, 1994.

Day, William Patrick. *Vampire Legends in Contemporary American Culture: What Becomes a Legend Most*. Lexington: University of Kentucky Press, 2002.

Dixon, Wheeler Winston. *The Transparency of Spectacle: Meditations on the Moving Image*. Albany: State University Press of New York, 1998.

———. *A History of Horror*. New Brunswick, NJ: Rutgers University Press, 2010.

Flynn, John L. *Cinematic Vampires: The Living Dead in Film and Television*. Jefferson, NC: McFarland, 1992.

Fojas, Camilla. *Border Bandits: Hollywood on the Southern Frontier*. Austin: University of Texas Press, 2008.

Gelder, Ken. *Reading the Vampire*. New York: Routledge, 1994.

Goddu, Teresa A. "Vampire Gothic." *American Literary History* 11.1 (1999): 125–41.

Golden, Christopher, Stephen R. Bissette, and Thomas E. Sniegoski. *Buffy the Vampire Slayer: The Monster Book*. New York: Simon and Schuster, 2002.

Green, Paul. *Encyclopedia of Weird Westerns: Supernatural and Science Fiction Elements in Novels, Pulps, Comics, Films, Television, and Games*. Jefferson, NC: McFarland, 2009.

Hearne, Joanna. "'The Ache for Home': Assimilation and Separatism in Anthony Mann's *Devil's Doorway*." In *Hollywood's West: The American Frontier in Film, Television and History*, edited by Peter C. Rollins and John E. Connor, 126–59. Lexington: University of Kentucky Press, 2005.

Herschfield, Joanne. *The Invention of Dolores Del Rio*. St. Paul: University of Minnesota Press, 2000.

Islam, Needeya. "'I Wanted to Shoot People': Genre, Gender, and Action in the Films of Kathryn Bigelow." In *Kiss Me Deadly: Feminism and Cinema for the Moment*, edited by Laleen Jayamanne, 102–3. Sydney: Power Institute of Art, 1995.

Jones, Sara Gwenllian. "Vampires, Indians, and the Queer Fantastic: Kathryn Bigelow's *Near Dark*." In *The Cinema of Kathryn Bigelow: Hollywood Transgressor*, edited by Deborah Jermyn and Sean Redmond, 57–71. London: Wallflower Press, 2003.

Lane, Christine. "*The Loveless* to *Point Break*: Bigelow's Trajectory in Action." *Cinema Journal* 37.4 (1998): 59–81.

———. *Feminist Hollywood: From* Born in Flames *to* Point Break. Detroit: Wayne State University Press, 2000.

McNally, Raymond, and Radu Florescu. *In Search of Dracula: The History of Dracula and Vampires*, revised edition. New York: Mariner Books, 1994.

Muir, John Kenneth. *Horror Films of the 1990s*. Jefferson, NC: McFarland, 2011.

Newman, Kim. *Nightmare Movies: Horror on the Screen since the 1960s*, revised edition. London: Bloomsbury, 2011.

Nichols, Mary P. "Heroes and Political Communities in John Ford's Westerns: The Role of Wyatt Earp in *My Darling Clementine*." In *Print the Legend: Politics, Culture, and Civic Virtue in the Films of John Ford*, edited by Sidney A. Pearson, 78–85. New York: Lexington Books, 2009).

Prasch, Thomas A. "Vampirism as Subculture: Trends in Bloodsucking." *Ryder Magazine*, October–November 2010, 22–26.

Rufus, Anneli S. *Party of One: The Loner's Manifesto*. New York: Marlowe, 2003.

Slotkin, Richard. *Gunfighter Nation: The Myth of the Frontier in Twentieth-Century America*. Norman: Oklahoma University Press, 1998.

Tudor, Andrew. *Monsters and Mad Scientists: A Cultural History of the Horror Movie*. London: Basil Blackwell, 1989.

Tusker, Yvonne. *Spectacular Bodies: Gender, Genre, and the Action Cinema*. New York: Routledge, 1997.

Vampires. Directed by John Carpenter. Culver City, CA: Sony Pictures Home Entertainment, 1998. DVD.

Vampires: Los Muertos. Directed by Tommy Lee Wallace. Culver City, CA: Sony Pictures Home Entertainment, 2002.

CHAPTER NINE

Colliding Modalities and Receding Frontier in George Romero's *Land of the Dead*

Outi J. Hakola

In George Romero's zombie film *Land of the Dead* (2005), zombies have colonized the earth and humans are struggling for survival. This horror film uses the genre's conventionalized characteristics—undead and cannibalistic monsters, graphic violence, widespread destruction—to present an apocalyptic vision of a human society disintegrating in the face of a threat from outside its borders. In addition, it uses the conventions familiar from Westerns, such as frontier thematics and the figure of the cowboy, to examine the values—individualism and self-reliance—that lie at the core of Westerns' mythology of the frontier. In the resulting hybrid, civilization becomes the central theme that links two seemingly disparate genres: zombie horror traditionally narrates the destruction of civilization, whereas Westerns mythologize its spread on the frontier. In this chapter, I discuss how the combination of two generic practices expands the negotiation over civilization in ways that would not have been possible in the isolated generic contexts.

In *Land of the Dead*, intertextuality is present from the opening of the film, where the connections to Romero's earlier zombie films and Westerns are highlighted. *Land of the Dead* is the fourth zombie film directed by Romero, and it follows the same story line as *Night of the Living Dead* (1968) and its other sequels, *Dawn of the Dead* (1978) and *Day of the Dead* (1985). Although these four films are rather loosely linked, they all share the same apocalyptic setting: a world where zombification escalates and the living are cornered. During the opening credits of *Land of the Dead*, quotes from reporters are used as self-conscious references to the earlier films and events. The reporters' voices describe zombies: "Unburied corpses are returning to life and feeding on the living"; their destructive powers: "If you are bitten, you just become one of them that much sooner"; their global presence: "This is not a local or a regional phenomenon"; and the need for disposal: "They must be destroyed as quickly as possible. There's no time for funeral arrangements."

Whereas the earlier films narrated conflicts between small groups of survivors and masses of zombies, Land of the Dead reduces the chaotic conflicts to a more settled front where masses of zombies rule the wilderness and people are trying to survive in fortified cities. The scene is set by a reporter's statement: "People are said to be establishing outposts in big cities and raiding small rural towns for supplies, like outlaws." This quotation provides the viewer with context and with the film's first reference to Westerns, establishing its setting as the frontier that exists between the zombified wilderness and "Fiddlers Green," the city of the living.

In the film, the theme of civilization is approached through the frontier myth, which acquires meaning from two different cinematic contexts: horror and the Western. As a Western, Land of the Dead renews the existence of the frontier myth, but as a horror film, its destructiveness challenges the individualism often emphasized in Westerns. These differences can be approached through the concept of genre modality—a typical cultural and aesthetic practice created by a certain genre—and by examining how Land of the Dead's colliding genre modalities provide fruitful discussion of the values of American civilization.

Colliding Modalities at the Zombified Frontier

Modality becomes a useful concept when cinematic genres are understood as cultural practices and processes, which affect and are affected by reception, production, and other textual practices. Within cinema studies, the dynamic and processual view of genre has been well developed by Rick Altman, Stephen Neale, and Richard Maltby.[1] Instead of emphasizing the merely classificatory functions of genres, they have insisted on viewing genre as a communicative process in which films can change, cross generic borders, and use different conventional practices—modalities—for their own purposes. John Frow clarifies this approach in his remark that individual films do not belong to genres but rather participate in generic processes (perhaps even in several genres at once). Films use generic processes for particular purposes and thus construct genres.[2] Thus, instead of forcing Land of the Dead into a single category, it is important to look into the ways in which it makes use of different generic practices.

A genre's practices, conventionalized meanings, and intertextual references can be defined as modalities. Although the concept of modality is used differently in different fields, it refers to ways of being—either actual (what is) or potential and imaginative (what could be). In fiction, modality is often connected to the idea of possible worlds. Daniel Nolan argues that possible worlds, even though limited and artificial, are a way to imagine hypothetical situations and broaden the reader's perspectives without having to be limited by actual historical or practical facts.[3] In a similar way each genre imagines a possible world with its own logic, conventions, narrative structures, and themes. In horror films, the existence of undead monsters is well established, and we readily accept that Westerns are not historical reconstructions of the American West, but an adaptation of it.

Each genre film creates its own story world where the chosen generic practices actualize and are believable—what Neale calls the "probable," "plausible," and "likely," as verisimilitude. In other words, a genre's correspondence with the real world (actual being) is always filtered through its discursive/textual forms and aesthetic conventions.[4] With respect to cinema genres, modality refers to the distinctively expressed cultural meanings and aesthetic articulations of a genre. Christine Gledhill, for example, argues that each genre creates certain repetitive articulations of particular themes or conventions, which start to function symbolically inside that genre. These articulations become recognized and expected by the audience, and thus become modalities of the genre.[5] In other words, within a genre, some elements become so repetitious and formulaic that they start to function as recognizable signs. At an iconographic level, these signs could be decayed castles in horror films or saloons in Westerns. However, modalities are more than collections of iconic images or aesthetic conventions. Instead, they carry with them ideological and mythical elements, such as the use of monsters in horror or frontier conflicts in Westerns. When these themes travel across genre boundaries, the mythologies, ideologies, and narrative structures created within one fictional world travel with them.

Modalities are both productive and intertextual. Gledhill argues that the capability to cross the boundaries of medium and genre reveals the cultural productivity of modalities, which can also "circulate back to form social expectations and practices."[6] Westerns, for example, are set on the actual frontier, and they recreate a version of it through their use of historical settings, landscapes, and characters. They also, however, burnish the myths of the frontier by repetitiously acting them out, and so create not only a cinematic model of frontier but also a socially shared image of the frontier experience.

Thus, modalities emphasize the circulation of ideas. Paul Watson argues that any film genre is a "metaphorical" process that explores specific dimensions of cinematic expression, which can then be reused in other contexts. Consequently, a film genre's power and productivity lies in its intertextual relationships, not in any individual practices.[7] The productivity arises from the combination or collision of different ideas. Peter Stanfield argues, for example, that early Westerns' hybridization with romances, musicals, and comedies allowed the genre to transform, create new ideas, and connect with a larger audience than any "pure" genre film would do.[8] In the case of Western parodies, Matthew R. Turner contends that the genre hybrid makes visible, overdoes, and mocks the conventions of the Westerns, but by doing so, it also reinforces these conditions and modalities. He argues that the mocking of Westerns does not erase the existence of Western myths, but rather, comments on them.[9]

In *Land of the Dead*, the horror genre's conventions create the general story world into which the modalities of the Western intrude, colliding with horror modalities. In the horror genre, especially, the articulation of monstrosity is a recognizable modality. Horror narration features the monster as a key character that triggers events and necessary emotional reactions.[10] Monsters play a key role also in Robin Wood's definition of the horror genre: "monster threatens normality." Wood's straightforward formula provides three variables: "normality, the Monster, and, crucially, the relationship between the two."[11] This reciprocal relationship creates the negotiation where both monstrosity and normality—or civilization, as in *Land of the Dead*—are defined.

Zombies—part of the Hollywood horror film's cavalcade of the living dead—play the role of monsters in *Land of the Dead*. The living dead are located on the borderline between life and death. Most commonly, they are characters whose unnatural relationship to dying and death has turned them into appalling, undead, and unnatural creatures. Similarly, zombies are unburied corpses that become reanimated and threaten the living with their existence—both physically, by their power to kill, and metaphysically, by their power to transform the living into the undead.

This modern image of the zombie is, itself, Romero's creation, first put on screen in *Night of the Living Dead* (1968). The director is often referred to as the father of modern zombies, since he transformed zombies from mindless slaves controlled by Caribbean voodoo masters into modern cannibalistic corpses feeding on the flesh of the living. His depiction of them highlights their corporeality by mixing their trancelike ambulation with the grotesque and graphic appearance of their corpses.

Zombies' means for self-expression are limited to aggression and violent destruction. They are characters that act, often threatening others physically, but do not speak or think. They do not serve rationality; their actions are instinctual, and their obsessive and consuming cannibalism is the result of the need to feed. Zombies, as Gregory A. Waller argues, act like animals, basing their existence on instinctual behavior, repressed desires, or repressive control instead of making conscious decisions.[12] Zombie cannibalism threatens individuals, but by infecting their victims and zombifying *them*, they create a mass phenomenon that paralyzes the structures of society by robbing more and more of its citizens of the power of conscious choice or thought. As Waller says, they "are the projection of our desire to destroy, to challenge the fundamental values of America, and to bring the institutions of our modern society to a halt."[13]

Westerns, in contrast, have concentrated on the frontier myth that forms Americans' political and cultural self-image. Fredrick Jackson Turner, in his influential essay "The Significance of the Frontier in American History" (1893), argues that frontier refers to the "West" of America, where the pioneers encountered wilderness and created culture and civilization shaped by their borderland experience.[14] For Turner, the historical frontier defined the American character and reinforced the uniqueness of the United States; the effect of the frontier on America was, for him, tangible, measurable, and real. Later scholars have extended his argument by focusing on the frontier as a myth central to the American imagination. Richard Slotkin, for example, argues that although debates about the cultural significance of the frontier were based on historical realities, the frontier became—after its symbolic closing in 1893—an ideological reference that has had enormous mythological, political, and cultural power. Mass culture, especially Western films, has channeled that power by narrating, reimagining, and reinforcing familiar, shared ideas about the frontier experience.[15]

The imagined frontier is the site for, and derives much of its mythological power from, the "winning of the West." As Slotkin argues, the myth of the frontier is about "progress," achievement, and winning. Progress can refer to actual conquest of the West, but also—for example—to the creation of democracy and national identity, and to the expansion of commerce and industry.[16] In all cases, however, the myth of the frontier is about the expansion of civilization. *Land of the Dead* brings zombies—metaphors of destruction—to a frontier: a borderland where civilization is created. It thus transforms the frontier into a place where civilization is threatened, and where the colliding generic modalities of horror and the Western challenge the viewer's understanding of civilization.

Redefining Frontier Values

Most Westerns are located on a historically and geographically specific frontier: the American West sometime between the mid-nineteenth century and the early twentieth century. As Neale argues, because of their direct relationship with the frontier myth, Westerns have been uniquely connected to "US history, culture and identity."[17] Westerns have a strong tradition of imagining the frontier, but the once-substantial output of this particular genre has slowed to a handful of widely separated films. At the same time, other genres have taken over the role of Westerns in the renegotiation of the meaning of the frontier. Geoff King, for example, argues that the use of frontier themes in other genres has "expanded, developed and reinforced" the original Western use of frontier.[18] In the horror genre, the frontier is often an allegorical space where moral values of civilization encounter impulsive and instinctual values of the wild.

In *Land of the Dead*, the frontier is given allegorical, historical, and geographical dimensions. Allegorically, zombies—the contemporary savages—can be compared to the Indians familiar from Westerns, with the world they inhabit representing the wilderness. The world of the living survivors, meanwhile, corresponds with the civilization being built on the frontier. The historical frontier conflict is updated to the contemporary world by connecting the film to post-9/11 America and the War on Terror. References to 9/11 are used, especially, by Kaufman (Dennis Hopper)—the leader of the tower-dwellers—who sees both internal threats (a resistance movement) and external threats (zombies) to society as forms of terrorism against his creation of civilization. However, as Kyle Bishop argues, 9/11 did not bring anything new to zombie films, as such. The themes of apocalypticism, death, destruction, violent attacks, and mistrust already existed; 9/11 simply created a new cultural context for zombies.[19] The 9/11 connection also gives historical intertextuality to *Land of the Dead*, although the film continues to comment on the mythical dimensions of the frontier—especially those involving civilization and individualism.

Geographically, *Land of the Dead* creates an actual borderline between zombified territory and the barricaded survivors' city. The zombies colonize the rural areas and small towns around the city, creating a "natural" space that compares to mythical Indian territory, "linked to wildness, freedom, escape, impulsive behavior and liberation."[20] The survivors' city has three different areas: the tower where the elite live, the surrounding areas of the city where common people live, and the front, which is inhabited by soldiers who defend against zombies attempting to infiltrate the city and suppliers who make incursions into the zombified territory in order to fetch supplies for the city. In this world, the tower represents the settled society and civilization, just as the settled town of the Western "with its church, schoolhouse, thriving ranches and farms" symbolized moral order, control, and purification.[21] The physical conflicts between zombies and survivors take place at the front, but the common people who have been denied an access to the tower also live on a kind of social frontier where the previous moral codes have decayed.

Because the survivors' city is internally divided, *Land of the Dead* has two borders: one between zombies and survivors, and the other between the common people and the elite. The first division is familiar from Westerns' portrayal of the frontier experience, and the latter from Romero's earlier zombie films. Since *Night of the Living Dead*, zombies have created an external threat, but the real problem has been dysfunctional relationships among the living, who are unable to unite to face the threat. *Land of the Dead* takes place in a two-tiered community where the classes are separated by lifestyle and future prospects, as well as concretely, by fences. Thus, reactions to the zombie threat have not unified the people but intensified their divisions, as their inequality grows more visible and the elite's imposition of fences and

Commoners scrape out a meager existence on the streets of the walled city in *Land of the Dead*, while the elite live in luxury in the tower that looms over them.

other methods of control cause tensions to grow. The narration thus follows the horror genre's tendency for monsters to reveal the weaknesses of humanity and normality. In *Land of the Dead*, the civilization is fragile and challenged to the breaking point, which enables zombies to invade and destroy the survivors' city.

The distinction between this story and typical Westerns is remarkable. Westerns celebrate civilization's emergence from frontier conflicts through the displacement of frontier morality by civilized morality. By doing the contrary, Romero challenges the Western's idea of the stable, invulnerable, and victorious role of civilization. The frontier, in the postapocalyptic world of the film, is no longer advancing and spreading the civilization, but instead receding. By changing the direction of the frontier experience, *Land of the Dead* questions and critiques the American values sustained and validated by the frontier myth.

Frederick Jackson Turner argues that the frontier shaped the United States: that encounters with the wilderness guided Americans away from European culture and toward a new society where democracy was based on liberty, individualism, and opportunism, rather than organized institutions.[22] A similar emphasis on individualism is found in Westerns. Richard Slatta argues that, although in the actual West cooperation was the key to survival, the mythologized version of the West highlights self-reliance and individualism, embodying them in the lonely cowboy figure even as cowboys helped to preserve communal values.[23] In *Land of the Dead*, individualism is called into question through the collision of modalities. It turns into egoism, especially when Kaufman's desire to stay in power causes him to impose social control and destroy communal values.

Leah A. Murray argues that these colliding forces—individualism and communitarianism—have been the two dominant ideologies in American political philosophy since the founding of the nation. Murray defines individualism as the idea that society depends on self-reliance, values individual hard work and entrepreneurship, and devalues communitarianism as a limitation on individual freedom. She defines communitarianism as the notion that co-operation makes society prosper, and that community and self-sacrifice should be respected and valued. Romero's zombie films, she argues, address the value of communitarianism while dramatizing the problems of individualism.[24]

In *Land of the Dead*, individualism fails to provide morality and communality; individualist endeavors are doomed, or shown to be corrupt, and those who try to work together are rewarded. For example, gamblers allow a young girl to be fed to the zombies in the name of entertainment, momentary pleasure, and greed. Riley, the communitarian hero of the film, saves the girl at the last moment. A moment later, she helps to save Riley's life and they remain together in order to survive, reinforcing the film's message that cooperation and attention to the needs of others are the keys to meeting the zombie threat.

A similar duality is visible in the leaders of the two factions of the living. Kaufman, who rules over the tower-dwelling elite, is an individualist who is interested in maintaining the social structures he has created, and he is unwilling to acknowledge the growth of both internal resistance to his leadership and the zombie threat. He abuses his power by controlling the borders and by arresting or otherwise eliminating people he deems undesirable. His actions serve as a warning of how individualist goals can limit the individual liberty of others. As a counterpoint to Kaufman, the resistance leader Mulligan (Bruce McFee) exhibits communal values, trying to convince others to take action and claim what should belong to all, instead of to only a few. At the end of the film, it is Kaufman who is punished by death and Mulligan who survives.

Romero's zombie films propose that the American social contract should be based on communitarianism.[25] The same desire, in fact, can be detected in some recent Westerns that have reinterpreted the frontier story. Mary P. Nichols argues that, while classic Westerns celebrated the role of individualism and self-reliance in protecting the community, recent films—including *No Country for Old Men* (2007) and *3:10 to Yuma* (2007)—have given increased visibility and importance to communities that defend themselves through the cooperative action of communitarian-minded frontier citizens.[26]

Regardless of the desire for communal values, the possibility for communitarianism seems far-fetched in *Land of the Dead*, because those who embrace communitarian values are in the minority and cannot stop the apocalyptic destruction. The film offers an intimidating vision of how individualism can turn against the positive values that it represents in American ideology. When individualism turns into egoism, it can create social structures that support neither democracy nor the equal distribution of personal freedom and liberty. Instead, the film suggests that individual efforts should be guided by communitarian responsibility and the willingness to work together.

Emerging and Degenerating Civilizations

A key element of the frontier myth is the idea that the frontier is a site for learning and character building, both individual and collective. As Slotkin writes: "American must cross the border into 'Indian country' and experience a 'regression' to a more primitive and natural condition of life so that the false values of the 'metropolis' can be purged and a new, purified social contract enacted."[27] The founding experience of American civilization is rooted in violent conflict with the wild or savages: on the one hand, violence brings order into chaos and turns savagery into civilization; on the other, violence is only a resource, not a value in itself. It is the judicious, necessary use of violence to achieve a positive effect that differentiates the civilized Westerner from the violent savage.[28]

In *Land of the Dead*, however, people appear incapable of learning from the conflicts with zombies. Furthermore, their use of violence appears unnecessarily brutal and fails to bring order to the chaos. The soldiers, for example, do not simply kill the zombies, but inflict demeaning violence on them. They use the zombies for target practice, force them into gladiatorial fights, and hang their bodies as trophies for everyone to see. Violence against the zombies thus becomes a form of entertainment, and living people turn into savages. Instead of using violent frontier conflict to create civilization, their use of violence destroys what is left of it. Thus, the civilization-in-the-making depicted in traditional Westerns first degenerates back to frontier morals—with prostitutes, gambling, liquor, and violence—and then into complete savagery.

While the living fail to learn from the violent conflict, the zombies *are* learning. This possibility is suggested in the prologue, where a reporter observes—"if these creatures ever develop the power to think, to reason, even in the most primitive way"—they would be a threat. In the opening scene, this threat becomes reality. Two suppliers are watching zombies outside the city. They observe them trying to perform tasks they used to do as humans: playing instruments or, in the case of the main zombie character, Big Daddy (Eugene Clark), working at the gas station. Riley, the hero of the story, comments, "They used to be us. Learning how to be us again." When his companion, Mike (Shawn Roberts), disagrees, Big Daddy recognizes them and tries to communicate this to other zombies. Riley notes the change: "It's like he's talking to them."

This is a turning point, after which the zombies quickly learn new things. They discover that the people who kill them and steal supplies come from the fortified city, and they realize that the living use fireworks, or "sky flowers," to control them. They figure out how to break barricades, avoid traps, and eventually, how to use weapons. Most importantly, they learn how to communicate and how to show emotions. One of the most powerful moments of the film comes when the zombie leader, Big Daddy, has figured out the meaning of the fireworks and desperately tries to alert the other zombies

Flesh-eating zombie Big Daddy, a former garage owner, emerges as the leader of the undead, and perhaps of a nascent zombie society, in *Land of the Dead*.

to the threat. He tries to save other zombies' lives, but he is unsuccessful, and he has to watch some of them die in front of his eyes.

The film contrasts the learning process taking place among the zombies with the accelerating disintegration of the society of the living. While the living continue to pursue their individual goals and are at war not only with zombies but also with each other, the zombies are learning to be a group. When they attack the city, they even manage to set aside their instinctual self-serving need to feed on humans in order to execute the invasion and bring down the tower—the ultimate symbol of civilization. Individualism—when it devolves into egoism—breaks down civilization, but communitarianism can produce civilization.

In the end of the film, after avenging their mistreatment, the zombies travel back into the wilderness. Romero leaves their fate ambiguous, but Simon Clark sees this ending to open a possibility for a new zombie society different than that created by the living: one that celebrates instinctual freedom. Clark bases his claim on the zombies' instinctual characteristics and on the Freudian explanation model of the psyche. In the Freudian model, individuals would like to act on their instincts, but social norms have forced them to suppress these desires. Thus, Clark argues, social structures have distanced human beings from nature, but the zombies—having returned to the wilderness—would have a direct relationship with the wild and could create a society that combined personal liberty with communality.[29]

Clark's idea of an emerging zombie society recalls the frontier myth, wherein wilderness, freedom, and liberty are productive forces for civilization. However, whereas Clark connects the creation of civilization to a continued relationship with instincts, I argue that *Land of the Dead* promotes a combination of individualism and communitarianism. The zombies who learn to work together, despite their own solitary goals, create the progressive civilization of the traditional Western, whereas the survivors who learn to mistrust each other and rely only on themselves face the degeneration of their civilization.

Examples of Individualism:
A Hero and an Outlaw

In Westerns, as John Cawelti argues, the responsibility of importing the positive values of the wilderness into the community was given to the heroic individuals who crossed the boundaries of civilization, entered the wilderness, and there learned to defeat savagery.[30] In *Land of the Dead*, it is suppliers who enter the realm of wilderness and have the opportunity to learn from encounters with savages and their own dark sides. The two main supplier characters, Cholo (John Leguizamo) and Riley (Simon Baker), react differently to this encounter. They have different attitudes to individualism, and they come to represent the Western archetypes of the outlaw and the cowboy.

Cholo is an outlaw who refuses to work as a mediator between wilderness and civilization. Rather than trying to understand the wilderness, he violently attacks the zombies and kills them in order to attain a feeling of supremacy. He sees himself as having no connection to the wilderness and belonging only to civilization. By doing unpleasant favors for Kaufman he saves enough money to buy a place in the tower, and—though Riley tries to warn him that in the end the tower-dwellers will never accept him—he doesn't listen. When Kaufman rejects Cholo, the henchman loses his trust in society and steps outside of it, stealing an armed truck and threatening to blow up the tower unless he is given $5 million. This reaction, like his earlier behaviors, is opportunistic, egoistic, and disrespectful to communal values. He wants to avenge Kaufman's betrayal of him, even if it means killing innocent people. In the end, he is turned into a zombie, which is the final statement that his morals are those of the savages, not of the frontier or civilization.

Riley, on the other hand, represents an iconic frontier figure: the hero—a cowboy or reluctant gunfighter—who works as a mediator between society and wilderness. When Riley enters zombie territory, he shows respect for the

"Dead Reckoning," a heavily armed and armored truck built by Kaufman for forays into the zombie-controlled wilderness beyond the city, is turned against him by Cholo, his disaffected former henchman.

zombies and focuses on the straightforward fetching of supplies. He distracts zombies with fireworks rather than taking unnecessary risks of violent encounters. He kills zombies, but only in self-defense, not for fun like Cholo does. At the end of the film, Riley even refuses to kill the zombie leader. He comments, "They're just looking for a place to go, same as us." His empathy for the zombies allows him to act as a mediator between the living and the undead.

Riley's mediating skills and strong sense of moral and communal values are needed within the internally divided civilization, as well. He can negotiate with Kaufman and Cholo alike, and while he does not agree with Kaufman's goals and values, he agrees to defend the city people against the threats posed by both the zombies and Cholo. Riley agrees to work as a mediator because he wants to protect the citizens, but he takes on the role as reluctantly as any classic Western hero. In the process of protecting civilization and moral values the Western heroes are often forced to act questionably, and they end up as lonely figures that belong to the frontier, fully at home neither in civilization nor savagery.[31] Riley also belongs to the frontier, but unlike Cholo, he has actively chosen to embrace it. Riley recognizes the fractures in civilization and takes a pessimistic view of organized society, arguing that all the places inhabited by the living are the same: corrupted and class divided. Thus, although Riley is protective of the community, he does not want to be part of it, preferring to find refuge in solitude.

At the end of the film, when civilization in its current form is destroyed, Riley's responsibility for the city people ends. He refuses to join Mulligan, the resistance leader, in forming a new society, because for him the concept of society necessarily includes the possibility of the abuse of power. Instead, he sticks to his earlier plan to leave society behind: "I'm going to find a place where there is no people." Like the classic Western loner-hero, Riley recognizes that the independence he values is incompatible with the civilization he has protected.

This moment renews the frontier mythology. Although horror's modalities have challenged the frontier values throughout the film, in the end the idea of individual freedom reappears. Through the iconic cowboy figure of Riley, *Land of the Dead* suggests that the frontier mythology is still productive, but that the role of individualism in civilization needs to be reevaluated. Individualism should not mean egoism, as in the case of Cholo and Kaufman, but communitarianism, where freedom comes with moral responsibility, as in the case of Riley. The film ends with Riley deciding to head north, but his independent intentions are softened by communitarian urges when he agrees to take a small group of his friends with him. In a final nod toward classic Western iconography, they ride together toward the wilderness and into the sunrise.

Reevaluating American Values

Land of the Dead exists within the horror genre's story world, but it includes elements from Westerns. The collision of two sets of generic practices brings new dimensions to the story and its themes. The film's intertextuality is used to comment on the value of individualism in the shaping of American civilization, showcasing the idea that when individualism is taken for granted and given too much emphasis, it can easily lead into corruption and the inability to work together and protect the community. Thus, practices of individualism should, the film suggests, be subordinated to the communitarian values of those like Riley. At the same time, *Land of the Dead* suggests that blind acceptance of the frontier ideology can lead to disaster, causing civilization to degenerate instead of progress. The frontier experience, Romero contends, may justify American exceptionalism, but frontier values and the vision of American civilization that rests on them should be constantly reexamined and reevaluated.

Notes

1. Rick Altman, *Film/Genre* (London: British Film Institute, 1999); Stephen Neale, *Genre and Hollywood* (London and New York: Routledge, 2002); Richard Maltby, *Hollywood Cinema* (Oxford: Blackwell Publishing, 2003).

2. John Frow, *Genre* (Abingdon and New York: Routledge, 2006), 2, 28.

3. Daniel Nolan, "Modal Fictionalism," in *The Stanford Encyclopedia of Philosophy (Winter 2011 Edition)*, ed. Edward N. Zalta, 2011. http://plato.stanford.edu/archives/win2011/ entries/fictionalism-modal/

4. Neale, *Genre and Hollywood*, 32–35.

5. Christine Gledhill, "Rethinking Genre," in *Reinventing Film Studies*, ed. Christine Gledhill and Linda Williams (London: Arnold, 2000), 228–29.

6. Gledhill, "Rethinking Genre," 235.

7. Paul Watson, "Genre Theory and Hollywood Cinema," in *An Introduction to Film Studies*, ed. Jill Nelmes (London and New York: Routledge, 2007), 110–20, 124–26.

8. Peter Stanfield, *Hollywood, Westerns and the 1930s: The Lost Trail* (Exeter: University of Exeter Press, 2001), 118–21.

9. Matthew Turner, "Cowboys and Comedy: The Simultaneous Deconstruction and Reinforcement of Generic Conventions in the Western Parody," in *Hollywood's West: The American Frontier in Film, Television & History*, ed. Peter C. Rollins and John E. O'Connor (Lexington: University Press of Kentucky, 2005), 219, 232–35.

10. Noël Carroll, *The Philosophy of Horror* (New York, London: Routledge, 1990), 16–17, 60–86. The monster-centrality proposed by Carroll has been criticized as well, as not all horror films have (unnatural) monsters on which the narration could center. Still, horror films are dependent on the sense of threat, and whether the monster is real or imagined is a different issue.

11. Robin Wood, "An Introduction to the American Horror Film," in *Planks of Reason: Essays on the Horror Film*, ed. Barry Keith Grant and Christopher Sharrett (Metuchen, NJ: Scarecrow Press, 1984), 175–76.

12. Gregory A. Waller, *The Living and the Undead: From Stoker's* Dracula *to Romero's* Dawn of the Dead (Urbana and Chicago: University of Illinois Press, 1986), 276–78.

13. Waller, *The Living and the Undead*, 280.

14. Frederick Jackson Turner, "The Significance of the Frontier in American History," [1893] in *Rereading Frederick Jackson Turner: The Significance of the Frontier in American History and Other Essays*, ed. John Mack Faragher (New York: Henry Holt, 1994), 31–60.

15. Richard Slotkin, *Gunfighter Nation: The Myth of the Frontier in Twentieth-Century America* (Norman: University of Oklahoma Press, 1998), 3–4, 24.

16. Slotkin, *Gunfighter Nation*, 11.

17. Neale, *Genre and Hollywood*, 134.

18. Geoff King, "Spectacular Narratives: *Twister, Independence Day*, and Frontier Mythology in Contemporary Hollywood," *Journal of American Culture* 22.1 (1999): 38.

19. Kyle Bishop, "Dead Man Still Walking: Explaining the Zombie Renaissance," *Journal of Popular Film & Television* 37.1 (2009): 17–19, 24.

20. John Cawelti, *Mystery, Violence and Popular Culture* (Madison: University of Wisconsin Press, 2004), 144–45.

21. Cawelti, *Mystery, Violence and Popular Culture*, 144–45.

22. Turner, "Significance of the Frontier," 32–45.

23. Richard W. Slatta, "Making and Unmaking Myths of the American Frontier," *European Journal of American Culture* 29.2 (2010): 85.

24. Leah A. Murray, "When They Aren't Eating Us, They Bring Us Together: Zombies and the American Social Contract," in *The Undead and Philosophy: Chicken Soup for the Soulless*, ed. Richard Greene and K. Silem Mohammed (Chicago: Open Court, 2006), 211, 212, 215.

25. Murray, "When They Aren't Eating Us," 212, 220.

26. Mary P. Nichols, "Revisiting Heroism and Community in Contemporary Westerns: *No Country for Old Men* and *3:10 to Yuma*," *Perspectives on Political Science* 37.4 (2002): 207–15.

27. Slotkin, *Gunfighter Nation*, 14.

28. See also Cawelti, *Mystery, Violence and Popular Culture*, 212; Slotkin, *Gunfighter Nation*, 11.

29. Simon Clark, "The Undead Martyr: Sex, Death and Revolution in George Romero's Zombie Films," in *The Undead and Philosophy: Chicken Soup for the Soulless*, ed. Richard Greene and K. Silem Mohammed (Chicago: Open Court, 2006), 197–209.

30. Cawelti, *Mystery, Violence and Popular Culture*, 212.

31. See for example Cawelti, *Mystery, Violence and Popular Culture*, 147–50.

Bibliography

Altman, Rick. *Film/Genre*. London: British Film Institute, 1999.

Bishop, Kyle. "Dead Man Still Walking: Explaining the Zombie Renaissance." *Journal of Popular Film & Television*, 37.1 (2009): 16–25.

Carroll, Noël. *The Philosophy of Horror*. New York, London: Routledge, 1990.

Cawelti, John. *Mystery, Violence and Popular Culture*. Madison: University of Wisconsin Press, 2004.

Clark, Simon. "The Undead Martyr: Sex, Death and Revolution in George Romero's Zombie Films." In *The Undead and Philosophy: Chicken Soup for the Soulless*, edited by Richard Greene and K. Silem Mohammed, 197–209. Chicago and La Salle, IL: Open Court, 2006.

Frow, John. *Genre*. Abingdon and New York: Routledge, 2006.

Gledhill, Christine. "Rethinking Genre." In *Reinventing Film Studies*, edited by Christine Gledhill and Linda Williams, 221–43. London: Arnold, 2000.

King, Geoff. "Spectacular Narratives: *Twister, Independence Day*, and Frontier Mythology in Contemporary Hollywood." *Journal of American Culture* 22.1 (1999): 25–39.

Land of the Dead. Directed by George Romero. Universal City, CA: Universal Home Entertainment, 2005. DVD.

Maltby, Richard. *Hollywood Cinema*. Oxford: Blackwell Publishing, 2003.

Murray, Leah A. "When They Aren't Eating Us, They Bring Us Together: Zombies and the American Social Contract." In *The Undead and Philosophy: Chicken Soup for the Soulless*, edited by Richard Greene and K. Silem Mohammed, 211–20. Chicago and La Salle, IL: Open Court, 2006.

Neale, Stephen. *Genre and Hollywood*. London, New York: Routledge, 2002.

Nichols, Mary P. 2008. "Revisiting Heroism and Community in Contemporary Westerns: *No Country for Old Men* and *3:10 to Yuma*." *Perspectives on Political Science* 37.4 (2002): 207–15.

Nolan, Daniel. "Modal Fictionalism." In *The Stanford Encyclopedia of Philosophy (Winter 2011 Edition)*, edited by Edward N. Zalta, 2011. http://plato.stanford.edu/archives/ win2011/entries/fictionalism-modal/

Slatta, Richard W. "Making and Unmaking Myths of the American Frontier." *European Journal of American Culture* 29.2 (2010): 81–92.

Slotkin, Richard. *Gunfighter Nation: The Myth of the Frontier in Twentieth-Century America*. Norman: University of Oklahoma Press, 1998.

Stanfield, Peter. *Hollywood, Westerns and the 1930s: The Lost Trail*. Exeter: University of Exeter Press, 2001.

Turner, Fredrick Jackson. "The Significance of the Frontier in American History." [1893] In *Rereading Frederick Jackson Turner: The Significance of the Frontier in American History and Other Essays*, edited by John Mack Faragher, 31–60. New York: Henry Holt, 1994.

Turner, Matthew R. "Cowboys and Comedy. The Simultaneous Deconstruction and Reinforcement of Generic Conventions in the Western Parody." In *Hollywood's West: The American Frontier in Film, Television & History*, edited by Peter C. Rollins and John E. O'Connor, 218–35. Lexington: University Press of Kentucky, 2005.

Waller, Gregory A. *The Living and the Undead: From Stoker's Dracula to Romero's Dawn of the Dead*. Urbana and Chicago: University of Illinois Press, 1986.

Watson, Paul. "Genre Theory and Hollywood Cinema." In *An Introduction to Film Studies*, edited by Jill Nelmes, 110–27. London and New York: Routledge, 2007.

Wood, Robin. "An Introduction to the American Horror Film." In *Planks of Reason: Essays on the Horror Film*, edited by Barry Keith Grant and Christopher Sharrett, 164–200. Metuchen, NJ: Scarecrow Press, 1984.

CHAPTER TEN

Zombie Nationalism

Robert Rodriguez's Planet Terror *as* Immigration Satire

Christopher Gonzalez

Two creatures tend to evoke fear or disgust in many a moviegoer: the cock-roach and the zombie. Like kindred spirits, these creatures do not know the meaning of "quit"; they are consumers of the highest order, with a preternatu-ral ability to outlive and outlast. A strange mix of prehistoric and postatomic bug, the cockroach notoriously can survive under even the most draconian of conditions; it is scarcely even affected when its head is severed. The zombie, on the other hand, is the human transmogrified—degraded and cursed by technology and chemistry of his own making. Like the cockroach, it is also a consumer, drawing subsistence from the land of the living with a sense of inevitability. The zombie, in this modern incarnation, emerged in George A. Romero's *Night of the Living Dead* (1968), and it can now be found in set-tings ranging from Robert Kirkman's comic *The Walking Dead* (2010–) and its highly rated AMC television adaptation, to the zombie survival guides of Max Brooks and Seth Grahame-Smith's parody novel *Pride and Prejudice and Zombies*. There seems to be no terrain that is safe from the undead in contemporary popular culture, and the repeated metonym of the Mexican as cockroach—as something to be exterminated and eliminated—is at the very heart of the zombie film. It seemed only a matter of time, then, that Austin-based director Robert Rodriguez, who brought Texas and vampires together in *From Dusk Till Dawn* (1996), would unite Texas, cockroaches, and zom-bies in his films *Machete* (2010) and *Planet Terror* (2007).

In this chapter, I argue that Rodriguez uses the zombie narrative as a means of creating an innovative commentary on the troubled issue of illegal immigration. As a Texas-based filmmaker, Rodriguez often deals overtly with issues of immigration and Latinidad in the United States within his films such as *Machete*. Additionally, Rodriguez typically appropriates multiple genres—especially the speculative genres—as vehicles for his films. His films often intertextually overlap in interesting ways, creating intriguing inroads for thematics that connect his seemingly disparate films. Ultimately, Rodriguez uses the zombie genre to satirically comment on real life-or-death situations and material realities that compel people to cross human-made borders at all. Rodriguez, I maintain, makes this most stringent commentary in his film *Planet Terror*.

A counterpart piece to Quentin Tarantino's film *Death Proof* (2007), Rodriguez's *Planet Terror* forms part of the collaborative *Grindhouse* double-feature project—a project that was meant to be a holistic viewing experience, complete with fabricated movie trailers and special effects that lent the collaboration the feel of an exploitation flick, complete with the recreation of scratched and burned celluloid.[1] These effects are very much a part of the film, and the entirety of *Grindhouse* was intended to be viewed in one sitting. *Planet Terror*, the first half of *Grindhouse*, tells the story of the inhabitants of a small Texas town who must fight to fend off assimilation (or death) at the hands of a quickly proliferating zombie outbreak created by military experiments gone awry. Following the generic convention established by George A. Romero's *Night of the Living Dead*, these small-town citizens—led by El Wray (Freddy Rodriguez) and Cherry Darling (Rose McGowan)—work feverishly to survive the onslaught of hungry zombies over the course of one night. The various survivors make their final stand at an appropriate venue for a Texas-style zombie standoff: a barbecue joint named The Bone Shack. Understanding that they cannot survive the zombie outbreak indefinitely, El Wray devises a plan to leave Texas and cross the border into Mexico until they have the Pacific Ocean at their back. Rodriguez, however, demonstrates his loyalty to the *Grindhouse* project by suffusing his zombie film with black humor, gratuitous scenes of gore and violence (perhaps even more than expected of a zombie narrative), and a deliberately rendered low-budget aesthetic. Arguably, Rodriguez is more interested in adhering to the exploitation tradition in film than he is exploring the possibilities of the zombie genre.

Yet Rodriguez's influences go far beyond Romero. The *Grindhouse* collaboration is, itself, an homage to the exploitation B-flicks of the 1970s, mingled with references to Dan O'Bannon's *The Return of the Living Dead* (1985) and the work of John Carpenter, among others. This mix of influences may have helped bring about the general panning of *Planet Terror* by critics. It is often the case that films or literature "in the style of" bygone directors or authors are typically disparaged because they often do nothing more than simulate something already created and thus seem like cheap imitations. But is *Planet Terror* simply a cheap imitation?

My argument is that it is not. Though it may not be readily apparent how a zombie film connects with Rodriguez's more recent film *Machete*, there is an intriguing correlation between them. *Planet Terror* is preceded by a "fake" trailer for the film *Machete*, and though Rodriguez's film that bears that name would not be made for another three years, the trailer provides a crucial lens for viewing *Planet Terror*. While the Machete character is himself based on any number of 1970s vigilante figures—specifically those played by Charles Bronson in films such as *Death Wish* and *Mister Majestyk* (both 1974)—it is what Jeff Fahey's character Michael Booth says to Machete that is salient here, for it informs the remainder of my analysis: "As you may know, illegal aliens such as yourself are being forced out of our country at an alarming rate . . . For the good of both our people." The issues of "aliens" and "being forced out of our country" are foregrounded in both *Machete* and *Planet Terror*, and as the *Machete* trailer serves as a sort of introduction for *Planet Terror*, we can view the film as a commentary on the politics of immigration.

Rodriguez flips the zombie trope in *Machete*, wherein Mexican immigrants want to be a part of the dominant culture and actively seek assimilation with the help of "The Network"—a group of legal citizens who provide aid to immigrants in the form of money, food, shelter, employment, and other necessities. Conversely, the capitalistic drug lords and self-serving politicians seek literally to exterminate the Mexican immigrants, whom they see as vermin—specifically cockroaches or *cucarachas*, as they are called. In *Machete*, Rodriguez guides the spectator to identify with the immigrant group—the group that seeks to destabilize the established culture. Therefore, it is useful to examine how Rodriguez appropriates both filmic and cultural narratives in these two films.

Rodriguez's Intertextuality

Generally speaking, the heightened intertextuality of Rodriguez's films creates a type of "insider knowledge" that provides certain audiences—those viewers who, for instance, are familiar with blaxploitation films, zombie movies, or immigrant narratives—with a richer experience. In effect, Rodriguez relies on the prior experience the audience may have with these intertexts by often subverting audience expectations or re-presenting them in a new way.

For example, *Machete* makes use of the trope of the illegal border crosser who only wishes to unobtrusively make a living wage in the United States. Cary Fukunaga's *Sin Nombre* and Chris Weitz's *A Better Life* are examples of exactly this type of immigrant narrative. Rodriguez, on the other hand, deviates from this narrative by having a Charles Bronson-type vigilante who poses as a day laborer but is actually a Mexican *federale*, code-named "Machete." *Machete* also works with audience expectations of blaxploitation films, as Rodriguez creates his Latino version of such films. Rodriguez, and Tarantino as well, are both very mindful of the intertexts they invoke and understand how valuable audience familiarity and experience with these intertexts can be for their own films.

In addition, the films share key components: the sexy-woman-with-huge-gun figure, the quiet-outsider protagonist, the actor Jeff Fahey, and so on. Though the story world of *Machete* appears not to be that of *Planet Terror*, there is a transworld feel about them, as if they exist in the same universe. Brian McHale describes this phenomenon of "transworld identity" in *Postmodernist Fiction*, where characters that belong to "different fictional worlds" are brought together, resulting in an "intertextual boundary-violation."[2] For viewers familiar with Rodriguez's oeuvre, these intertextual moments resonate in significant ways. The result is that many of Rodriguez's films seem to overlap, ontologically speaking. One cannot help but see the antagonism between respective groups in both films. Indeed, in *Machete*, Senator John McLaughlin (Robert De Niro) calls the immigrants "terrorists," a word that clearly relates to a film with the title *Planet Terror*.

In *Planet Terror*, the zombies are a product of governmental experimentation and scientific hubris, and the film accordingly owes a huge debt to the zombie and science fiction genres and relies heavily on intertexts such as *The Return of the Living Dead*. Conversely, the "illegals" in *Machete* ultimately rise up in revolution to become an assimilating, zombielike force in their own right. Churning these waves of revolution is Machete—a Bronsonesque badass who is a nativist's worst nightmare. Rodriguez's intertexts even extend beyond fiction. Audiences aware of the so-called Minuteman Project, whose members take it upon themselves to patrol the U.S.-Mexico border, will see it reflected in a scene from *Machete* where a member of a fictional version of the Minutemen shoots and kills a family of border-crossers, one of whom is a pregnant woman. Audience familiarity with these intertexts allows Rodriguez access to an already activated emotional response to this issue as well as providing him with a larger canvas upon which to detail his satirical take on immigration.

Led by ex-lawman "Machete," illegal aliens rise up in revolution against white racists and nativists—wielding their leader's signature weapon—in Robert Rodriguez's *Machete*.

Conventions of the Zombie Narrative

Rodriguez's approach to immigration in *Planet Terror* can be contextualized by reviewing a few conventions of the zombie film genre. In a typical zombie narrative, the viewer is carefully guided to empathize with those characters that struggle to survive, even those characters that may be reprehensible or downright unlikable. In fact, this artificial social dynamic is partly responsible for the dramatic tension in zombie films. *Night of the Living Dead*, for example, featured a black man and a white woman relying on one another in a desperate attempt to survive—an unexpected and potentially controversial development for 1968 audiences. Even in more recent zombie narratives—such as the AMC series *The Walking Dead*—there is still a tradition of bringing survivors from disparate social groups together so that they must depend on one another.

In Season 1 of the show, there is a white supremacist and an African American amidst the group of survivors. Tension arises almost immediately when the two must work as a unit. Here, despite the disdain any sensible viewer has toward the white supremacist, there is a moment when the character finds himself alone, handcuffed to a pipe on a rooftop. He may be an unlikable character, but he is still human. Thus, the creators of *The Walking Dead* play with the tension the audience feels in this scene. Zombies are the built-in antagonists, but in this scene audiences are torn. As zombies are generally blank slates with no affect, audiences may empathize with a human character, even if he is despicable.[3] Because of the ubiquity of the zombie genre in popular culture, there is already a firmly established identification audiences have with uninfected, non-zombie characters. In fact, this willingness to identify with a character creates tension within an audience, just as it does among the characters that are united of purpose but may not trust one another. But more importantly, as Gerry Canavan notes, "Zombie apocalypses, like imperialistic narratives of alien invasion, repackage the violence of colonial race war in a form that is ideologically safer. Zombie films depict total, unrestrained violence against absolute Others whose very existence is seen as anathema to our own, Others who are in essence living death."[4] In essence, zombies function as a near-automatic Other that cannot be dealt with reasonably. As a result, members of widely divergent social groups must coalesce around a common purpose, even when those group members would otherwise avoid one another.

Thus, as a standard, we often identify with the protagonist of the zombie narrative while seeing the zombie as Other. Consequently, audiences generally want the protagonists to survive the zombie apocalypse, and the struggle for survival is what drives the narrative progression. In zombie films we crave homeostasis of the story world despite knowing it will be denied; zombie narratives function like a Pandora's box, with no return to the world as it was before the box was opened.[5] There are typically two reasons for this characteristic of a zombie film: either there are just too many zombies to contend with and they overwhelm the world, or the thing that generated the zombies in the first place (say, top-secret biochemical agents) is still out there to begin the zombie apocalypse anew.

Horror and Humor

Planet Terror falls partially in the horror genre, but it also makes strong use of dark comedy throughout the film. This of course follows a rich tradition in film and literature of blending what seem to be antipodal emotions: amusement and horror.[6] Noël Carroll encapsulates the counterintuitive pairing of horror and humor this way: "There is some intimate relation of affinity between horror and humor. [. . .] it appears that these two mental states—being horrified and being comically amused—could not be more different. Horror, in some sense, oppresses; comedy liberates. Horror turns the screw, comedy releases it. Comedy elates; horror stimulates depression, paranoia, and dread."[7] Rodriguez's film revels in its gore, just as the exploitation films of the 1970s were apt to do. One brief example from the film will serve to illustrate the point.

Dr. William Block (Josh Brolin) discovers his wife, Dr. Dakota Block (Marley Shelton), is having a lesbian affair. He is enraged, and he menaces her with a set of hypodermic needles, aping Dakota's own routine for administering a series of three color-coded, anesthetizing shots. But this time Dakota is at the other end of her own needles, and she puts her hands up to protect her face. Her husband jabs the needles into her hands, anesthetizing them in the process. Just at the moment when the audience is led to believe William will murder Dakota, a nurse breaks into the small room to report the hospital is under siege. This scene simultaneously relies on the apprehension that William may murder Dakota at any moment, but also the slapstick absurdity of having one's hands completely numbed. Later, as Dakota flees the hospital as it is overrun by the undead, her attempts to open her car door with her numbed hands are farcical. The humor of the scene, however, is immediately undone when Dakota slips her hand into the door handle and subsequently slips to the ground, gruesomely breaking her wrist in the process. Despite such repeated juxtapositions of slapstick humor and exploitative horror, no one will mistake *Planet Terror* for a comedy. It is, above all else, an homage to splatter films that occasionally use outrageous comedic situations.

"Horror films," as Fred Botting notes, "deal primarily in the production of extreme affects, affects evoked by taboos, shocks, suspense, and violence, by the promise and delivery of blood and gore, by repulsive eviscerations, decapitations, and destructions of bodies on screen and calibrated through an array of special and technical effects, to assault the eyes and sensibilities of spectators before the screen."[8] This idea of "extreme affects" is manifest in Rodriguez's willingness to depict the horrific with slapstick humor. Thus, by using the zombie narrative within the horror genre, coupled with gritty humor, Rodriguez has selected the perfect filmic combination to engage his audience's emotions, a significant point that has specific consequences as it relates to larger issues of immigration in the United States in *Planet Terror*, as I argue below.

The juxtaposition of a zombie apocalypse with the issue of illegal immigration seems even more unlikely than the juxtaposition of humor and horror. In fact, however, the idea of the zombie and the illegal immigrant as being linked is one that has been explored before, such as when Jon Stratton maintains that

> excluded from the rights and privileges of the modern state, those displaced people are positioned legally as bare life; and that in this legal limbo, these people can be treated in a way that enables them to become associated with a condition mythically exemplified in the zombie. The consequence is that not

only can the zombie texts of films and other media be read as reproducing this connection, drawing on present-day anxieties to increase the terror produced by these texts, but displaced people are characterized using the same terminology that describes the threat that zombies generate in zombie apocalypse texts.[9]

Yet in *Planet Terror*, the zombies are not metonyms for illegal immigrants. Rather, Rodriguez ingeniously subverts the archetypical zombie trope of defending a small space by having his survivor group—a group the audience is cued to identify with—leave their nation and cross a border because their lives depend on it. In essence, it allows the audience to simulate crossing a border in order to actuate a survival plan.

Zombie Nationalism

In choosing a genre made prominent by Romero, Rodriguez understands the political valences available to him in the genre's ability to reflect difficult contemporary issues such as racism, capitalism, consumerism, unabated military powers, and immigration. For example, Botting notes that "George Romero's deployment of the zombie in his politically calibrated series of movies spanning five decades remains attuned to the shock effects of mass culture and media. His first, *Night of the Living Dead*, offers a zombie reading of a United States negotiating the Vietnam War, the Civil Rights movement, and the Space Race potlatch against Communism."[10] To be sure, Rodriguez establishes the idea of "alien" bodies being forced out of the country before the beginning of *Planet Terror* proper via the *Machete* trailer. When considering the final scene of the film, however, the idea of being forced out of the country takes on a new meaning. I will come to the final scene momentarily. But before I do, I would like to introduce one more link between the two films.

Each film takes place in Texas: a border state with a high-profile governor, a rebellious spirit, and a frontier attitude toward the challenges it faces. Texas is a centerpiece in discussions of illegal immigration and is the driving force both in *Machete* and in *Planet Terror*, which examines the possibility that some people could find life so intolerable at home that they would have no choice but to leave the country of their birth. Putting it differently, the film asks: What could force a group of Texans—whose pride is rooted in their history of independence and the state's one-time status as an independent republic (represented in the state's flag as a "Lone Star")—to cross their own southern border into the safety of Mexico? If we view Rodriguez's film through the lens of immigration and the question of illegality, we see that

Mirroring the experience of countless real-world migrants and refugees, survivors of a zombie plague flee their ruined city, leaving home behind in the hope of creating a new life elsewhere.

Planet Terror is an intriguing commentary on one of the most volatile issues of our time.

Patrick Colm Hogan's notion of "affectivity" is particularly useful in this context, as it can help us think about the depiction of in-group/out-group movement under the process of assimilation.[11] The emotions evoked by a text or film—provided they are not boredom or frustration—are, Hogan argues, a crucial aspect of story world reconstruction in the viewer's mind, which is directly related to our capacity to empathize and identify with fictional minds and characters. Emotions are thus especially important in creating in-group/out-group categories, and affectivity is the "infusion of emotion into our ideas about identity."[12] For Hogan, emotion, narrative, and identity categories are inextricably linked. Accordingly, it stands to reason that the better one is able to decode and process a narrative, the better understanding of the fictional mind a reader will have, and the stronger emotional engagement they will have with the story world, providing the potential for a restructuring of how, say, an out-group national identity is conceived of by the spectator.

With this understanding of how social groups function, we see that zombie narratives rely on a motley crew of characters who are forced to come together and function as a unit, drawing on the specific talents of the group members for the greater good. The tension created by the group dynamic—individuals who would not, under ordinary circumstances, form a cohesive social group—is, as noted above, one of the driving forces of the zombie narrative. The objective in a zombie narrative is to survive, but this is typically delineated in a specific time and space. Most often the zombie narrative unfolds in specific geographical space over the course of several hours. The relative speed of the zombies' proliferation contributes to the drastic actions non-zombie characters must take—such as "killing" zombies who were former friends, lovers, or children. In short, despite other social factors that determine how characters identify in a prezombie world, two new superordinate groups begin to cohere in a zombie narrative: zombie and non-zombie. After the zombie event, social groups effectively become a matter of "us" versus "them."

"Us" versus "them" policies are, in the real world, often rooted in racism, with proponents of them ascribing extreme qualities and nefarious behaviors to "outsiders" as a means of dehumanizing them. These propaganda tactics, ubiquitous and well documented in wartime, are also used in domestic political controversies, such as that over so-called illegal aliens in the United States. Priscilla Huang notes, for example, that "the image of pregnant immigrant women crossing the border to have children in the United States is a familiar one in the media and in immigration reform debates. The myth capitalizes on the stereotype that immigrant women of color are overly fertile and conspire to give birth to 'anchor babies'" who by law would then be U.S. citizens.[13] The use of "anchor baby" to describe the children born, on American soil, to undocumented parents reduces them from a person to a tool, and it reduces onlookers' sympathy for parents separated from their children because of immigration status. The reduction of the immigration debate to an "us" versus "them" situation also obscures the fact that a significant portion of the U.S. population has a connection to someone directly affected by illegal immigration.

Issues of Latino immigration and forces of assimilation creatively play out in *Planet Terror*, where Rodriguez uses the trope of illegal immigration and turns it on its head in the guise of a zombie narrative. Beneath its B movie surface, it actually textures the tensions that arise when two communities—"alien" and human—come together. The proliferating "alien" or zombie group—the result of military science gone horribly wrong—causes panic and fear among the small-town inhabitants, a fear driven by the "alien" culture. In this reversal of the assimilation narrative that was so popular in the early twentieth century—one where the immigrant works through hardship to become a success in a new land and ultimately assimilates by marrying a local girl and raising a family—Rodriguez models a *fear* of assimilation into the alien culture through specific aural and visual devices to trigger the audience's emotive—even empathetic—response to the town folk. This is a long-established convention of horror films generally, and zombie films specifically. The audience, despite racial, cultural, political, national, or linguistic differences with specific characters, will consistently gravitate to the non-zombie group. (No one has yet created an easy-to-identify-with zombie character, or created a first-person zombie narrative.) Rodriguez uses this convention to encourage audiences to align themselves with the non-zombie group in his film, which has significant ramifications given the immigration subtext of *Planet Terror*.

Rodriguez later reverses the assimilatory forces in *Machete*, where the immigrant community rises up to become the dominant group, forcing the Anglo-as-Other to assimilate. Though *Machete* is not the focus of this chapter, it does bear some mention in this examination of *Planet Terror* as a satirical comment on current policy on immigration. It is important to note that Rodriguez deploys a heightened sense of what I call "Rodriguez-intertextuality" (the thick cross-referencing between his films) that itself creates an assimilatory flow from audience out-group to a Rodriguez-intertextual in-group—a flow that he rewards in the experience of watching his films cumulatively. The net effect is that Rodriguez's creative couching of the so-called Latino question at the level of form and content in *Planet Terror* urges viewers to reframe the current political debate on immigration.

Whether the cast of characters in a zombie narrative will survive depends on how well they can function as a unit. This is why an already established group—a military unit, for example—never forms the entire cast of a zombie film; there must be doubt that the group will continue to cohere through the various challenges posed by the zombies. Yet while differences are always present in an in-group—enabling the narrative to explore group dynamics against a common enemy—research suggests that identity categories are prioritized depending on social situations.

In *Planet Terror*, the range of socioeconomic strata represented among the survivors takes precedence over the cohesion of the group in the face of the zombie assault. Rodriguez uses this commonplace of the zombie genre to great comedic effect. Protagonists Cherry Darling and El Wray, having once walked out on one another, are thrust together because of the zombie event. Dr. Dakota Block, forced to seek help from her estranged father, is only allowed to enter his house after he disgustedly concludes that he has no choice. Sheriff Hague (Michael Biehn) and J. T. (Jeff Fahey), brothers whose tense relationship is strained by J. T.'s refusal to reveal his secret techniques for cooking award-winning barbeque, are united in their fight against the zombie horde. The rupture in their relationship is healed only when both are dying from gunshot wounds, and, as an act of brotherly love and kindness, J. T. begins to explain his cooking process, which an eager Sheriff Hague jots in his memo pad.

Two relationships in the film in particular demonstrate how the "us" versus "them" binary present within the social dynamic of zombie narratives functions. Though the specifics are never actually revealed (Rodriguez keeps many plot points hidden in *Planet Terror*), there is a backstory that creates distrust between Sheriff Hague and El Wray. When the two characters encounter each other for the first time in the film, Hague cannot bring himself to trust El Wray. His determination to keep El Wray from having a gun is a running gag for most of the film. Once Hague learns El Wray's true identity as a significant military or law enforcement agent (a moment that is literally cut out of the film via a deliberately "missing reel"), Hague tells the rest of the group concerning El Wray: "Give him the guns. Give him all the guns." Despite all prior differences, Sheriff Hague finally understands that he and El Wray are members of the same group.

On the other hand, there is William and Dakota Block. Married with problems (which lead to his murder attempt), their relationship seems doomed when Tammy, Dakota's lover, is brought into the emergency room dead as a result of a zombie attack: "It's a no-brainer," a nurse jokes as Tammy is revealed to be missing her brain. William, now understanding the betrayal of his adulterous wife, confronts her with murderous intent. As their relationship seems

Planet Terror's band of survivors—including (left to right) Deputy Tolo, Sheriff Hague, El Wray, and Cherry Darling—must cooperate in order to survive the zombie onslaught.

irreparable, it fits the zombie-film trope to have one of them become one of the undead, and there is little surprise when William "dies" at the hands of his own father-in-law and becomes a zombified Other. So, while members of the non-zombie group can ultimately overcome other important differences, identity categories that unite members of the group are rendered meaningless when zombification occurs.

In fact, *Planet Terror* uses a Russian doll structuring of identity—smaller identity categories located within larger ones. Each of the major characters carries on in a way that has isolated them from their most salient group. Cherry is a go-go dancer who longs to be a stand-up comedian; Dr. Dakota Block is married to a man but longs to be with a woman; El Wray, apparently a retired member of a law enforcement or military organization, is treated as an ex-convict for most of the film. Each of these characters, through the imposition of the zombie force, must cohere with the others to form a new in-group. As the characters come together, Rodriguez structures the film so as to allow audience movement into the new in-group along with the characters. The result is affinity for, and identification with, these disparate on-screen personalities. The audience is then aligned to identify with the same goals as the group on screen. Beyond simply surviving to see the next day, the superordinate goal of the survivors in *Planet Terror* is voiced by El Wray to Cherry Darling: to move from Texas (the center of the zombie outbreak) to Mexico, with, as he says, "the ocean at your back," and thus in a defensible position. The film's final scene shows the group, grown larger as they find others seeking safety in numbers, on a Mexican coastline with easily identifiable, iconic pre-Columbian pyramids.

This outcome illustrates the different tack Rodriguez takes in concluding his zombie narrative. Stratton has theorized how Romero's pioneering zombie films explore their connections to illegal immigration: "The trope of a group of humans defending a space from threatening zombies has become a common theme in zombie apocalypse texts, and it is now even more open to be read in terms of the threat considered to be posed by illegal immigrants than in Romero's first film. In Romero's fourth zombie film *Land of the Dead*, released in 2005, the parallel between the zombie siege of Pittsburgh and the fear over illegal entry to the USA across the Mexican border is easily made."[14] In his final scene in *Planet Terror*, however, Rodriguez has his survivor group migrate across a border to defend a position in Mexico, making any American-made zombies the trespassers of a new promised land. Indeed, this scene complements the fake *Machete* trailer at the beginning, creating a significant frame for viewing *Planet Terror*. Rodriguez has satirized the fear of an alien presence manifest as an easily identifiable zombie Other—a group that has the ability to elide differences among groups who would otherwise not be members of the same social groups. It is a strong critique of nationalism that depicts a solution that rests in completely eradicating the other group: zombies and human Others alike are purged from the landscape.

What ultimately makes the final scene so powerful is the very fact that the survivors must move south into Mexico. Here Rodriguez takes a problematic issue for both nations and recasts it as the solution of his film. In order to survive, the group must cross into Mexico, as an untold number of Mexicans must, in reality, brave the crossing of the border northward as they seek a better life with the prospects of a future worth having. These realities often go unnoticed in prominent discussions of immigration reform because it is difficult for many U.S. citizens to empathize with Mexicans who cross the border, since the United States does not have a history of its citizens wishing to flee to another nation.[15] In fact, the opposite is true; the United States tends to be a nation of possibility for many of the world's citizens. Those who cross the border into the United States often hide themselves in an effort to be unobtrusive, and so quite often their story may be known in trusted intimate social groups while remaining untold outside their communities for fear of reprisals, and they are thus unknown.

Conclusion

In *Planet Terror*, Rodriguez depicts how U.S. citizens—even famously proud Texans—might wish to flee across their own nation's expansive borders. And while *Planet Terror* is a work of fiction, it is rooted in a plausible reality as all fiction is (otherwise we would not recognize it). We have seen the mass of people who fled during the devastation caused by Hurricane Katrina and the failed human-made levees in New Orleans. In those moments of desperation, rules and regulations instituted by human-made committees often seem silly and superfluous. We recognize the human instinct for self-preservation when unimaginable decisions must be made. There is a level of empathy that is inculcated when watching those moments, even many years after the fact.

Though Rodriguez uses the trappings of a B movie in *Planet Terror*, the social factors operating in the film are no different than those we encounter in everyday life. Sometimes disasters happen. Sometimes we are forced to leave our homes, our native lands, in search of safety or refuge. Rodriguez's film—a tale of a disparate but cohesive band, able to look past individual differences for the common good—is an instructive commentary on how U.S. citizens might show empathy toward their southern neighbors. Policies that respect the common ground among groups rather than simple characterizations that render people as Other are warranted even in difficult situations.

Rodriguez's method is far from perfect, but his emphasis on identity negotiation among contesting groups—from *Machete* to *The Faculty*, and in both *Planet Terror* and *From Dusk Till Dawn*—is worth noting. These films exemplify Viktor Shklovsky's concept of *ostranenie*—what he describes as "to make a stone feel stony."[16] Rodriguez expertly defamiliarizes the ways in which social groups can be united in the face of terror despite differing identities. By including characters who defy our expectation of particular groups, such as El Wray, the Latino ne'er-do-well who is actually a high-ranking military agent or Cherry Darling, the go-go dancer who ultimately has the courage to lead her people to safe haven, he opens the door for audiences who may not have the cultural or experiential capital to identify with an out-group. The fact that these are works of fiction, conjurations on celluloid or digital media, does not preclude the fact that the emotions an audience experiences are real. Rodriguez presents viewers with the possibility of transferring a similar empathetic response for real people—people they know little to nothing about—to real human beings who otherwise might only register as statistics on a CNN ticker at the bottom of their television set. Ultimately, such an inference suggests the power of narrative fiction and the human capacity for reconstructing fictional worlds that move us as impressively as events in the real world. It evokes emotions that linger long after we have left the cinema—emotions that may leave us, and our minds, changed.

Notes

1. Besides using the similar exploitation aesthetic, Tarantino also cast many of the same actors that appear in *Planet Terror*. As a result, not only is *Grindhouse* a highly intertextual work, it is arguably *intra*textual as well.

2. Brian McHale, *Postmodernist Fiction* (New York: Methuen, 1987), 17. McHale credits Umberto Eco with coining the term *transworld identity*, 35.

3. This may hold true with audiences until a threshold is breached where the character seems to deserve his end at the hands of the undead. But my point here is to suggest that in the survivor-zombie dyad, audiences tend to root for the survivor until led by the author or director to do otherwise.

4. Gerry Canavan, "We *Are* the Walking Dead: Race, Time, and Survival in Zombie Narrative," *Extrapolation* 51.3 (2010), 439.

5. It is interesting that in most zombie narratives, whatever caused the zombie outbreak is never reversed. Instead, the aim seems to be survival. One exception to this is Richard Matheson's *I Am Legend*, where the protagonist works frantically to find a scientific cure for the vampirism outbreak.

6. For a brief but enriching recapitulation of this horror/humor dichotomy in film and literature, see Noël Carroll, "Horror and Humor," *Journal of Aesthetics and Art Criticism* 57.2 (1999): 145.

7. Carroll, "Horror and Humor," 146–47.

8. Fred Botting, "A-ffect-less: Zombie-Horror-Shock," *English Language Notes* 48.1 (2010), 180.

9. Jon Stratton, "Zombie Trouble: Zombie Texts, Bare Life and Displaced People," *European Journal of Cultural Studies* 14.3 (2011): 267.

10. Botting, "A-ffect-less," 183.

11. Patrick Colm Hogan, *Understanding Nationalism: On Narrative, Cognitive Science, and Identity* (Columbus: Ohio State University Press, 2009), 93–123.

12. Hogan, *Understanding Nationalism*, 93.

13. Priscilla Huang, "Anchor Babies, Over-Breeders, and the Population Bomb: The Reemergence of Nativism and Population Control in Anti-Immigration Policies," *Harvard Law & Policy Review* 2.2 (2008): 400.

14. Stratton, "Zombie Trouble," 274.

15. One notable exception here are those individuals who during the Vietnam War fled the United States rather than be conscripted.

16. Viktor Shklovsky, *Theory of Prose*, trans. Benjamin Sher, intro. Gerald L. Bruns (Elmwood Park, IL: Dalkey Archive Press, 1991), 6.

Bibliography

Botting, Fred. "A-ffect-less: Zombie-Horror-Shock." *English Language Notes* 48.1 (2010): 177–90.

Canavan, Gerry. "We *Are* the Walking Dead": Race, Time, and Survival in Zombie Narrative." *Extrapolation* 51.3 (2010): 431–53.

Carroll, Noël. "Horror and Humor." *Journal of Aesthetics and Art Criticism* 57.2 (1999): 145–60.

Hogan, Patrick Colm. *Understanding Nationalism: On Narrative, Cognitive Science, and Identity.* Columbus: Ohio State University Press, 2009.

Huang, Priscilla. "Anchor Babies, Over-Breeders, and the Population Bomb: The Reemergence of Nativism and Population Control in Anti-Immigration Policies." *Harvard Law & Policy Review* 2.2 (2008): 385–406.

Machete. Directed by Robert Rodriguez. 2010. Los Angeles, CA: Twentieth Century Fox Home Entertainment, 2011. DVD.

May, Jeff. "Zombie Geographies and the Undead City." *Social & Cultural Geography* 11.3 (2010): 285–98.

McHale, Brian. *Postmodernist Fiction.* New York: Methuen, 1987.

Planet Terror. Directed by Robert Rodriguez. 2007. Santa Monica, CA: Genius Entertainment, 2007. DVD.

Shklovsky, Viktor. *Theory of Prose.* Translated by Benjamin Sher, introduction by Gerald L. Bruns. Elmwood Park, IL: Dalkey Archive Press, 1991.

Stratton, Jon. "Zombie Trouble: Zombie Texts, Bare Life and Displaced People." *European Journal of Cultural Studies* 14.3 (2011): 265–81.

CHAPTER ELEVEN

Undead and Un-American

The Zombified Other in Weird Western Films

James Hewitson

As a film genre, the Western has been central to creating and responding to the evolving vision of America's self-definition as a nation. In its earliest articulations it explicitly embodied the nineteenth-century concept of Manifest Destiny, in which America was fated to encompass the entire continent. Typically set in sparsely populated frontier environments or along the paths to these emerging settlements, the Western most basically represents the development of a specific idea of civilization in an otherwise hostile wilderness. The ideal vision, particularly in earlier films, is generally predicated on the creation of an egalitarian community of families who settle and develop the land in cooperation—democracies in miniature, comprised of self-sufficient individuals who work together to create a viable and peaceful political and economic society. In the process, however, this ideal could only come to fruition through confrontation with hostile forces that threaten it. The threats to the emergence of such communities in the Western vary, but they tend to manifest themselves through antagonistic groups or organizations—violent Native American tribes, psychopathic criminal gangs, greedy ranchers, powerful bankers, or encroaching railway and mining companies—that imperil the freedom and individualism on which the new democratic community is to be based. Although the conflicts described are local, they metaphorically involve the survival of the nation and its egalitarian values. Ultimately the threats express a series of alternative, dystopian visions of what America could become, should its democracy be thwarted and the destructive forces prevail.[1]

The insertion of supernatural elements into the filmic frontier metanarrative began quite early: *The Phantom Empire* (1935) combined the Western and science fiction, *Riders of the Whistling Skull* (1937) incorporated mummies, and *Curse of the Undead* (1959) included a vampire. Later Westerns with elements of the fantastic included films such as *High Plains Drifter* (1973), *Pale Rider* (1985), *Purgatory* (1999), and, more recently, *Gallowwalker* (2010), *Jonah Hex* (2010), and *Cowboys and Aliens* (2011). This generic hybridity has resulted in the creation of the "weird Western" as a recognized subgenre in itself. Although many such films are parodic and vary profoundly in terms of budget and commercial appeal, the generic interpenetration inherent in the very definition of the weird Western—in which the conventions and narrative expectations associated with different kinds of films are combined in a single context—nonetheless provide alternative ways of understanding the shifting nature of the Western. In many films that include elements from other genres—such as aliens, ghosts, vampires, or zombies—the resulting hybridization offers a reconsideration of the ideological assumptions upon which the Western genre itself is founded. In particular, the inclusion of monsters that have their own film history can lead to a new interpretation of the forces in conflict. In such cases the danger to the idealized vision of the nation is exaggerated, the competition between value systems is made more absolute, and the resulting violence is amplified.

In the wake of the increasing popularity of the zombie film genre in the 2000s, a series of low-budget Westerns have appeared in which zombies are the central threat. These include films such as *Death Valley: The Revenge of Bloody Bill* (2004), *The Quick and the Undead* (2006), *Dead Noon* (2007), *Undead or Alive* (2007), *Devil's Crossing* (2011), and *The Dead and the Damned* (2011). The inclusion of the zombie in this context provides a new means of analyzing the articulation of idealized American identity in the traditional Western. While zombies are the animated dead, in a larger sense the category can be understood as embracing all creatures who have lost their humanity and have been made subservient, either to the will of another or to their own base physical needs. As such, the zombie Western provides a means of analyzing and reconsidering key themes from traditional Westerns: in particular, the stock figure of the henchman, an antisocial entity who acts violently in the interest of some larger authority for financial reward; the creation of community in a violent, hostile environment predicated on individualistic self-advancement; and the ways in which the Western excludes individuals and groups that threaten a normative American identity. The development of these issues cannot be easily systematized, but all three nonetheless can be

The zombie lawman from *Undead or Alive*—leading citizens in a community made up entirely of the undead.

seen as working within a general spirit of revisionism, in which the idealized American history portrayed in the classic Western is dismantled.

The examination of the zombie in the Western is foregrounded by a consideration of the figure of the henchman in George Stevens' *Shane* (1953), a classic example of the genre. Here the henchman is a stock character, typically self-interested and debased, operating under the control of a rapacious, authoritarian individual. Clint Eastwood's revisionist remake of *Shane*, *Pale Rider*, reinterprets the henchman as a depersonalized, mindless minion, thoughtlessly serving sinister interests. Many weird Westerns, however, more aggressively questioning the settlement of the West and the actual nation that emerged from this process, expand upon both the generality of this figure and the loss of humanity that it involves. In these later examples, the henchmen become actual zombies, in thrall to violent needs that they cannot control; rather than merely being an isolated group in the larger population, they become the community itself.

Shane and the Henchman

The henchman is a familiar figure in classic Westerns and action films. While the plots of such films typically describe the primary struggle as existing between a protagonist and an antagonist, and as representative of the fundamental moral conflict in the film, the protagonist is often challenged by a number of minions who are employed by the antagonist before confronting the antagonist himself. Episodes involving these henchmen are often formulaic—they are merely anticipatory to the engagement of the principal characters and exist primarily to establish the prowess of the protagonist. For this reason, the figure of the henchman has become a source of humor to audiences versed in the narrative conventions of the genre. Henchmen nonetheless help to elaborate the principal philosophic differences between the main characters and, in the Western, establish the consequences of failing to properly embrace and actualize dominant American democratic values.

Shane provides a perfect example of this function of the henchman. The plot centers on the conflict between a powerful rancher, Ryker, who wants to control all of the land in a Western valley, and a small group of homesteaders who are trying to settle and develop the area as farmland.[2] Because of his wealth and large holdings, Ryker is able to employ a number of men to help him control the territory and drive out the homesteaders. These men are fairly typical "henchmen" in that they are largely undifferentiated: they have few distinguishing features—not even names—and are referred to as a single unit, "Ryker's Boys." They are all independent agents for hire, but their grouping reduces them to a state of mindless minionhood, and they are generally shown lounging around the saloon doing very little except drink: they act only when called upon by Ryker. They have no allegiance to a larger community, the place they live, or to each other; they simply exist to do Ryker's bidding.

The depiction of these men, any one of whom might be a self-reliant "cowboy" in another Western, contrasts strongly with that of the homesteaders. Where Ryker's Boys are isolates gathered together and acting purely for economic reasons, the homesteaders are distinguished from one another through specific names, origins, and even accents. They also have families (numerous children populate the film) and a clear commitment to the land and each other beyond basic economic survival. They meet regularly to democratically discuss

"Ryker's Boys" from *Shane* represent the classic Western version of the henchman.

matters of local importance, support each other in times of duress, and are hard workers intent upon building a strong community of "Americans" through the consistent development of its land.[3] As Shane tells the homesteaders, their struggles and poverty are ennobled by the vision of the America they are working to realize. It is a world in which money is not the only objective—there must be "something that means more to you than anything else—your families. Your wives and kids . . . They've got a right to stay here and grow up and be happy. That's up to you people to have . . . nerve enough to not give it up." The farmers' idea of America as a place of opportunity for everyone is actively derided by the henchmen, however, who see the homesteaders as debased by poverty, and they repeatedly humiliate them and compare them to animals. Focused almost exclusively on profit and pleasure, the henchmen are unable to appreciate the higher value of community. They cannot respond to these ideals because they can only envision life in the most basic and brutal terms.

The ongoing conflict between the homesteaders' and Ryker's interests possesses a larger historic dimension, which touches upon the question of the future of the nation. Each communicates a different vision of what the West, and, by implication, America, is to become. Ryker justifies his right to the land by emphasizing his original role in settling the wilderness. As he explains to Starrett, one of the homesteaders:

> When I came to this country, you weren't much older than your boy there. And we had rough times, me and other men that are mostly dead now. I got a bad shoulder yet from a Cheyenne arrowhead. We made this country. Found it and we made it, with blood and empty bellies. The cattle we brought in were hazed off by Indians and rustlers. They don't bother you much anymore because we handled 'em. We made a safe range out of this. Some of us died doin' it. We made it. And then people move in who've never had to rawhide it through the old days. They fence off my range, and fence me off from water. Some of 'em like you plow ditches, take out irrigation water. And so the creek runs dry sometimes. I've got to move my stock because of it.

While not disputing Ryker's own role in the development of the region, Starrett represents the next stage in a progressive vision of American history, within which Ryker represents a single and now-passed phase. Starrett counters Ryker's claim by acknowledging the Native Americans, trappers and traders who preceded the ranchers, and arguing that small farms will, in turn, replace open-range ranching:

> These old-timers, they just can't see it yet, but runnin' cattle on an open range just can't go on forever. It takes too much space for too little results. Those herds aren't any good. They're all horns and bone. Now, cattle that is bred for meat and fenced in and fed right—that's the thing. You gotta pick your spot, get your land, your own land. Now a homesteader, he can't run but a few beef. But he can sure grow grain and cut hay. And then what with his garden and the hogs and milk, well, he'll make out all right.

Ryker is remade as a remnant of an earlier and more primitive phase of economic development, his large operation destined to be superseded by the homesteaders capable of making the land more productive. To avoid his own extinction and preserve a disappearing and outdated mode of life, Ryker struggles to maintain his status by interfering with the natural development of the region as a whole: first through bribery, then through threats and vandalism, and finally by bringing in Wilson, a hired killer, to terrorize the farmers.[4]

The inevitability of Ryker's demise as a representative of an older, obsolete vision of America is most clearly articulated in an exchange with Shane, the titular hero, when he confronts Ryker at the end of the film: "You've lived too long. Your kind of days are over." When Ryker challenges him in turn, saying, "My days? What about yours, gunfighter?" Shane replies, "The difference is that I know it." Shane, himself a representative of the older, more violent period of history, realizes that he, like Ryker and Wilson, does not have a place in the new, ideal America that is coming into being through the efforts of the homesteaders. After shooting both Ryker and Wilson, Shane rides into the mountains, possibly dying, and leaves the valley to the settlers who will make it productive.

Ryker's henchmen are also part of the older order, despite the possibilities offered them by the emergence of a more democratic and egalitarian system. They remain invested in the debased economic relationship that they have developed with Ryker as thugs for hire, preferring to earn a living through mayhem on the behalf of larger and more indifferent interests—as such, they are and remain quasi-zombified in their material greed and violent tendencies. They have rejected their chance at a more vital and fruitful role in shaping the nation, both as individuals and as citizens. Their commitment to Ryker's and to some extent Wilson's autocratic, purely capitalistic system is further underscored by their consistent lack of fellow feeling for the homesteaders and their mission to develop the land. They literally fade from the film, with the exception of a single character—Calloway—who comes to warn Shane of Ryker's schemes before announcing that he is "quitting Ryker" because, as he states, "something has come over [him]." Unlike the other henchmen, he has been touched by the determination evident in the homesteaders and has individuated to the point of having a name.

Henchmen, Deputies, and Zombies

Shane is obviously not a zombie film, but its representation of the henchman corresponds to zombies in a number of ways that underscore the power relationships that it shares with them. The figure of the zombie has had a number of filmic iterations. As a fictional construct, of course, zombies can be given any set of features an author or filmmaker requires, and the "rules" that zombies follow—how they are created or killed, to what extent they may be self-aware and so on—may vary a great deal in different narratives. It is common, however, to distinguish between the zombies that appear in Haitian folklore—popularized in American films of the early and mid-twentieth century—and the current image of zombies as flesh-eating ghouls that originated with George Romero's *Night of the Living Dead* (1968) and its sequels. Romero's zombies are damaged, decaying, animated corpses, fixated on eating living humans. Haitian zombies, however, are reanimated corpses, disinterred by a voodoo priest and turned into slaves: they act as mindless automatons, obeying their masters without question.[5]

Ryker functions in a manner consistent with that of the zombie master of the Haitian tradition: he has complete control over his "boys," holding them in a state of arrested development, where they seem to live largely as mindless adolescents.[6] Their lack of sympathy for others, their isolation, and their complete dependence on Ryker for their livelihood render them subhuman and without autonomy. Their evocation of the zombie, moreover, suggests significant parallels that illuminate points of cultural continuity between *Shane* and later revisionist and weird Westerns. Viewing *Shane*—and, by extension, other classic Westerns—as a part of a zombie discourse in American culture allows it to be understood as a participant in a continuing dialogue about what it means to be American; that is, as part of an ongoing examination of the capacity of the nation to provide its citizens with a sense of community and of the various forces conspiring against the fulfillment of the human subject.

Shane concludes with the community intact, Ryker dead, and his henchmen presumably dispersed and condemned to nomadic lives. The satisfaction of this ending rests on the idealization of the community and American history: forces with clear moral values are brought into conflict, and the survival of the homesteaders and the opportunities for civilized self-advancement that they represent constitute a victory for the best aspects of America over all of the corrupting forces that threaten it. Later, explicitly supernatural Westerns, however, present this kind of resolution as far more difficult to achieve. In these cases, the zombie is not so easily dispersed nor is its identity so certain. *Pale Rider* describes a similar conflict, but it relocates it to a mining community, in which a large operation working on an industrial level is attempting to drive out a number of independent tin-pan miners in order to assume control of the mineral rights of the whole region. The character of Wilson is replaced by Stockburn—a corrupt marshal with six seemingly identical deputies—who is hired by LaHood, the owner of the corporation, to drive out the small miners. Shane's part is taken by "Preacher," a supernatural figure who, the film intimates, is already dead and has returned to protect the miners and possibly to take revenge on Stockburn, who, it is strongly implied, has had some responsibility in his death. Their confrontation is thus given metaphysical overtones, involving issues of guilt and divine retribution.

The differences between *Shane* and *Pale Rider* all work to emphasize the inhumanity of the large mining operation, the extent of the forces it can call upon to ensure its economic dominance, and the general abjection of the tin-pan miners themselves. In *Shane*, Wilson is a hired killer, and the need to find legal justification for his attacks upon the homesteaders is constantly emphasized. In *Pale Rider*, however, Marshal Stockburn represents a kind of law that can be bought and which will accordingly always operate in favor of the largest and richest economic concerns without legal justification. The setting for the story, too, works to deemphasize the importance of the miners themselves. Homesteading was a significant event in American history, and it contributed to the settlement of the nation. Tin-pan mining, however, was taken up for entirely personal gain and was a transient activity that rarely resulted in long-term development of, or lasting settlement in, a region.[7] Without the assistance of the seemingly superhuman Preacher the independent miners would clearly be no match for the forces arrayed against them.

Pale Rider centers primarily on the figure of the Preacher and his climatic encounter with the marshal, and with this the film itself moves away from historical engagement and community formation and is instead focused upon metaphysical concerns. With this redirection of the action, the significance of a number of the secondary characters also undergoes alteration from their representation in *Shane*. While Ryker represents an earlier and necessary phase of American history that needs to be brought to an end, LaHood is a figure of rapacious corporate greed and exploitation. Ryker's cattle operation uses the land inefficiently, but LaHood destroys the environment with hydraulic mining in order to extract gold cheaply and quickly. In *Shane*, Wilson is clearly dangerous and possibly psychopathic, but his emotional reactions reflect the violent nature of that earlier period of American history, and he is also an independent operator—a corollary to Shane himself. Stockburn, however, represents a kind of institutionalized and legally sanctioned violence that can only exist because of systemic political and social corruption. His deputies—who have no real counterpart in *Shane*—further emphasize a degree of organized and dehumanized violence and injustice that does not exist in the earlier film. They dress identically, are silent and expressionless, and obey Stockburn's orders flawlessly and in perfect synchronicity. If the henchmen in *Shane* illustrate a lack of social or psychological development that has kept them in adolescent roles, the deputies of *Pale Rider* represent the complete suppression of personality that is necessary for participation in the corrupt new West. Again, while they are not zombies in a generic sense, the deputies' complete allegiance to Stockburn and absence of all sympathy or emotional effect mark them as dehumanized by the position they occupy and the interests they serve.

The othering of the deputies, the sense of supernatural augury surrounding the Preacher, and the film's emphasis upon the Preacher's confrontation with

Stockburn and his interchangeable, zombielike deputies in *Pale Rider*.

Stockburn all work to redefine the significance of the basic conflict. Instead of being about the creation of an idealized America, as in *Shane*, *Pale Rider* essentially describes otherworldly justice being visited upon a corrupt land. LaHood is judged guilty and his operation destroyed, but when the Preacher rides off into the mountains, there is little sense that the tin-pan miners will be able to create a viable community. Unlike the farmers in *Shane*, the mining community in *Pale Rider* remains economically dependent upon the successful extraction of exhaustible resources from the earth. They can only settle and develop the area for as long as the environment is able to provide them with saleable commodities, and at some point will have to change their métier or leave the area, despite the ennobling speech to the contrary made by Barret. The reduction of their role in the narrative is reflective of their historical marginalization and is underscored by their subsistence-level occupation. They are reduced to the role of bystanders and witnesses to the larger drama being played out, and, since the Preacher's justice does not extend beyond the range of LaHood's operation, they will presumably remain in the role of drifters in the nation itself, attempting to eke out a living on the edges of a larger economy that will not provide them with the stability they seek.

Go West Young Zombie

The representation of the West in *Pale Rider* evinces a marked deterioration from that in *Shane*, and in later weird Westerns this tendency is typically exacerbated. In these films, the distinction between the virtuous proto-American settler and the un-American element becomes increasingly fraught. While the small miners in *Pale Rider* are distinguished from the corruption represented by LaHood and Stockburn, in later films such figures are often shown to be the primary threat to the establishment of any kind of order. In these instances, however, they fail to become the idealized figures of classic Westerns not by surrendering their freedom to a larger organization, but rather by giving into and acting on their own worst impulses in order to survive in a hostile environment. Here, the figure of the henchman, who has failed to recognize the promise of the West and the humanity of others, is remade as a zombie, which has lost its own humanity altogether. This shift is illustrative of a larger transformation of the Western genre. While becoming a henchman is at least theoretically a choice individuals make, and one that in some instances can be reversed, becoming a zombie is almost invariably involuntary and a consequence of uncontrollable factors in the environment itself. It is, then, something that will happen to everyone because larger forces behind it cannot be resisted.

The Dead and the Damned illustrates the relationship between the economy of the West and the loss of humanity that is typical of these films. The Dead and the Damned is, like Pale Rider, set in a mining community during a gold rush. A zombie plague is unleashed by a miner who unearths a strange green rock, which he takes back to town because he believes it may be valuable. It soon unleashes a gas that transforms the townspeople into rampaging, canni-balistic zombies. The zombie plague here, however, is clearly an extension of the gross displays of greed and unprincipled behavior already evident in the town. In this context, even the protagonist, Mortimer, a bounty hunter who accepts contracts indiscriminately, is hired to capture a Native American who has been falsely accused of a crime for racist reasons, and at one point even buys a woman to use as bait. The secondary characters also are typically willing to sell themselves and others, as well as to lie, cheat, and steal at will. This film concludes with the two surviving and uninfected characters at a cliff's edge facing a surging zombie horde, with no route to safety. The final frame shows them running toward the zombies, doomed. The rapacious greed and general exploitation of the zombies inevitably will consume them as well. Rather than focusing on a purely external threat to the young commu-nity, as is the case in Pale Rider, The Dead and the Damned instead emphasizes the psychic collapse of its citizenry through their collective failure to create an environment in which it is impossible to act on any but the most debased and self-interested motives. The zombie, who survives by killing and feeding on humans, literalizes how individuals must radically adapt to survive in a savage world. In another example, Death Valley: The Revenge of Bloody Bill, a whole town has been stopped in time and its inhabitants transformed into zombies as revenge for the lynching of Bill Anderson, the titular Bloody Bill, a murderous Confederate soldier, and his otherwise innocent sister. Visitors to the town are systematically killed by the zombies and made part of the undead citizenry. The past here has become a nightmare, and the only escape is not to correct any of the wrongs that have occurred, but rather to find a means to destroy its power altogether. These and other films with similar themes and storylines, such as the *Quick and the Undead* and *Dead Noon*, are primarily topical to the current popularity of the zombie genre; nonetheless, however, they collectively illustrate a number of presuppositions that are illustrative of the ways in which the understanding of the West has been transformed. Viewed collectively, these weird Westerns reflect an ongoing emphasis on revisionist interpretations that were established in earlier cinema, to the point at which the genre itself becomes a Western-horror hybrid.

One of the most intriguing examples of recent Western zombie films is the horror-comedy *Undead or Alive: A Zombedy* (2007). In this film, the threat to the community derives from the town's very claim to the land itself. Here, the zombies are created by the "White Man's Curse": a plague placed on the land by the legendary Native American leader Geronimo as punishment for the genocide of his people. Two hapless misfits, Luke and Elmer, run afoul of a corrupt sheriff, who becomes a zombie early in the film but maintains his role as legal enforcer; they spend the majority of the film running from him and his posse of zombie deputies, meeting Geronimo's niece, Sue, along the way. Eventually the three, at this point the sole surviving humans, are trapped in an army fort surrounded by the sheriff and his zombie henchmen, as well as a regiment of soldiers—the federal government's henchmen—all of whom have also

A zombie citizen from *The Dead and the Damned*—condemned, for his greed, to live a life defined by mindless consumption.

become zombies. While escaping, Elmer is bitten and he in turn infects Luke. Once outside of the fort and safely in the desert, Sue learns that her allies are now zombies. Suddenly the narrative skips forward in time to reveal Elmer and Luke restored to their human state. According to the mythology established in the film, the only way to undo Geronimo's curse is to eat the living flesh of whomever created it; as Elmer explains, he realized that Sue, as Geronimo's surviving blood relative, might prove a substitute for Geronimo himself.

By consuming Sue to save themselves, Luke and Elmer ironically and viscerally reenact the exploitation and destruction of the Native American population intrinsic to the settlement of America in general and the West in particular; their cannibalism recreates the circumstance that had originally caused the invocation of the curse. Paradoxically, however, this inhuman act is the only means of escaping the dehumanizing indignity of zombie existence. Their narrative concludes with an image of the two riding into a classic Western landscape at sunset—with Luke consoling himself over the death of Sue with visions of the adventures ahead with Elmer. While they have escaped zombification and absorption into the mass, this ending nonetheless recalls the family-free and nomadic henchmen in *Shane*, who have also failed to form the vital, reproductive relationships necessary to the creation of established community. A self-absorbed, arrested state of adolescence that obliviously profits from ongoing racial injustice is the only way to remain truly free from what seems to be the totalizing state of corruption embodied by the zombie mass. The final scene of the film, however, returns to the town in which the plague began and shows a zombie father digging up his dead daughter and his wife to reconstitute as a zombie family, complete with a zombie dog. Again, while the image is humorous, it shows life continuing as before, only horribly diminished. The implication is that the town, too, will recreate itself as a community of zombies. Society has been entirely zombified, from its legal and military institutions to its nuclear families and towns, and this becomes the film's new America. The zombie curse is normalized, and despite the fact that the ending shows the town deeply compromised in every possible sense, a simulacra of life persists.

In *Undead or Alive*, the relationship between the community and the nomadic outcasts has been inverted. By remaining detached, Luke and Elmer have been able to escape the curse. The larger implications, of course, is that in a corrupt society it is only by remaining willfully oblivious of the crimes and injustices that make life comfortable that it is possible to escape contagion. The perpetual adolescence of the protagonists is their refusal to grow up to become zombies like the townspeople. The zombie state is in this sense a cultural destiny that can only be evaded; to do so and remain human, however, is to become outlaw. The Western-zombie hybrid can in this way be seen as the ultimate revisionism, from the ideal site of a new democratic community as shown in *Shane* to an inhuman world of half-dead citizens and debased consumption. The insertion of zombies into a genre as strongly tied to national self-definition as the Western necessarily makes American history itself monstrous. While classic Westerns celebrate that history and use it to inform and shape an understanding of the present, the zombie Western typically repudiates it, forcing an interrogation of the premises underlying America's foundational myths. At the same time, however, the fact that the Western by definition involves events of the past also establishes that history as, literally, history, and our temporal distance removes the need to take responsibility for it. It becomes just another scary movie.

Notes

1. The mythic understanding of the Western frontier as the site of an archetypal competition between savagery/wilderness and civilization was established in Henry Nash Smith's foundational work *Virgin Land: The American West as Symbol and Myth* (Cambridge: Harvard University Press, 1950); the thematic tensions between civilization and wilderness are further explored in relation to the Western as a genre in Jim Kitses, *Horizons West* (Bloomington: Indiana University Press, 1969) and Will Wright, *Sixguns and Society: A Structural Study of the Western* (Berkeley and Los Angeles: University of California Press, 1975), as well John Cawelti, *The Six-Gun Mystique Sequel* (Bowling Green: Bowling Green University Popular Press, 1999); and Richard Slotkin, *Gunfighter Nation: The Myth of the Frontier in Twentieth-Century America* (New York: Atheneum Press, 1992).

2. Michael Coyne, *The Crowded Prairie: American National Identity in the Hollywood Western* (New York: St. Martin's Press, 1997), argues that "conflict is between democracy (the homesteaders) and charismatic authoritarianism (Ryker)," 76.

3. John Saunders, *The Western Genre: From Lordsburg to Big Whiskey* (London and New York: Wallflower Press, 2001) points out (20) that ethnic identities of the homesteaders even establish it as a melting pot "healing the North/South divide and uniting the races in a common purpose."

4. Coyne observes (75) that "*Shane* represented the culmination of the classic community Western . . . retain[ing] a romantic optimism in the value of community. The sodbusters in *Shane* are family men and no match for Ryker's strong-arm tactics"; Edward Countrymen and Evonne von Heussen-Countrymen, *Shane* (London: British Film Institute, 2007), note that this aspect of the film was strongly indebted to Frederick Jackson Turner's 1893 essay on the end of the Western frontier, "The Significance of the Frontier in American History," [1893] in *Rereading Frederick Jackson Turner: The Significance of the Frontier in American History and Other Essays*, ed. John Mack Faragher (New York: Henry Holt, 1994), 35.

5. The Haitian zombie was popularized in the play *Zombie* (1932), and in popular films such as *White Zombie* (1932), *Ouanga* (1936), *Revolt of the Zombies* (1936), and *I Walked with a Zombie* (1943). For more on this see Kyle William Bishop, "Raising the Living Dead," in *American Zombie Gothic: The Rise and Fall (and Rise) of the Walking Dead in Popular Culture* (London: McFarland & Company), 37–63; Chera Kee, "'They are not men . . . they are dead bodies!': From Cannibal to Zombie and Back Again," in *Better off Dead: The Evolution of the Zombie as Post-Human*, ed. Deborah Christie and Sarah Juliet Lauro (New York: Fordham University Press, 2011), 9–23.

6. Countryman also observes that in "Ryker's world without women there can be no children, and there definitely are no homes. For all his presumed wealth, Ryker sleeps in a room above Grafton's bar," 16; interestingly Saunders says something similar about Shane: "The hero's celibacy condemns him to a kind of immaturity; in this society where marriage is the norm he is an outsider," 26.

7. The conflict between LaHood's large enterprise and the tin-pan miners in *Pale Rider* is largely constructed for narrative purposes. After the 1850s (thirty years before the events described in *Pale Rider*), hydraulic mining became increasingly common and was often used by collectives of miners, who would invest in the machinery together. By the 1880s, when the film is set, only the most impoverished or desperate would use pans. The amount of gold one might collect would also be negligible, which resulted in a great deal of mobility as miners searched for new sources. Mining in general proved limited in terms of its capacity for developing an area. For more on this see *A Golden State: Mining and Economic Development in Gold Rush California*, ed. James J. Rawls and Richard J. Orsi (Berkeley and Los Angeles: University of California Press, 1999).

Bibliography

Bishop, Kyle William. "Raising the Living Dead." In *American Zombie Gothic: The Rise and Fall (and Rise) of the Walking Dead in Popular Culture*, 37–63. London: McFarland & Company, 2010.

Cawelti, John. *The Six-Gun Mystique Sequel*. Bowling Green: Bowling Green University Popular Press, 1999.

Countrymen, Edward, and Evonne von Heussen-Countrymen. *Shane*. London: British Film Institute, 2007.

Coyne, Michael. *The Crowded Prairie: American National Identity in the Hollywood Western*. New York: St. Martin's Press, 1997.

Dead and the Damned. Directed by Rene Perez. Santa Monica, CA: Inception Media Group, 2011. DVD.

Death Valley: The Revenge of Bloody Bill. Directed by Byron Werner. Los Angeles, CA: Asylum Home Entertainment, 2004. DVD.

Kee, Chera. "'They are not men . . . they are dead bodies!': From Cannibal to Zombie and Back Again." In *Better off Dead: The Evolution of the Zombie as Post-Human*, edited by Deborah Christie and Sarah Juliet Lauro, 9–23. New York: Fordham University Press, 2011.

Kitses, Jim. *Horizons West*. Bloomington: Indiana University Press, 1969.

Pale Rider. Directed by Clint Eastwood. 1985. Burbank, CA: Warner Home Video, 2010. DVD.

Rawls, James J., and Richard J. Orsi, ed. *A Golden State: Mining and Economic Development in Gold Rush California*. Berkeley: University of California Press, 1999.

Saunders, John. *The Western Genre: From Lordsburg to Big Whiskey*. London and New York: Wallflower Press, 2001.

Shane. Directed by George Stevens. 1953. Hollywood, CA: Paramount Home Video, 2000.

Slotkin, Richard. *Gunfighter Nation: The Myth of the Frontier in Twentieth-Century America*. New York: Atheneum Press, 1992.

Smith, Henry Nash. *Virgin Land: The American West as Symbol and Myth*. Cambridge: Harvard University Press, 1950.

Undead or Alive: A Zombedy. Directed by Glasgow Phillips. Chatsworth, CA: Image Entertainment: Odd Lot Productions, 2007. DVD.

Wright, Will. *Sixguns and Society: A Structural Study of the Western*. Berkeley and Los Angeles: University of California Press, 1975.

CHAPTER TWELVE

Hungry Lands

Conquest, Cannibalism, and the Wendigo Spirit

Robert A. Saunders

"The red man, whom our hardy sires found in possession of the land
. . . Their world was wanted; far and fast we drove them towards the
setting sun."

—R. H. Stoddard, "Manifest Destiny," 1872

This chapter explores the indigenous myth of the wendigo spirit as depicted in Antonia Bird's horror film *Ravenous* (1999), a blackly comedic exploration of the American colonization of mid-nineteenth-century California. From opening scene to closing credits, *Ravenous* presents a cautionary tale condemning militarism, imperial conquest, and the "manly values" of the American West. In the film, a stranger arrives at a remote California outpost as the sole survivor of a snowbound wagon train in the Sierra Nevada Mountains and recounts a story of murder and cannibalism that decimated his party. As preparations are made to rescue any survivors, the camp's Native American scout, George, relates the Algonkian myth of the wendigo, an insidious spirit that drives its victims into obsessive cannibalistic rages. Originally a "native" affliction that merged real-world causes (hunger and extreme isolation) with otherworldly explanations (spirit possession), "wendigoism" evolves into a violent contagion in *Ravenous*, spreading through the garrison and wreaking havoc on the U.S. government's attempts to bring "civilization" to the American West. Through a fusion of elements of the vampire (the wendigo's host purportedly gains the "power" of its prey) and the zombie (the afflicted will continue to experience a ravenous hunger no matter how much flesh they consume) with an indigenous Native American myth, I argue that the wendigo spirit has been adapted by Western cultural producers to create a powerful postcolonial avenger, but one that can also be read as the embodiment of America's insatiable appetite for consumption.

Salon.com described *Ravenous* as the "best cannibal tragicomedy ever made."[1] While such overly specific qualifications might render this plaudit meaningless, reviews of the film were mostly positive, with the notable exception of Janet Maslin's (1999) *New York Times* review: "If there's anything worse than a cannibal movie, it's an undead-cannibal movie with pretensions about Manifest Destiny."[2] Buoyed by Antonia Bird's direction, *Ravenous* tended to be received by critics as something more than a simple horror film, though at times "overreaching,"[3] "muddled,"[4] or "halfhearted"[5] in its analogies, symbolism, and feints. Yet, according to Roger Ebert, "*Ravenous* is clever in the way it avoids most of the clichés of the vampire movie by using cannibalism, and most of the clichés of the cannibal movie by using vampirism. It serves both dishes with new sauces."[6] With its ambiguous juxtaposition of a spirited, vivacious cannibal antihero against a forlorn, moralizing protagonist, the film was interpreted as a "celebration and glorification of cannibalism,"[7] while providing a indictment of military conquest and questioning the very notion of "Western" civilization, thus flying in the face of Hollywood conventions. While failing to delight critics in its treatment of the spirit of the American West, the film was recognized for its originality within a well-worn genre, atmospheric allure, and (sometimes literal) tongue-in-cheek humor.

Bringing together analytical approaches informed by popular geopolitics and cultural anthropology, I interrogate the use of the wendigo spirit as a threat not to the Native American populations that have historically been its victims but as an agent of vengeance upon European interlopers as they conquer and transform the sacred landscapes of "Native" America. Following a synopsis of *Ravenous*, I explore the film's geopolitical representations, including the use of forbidding landscapes, representations of the Native American "other," and various constructions of "Americanism" associated with bravery, morality, and conquest. I also interpolate the notions of "dead" and "undead" that underpin the film's characters, as they ultimately complicate Bird's otherwise straightforward critique of colonization. In the conclusion, I draw comparisons between *Ravenous* and other horror films that depict horrific vengeance upon European/Euro-American interlopers who violate indigenous space. In doing so, I situate Bird's filmic storytelling within the realm of popular critical geopolitics, arguing that *Ravenous* is more than a fanciful tale of lustful anthropophagy.

Patriotic Consumption: Flagging the
Cannibal/Colonial Spirit in *Ravenous*

Ravenous opens with a fluttering American flag filling the screen. The prologue, set in 1847, depicts a banquet in honor of Captain John Boyd (Guy
Pearce), a Texan serving in the Mexican-American War. As his fellow officers set upon their steak dinners, flashbacks depict the captain's cowardice
during a Mexican advance on his unit. We learn that, after feigning death,
Boyd was thrown into a pit of slain American soldiers, where blood dripped
into his mouth and covered his face. Unable to stomach the site of the
bloody meat as he remembers his past travails, Boyd—under the disdainful
eye of his commander, General Slauson (John Spencer)—flees the table and
vomits. The general, recognizing Boyd for the craven that he is, banishes
him to Fort Spencer in the Sierra Nevada of northern California. There he
joins a "skeleton crew" assigned to a former Spanish mission, now a way station for emigrants on the way to the Pacific Coast. As Boyd speaks with the
camp's senior officer, Colonel Hart (Jeffrey Jones), another flashback shows
Boyd, invigorated by the blood of his comrades, which had "changed" him,
escaping the pit, killing a Mexican with his bare hands, and taking over an
enemy-controlled command post.

That night, Boyd catches sight of bearded stranger peering through the
mess hall window. Seemingly half dead from hunger and frostbite, the man is
brought into camp and revived with a hot bath, which shows him to be gaunt
but otherwise perfectly healthy. Boyd, Hart, and the other members of the
camp, privates Reich (Neal McDonough) and Toffler (Jeremy Davies) and
the Native American scout George (Joseph Runningfox), gather to hear the
tale of the mysterious "servant of God," F. W. Colqhoun (Robert Carlyle).
Upon learning he had been three months in the snowbound mountains,
Colqhoun is forced to explain how he survived, beginning his yarn: "I said
there was no food. I did not say there was nothing to eat. Do you understand?"[8] Colqhoun, a Scotsman, had been part of a six-member wagon train
that also included an Irish couple, the MacCreadys; a wealthy Virginian
farmer and his African American "servant"; and Colonel Ives, "a detestable
man and a most disastrous guide." The first snowfall caught the party in the
High Sierras, where they took refuge in a cave. Their hopes to push on were
ultimately dashed by the worsening elements.

> We ate the oxen. All the horses. Even my own dog. And that lasted us about a
> month. After that we, we turned to our belts, shoes, any roots we could dig up,
> but you know there's really no nourishment in those. We remained famished. The

day that Jones (the African American) died, I was out collecting wood. . . . When I returned, the others were cooking his legs for dinner. Would I have stopped it had I been there? I don't know. (George paces nervously and grows more agitated with each word.) But I must say that when I stepped inside that cave . . . the smell of meat cooking . . . I thanked the Lord. Then things got out of hand. I ate sparingly, others did not. . . . This time our hunger was different—more severe, savage—and Colonel Ives *particularly* could not be satisfied.

Colqhoun recounts how the Irishman was murdered, prompting him to flee, leaving Mrs. MacCready to the mercy of Ives. Hart begins preparations for a rescue party to save the widow and arrest Ives, but before they leave George produces a buckskin adorned with a fearsome creature devouring the flesh of an Indian man. In the presence of Boyd, George tells Hart the Ojibwa legend of wendigo: "A man eats another's flesh—it's usually an enemy—and he steals his strength, his essence, his spirit. And his hunger becomes insatiable. And the more he eats, the more he wants, too. And the more he eats, the stronger he becomes." Hart doubts the scout's concerns, asking, "George, people don't still do that do they?" George reminds the two Euro-Americans that "[the] white man eats the body of Jesus Christ every Sunday."

Trekking over the mountains, young Toffler tumbles off a cliff, sustaining a severe laceration to his abdomen. Later that night, he awakens to find Colqhoun slurping at the wound. Horrified, he tells the others: "He was licking me." The consummate soldier Reich is ready to run the Scotsman through, but Colqhoun entreats Hart to restrain him for the remainder of the journey. From this point on, George is convinced that Colqhoun is wendigo. Once at the cave, Colqhoun enters into a frantic state, sowing confusion and distress as Boyd and Reich plunge into the subterranean depths. The pair soon discovers the inner sanctum of the cavern to be a charnel house, littered with the bones of the entire wagon train. Reich deduces that Colqhoun has set a trap and scrambles back to the surface.

Meanwhile, Colqhoun sheds his bonds and unearths a knife with which he stabs Hart before killing George. A petrified Toffler drops his own weapon and runs into the forest, pursued by the villain. Boyd and Reich give chase; however, it quickly becomes apparent that the hunters are now the hunted. Colqhoun slays Toffler and Reich, sending the latter off a cliff, before turning on Boyd, who stoically jumps rather than face Colqhoun. After breaking his fall in the canopy and tumbling down the hillside, Boyd finds himself entangled in a pit with Reich's corpse, once again spattered with the blood of a fallen comrade.

Hobbled by a broken leg, Boyd languishes in the deathly hollow for ten days, while Colqhoun returns to the cave with Toffler's body, resuming his

The cannibal and his kill. *Courtesy of Photofest/Twentieth Century Fox*

anthropophagic ways. Eventually, Boyd succumbs to his hunger and eats some of Reich. Invigorated, but still lame, he makes his way back to Fort Spencer. He seeks the counsel of Martha (Sheila Tousey), a Native American woman who had been away from camp with Private Cleaves (David Arquette) when Colqhoun arrived, on how to stop wendigo. She mournfully informs him that there is no solution: "You ever give yourself, wendigo eats . . . must eat more. He takes . . . never, *never* gives. You give yourself, you must die." General Slauson soon arrives at the post, but he does not believe Boyd's story as no evidence of the search party or the wagon train can be located at the cave. Hart's replacement then arrives in the form of Colonel Ives (Colqhoun), and the only person who can corroborate Boyd's accusations is the camp drunkard, Major Knox (Stephen Spinella), who does not recognize "Ives."

Unable to prove his accusation that Ives is actually Colqhoun, Boyd is viewed as a lunatic. Eventually, Colqhoun comes clean to Boyd, expressing his disappointment that the captain did not "finish off" Reich in the woods. We learn that Colqhoun only recently suffered from tuberculosis and "suicidal ambitions," but on the way to convalesce in the West, he met a Native American guide in the Plains who told him of the wendigo legend. "Well, I just had to try," Colqhoun wryly states. "Consequently, I ate the scout first. I grew stronger. Later through circumstance, my wagon train grew lost in the Rockies." A debate over morality—"the last bastion of a coward" according to Colqhoun—ensues, before a slaughtered Cleaves is found, leading to Boyd's incarceration on suspicion of murder. The real culprit, a very much alive Colonel Hart, soon appears and violently dispatches Knox. He tells Boyd how Colqhoun nursed him back to health with Toffler's flesh. Evoking classic vampire camp, Hart tries to persuade Boyd to become one of them: "It's lonely being a cannibal. It's tough making friends."

Unconvinced by Colqhoun's mock-patriotic soliloquy on Manifest Destiny, which links his own hungers to the United States' "limitless appetite" for expansion,[9] Boyd refuses the boon, prompting the Scotsman to mortally wound the recalcitrant captain. Forced to choose between further cannibalism and a painful death, Boyd eventually opts for the former, eating the stew made from Major Knox. Upon his recovery, Boyd convinces Hart to let him go in return for killing him. A superherolike battle between Boyd and Colqhoun ensues as a small party of reinforcements approaches the fort. After exchanging blows with daggers, pitchforks, and clubs, Boyd lures Colqhoun into a bear trap, which kills them both (the unrepentant anthropophagus Colqhoun conveniently perishes first). General Slauson is then seen tasting the stew à la Knox, suggesting that the wendigo curse may yet live on (or perhaps that Slauson was the master cannibal all along).

Geographical Imagination, Hostile Spaces, and Manifest Destiny

Popular geopolitics concerns itself with contemporary myth making and geographic imagination, seeking to uncover the sociocultural fundaments that inform workaday national identity, our images of other nations, and how the world "actually" works. Marcus Power and Andrew Crampton indicate the importance of films in providing "logistics of perception" and "crystallizing" the role of the United States and Americans in global political dramas, particularly during moments of crisis: "Important questions can be raised about the ways in which geopolitical imaginations are expressed through film and about how different 'threats' and 'dangers' are constructed through various Hollywood narratives."[10] In his description of the unique power of motion pictures on geographical imagination, Klaus Dodds states: "As an immensely popular form of entertainment, films are highly effective in grabbing the attention of mass audiences. The power of film lies in not only in its apparent ubiquity but also in the way in which it helps to create (often dramatically) understandings of particular events, national identities and relationships to others."[11] While the focus of popular geopolitics is typically on America's role in the international system,[12] in this chapter, I explore similar concerns within the context of making the American "West" part of "Western Civilization"; that is, Euro-American.

Reflecting the field's origins in critical geopolitics, popular geopoliticians adopt a jaundiced eye when confronted with the unalloyed triumphalism resident in filmic depictions of American "geography." This is particularly true when "America" is cast against its various "Others"; for example, a barbarous Middle East, a forbidding Russia, or a recondite Orient. However, in the case of *Ravenous*, a somewhat different reading is in order. Like all Westerns, *Ravenous*, regardless of its critical intent, serves as an important component of the popular geographical imagination of America-in-the-making, a country and a people defined by its (transient) frontier rather than its (fixed) borders.[13] Characterized by "consumer worlds saturated by image-making" where the visual reifies "fictional stories of subject territories" and "factual control on the ground,"[14] films set in the "Wild West" situate knowledge and reinforce topographies of power associated with American national identity in its adolescent phase. As popular geographies of American expansion, Westerns can be read as "ideological landscapes"[15] that favorably posit the agents and effects of Western Civilization (however untoward) against the chaos of the "non-West" (either in the form of the wilderness, the Native American, or the lawlessness of the frontier). In film, the West is seen/scene—it is both a visual representation of a purported reality, as well as a cinematic backdrop for contemporary issues of society, politics, and culture.

Antonia Bird, working with Ted Griffin's screenplay, clearly aimed to construct a critical geography of the American West. Bird, whose works include the controversial gay-themed *Priest* (1994) and the fictional tale of the 9/11 hijackers *The Hamburg Cell* (2004), has stated that she is "interested globally in inequality and injustice."[16] Such concerns repeatedly manifest in her Director's Commentary on the DVD version of the film, most dramatically when she issues a mea culpa as a "European," stating, "We [i.e., European immigrants in America] are responsible for the Indian genocide."[17] She then draws a link between the identity issues of the Irish and Scottish who were "pushed out of their own countries" and came to form the bulk of the U.S. Armed Forces during the mid-nineteenth century. According to Bird, it is at the feet of these "Lost Europeans" that we should lay the cultural destruction of the Native Americans and the ecological rape of "Native America" on the altar of westward expansion.[18]

Perhaps no two words resonate more clearly when describing nineteenth-century American history than *Manifest Destiny*. The phrase entered into the popular lexicon through John O'Sullivan's midcentury essay "Annexation" in *United States Magazine and Democratic Review*, in which he urged the "fulfillment of our manifest destiny to overspread the continent allotted by Providence for the free development of our yearly multiplying millions."[19] A year later, Robert C. Winthrop addressed his fellow congressmen, marking the end of the Anglo-American condominium in Oregon, by affirming the "right of our manifest destiny to spread over this whole continent."[20] Within a few months, the expression blossomed into a propaganda tool for rapine territorial aggression directed at the United States' southern neighbor, Mexico: "With deep roots in American culture, the doctrine legitimized the assumed superiority of the Anglo-Saxon race."[21] The *Volksgeist* of the day endowed Americans not only with the feeling that the conquest of the continent was ineluctable but also righteous, thus leaving the conquerors with a clear conscience (something that Bird's film seeks to challenge). In order to make the lands of America fruitful, the Americans were forced by the hand of destiny to displace the "mongrel" Mexicans and annihilate the "savage" Indians. In the words of C. Vann Woodward, "It would be most convenient of all if the blame could be laid upon the victims themselves for their racial weaknesses

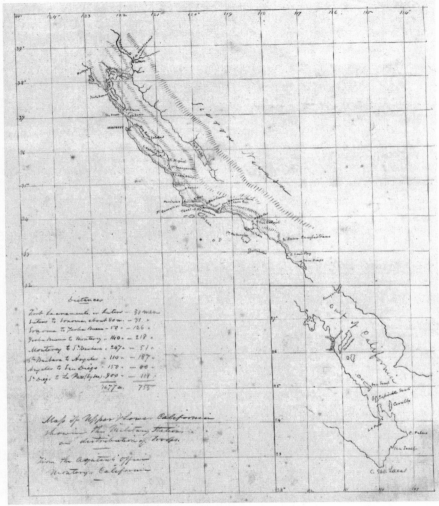

Map of U.S. military installations and troops in California, 1847. *Author's collection*

and the conquest could be seen as inevitable because of the superiority of the advancing race."[22] Thus it is fitting that *Ravenous* begins on a battlefield of the U.S.-Mexican War; however, the focus quickly turns to the sparsely populated but potentially productive West. According to one historian, "The west is the compass point that still stands metaphorically for national destiny as well as for good prospects, freedom, and personal rebirth. The nation realized itself by expanding westward, and this movement over the horizon toward California and the Pacific is embedded in our consciousness."[23] It is in the mountains of California that Bird and Griffin sculpt a nightmarish effigy of American expansion.

Hawking her film at the Sundance Film Festival, Bird remarked, "This is a fantastic fable about taking power";[24] this statement can be read both from a personal and national perspective. On the personal level, Colqhoun assumes the role of a proto-Nietzschean *übermensch* (underscored by one of the German philosopher's quotes, which precedes the film's opening scene), freed from slavish Judeo-Christian morality and emboldened by the sheer "freedom" of the American West. On the national level, *Ravenous* functions as an allegory of Anglo-American expansion across the North American continent, linking Manifest Destiny and American exceptionalism to the most visceral form of consumption imaginable: cannibalism.

Throughout the film, cannibalism serves as a metaphor for imperialism, although it is worth interrogating other ways to read the consumption of human flesh in the context of American history. In her essay on cannibalism, Shirley Lindenbaum points out that eating human flesh is not a crime in the United States; she goes on to argue that the country's performative obsession with competitive overeating and altereating ("reality TV" displays of the consumption of insects, entrails, and other nontraditional foodstuffs) give lie to the "opposed concepts of the primitive other and the civilized self" in a society stripped of its food-based taboos."[25] Cheekily rejecting the hoary European discourse that used anthropophagy as calumny to justify "predatory" imperialism,[26] *Ravenous* is brutally honest about the processes of colonial acquisition as the paradigmatic form of ingestion, one which exposes the Western culture's "unhealthy and systemic commitment to over-consumption."[27] Attempting to entice Boyd into a life of colonially abetted cannibalism, Colqhoun pontificates:

> Manifest Destiny. Westward expansion. You know come April, it will all start again. Thousands of gold-hungry Americans will travel over those mountains on the way to new lives, passing right through here. We won't kill indiscriminately, no . . . selectively. Good God, we don't want to break up families. . . . This country is seeking to be whole. Stretching out its arms and consuming all it can. And we merely follow.

Later, Colqhoun attempts to reinforce his patriotic leanings through the use of one of Benjamin Franklin's famous aphorisms, counseling Boyd, "Eat to live, don't live to eat," thus providing a textual "flagging" of American nationalism[28] to accompany the frequent visuals of the stars-and-stripes and other symbols of Americana.

Bird underlines the link between the "spirit" of her cannibalistic Wild West and late twentieth-century Los Angeles, a city populated with people worried about "what they put in their bodies" just as they are "having bits of their bodies hacked off." In the DVD commentary, both the director and the screenwriter comment on the semantics of the commanding general's name (Slauson) and its purposeful evocation of contemporary Californian geographies of power. Slauson Avenue, named for land developer Jonathan Sayre Slauson (1829–1905), is LA's main east-west thoroughfare in the southern part of the county. Fittingly, Slauson's entry in *Men of Achievement in the Great Southwest* reads: "It was well when Destiny ordained that an empire be builded [*sic*] in the western wilderness that there were men of J. S. Slauson's stamp to lay the foundation."[29] After emigrating from New York, Slauson established the citrus industry, built Protestant churches, and became president of the Chamber of Commerce in what would become Los Angeles. Lamentably, a politicized exposition on the need to keep settlers streaming over the mountains did not make the final cut, as General Slauson adjures Boyd to recant his tale of cannibalism, fearing such rumors would interrupt colonization, capitalism, and the imminent gold rush.

Slauson serves as trenchant symbol of the imperial endgame, around which the plot of *Ravenous* pivots. In our geographical imagination, the Western frontier is a "landscape of inchoation," a place where new beginnings are possible, but only for those capable of overcoming its inherent dangers through the judicious use of "formative violence."[30] America's national identity as a "gunfighter nation" is rooted in the myths of "taming" the hostile geographies that confronted the westward-bound settlers. The frontier was fraught with multiple dangers; however, chief among these were the threats posed by an untamed wilderness and an equally "feral" population of Native Americans. According to Gayle Baldwin, "The fear of the wilderness and the call to conquer it was juxtaposed to the Enlightenment higher ideal of life and liberty for all," resulting in a "need to make order out of this wild environment and its inhabitants."[31] *Ravenous*, while treating the Native American with dignity, thus avoiding the clichés of the classic "Western," does present an extremely hostile terrain against which the murderous drama unfolds.

Filmed in Slovakia's High Tatras, *Ravenous* presents the viewer with a believable simulacrum of the Sierra Nevada. In the forward to his history of the Donner Party, esteemed chronicler of the American West George R. Stewart describes the Californian range as such:

[T]he mountains stand forth notable by the rich green of forests, the blue of lakes, the white of snow, and the clear shimmer of high, wind-swept granite. The Sierra and its foothills form a belt 100-miles wide and westward of them is Sacramento Valley. . . . [Emigrants] must by sheer power of oxen lift their wagons over the Sierra. It is a long road and those who follow it must meet certain risks: exhaustion and disease, alkali water, and Indian arrows will take a toll. But the greatest problem is a simple one, and the chief opponent is Time . . . let it come late October, or November, and the snow-storms block the heights, when wagons are light of provisions and oxen lean, then will come a story.[32]

Taking a page from Stewart, Griffin's script begins the second act of the film with such a "story"; that is, Colqhoun's yarn, which lures the inhabitants of Fort Spencer into those ominous mountains. Bird's masterful use of geography allowed her to achieve Griffin's vision of a frozen wasteland. In the words of Roger Ebert, "She does what is very hard to do: She makes the weather feel genuinely cold, damp, and miserable. So much snow in the movies looks too pretty or too fake, but her locations are chilly and ominous."[33] With such a backdrop, the desperation of the pioneers' struggle is visually realized.

Donner Lake Pass by T. H. O'Sullivan. *Courtesy of the U.S. Geological Survey*

With its setting against stark landscapes, *Ravenous* naturally draws allusions to the ill-fated expedition of the Donner Party, in which a band of westward-bound emigrants found themselves stranded in the Sierra Nevada during the winter of 1846 to 1847, ultimately resorting to cannibalism during the last days of their ordeal. However, the plot was actually based on the legend of Alfred Packer, a lesser-known figure, who led a group of twenty gold hunters into Colorado's San Juan Mountains. Despite admonitions from local Indians, Packer's party ventured into the mountains and ran out of food. According to the producer of the *Ravenous* DVD, David Prior:

> He finally made it back to civilization, alone of course, and told a story a lot like Colqhoun's story in *Ravenous*—they took shelter . . . and one day while he was out gathering wood one of the men had been killed for food. He admitted to killing one man named Shannon Bell, sort of the Colonel Ives of the yarn, but only in self-defense. His story seemed fishy to a lot of people, though. Packer started spending too much cash around, and he gave himself away very quickly. The authorities led him back up into the woods, but he led them everywhere except to the cabin. Finally, after trying to kill the man he was shackled to, Packer was sent back to jail and the lawmen found the cabin . . . along with five cured, partially eaten bodies.[34]

The subsequent media spectacle riveted the country, and it focused the national psyche on the primordial conditions of the American West that seemed to transform "civilized" men into savages capable of killing and eating their fellows. According to spatial psychologists Sander Koole and Agnes Van den Berg, when confronted with wilderness, for example, "anywhere human influences are not discernible and in which natural process are left free reign," ancient fears reemerge.[35] The vast wilderness of the American West represented an increase in the order of magnitude from anything Euro-Americans had experienced along the Atlantic seaboard or the Appalachian Range. In the American mind, these wilds became intimately linked with chaos and death, producing feelings of terror and anxiety. Keeping this in mind, the Western adoption of the wendigo myth as a preternatural adjunct to the overarching terror associated with the North American wilderness seems almost predictable.

Wendigoism: From Spirit Possession to Psychosis to Contagion

As *Ravenous* does little to inform the viewer of the sociocultural history of the wendigo psychosis, a brief précis of the phenomenon and its various popular-culture offshoots is in order. In contrast to popular culture depictions of wendigo as a stalking, anthropomorphic monster,[36] the original Algonkian myth characterizes wendigo (or *wiitiko*)[37] as a malevolent spirit that enters the human body. The wiitiko psychosis occurs when a person (usually male) spends an extended period of time in the boreal wilderness and fails in the hunt for food.[38] In such cases, humans become subject to the cannibalistic desires of the wiitiko spirit, resulting in steady dehumanization. Traditional foods (game, grains, and others) are rejected by the "host," who comes to crave human flesh alone, thus signaling a shift from "crisis cannibalism" (as was the case in the Donner Party ordeal) to something genuinely malevolent. Specific to the belief systems of the Northern Algonkian nations of the Cree and Ojibwa,[39] wiitiko are a "taxon of beings"[40] existing in the real world and interacting with human beings. Possession by such supernatural forces causes the victim's heart to turn to ice, a process that is seen as almost irreversible, although remediation may be attempted. In such a state, the possessed is prone to murder, but more often the person will be killed by their own community in self-defense, what anthropologists deem "triage homicide." From a cultural vantage, recognition of the wiitiko psychosis *qua* spirit possession is a psychological manifestation of the "human tendency to condemn most vigorously in others that which is most feared in oneself."[41] Among the Algonkian, whose realm is characterized by extreme cold and few edible resources, a premium is placed on self-reliance and emotional restraint, particularly the rejection of aggression.[42] Wiitiko-possessed people are paranoid, obsessive-compulsive, and—most importantly—unable to hunt (that is, anything other than humans). To become wiitiko is thus the epitome of failure as a human being.

In the postcontact era, wiitiko mania cascaded among the Northern Algonkian, primarily as a response to environmental pressures and societal stress. As the political economy of North America came under the influence of French and English settlers, the indigenous populations suffered greatly: overhunting of fur-bearing animals led to a deterioration of the resource base, and the system of debt peonage created by the European settlers resulted in the breakdown of native society.[43] Unsustainable population increases (to satisfy European labor demands) and the effects of European diseases on the vulnerable populations exacerbated the problem. As the Northern Algonkian peoples became enfolded into the Western imperial project, the tendency to recognize the presence of wiitiko—even among those who had not committed acts of cannibalism—became increasingly common. The close association of food and ego-esteem among the Algonkian created a sort of paradox around the wiitiko-possessed person.[44] Given the limitless supply of (easy) food available in the form of other humans, the wiitiko host,

Ojibwa brave. *Courtesy of the Library of Congress*

with its heightened strength, represents the embodiment of power, but as an aggressive, unrestrained force dependent on other humans as/for sustenance, the wiitiko personifies all the characteristics that the Algonkian reject. Consequently, this "witch fear" was a predictable reaction to the trauma associated with environmental degradation and social collapse in the face of the European onslaught.[45]

As the wendigo legend became embedded in non-native North American wilderness mythology, the links between endemic food scarcity and wiitiko possession were (conveniently) forgotten, and the focus shifted to notions of power.[46] In his analysis of the wiitiko psychosis, Carlson alludes to the idea of "contagion," suggesting that the flesh of animals and men alike can impart their "spirit power" if consumed.[47] *Ravenous*'s tale of the wendigo plays into this tradition, abandoning the notion of psychosis in favor of the more familiar trope of infection. Instead, wendigo is something you "catch" when you are hungry and opt to eat your friends (or enemies). In these fanciful, Eurocentric tales of wendigo, there is also an upside to eating other humans: puissance. As the "consummate predator of humanity," the wendigo is power personified.[48] By being able to consume the strength of others, one can truly become a Nietzschean superman. Colqhoun embodies this notion to a tee. Sickly and on the verge of death, he eats his Indian guide and becomes healthy again. After consuming his wagon party, he is able to survive the harshest conditions without injury. With a bellyful of soldier flesh, he is nigh invincible (a fact that is subtly highlighted by Carlyle's petite frame and slight build).

In his original screenplay, Ted Griffin took the character even further, having him ascending the boreal canopy and attacking from above, thus

Colqhoun as a Christlike figure. *Courtesy of Photofest/Twentieth Century Fox*

providing a "Darwinian element" to the cannibalistic transformation.[49] While such overt evolutionary references failed to make the final cut, certain elements of this theme can be read in the characterization of Colqhoun and Boyd. Leaving aside traditional morality, it is actually unclear who is protagonist and who is antagonist. Colqhoun, a genuine bon vivant, is an extremely round character, constantly developing and always draped in color; he is literally and figuratively *spirited*. Conversely, Boyd is two-dimensional, gray, and morose. The former loves life (though he has no compunctions about taking it), while the latter seems almost a revenant, bound to this plane by the weakest of tethers.

By making Colqhoun the (anti)hero of *Ravenous*, Bird sends mixed messages about the "taming" of the West. When Boyd rejects the boon of the wendigo, it does not seem to be solely on the grounds of morality but also because he simply has no desire to exist. Colqhoun, freed from Judeo-Christian morality (or, at the very least, Victorian mores of self-reserve and propriety), provides a pathway for instantaneous evolution, while Boyd holds back, and is thus—evolutionarily speaking—held back. In his time in the Sierras, Colqhoun has mastered the wilderness environment and plans to profit from it come spring, while Boyd—always shown cold and shivering—is chained to his "old ways," refusing to change. Unable to adapt to the hostile landscape that surrounds him, Boyd seems like a doomed Neanderthal confronting the lissome Cro-Magnon (Colqhoun), who is predestined to prevail. Herein, we see the complexity of *Ravenous*: while Antonia Bird is at pains to stress her contempt for imperialist consumption, she portrays Colqhoun as an almost Christlike figure (he even paints a bloody cross on his forehead), bringing to mind Mircea Eliade's soulful admonition: "Before passing judgment on cannibalism, we must always remember that it was instituted by divine beings."[50] With an insatiable appetite for life, Colqhoun scripts the future of the West: only those willing to consume this land will succeed.

Tellingly, screenwriter Ted Griffin stated that, after doing some research on the wendigo myth, he did not want to be constrained by it, but ultimately he decided to include it with liberal adaptations to fit the needs of his story.[51] As I have explored elsewhere, Western cultural producers feel free to borrow from indigenous traditions to create new, exotic threats that target colonial interlopers. Like the Haitian zombie, which was transformed from a pitiable, solitary creature into an ever-expanding stalking horde bent on the destruction of global order, prosperity, and security,[52] the wendigo spirit—upon entering the collective consciousness of Anglo-American society—no longer threatened the Native American, but instead menaces (white) civilization. Just as zombieism was molded in the hands of fantasy authors and Hollywood screenwriters from an affliction confined to superstitious Haitians to a global viral pandemic, so, too, does "wendigoism" make the leap from an indigenous danger to an infectious "political" contagion, and one that disrupts the balance of power in the Western-dominated world of order and progress. However, this superficial reading of the wendigo curse in *Ravenous* does not tell the whole story. By positioning Colqhoun as Nietzschean-Darwinian master of the Western wilderness, *Ravenous* provides a rather more complex staging of the American imperial project. In its treatment of the "winning of the West" and the taming of "dangerous environments," *Ravenous* presents a paradox: on the one hand, it is an indictment of militarism and formative violence, while on the other, a visual and textual reaffirmation of the "evolutionary" conflict that was required to realize the promise of Manifest Destiny. The film's coda—which shows the apocryphal founder of Los Angeles, General Slauson, tasting the man-stew and thus ostensibly continuing the curse of the wendigo—reminds us of this ambiguity. Carnivorous, infectious consumption truly is the "spirit" of the West.

Notes

1. Andrew O'Hehir, "Dark Meat," Salon.com, March 19, 1999. http://www.salon.com/ 1999/03/19/reviewb_26/

2. Janet Maslin, "His Favorite Dessert? Ladyfingers, of Course!" *New York Times*, March 19, 1999.

3. Joe Morgenstern, "In Ghoulish 'Ravenous,' The Joys of Cannibalism Are Just a Matter of Taste," *Wall Street Journal Europe*, March 19, 1999.

4. Dann Gire, "Hungry? 'Ravenous' May Spoil Your Appetite," *Chicago Daily Herald*, March 19, 1999.

5. Bob Campbell, "Gothic 'Ravenous' Tests Appetite for Horror," *Times-Picayune*, March 26, 1999.

6. Roger Ebert, "Ravenous," *Chicago Sun-Times*, March 19, 1999. http://rogerebert.suntimes.com/apps/pbcs.dll/article?AID=/19990319/REVIEWS/903190304.

7. Stephen Thompson, "Interview: Antonia Bird—Blood and Guts," *A. V. Club*, 1999. http://www.avclub.com/articles/antonia-bird,13587/

8. All quotes, unless otherwise specified, are from *Ravenous* (1999).

9. See Danette DiMarco, "Going Wendigo: The Emergence of the Iconic Monster in Margaret Atwood's *Oryx and Crake* and Antonia Bird's *Ravenous*," *College Literature* 34.8 (2011): 134–55.

10. Andrew Crampton and Marcus Power, "Reel Geopolitics: Cinemato-graphing Political Space," *Geopolitics* 10 (2005): 194.

11. Klaus Dodds, "Hollywood and the Popular Geopolitics of the War on Terror," *Third World Quarterly* 29.8 (2008): 1621.

12. See, for example: Joanne P. Sharp, *Condensing the Cold War: Reader's Digest and American Identity* (Minneapolis: University of Minnesota Press, 2000); Klaus Dodds, *Global Geopolitics: A Critical Introduction* (Harlow, UK: Prentice Hall, 2005); Jason Dittmer, *Popular Culture, Geopolitics, and Identity* (Lanham, MD: Rowman & Littlefield, 2010).

13. Richard Slotkin, *Gunfighter Nation: The Myth of the Frontier in Twentieth-Century America* (Norman, OK: University of Oklahoma Press, 1998).

14. Stephen Daniels, "Geographical Imagination," *Transactions of the Institute of British Geographers* 36 (2011): 183.

15. Derek Gregory, *Geographical Imaginations* (Cambridge, MA: Blackwell, 1994).

16. Quoted in Susan Shacter, "Antonia Bird," *Bomb* 51 (1995). http://bombsite .com/issues/51/ articles/1854.

17. Antonia Bird and Damon Albarn, "Commentary with Director Antonia Bird and Composer Damon Albarn." In *Ravenous* [DVD], Fox 2000 Pictures.

18. Antonia Bird and Damon Albarn. 1999. "Commentary with Director Antonia Bird and Composer Damon Albarn." In *Ravenous* [DVD]: Fox 2000 Pictures.

19. John O'Sullivan, "Annexation," *United States Magazine and Democratic Review* 17.1 (1845): 5–10.

20. Quoted in Julius W. Pratt, "The Origin of 'Manifest Destiny,'" *American Historical Review* 32.4 (1927): 795.

21. María del Rosario Rodríguez Díaz, "Mexico's Vision of Manifest Destiny during the 1847 War," *Journal of Popular Culture* 35.2 (2004): 41–50.

22. C. Vann Woodward, "The Tainting of America," *New Republic* 186.11 (1982): 32.

23. Roger Cushing Aikin, "Paintings of Manifest Destiny: Mapping the Nation," *American Art* 14.3 (2000): 87.

24. Quoted in Dan Webster, "Whet Your Appetite for 'Ravenous,'" *Spokesman Review*, March 19, 1999.

25. Shirley Lindenbaum, "Thinking about Cannibalism," *Annual Review of Anthropology* 33 (2004): 478.

26. Lindenbaum, "Thinking about Cannibalism," 476.

27. DiMarco, "Going Wendigo," 135.

28. Michael Billig, *Banal Nationalism* (London: Sage Publications, 1995).

29. George Ward Burton, *Men of Achievement in the Great Southwest: A Story of Pioneer Struggles during the Early Days in Los Angeles and Southern California* (Los Angeles: Los Angeles Times, 1904), 44.

30. Gilberto Perez, "The Frontier Dialectic." *National Interest* 257.13 (1993): 466–67.

31. Gayle R. Baldwin, "World War Z and the End of Religion as We Know It," *Crosscurrents* 57 (2007): 413–17.

32. George R. Stewart, *Ordeal by Hunger: The Story of the Donner Party* (1936; New York: Houghton Mifflin Harcourt, 1992), 4–5.

33. Ebert, "Ravenous."

34. Bill Hunt, "Jerky Treats! An Interview with Ravenous DVD Producer David Britten Prior," The Digital Bits.com, October 27, 1999. http://www.thedigitalbits .com/articles/jerkytreats.html

35. Sander L. Koole and Agnes E. Van den Berg, "Lost in the Wilderness: Terror Management, Action Orientation, and Nature Evaluation," *Journal of Personality and Social Psychology* 88.6 (2005): 1014–28.

36. Perhaps the first was Theodore Roosevelt's campfire tale "The Wendigo" (1893), which introduced the wendigo as an anthropomorphized "monster" rather than a spiritual force. Given its utility as trope for Canadian/boreal wilderness-themed horror (see Atwood 2004), the wendigo monster has enjoyed a recent renaissance in a number of media, from children's fiction like *The Curse of the Wendigo* (2010) and graphic novels such as *Curse of the Wendigo* (2012) to science fiction/fantasy television programs including *Charmed, Supernatural,* and *Haven* among others.

37. To avoid confusion, I shall refer to the psychosis associated with spirit possession and cannibalism as *wiitiko,* following Seymour Parker, "The Wiitiko Psychosis in the Context of Ojibwa Personality and Culture," *American Anthropologist* 62.4 (1960): 603–23.

38. Parker, "Wiitiko Psychosis."

39. Thomas H. Hay, "The Windigo Psychosis: Psychodynamic, Cultural, and Social Factors in Aberrant Behavior," *American Anthropologist* 73.1 (1971): 1–19.

40. Nathan D. Carlson, "Reviving Witiko (Windigo): An Ethnohistory of 'Cannibal Monsters' in the Athabasca District of Northern Alberta, 1878–1910," *Ethnohistory* 56.3 (2009): 356.

41. Carlson, "Reviving Witiko," 356.

42. Parker, "Wiitiko Psychosis"; Hay, "Windigo Psychosis."

43. Lou Marano, "Windigo Psychosis: The Anatomy of an Emic-Etic Confusion," *Current Anthropology* 23.4 (1982): 385–412.

44. Parker, "Wiitiko Psychosis."

45. Carlson, "Reviving Witiko."

46. Margaret Atwood, *Strange Things: The Malevolent North in Canadian Literature* (London: Virago Press, 2004); DiMarco, "Going Wendigo."

47. Carlson, "Reviving Witiko."

48. Carlson, "Reviving Witiko," 359.

49. Ted Griffin and Jeffrey Jones. "Commentary with Screenwriter Ted Griffin, Antonia Bird and Actor Jeffrey Jones," in *Ravenous* [DVD], Fox 2000 Pictures, 1999.

50. Mircea Eliade, *The Sacred and Profane: The Nature of Religion* (1957; New York: Harper & Row, 1961), 103.

51. Griffin and Jones, "Commentary."

52. Robert A. Saunders, "Undead Spaces: Fear, Globalisation, and the Popular Geopolitics of Zombiism," *Geopolitics* 17 (2012): 1–25.

Bibliography

Aikin, Roger Cushing. "Paintings of Manifest Destiny: Mapping the Nation." *American Art* 14.3 (2000): 78–89.

Atwood, Margaret. *Strange Things: The Malevolent North in Canadian Literature.* London: Virago Press, 2004.

Baldwin, Gayle R. "World War Z and the End of Religion as We Know It." *Crosscurrents* 57 (2007): 412–25.

Billig, Michael. *Banal Nationalism*. London: Sage Publications, 1995.

Bird, Antonia. *Ravenous*. United States: Twentieth Century Fox, 1999. DVD.

Bird, Antonia, and Damon Albarn. "Commentary with Director Antonia Bird and Composer Damon Albarn." In *Ravenous* [DVD]: Fox 2000 Pictures, 1999.

Burton, George Ward. *Men of Achievement in the Great Southwest: A Story of Pioneer Struggles during the Early Days in Los Angeles and Southern California*. Los Angeles: Los Angeles Times, 1904.

Campbell, Bob. "Gothic 'Ravenous' Tests Appetite for Horror." *Times-Picayune*, March 26, 1999.

Carlson, Nathan D. "Reviving Witiko (Windigo): An Ethnohistory of 'Cannibal Monsters' in the Athabasca District of Northern Alberta, 1878–1910." *Ethnohistory* 56.3 (2009): 355–94.

Crampton, Andrew, and Marcus Power. "Reel Geopolitics: Cinemato-graphing Political Space." *Geopolitics* 10 (2005): 193–203.

Daniels, Stephen. "Geographical Imagination." *Transactions of the Institute of British Geographers* 36 (2011): 182–87.

DiMarco, Danette. "Going Wendigo: The Emergence of the Iconic Monster in Margaret Atwood's *Oryx and Crake* and Antonia Bird's *Ravenous*." *College Literature* 34.8 (2011): 134–55.

Dittmer, Jason. *Popular Culture, Geopolitics, and Identity*. Lanham, MD: Rowman & Littlefield, 2010.

Dodds, Klaus. *Global Geopolitics: A Critical Introduction*. Harlow, UK: Prentice Hall, 2005.

———. "Hollywood and the Popular Geopolitics of the War on Terror." *Third World Quarterly* 29.8 (2008): 1621–37.

Ebert, Roger. "Ravenous." *Chicago Sun-Times*, March 19, 1999. http://rogerebert.suntimes.com/apps/pbcs.dll/article?AID=/19990319/REVIEWS/903190304

Eliade, Mircea. *The Sacred and Profane: The Nature of Religion*. New York: Harper & Row, 1961.

Gire, Dann. "Hungry? 'Ravenous' May Spoil Your Appetite." *Chicago Daily Herald*, March 19, 1999.

Gregory, Derek. *Geographical Imaginations*. Cambridge, MA: Blackwell, 1994.

Griffin, Ted, and Jeffrey Jones. Commentary with Screenwriter Ted Griffin, Antonia Bird, and Actor Jeffrey Jones. In *Ravenous* [DVD]: Fox 2000 Pictures, 1999.

Hay, Thomas H. "The Windigo Psychosis: Psychodynamic, Cultural, and Social Factors in Aberrant Behavior." *American Anthropologist* 73.1 (1971): 1–19.

Hunt, Bill. "Jerky Treats! An Interview with *Ravenous* DVD Producer David Britten Prior." The Digital Bits.com. 1999. http://www.digitalbits.com/articles/jerkytreats.html

Koole, Sander L., and Agnes E. Van den Berg. "Lost in the Wilderness: Terror Management, Action Orientation, and Nature Evaluation." *Journal of Personality and Social Psychology* 88.6 (2005): 1014–28.

Lindenbaum, Shirley. "Thinking about Cannibalism." *Annual Review of Anthropology* 33 (2004): 475–98.

Marano, Lou. "Windigo Psychosis: The Anatomy of an Emic-Etic Confusion." *Current Anthropology* 23.4 (1982): 385–412.

Maslin, Janet. "His Favorite Dessert? Ladyfingers, of Course!" *New York Times.* March 19, 1999.

Morgenstern, Joe. "In Ghoulish 'Ravenous,' The Joys of Cannibalism Are Just a Matter of Taste." *Wall Street Journal Europe*, March 19, 1999.

O'Hehir, Andrew. "Dark Meat." Salon.com, March 19, 1999. http://www.salon.com/1999/03/19/ reviewb_26/

O'Sullivan, John. "Annexation." *United States Magazine and Democratic Review* 17.1 (1845): 5–10.

Parker, Seymour. "The Wiitiko Psychosis in the Context of Ojibwa Personality and Culture." *American Anthropologist* 62.4 (1960): 603–23.

Perez, Gilberto. "The Frontier Dialectic." *National Interest* 257.13 (1993): 466–70.

Pratt, Julius W. "The Origin of 'Manifest Destiny.'" *American Historical Review* 32.4 (1927): 795–98.

Rodríguez Díaz, María del Rosario. "Mexico's Vision of Manifest Destiny during the 1847 War." *Journal of Popular Culture* 35.2 (2004): 41–50.

Saunders, Robert A. "Undead Spaces: Fear, Globalisation, and the Popular Geopolitics of Zombiism." *Geopolitics* 17 (2012): 1–25.

Shacter, Susan. "Antonia Bird." *Bomb* 51 (1995). http://bombsite.com/issues/51/articles/1854

Sharp, Joanne P. *Condensing the Cold War: Reader's Digest and American Identity.* Minneapolis: University of Minnesota Press, 2000.

Slotkin, Richard. *Gunfighter Nation: The Myth of the Frontier in Twentieth-Century America.* Norman, OK: University of Oklahoma Press, 1998.

Stewart, George R. *Ordeal by Hunger: The Story of the Donner Party.* New York: Houghton Mifflin Harcourt, 1992.

Thompson, Stephen. "Interview: Antonia Bird—Blood and Guts." *A. V. Club.* 1999. http://www.avclub.com/articles/antonia-bird,13587/

Webster, Dan. "Whet Your Appetite for 'Ravenous.'" *Spokesman Review*, March 19, 1999.

Woodward, C. Vann. "The Tainting of America." *New Republic* 186.11 (1982): 30–32.

PART III

AND HELL
FOLLOWED WITH HIM

CHAPTER THIRTEEN

The Ghost from the Past

The Undead Avenger in Sergio Leone's Once Upon a Time in the West

Matthias Stork

"People like that have something inside . . . something to do with death."

—Cheyenne (Jason Robards)

Two gunslingers—the villain dressed all in black, the hero in light tan—face each other in the desert, framed against the rocky buttes of Monument Valley, the landscape with which John Ford symbolized the grandeur, promise, and precariousness of the American West. The wind rustles through the dry air, emphasizing the deadly silence that defines this moment. It is a classic scene, depicting the ritualized duel between two men. They are cowboys, frontier men, embodiments of a way of life that is continuously threatened by the progress of civilization. The scene is emblematic of the classic Hollywood Western—reflecting its distinctive iconography and its discourse on frontier life—but also of the oeuvre of Italian director Sergio Leone, who filtered the genre's conventions through his own artistic lens to produce works of unbridled stylistic extravagance.

The two cowboys stare at each other, ready to draw, to engage in the *dance of death*. Tight close-ups dictate the rhythm of the wordless battle, juxtaposing fearful determination against contemplative placidity. A wailing musical strain disrupts the atmospheric vacuum and leads into a flashback. The villain slowly comes into focus, younger, disheveled, sadistically growling the words, "Keep your loving brother happy," before shoving a harmonica into the mouth of a teenage boy, the hero's *former*, younger self, linking the past

207

to the present. An explosive electronic guitar intrudes onto the soundtrack, and the camera pulls back to reveal a lone arch crowned by a bell, standing in the middle of nowhere. The young boy's hands are tied behind his back, his older brother standing on his shoulders with a noose around his neck. The music swirls into a startling crescendo, accompanied by a barrage of reaction shots of the villainous posse, with their cruel grins and impassive stares forming a montage of inevitability. The doomed man curses at his executioners, then pushes away the boy, who falls into the dust. The boy sprawls there, exhausted, as symbolic church bells ring on the soundtrack and his brother swings from the rope in the background, caught in death's grip. The flashback ends with a final mournful bell chime; the two men draw. A gunshot reverberates through the desert.

Sergio Leone's *Once Upon a Time in the West* (1968) is a film about death, and more than just one. As a historical work, it portrays the demise of the Old West, as constructed in the mythical Western narrative of cinema. As a genre film, it is a eulogy for the Western's generic texture, including its archetypal characters (lone drifters, bandits, bounty hunters, mysterious outsiders), its distinctive frontier spaces (ghost towns, stretches of hot sand and scruffy rock formations, vast areas of untouched vegetation), as well as its iconic scenarios—most notably, the fight to the death: the duel. This passing of the West(ern) is specifically linked to the notion of conquest: the taming of the wilderness and the emergence of modern civilization and the erasure of the old primitivism by a new era of industrialization and capitalism, symbolized by the arrival of the railroad. Within this realm of Social Darwinism, representatives of the old and the new West confront each other, seeking the means to survive, to profit, and to rule. Businessmen and gunmen collide. Bodies abound.

The essential conflict of the film, however, concerns only two individuals, members of an ancient race. The conflict is more mythical than historical, unaffected by the tremendous social paradigm shift. It is an act of retribution. Harmonica, the film's mysterious stranger, avenges the murder of his older brother by killing Frank, the villain. Their final duel attaches several layers of meaning to death, underscoring its central place in the film. First and foremost, it establishes death as the narrative's red thread. The execution of Harmonica's brother provides the impetus for him to hunt down and kill Frank. The flashback sequence concludes with the brother's legs flailing in the air in the upper right corner of the screen, before the camera pans down to show Harmonica falling to the ground in the lower left corner, and then cutting to two parallel low-angle, deep-focus shots of the draw. This compositional symmetry establishes a connection between the two deaths and explains Harmonica's need for revenge. It also, in setting the story in motion, reveals yet another layer of death that connects the killing of the brother in the past and Frank in the present: the trauma imposed on Harmonica's former self, a young Mexican boy too exhausted and weak to save his brother's life. Surrounded by death (his brother's lifeless body indeed hovers over him, while Frank and his posse form a circle of death around him), Harmonica may not die physically, but he loses his innocence, and he is burdened with the weight of guilt. The sequence portrays his emotional death, the brutal crushing of his soul. He is as much a victim of Frank's deadly act as is his brother. Years later, when he reemerges to confront his tormentor, he exhibits unusual—at times even otherworldly—characteristics, including a supernatural command of time and space, superhuman instincts, and seeming invincibility.

Through its exploration of those characteristics and its examination of the film's aesthetics, this essay approaches Harmonica as one of Sergio Leone's *living dead* characters: a ghost from the past, a faded memory in material form, returning to confront his traumatic experience and exact revenge upon his tormentor in order to find inner peace and move on. *Once Upon a Time in the West* should not, however, be mistaken for a ghost Western. It is, rather, a double-helix Western, interweaving its elaborate discursive structure of traditional genre conventions with postmodern metareflections. Within this hermeneutic space, however, it borrows from the horror film in presenting the central character as an atypical creature—the *other*.

Leone's distinctive frontier iconography and character dispositions reveal a tenacious, sometimes even assaultive, fascination with death, but death is not exclusively posited as the end of existence. Rather, it is shown to facilitate a new experience of life—albeit one framed by the shadow of death. For Leone's characters, the frontier is a shelter for the undead, and life is nothing but living *as* the dead. *Once Upon a Time in the West* and its hero, Harmonica, are thus an early, admittedly rather subtle, instance of the appearance of the undead in the West.[1]

A Landscape of Death—Sergio Leone's Frontier of the *Living Dead*

The landscape of Sergio Leone's Westerns is dry and dirty, rusty and austere, filled with endless stretches of hot desert, parched riverbeds, and piercing rocks. It is essentially barren and strictly anti-Fordian; it does not offer the promise of a better life—the credo of Manifest Destiny. The rural peripheries are laden with graveyards, abandoned mission houses, and deserted shacks, and the few spaces of communal life are largely devoid of civilized culture. They are ghost towns populated by scavengers, pillagers, and other criminals. Women, other than prostitutes, are generally absent, and the institutions of law and religion[2] (if they exist at all) are corrupted and flawed. These communal areas are not a space for social progress, not an environment in which to settle down, raise families, and build communities. Townsfolk are portrayed as powerless bystanders, mere pawns in the game of the power-ful—usually passing bounty hunters—who impose their own laws and act as agents of destruction. Early scenes from *The Good, the Bad and the Ugly* (1966) illustrate this constellation. Blondie (Clint Eastwood) and the noto-rious, sought-after bandit Tuco (Eli Wallach) are partners in an ingenious, yet risky, money-making scheme. Blondie delivers Tuco to the authorities in exchange for the reward money and later frees him from his execution. The scam is a rehearsed routine. Blondie comes to Tuco's rescue at the eleventh hour, severing the tightening rope around his neck with a bullet and prevent-ing him from being hanged, and blasting the hats from the heads of the on-lookers—including the sheriff and his posse—as if to underscore the town's impotence in the face of the gun. It is a play battleground for skilled, intrepid gunmen, as Michael Carlson describes it: "a stage, an arena, a chessboard, a tabula almost rasa on which the main players play."[3]

There are no stereotypical threats to civilization on this frontier. Indians do not form part of Leone's quasi-apocalyptic vision. Instead, the noble pioneer spirit, the embodiment of civilization, is buried under the weight of a chaotic wilderness, nurturing savagery, immorality, and recklessness from within. His frontier is thus an extremely precarious sphere, where profes-sional killers abound, and death does not lurk outside the protective realm of the settlements but exists within them. Jim Kitses accordingly observes: "Death rules: the logic of the action and imagery of the films is to see the frontier as a vast cemetery."[4] Those who manage to persist in this hellish environment have no aspirations to settle down, let alone build or advance a community. They are restless soldiers of their own fortune, not evading, but consciously seeking the ultimate mortal confrontation, the ritual of the duel. In other words, Leone's characters live to die. Their existence is defined by the ubiquity and unpredictability of death. As a result, they continually find themselves right on the verge of life and death, engaging in near-death experiences. They live in the shadow of death, in a liminal stage, similar to Johnny Depp's character of William Blake in Jim Jarmusch's *Dead Man* (1995). They are the *living dead*.

Leone's *Dollars* trilogy offers several paradigms of this deadly lifestyle, beginning with the character of Joe—the foundational Man with No Name—in *A Fistful of Dollars* (1964), a remake, or rather retelling, of Akira Kurosawa's *Yojimbo* (1961). Joe is an enigmatic drifter with no past who, one day, passes through the border town of San Miguel. When he learns about the bloody conflict between the Rojo brothers and the Baxter clan, he sees an opportunity to make money and resolves to play the two families against each other.

Leone, as a storytelling device, associates the character of Joe with the presence of death. When Joe first arrives in San Miguel the Baxters harass him and shoot at his mule. Before Joe challenges them to a deadly duel, he asks the local undertaker to prepare coffins for his soon-to-be victims, adding an ironic dimension to his character's laconic disposition. Leone uses the character to create anticipation of a deadly shootout and to build suspense for the audience. Joe's association with death is reinforced in his first major scheme against the two families, in which he transports two dead Mexican soldiers to a nearby cemetery and labels them as still alive. Later in the film, when the Rojos take revenge on Joe in an extended torture sequence, Leone confronts Joe with his own mortality and reveals the character's vulnerability. The Rojos' brutal beating of Joe is a reminder that, after all, he is just a man and—although he is associated with death—he cannot control it.

Joe only manages to escape from the Rojos' impenetrable bulwark by hiding in a coffin. Peeking out from under its worn wooden boards, he witnesses the slaughter of the Baxter family, and so he becomes one of the *living dead*, seeing his own fate replayed while still drawing breath. His makeshift funeral is a return to life, but he reemerges from the Rojos' lair transformed into an otherworldly being. At the climax, Joe manifests himself as a demonic figure, materializing from the thick dust of a massive explosion and wearing a steel chest plate under his poncho so that not even a shot to the heart can kill him. No longer an ordinary hero, he has become an invincible avenger, an agent of death.

In the sequel, *For a Few Dollars More* (1965), Colonel Douglas Mortimer (played with wistful grace by Lee Van Cleef) fills the role of the living dead as a mourning brother seeking revenge for the death of his sister, who committed suicide while being raped by the psychopathic bandit, Indio. Dressed in black, Mortimer bears a striking resemblance to a Catholic priest: a mediator between the living and the dead.[5] Mortimer straddles the line between life and death in other ways as well. Caring more for the memory of his dead sister than for his own life, he throws himself into gunfights with an eagerness that is unusual even among Leone's gunfighters, all of whom freely and repeatedly dance with death. He is assisted, in the final showdown with Indio, by the Man with No Name (Clint Eastwood),[6] who is once again an otherworldly—even supernatural—being capable of appearing out of nowhere to dispatch his enemies with deadly precision and superhuman skill. Leone designs the frame, commanded by the Man with No Name, as a supernatural space. To put it differently, Leone does not turn the camera on Eastwood but has Eastwood penetrate the frame of the camera, creating an unsettling and dramatic effect. The Man with No Name's movements through space are so elaborate and unexpected that not even the mechanical eye of the camera is aware of them.

The Good, the Bad, and the Ugly offers the trilogy's most explicit example of the living dead. Blondie leaves Tuco to die in the desert and rides off with their bounty, but not before informing his victim that the next town is only seventy miles away—that is, almost impossible to reach on foot. Tuco somehow manages to elude death and reach the town, and though his fight for survival occurs off screen, his appearance clearly demonstrates that he went through hell. Like Joe and Mortimer in the two previous films, he has descended into the realm of death and escaped, and—like them—it is clear that the driving force that kept him alive has been his desire for revenge. He later forces Blondie to walk through the desert as well, taunting, humiliating, and torturing him along the way, denying him water, rest, and shadow. Blondie's skin burns, his lips burst open, and his throat becomes parched; eventually he, too, is left stumbling through the desert like a zombie—one of the *walking dead*.

Death is also explicitly inscribed in the texture of the narrative as it deals—both historically and generically—with the end of the Old West and its inhabitants, most notably the lone gunslinger. In certain respects, the film itself is one of the living dead, released in 1968, many years after the genre's golden age and freely and consciously referencing its history, in postmodern fashion, as a "cinema of frozen archetypes," as Umberto Eco observed. On a discrete level, death rears its ugly head on several occasions: in the form of a shocking family execution, an unexpected and abrupt funeral reception, a paraplegic's agonizing and ultimately futile fight for survival, the slow and painful passing of the archetypal cowboy (Cheyenne, played by Jason Robards). The dead characters do not remain among the living, but Harmonica proves to be an exception to the rule. He is, as we shall see, transcendent rather than earthbound, and he is removed from the central elements of the story.

A Language of Death—
The Film's Deadly Discourse

The discursive strategy of *Once Upon a Time in the West* equally emphasizes the film's thorough engagement with death. Actions may speak louder than words, but not in this case. The principals' comments on the film, along with its dialogue, are roaring thunderbolts that light up the dusty prairie of the frontier and open the gate to the underworld. Sergio Leone himself generally referred to the film as "a ballet of death," "a dance of death," or "an opera of death,"[7] implying an underlying tangibility of death—an unforeseen seriousness—absent, for the most part, from his previous work. The film's German title was translated as *Spiel mir das Lied vom Tod* (*Play the Song of Death to Me*),[8] a complete reinterpretation of the original title, underlining the significance of death in relation to the central characters. Their dialogue is equally laden with allusions to death, which creep into almost every scene and pervade almost every exchange. Harmonica, for example, refuses to explicitly reveal his true identity to Frank until the very end of the film, but he gives him a number of cues as to who he is: one of the undead, one of Frank's victims, slain yet unforgotten.

Harmonica did not die at Frank's hand, and as the sole survivor, he uses the names of those who are unable to speak to confront Frank with his guilt. This use of names establishes an intimacy between Harmonica and the victims. He acts as their spokesperson, speaking the language of the dead, and by uttering their names, he brings them back to life.

Frank: "What do you want? Who are you?"

Harmonica: "Dave Jenkins."

Frank: "Dave Jenkins is dead a long time ago."

Harmonica: "Calder Benson."

Frank: "What's your name? Benson's dead, too."

Harmonica: "You should know, Frank, better than anyone. You killed them."

Frank: "Who are you?"

Harmonica: "Jim Cooper, Chuck Youngblood."

Frank: "More dead men."

Harmonica: "They were all alive until they met you, Frank."

In this exchange, the dead return to the living in the form of remembrance. Harmonica, himself a victim of Frank, a survivor, physically unharmed, yet emotionally destroyed, becomes their representative, their voice. His language, however, is as much musical as verbal. The harmonica—the symbol of Frank's murder of his brother—is his main means of communication. Each tone he produces is an indictment of Frank's existence, a cry of outrage from the dead. As Christopher Frayling notes, "Harmonica is presented to us as an avenging ghost [. . .],"[9] the apex of the living dead archetype Leone establishes in the *Dollars* trilogy. He is also, however, an undead messenger—one whose message is death itself, wrapped in an unsettling melody, which persists even when words fail.

The Ghost from the Past:
Harmonica as the Undead Avenger

Harmonica is not presented as a typical ghost, or even undead being. Indeed, he is very much alive; but a closer view casts a different light on his supposed *alive*-ness. Harmonica rarely speaks. His trademark musical instrument constitutes his primary means of communication. Harmonica seems removed from the world and the people around him. He is unable to form emotional bonds with other people, let alone be part of a community (Jill clearly cares for him, yet he rebuffs her advances to stay with her and leaves the burgeoning town of Sweetwater at the end of the film). Tellingly, while almost all the characters in the narrative essay partake in the emerging process of civilization, for example, capitalist ventures, Harmonica never mentions money (in fact, he does not even pay for his own drink; Frank does). As John Fawell observes, "Harmonica, Cheyenne and Frank represent three archetypes from the mythic past [. . .] Of these three members of the 'ancient race' to which Harmonica says he and Frank belong, Harmonica stands out as the most ancient, the most primitive and the furthest removed from the contemporary West of capitalism and train tracks."[10] He is thus not earthbound. During the opening sequence, he kills three opponents by drawing and firing with superhuman speed. Though shot in the chest, he is not affected by the wound, and no mention of it is made in the remainder of the film. He cannot die if he is already dead.

Harmonica's undead status—his separation from the plane of the living—has metaphysical implications that set him apart from traditional Western characters. He withdraws from the world around him, separating himself from the material world (capitalism), the social world (love and friendship), and the physical world (flesh). He becomes an entirely different life form, consumed with a burning desire for revenge. The world has lost its meaning

An undead avenger, Harmonica (in the distance) is the deadliest gunfighter in the West.
Courtesy of Photofest

for him. As if touched by an intangible force, he moves beyond the physical sphere, transformed into an otherworldly, supernatural, undead being.

Harmonica's separation from the world of the living is underscored by his apparent disconnection from the physical plane within which the other characters—and the action of the film itself—are anchored. He glides into the frame from the side, as if materializing out of thin air. As Frayling puts it, "He just *appears*."[11] The spectators "are not given any spatial context, any sense of where he is or where he comes from [. . .]."[12] Aside from the obvious revelatory flashback, only a single scene portends, purely stylistically, a point of origin for Harmonica. When Cheyenne, after escaping from prison, arrives at the saloon and proceeds to quench his thirst with a jug of whiskey, the harmonica motif abruptly intrudes upon the diegetic soundtrack. Cheyenne, the bartender, and Jill, all surprised and confused, look around, scanning the interior. It is a disquieting moment. Leone then uses point-of-view shots to have Cheyenne locate the source of the music. The camera aligns itself with Cheyenne's movements, pans to the right, tracks forward, and focuses on the rear of the shack to reveal a figure sitting in darkness. Cheyenne grabs an oil lamp next to his face and swings it into the direction of the mysterious figure, completely in sync with the score's musical crescendo. As the light penetrates the darkness, harsh electronic guitar notes—the same music of death used in the opening flashback—sound, and Harmonica's face registers in extreme close-up, framed by shadow and cast in fire: a demonic creature, not of this Earth.[13] The aesthetic composition of the scene—the interplay of staging, acting, music, and camera movement—characterizes Harmonica as a dead man. It looks as if he had just escaped from the fires of hell.

Another crucial scene, the final duel, reemphasizes Harmonica's supernaturalism, his invincibility. The natural environment—the sun, the wind, the dust—does not affect him. He is a part of it. Frank circles around Harmonica to find the best possible position for the standoff, with his back against the sun (creating one of Leone's trademark circles of death for the shootout). Harmonica seeks no such tactical advantage. He stands still, eyeing Frank. Leone again photographs him in close-up, a slightly moving telephoto shot blurs the lines between Harmonica and the desert around him. Harmonica and the landscape merge and in effect, he comes to represent "some ancient, timeless force, as solid as granite."[14] When the gunslingers finally draw, Harmonica's hand moves first, almost a second earlier than that of Frank, the reputedly fastest shooter in the West. Harmonica kills him with a shot directly through the heart. Only one who has descended to the depths of hell, an undead, can slay the devil on Earth.

Already undead, Harmonica becomes—in the act of slaying his brother's killer—a ghost from the past. Mark Sanderson suggests that ghosts are "memories that materialize," and one of the primary motifs for their return to the living is revenge.[15] He is only a memory from Frank's past, a forgotten fragment from Frank's immoral life, to be reinserted in the puzzle that is his memory. Accordingly, Frank's death is punctuated by a brief glimpse into the flashback: Harmonica falling into the dust. Past and present are realigned, memory and truth reestablished. For the dead, justice is served; quite appropriately, with death. In this respect, Harmonica complicates the notion of the *undead*, functioning as a materialized memory come to life to exact revenge.

Till Death Do Us Part:
Leaving the Frame

Having exacted revenge, cleansed his conscience, and reinstated the order of the world, Harmonica leaves the earth behind, parting ways with the world of the living and returning to the world of the dead. This departure is, like Harmonica's undead status, conveyed via the film's aesthetic.

It is signaled first in a poignant scene between him and Jill McBain—the widow whose land, and life, he has been protecting from Frank throughout the film. When he returns to her after killing Frank she is relieved to see him still alive and clearly hopes for a future for the two of them. As she looks into Harmonica's eyes, however, she instantly realizes that he will not stay with her. Cheyenne's words put this moment in perspective: "People like that have something inside . . . something to do with death." With his purpose fulfilled, Harmonica's time is over. Nothing is left for him but death—he cannot remain among the living. Leone stages the scene almost silently, and the respective presences of life and death become almost palpable. Jill can only hope for his return to the new world that she is helping to create, once it has fully blossomed. *Someday*, is Harmonica's succinct and wistful answer. And Jill knows that it means *never*.

The second departure scene emphasizes the film's overarching narrative theme, the emergence of a new civilized world and the passing of the Old West, even more pointedly. It harkens back, stylistically, to one of Leone's most profound compositions: Harmonica whittling on a piece of wood and

Frank (center) and Harmonica (right), now the last of an "ancient race" that shaped the frontier, know that there is no place for them in the rapidly civilizing West. *Courtesy of Photofest*

Frank arriving on horseback from afar, framed against the construction of the railroad. This framing crystallizes the film's central conflict—juxtaposing the life of the new industrialized West against the death of the mythical frontier. This shot composition, even grander in scope, concludes the film as well. As the titles appear on screen, Jill walks toward the railroad workers to nourish them with water, fulfilling her role as Earth mother. The camera zooms in, then pans to the right, taking in the spectacle of a new developing civilization, before capturing in the lower right corner of the frame Harmonica's exit with the body of Cheyenne: another victim of the new West, shot by the industrial mogul Morton. Harmonica ascends up a small hill and then slides out of the frame, turning away from the living. He is no longer a ghost from the past. His mission has been fulfilled, and he can move on. The last member of the *ancient race* disappears.

Notes

1. The crossover between the Western and the horror film has notable antecedents, including *Riders of the Whistling Skull* (1937), *Curse of the Undead* (1959), and *Billy the Kid vs. Dracula* (1966). Here, the relation between the two genres was much more pronounced than in *Once Upon a Time in the West*, incorporating distinctive semantic elements from both genres, such as horror personnel (zombies, vampires, and mummies) and the Western landscape. But this trend would not reemerge as its own subgenre until the 1990s with films such as *Grim Prairie Tales* (1990) and *From Dusk Till Dawn* (1996). *Once Upon a Time in the West*'s more subtle approach to the undead is on display in Clint Eastwood's ghost Westerns *High Plains Drifter* (1973), *Pale Rider* (1985), and, to a certain extent, *The Outlaw Josey Wales* (1976).

2. By extension, the Christian notion of the *afterlife* is thus nonexistent. The transcendence of death is part of life in Leone's West—a supernatural act, performed by superhuman agents.

3. Michael Carlson, *Sergio Leone* (Harpenden: Pocket Essentials, 2001), 9.

4. Jim Kitses, *Horizons West: Directing the Western from John Ford to Clint Eastwood* (London: British Film Institute, 2004), 256.

5. Similar to the Greek mythological character of Charon, the ferryman of Hades who helps the souls of the recently deceased cross the river Styx, which divides the world of the living from the world of the dead.

6. The Man with No Name is referred to by other characters in *For a Few Dollars More* as "Manco"—Spanish for "one-armed," and an apparent reference to his habit of performing routine actions with his left hand only in order to keep his gun hand ready for action.

7. Edward Buscombe, *The BFI Companion to the Western* (New York: Da Capo Press, 1988), 254.

8. The title is seen as a reference to Harmonica's wailing musical tunes. In this regard, the creative translation shifts attention from the film's narrative about the end of the Old West and the emergence of civilization to the vengeance plot. When Harmonica plays his eponymous instrument, he communicates a message of death. The title is also inserted in one of the film's crucial scenes: the flashback. Frank's line *Keep your loving brother happy* is not translated literally (*Sorge dafür, dass dein lieber Bruder glücklich bleibt*) but as a reference to the new title (*Spiel mir das Lied vom Tod/Play the Song of Death to Me*). The grammatical form of the imperative classifies the title as Frank's line, but it equally points to the bond between Harmonica and Frank. The two are essentially a dual character, dependent upon one another. Harmonica's only purpose of existence is his revenge. And Frank will be eternally marked by his act against Harmonica.

9. Christopher Frayling, *Sergio Leone: Something to Do with Death* (London: Faber and Faber Limited, 2000), 275.

10. John Fawell, *The Art of Sergio Leone's* Once Upon a Time in the West: *A Critical Appreciation* (Jefferson, NC: McFarland, 2005), 56.

11. Christopher Frayling, *Spaghetti Westerns: Cowboys and Europeans from Karl May to Sergio Leone* (London, New York: I. B. Tauris, 1998), 203.

12. Fawell, *The Art*, 60.

13. This audiovisual motif reappears in Clint Eastwood's ghost Westerns *High Plains Drifter*, *Pale Rider* and, to a certain extent, *The Outlaw Josey Wales* to denote the main character as an avenging angel.

14. Fawell, *The Art*, 120.

15. Mark Sanderson, *Don't Look Now* (London: British Film Institute, 1996), 59; Rosemary Ellen Guiley, *The Encyclopedia of Ghosts and Spirits* (New York: Facts on File, 1992), 135.

Bibliography

Buscombe, Edward. *The BFI Companion to the Western*. New York: Da Capo Press, 1988.

Carlson, Michael. *Sergio Leone*. Harpenden: Pocket Essentials, 2001.

Fawell, John. *The Art of Sergio Leone's* Once Upon a Time in the West: *A Critical Appreciation*. Jefferson, NC: McFarland, 2005.

Frayling, Christopher. *Spaghetti Westerns: Cowboys and Europeans from Karl May to Sergio Leone*. London: I. B. Tauris, 1998.

———. *Sergio Leone: Something to Do with Death*. London: Faber and Faber Limited, 2000.

Guiley, Rosemary Ellen. *The Encyclopedia of Ghosts and Spirits*. New York: Facts on File, 1992.

Kitses, Jim. *Horizons West. Directing the Western from John Ford to Clint Eastwood*. London: British Film Institute, 2004.

Sanderson, Mark. *Don't Look Now*. London: British Film Institute, 1996.

CHAPTER FOURTEEN

Moving West and Beyond

Life in the Midst of Death in Purgatory

Hugh H. Davis

In John Ford's *The Man Who Shot Liberty Valance* (1962), a newspaperman, having discovered the truth about the death of Valance, declines to make it public, declaring: "When the legend becomes fact, print the legend." Ford's film is, in many ways, a meditation on the legacy of the West and its heroes, particularly in the face of those heroes' mortality. Uli Edel's *Purgatory* (1999), a made-for-cable film, is also a meditation on the legacy of the West, but it looks beyond the grave. It views immortality through the dual lenses of the cultural and the supernatural, contrasting its heroes' exalted place in shared memories and Western dime novels with their precarious position in a literal afterlife.

The undead in *Purgatory* simultaneously represent history, legend, and the fading of the Wild West. Outlaws and gunmen in life, they were transformed—while still alive—into larger-than-life heroes by the authors of sensationalistic dime novels. The dime novelists, like the newspaperman in *Liberty Valance*, preferred a good story to the truth. As the historical Wild West passed out of existence and the legendary Wild West took its place, the dime novels' outsized tales became the basis for the legends. The four undead gunfighters in the telefilm have, in this sense, already achieved a form of immortality when the story begins. By stepping from history into legend, they (or distorted images of them) have become part of the legendary West of the dime novels, which will in time become the West of film and television. *Purgatory* focuses, however, on their spiritual journey toward a more literal form of immortality: their quest to spend eternity in heaven rather than hell.

Purgatory differs from most other undead Westerns in that its undead characters are the protagonists, and ultimately, like their dime novel selves, heroes. Even more strikingly, where virtually all other undead Westerns feature the undead returning to the realm of the living—whether seeking redemption, exacting retribution, or mindlessly creating general mayhem—*Purgatory* takes place entirely on a spiritual plane, albeit one that is not revealed as such initially.

"The Rest of You, I'll See in Hell": Reaching Refuge in *Purgatory*

Purgatory is a supernatural saga of redemption and salvation—a fantastic view of a Wild West afterlife experienced by Western legends—but it begins with a conventional image: a gang robbing a bank in a small town and then fleeing after a shootout. On the run and under fire, Blackjack Britton (Eric Roberts) and his men ride through the night and into the next day, losing some of their wounded and all of their stolen money, before plunging through a dust storm and emerging on the outskirts of a town situated in an improbably lush valley.[1] Commenting that "this sure as Hell ain't Mexico," the men decide to follow the path that leads into this seeming oasis, passing by the Gatekeeper (Saginaw Grant)—an Indian sitting by an iron gate in a broken wall—and ending at the church that stands at the center of the town. There they are greeted by Sheriff Forrest (Sam Shepard), who welcomes them to Refuge and offers free drinks in the saloon, free board, free use of the stables, and free medical care from Doc Woods (Randy Quaid). He directs Deputy Glen (Donnie Wahlberg) to help them settle in, and he imposes only one condition in exchange for his hospitality, requesting them not to curse anywhere in Refuge, "'cept for the saloon, of course." The outlaws, believing themselves to be wolves who have stumbled upon a town full of sheep, accept the offer with delight.

The youngest and greenest of them, Sonny Dillard (Brad Rowe), is a dedicated reader of dime novels who hero worships their larger-than-life characters. Through his collection of these well-thumbed pamphlets, Sonny immerses himself in tales of glorious gunslinger heroes whose exploits are enhanced and exaggerated by the authors until the heroes themselves seem indestructible and immortal. Sonny is thus the only member of the gang to recognize any of Refuge's citizens for who they really are. Comparing the faces of Forrest, Glen, and Woods to the illustrations in his beloved dime novels, he realizes that—although they walk the streets of Refuge unarmed, and meet the taunts and threats of Blackjack's increasingly unruly gang with measured words rather than fists or guns—they are, respectively, Western legends Wild Bill Hickok, Billy the Kid, and Doc Holliday. Probing further, he discovers that general-store-owner Brooks (J. D. Souther) and farmer Lamb (John Dennis Johnston) are actually famed outlaw Jesse James and notorious gunfighter Lefty Slade, and that Rose (Amelia Heinle), the girl with whom he is smitten, is Betty McCullough, the first woman hanged in the Arizona territory.[2]

Suspecting that Refuge is a sort of retirement village for old gunslingers, Sonny begins asking more questions. He yells out "Draw!" to the unarmed Doc in order to call him out for his older life, and he is rewarded by the sight of him turning and reaching for a gun he no longer carries. He confronts "Farmer Lamb" while he works his fields, reciting details from the dime novel *The Blazing Guns of Lefty Slade* until the pretense of being a farmer falls away and Lamb/Slade growls that "that fool writer never even talked to me."[3]

Even as Sonny investigates, however, events suggest—to him and to the audience—that there is a supernatural dimension to Refuge. When three of Blackjack's men throw knives at Forrest (who has stepped between them and their target, the front door of the church), two of the blades are deflected, as if by an unseen hand, and the third man is struck dead by a bolt of lightning. The silent old Indian collects his body and carries it away through the wrought-iron gate at the edge of town, and the sky—which had darkened ominously—grows bright again. Newcomers to Refuge who step off a stagecoach later that day include the notorious gambler Dolly Sloan, who now calls herself Ivy (Shannon Kenny) and who died in Sonny's arms during the shootout that followed the gang's botched bank robbery. The coachman (R. G. Armstrong) tells Sheriff Forrest that his time is "about to be up," and he gives him a white rose to wear in his lapel. Farmer Lamb, when members of Blackjack's gang trample his crops beneath their horses' hooves and he kills one of them in a moment of rage, is led away, not to jail by Sheriff Forrest or Deputy Glen, but through the gate and into the mists beyond by the Gatekeeper.

Sonny learns the truth about Refuge only when—having overheard the gang planning to ransack the town, kill everyone who stands in their way, and take all they can carry—he rushes to the church to tell the assembled citizens. "Refuge," Doc explains, "is where the marginally good are gleaned from the hopelessly wicked." Ten years of compliance with its strict rules, Forrest explains, will earn them their reward: an invitation from the Coachman to board the stage that will take them to heaven.[4] The townspeople explain that they cannot fight back against the outlaws, since any act of violence will damn them forever. The significance of Lamb's behavior after his own act of violence—his murderous rage dissolving, in an instant, into despair and anguish—suddenly becomes clear. Having broken the rules of Refuge after eight years of compliance, Lamb woefully followed the Gate-keeper away to meet his fate, mourning not the life of the man he took but his own last chance at redemption, now irretrievably lost to him.

Sonny implores the townspeople to stand up for themselves, but they refuse. Forrest notes that they grow meeker with each moment they stay in the town, making their chances of fighting back slim at best anyway. Determined to defend Refuge alone, if necessary, Sonny goes to face the outlaw gang the following morning, but he finds he has help after all. He is soon joined by Glen, Brooks, and Woods, who discover—to their grim satisfaction—that their reflexes and aim are undiminished by their years in Refuge. The quintet, though badly outnumbered, is victorious, and Sonny—though shot and killed—immediately joins the four legendary gunfighters as an undead citizen of the town. Blackjack falls to Hickok's guns, but, as one of the "irredeemably wicked" for whom there is no place in Refuge, he is taken away by the Gatekeeper and thrown over the cliff's edge that lies beyond the gate and the mists, falling into the fiery canyon below to spend eternity condemned to hell.

Forrest and his partners believe that they, too, have damned themselves by their recent acts of violence, but instead the Coachman invites them to take the stage ride to heaven with him, declaring: "The Creator may be tough, but he ain't blind." Their final scene shows them staring in wonder from the windows of the coach, faces bathed in the white light of a beatific vision as they head to their eternal resting place. Sonny, meanwhile, turns down the Coachman's offer of a ride, instead pinning on Forrest's star and becoming the new sheriff, so that he can spend more time with Rose. Warned that the rules of Refuge are strict, Sonny insists on delaying his journey to heaven, confident that he can help others reach that goal. Having admired the gunslingers for years, Sonny at last has the opportunity to walk in the footsteps of Wild Bill Hickok as the new sheriff in town.

The film is nominally the story of Sonny's salvation. It traces his growing disenchantment with the realities of life as an outlaw; catalogs his acts of kindness, generosity, and respect toward the townspeople; and contrasts his affinity for the legends that abide in Refuge with his growing distance from Blackjack's gang. He is, inevitably, the only member of Blackjack's gang to attempt to follow the town's rules. More significantly, however, he is the only one to listen thoughtfully to their counsel. Indeed, Sonny is the only member of the gang to whom they *offer* such counsel, perhaps because they are aware that he—alone among the gang members—has not yet chosen a life of lawlessness over one of decency and goodness. When the final confrontation inevitably comes, Sonny (just as inevitably) aligns himself with the citizens of Refuge rather than with his fellow gang members. Doing so, he finds himself literally standing alongside his dime-novel heroes—Wild Bill, Billy, Jesse, and Doc—and proves himself worthy of joining their ranks. Both as counselors and as models of how a man should conduct himself in the West, the legendary inhabitants of Refuge are far more compelling to Sonny than are Blackjack and the members of the gang.

Purgatory is also, however, a story about the salvation of the four legendary gunfighters who stand with Sonny in the final showdown. Having lived and died by the gun—and been sent to Purgatory to atone for their less-than-righteous lives—their final steps toward Paradise are, ironically, made in the dusty streets of the town during a final gun battle. Having spent the majority of the film rejecting their past lives and even their old names, they triumph only when they embrace their legendary reputations. Their defense of the town of Refuge links their status as established heroes in the world of the living with their roles as heroes in the purgatorial world of the undead, and so completes their salvation.

Ultimately, however, the two stories of salvation—that of Sonny, and that of his undead heroes—converge. Sonny's salvation is made possible through his hero worship, for he desires for his life to match the glorious stories he has read in his dime novels, and he rises to the defense of Refuge in emulation of them. His understanding of heroism comes from his reading about, and his understanding of, these mythic Western figures, and his understanding is defined in terms of the mythic West. As the moral compass in this film, the innately good Sonny reminds the viewers of humanity's potential for redemption. Just as Wild Bill and Doc served on the side of the law but had shady pasts and cut violent paths through the West, Sonny is a member of Blackjack's gang who ultimately joins with the side of the law in Refuge. Like Billy and Jesse, who were outlaws but reputed to serve the people, Sonny is a bank robber who protects the town of Refuge from the oppression of Blackjack and his partners. It is only with the Coachman's final benediction—"The Creator may be tough"—that Sonny and his heroes realize how crucial such distinctions are.

"The Creator May Be Tough, But He Ain't Blind": Finding Salvation in *Purgatory*

Legend is deeply intertwined with the heroes' search for salvation in *Purgatory*. It is—however complex and even inconsistently presented from character to character—reality for them. The film's presentation of Jesse James and Billy the Kid as capable of redemption is clearly tied to legends that portrayed them as Robin Hood figures, committing crimes but helping those in need. Wild Bill Hickok's exploits—easily mythologized by writers, first of dime novels and then of movie and television scripts—allowed him to be cast as a heroic lawman of the plains despite also having notoriety as a gambler and gunfighter. Doc Holliday, also a gambler and gunslinger, achieved his greatest fame through his association with his friend, the equally mythologized Wyatt Earp, and for his exploits in the gunfight at the O.K. Corral. While *Purgatory* does not cite any specific legend for these heroes, their reputations rest in the background throughout the film. Sonny knows the claims made about them, and, although they insist the plots of the dime novels are more fiction than truth, they prove worthy of these reputations through their participation in the climactic gunfight. Billy, Jesse, Wild Bill, and Doc step into and fulfill the role of Western antihero, embracing their cultural immortality in order to claim their spiritual immortality. While they may have strayed from the path of the righteous in their lives, they find the path to salvation in the afterlife by confirming and taking on the expectations placed upon them as a result of their reputations. They claim redemption thanks to their acceptance of their legends. Early in the film, they deny and act contrary to these expectations, but they achieve their eternal reward through their glorious evocation of Western archetypes.

Purgatory further enhances these legends, bringing them to life—particularly in the climactic gunfight—and suggesting that the four undead gunfighters exemplify the heroic Code of the West. The gunfighters save the day, and their souls, by embracing rather than hiding their legendary talents, and so earn their redemption and salvation. The climactic gunfight also brings to life, for modern viewers, the dime-novel representations of the four as folk heroes. Sonny first recognizes these undead legends from the illustrations he has seen of them, and—thanks to the film's casting—viewers can readily connect their portrayals in the film to earlier pop-culture images. Visually, J. D. Souther recalls the most famous picture of Jesse James, and Donnie Wahlberg actually is more reminiscent of Billy the Kid than most of the actors cast in the role.[5] Sam Shepard and Randy Quaid, though they do not look like the most familiar images of their characters, evoke images of them in other ways. Shepard lacks Hickok's long hair and moustache, but he wears his twin guns in reversed holsters with the butts forward: a quirk that has, in popular culture, become Hickok's trademark. Quaid is taller and broader-shouldered than the tubercular Holliday, but his immaculate vest, frock coat, and walking stick—a uniform worn by many gamblers and gunslingers, but particularly favored by the Georgia-born dentist—recalls a legacy of actors tackling the role of the tormented character.[6] Each of these figures is an extension of his own legend, magnified in the undead town of Refuge.

The gunslingers' reputations are burnished by the final gunfight, both because they win against seemingly impossible odds and because they risk their souls by even taking part. Knowing the rules of Refuge and the price for breaking them—and having just seen both reinforced as Lefty was led away by the Gatekeeper—engaging the Britton gang in battle was an enormous and potentially damning risk. Their generosity and bravery in taking that risk, coupled with the fact that they take up their guns in the name of defending Refuge and in the name of Right allows them entry into paradise. Their actions in life were morally ambiguous, but the legends that grew up around them in life, inspiring the imaginations of reader and viewers alike, cast them in heroic lights. The final showdown in *Purgatory* represents the moment where, at last, their actions—reflective of their true selves—align with their larger-than-life heroic images. Their actions in the film also confirm and extend their legends, reinforcing their status as iconic Western heroes who inspire the imagination.[7]

Purgatory burnishes its heroes' reputations and further taps into viewers' collective imagination of the Wild West by evoking of imagery from earlier Western films.[8] Forrest's decision to stay in town and face the outlaw gang rather than leave on the stage—shadowed by the suspicion that he is condemning himself to hell—echoes Marshal Will Kane's (Gary Cooper) decision in *High Noon* (1952) to stand and face the Miller gang rather than board the train with his new bride. Forrest's symbolic confirmation of the decision—removing the Coachman's white rose from his lapel and dropping it into the dirt—is a visual quotation of the end of *High Noon*, when Kane drops his tin star in the dust and walks away. Forrest's dark hat, Western string tie, and vest (adorned with his badge) recall the ensemble worn by Kane throughout the older film, and—like Kane—he conveys a deep weariness that gives him considerable gravitas. Forest's reluctance to strap on the guns he believed he had hung up forever is, like Kane's, tinged with regret rather than anticipation or excitement. Where Kane merely fears that his life with Amy will be cut short in the gunfight, however, Forrest—as one of the undead—worries that using his guns will condemn him in the eyes of God and bring damnation. Both films feature pivotal scenes with the townspeople meeting inside the church. While the church is the center of the town in *Purgatory*, the church scene is the center of the narrative in *High Noon*, the critical point in which the town leaves Kane to face the outlaws on his own.

Forrest's moral dilemma evokes Kane's in *High Noon*, but—unlike Kane— he does not have to face the outlaw gang alone. Rather, as in Howard Hawks's

After living for nearly a decade in Refuge as mild-mannered, nonviolent "Sheriff Forrest," Wild Bill Hickok reclaims his true identity, and his immortal soul, by strapping on his guns in order to defend the town. *Courtesy of Photofest*

Rio Bravo (1959)—a Western made as a deliberate response to *High Noon*—he is backed by an eccentric, but capable, band of assistants. Outgunned and outnumbered by an outlaw gang determined to break their leader out of his jail, Sheriff John T. Chance (John Wayne) is prepared to face the assault on his own, but he is joined by three deputies: aging, hobbled Stumpy (Walter Brennan); young, impulsive Colorado (Ricky Nelson); and alcoholic Dude (Dean Martin). Forrest—knowing the risk he is taking by facing Blackjack's gang—refuses to ask for help from his friends, but, like Chance in *Rio Bravo*, he is joined by them at the last moment. Brooks/James, though much younger and healthier than Stumpy, is similarly regarded by the outlaws as weak and unthreatening (he is, until the final showdown, the least confrontational of the four). The impulsive Glen/Billy, who has to be calmed down more than once by Forrest when he wants to challenge Blackjack's men, is strongly reminiscent of Colorado.[9] Finally, like Dude, Doc Woods/Holliday struggles with the lure of drinking, telling Blackjack and his men he has given up alcohol. Whereas Dude is sobered up by Chance for the final battle in *Rio Bravo*, Doc—matching the archetype of the hard-drinking gunslinger, personified in the Doc Holliday of legend—joins the gunfight with a bottle in his hand.[10] Drinking is against the rules of Refuge, but Doc, presumably thinking he is already damned for fighting, returns to the bottle as well.[11]

Purgatory's evocation of and allusions to *High Noon* and *Rio Bravo* further link it to a line of Western and Western-influenced films. Hawks and Wayne twice remade *Rio Bravo*, first as *El Dorado* (1966) and then as *Rio Lobo* (1970). John Carpenter remade it twice more, using it as inspiration for the urban crime drama *Assault on Precinct 13* (1976), itself remade and updated in 2005, and then for the science-fiction horror story *Ghosts of Mars* (2001). The film was also reset in modern-day France as *The Nest* (2002). *High Noon*, in turn, was remade in 1981 as the science-fiction thriller *Outland*, set in a mining colony on one of Jupiter's moons, and it also influenced numerous other films. *Purgatory's* refitting of both stories into a fantasy-Western returns them to their roots while reconsidering the Western archetypes by setting them against a supernatural plane and suggesting possibilities for the Western as an afterlife drama. *Purgatory* evokes and appropriates tropes and ideas from a tapestry of Westerns, bringing together a variety of allusions and archetypes. These archetypes begin with the historical West but rapidly grow from a succession of dime novels, films, television series, and other legends. The characters in *Purgatory* represent and embody the archetypes of the Old West, using those character types to convey a parable for redemption.

"Most Moving Human Encounters": Determining Dantean Echoes in *Purgatory*

Purgatory, as a fantasy-Western, connects its characters not only to the long tradition of earlier Westerns but also to stories of the undead in the afterlife. Just as *High Noon* is a Western version of the medieval morality play *Everyman*, with Will Kane serving as Everyman, *Purgatory* is a Western version of Dante's *Divine Comedy*, with Sonny getting his tour of the afterlife and meeting the undead spirits of some of his heroes. Dante's epic poem has been adapted many times, but those adaptations have primarily focused on cantos from the *Inferno* canticle, showing elements of hell in a fantastic setting. Most Dantean adaptations showcase hell and dramatize elements of this aspect of the afterlife, showing sinners being punished and tormented. A few productions bring in aspects from *Paradiso*, showing the glories of heaven, but the adaptations of *The Divine Comedy* do not, with the exception of Edel's film-for-cable, recreate elements from *Purgatorio*. Despite being possibly "Dante's most original creation,"[12] the poet's Purgatory is the least-considered aspect of the tripart epic. Although it does not directly cite Dante, this film represents one of the few popular cultural representations of the middle canticle.

While Refuge is not on a mountain, like Dante's Purgatory, it is on a "solitary plain,"[13] and its lush greenness recalls the "eternally fruitful" slopes of the literary Purgatory.[14] Not a "genuine fortified city," it has a gateway guarded by an angel[15]—as the iron gate outside Refuge is guarded by the supernatural Gatekeeper—and is a place "simple, regular, and serene."[16] As Kevin Brownlee points out, the pagan Virgil, who has the role of gatekeeper, has no actual knowledge of Purgatory, so he serves as "no more than a silent witness to the entrance" to the Earthly Paradise. The mute Gatekeeper in the film takes a similar stance, regulating passage through the gate but offering no comment.[17] While the souls in *Purgatorio* "are all saved, and eager to act in accordance with divine will, [so] there is no place among them for violence, malice, fraud, rebelliousness, etc.," the souls in *Purgatory* are not all saved but have the rules of Refuge upon them, keeping them in line as they serve their penance.[18] The souls in Refuge are poised between heaven and hell and could potentially go to either, unlike the souls in Dante's epic, so they must behave with care to avoid damnation. The canyon of fire outside of Refuge, shown at the end of the film, when the Gatekeeper deposits Blackjack and his chief henchman in it, evokes the cliff that divides Ante-Purgatory from Purgatory proper, as well as the wall of fire that separates Purgatory and Eden in Dante's geography. The intense fire to which the Gatekeeper takes lost souls recalls how "from the inner wall, flames blast the ledge" in Dante's poem.[19] Taking its cue from medieval philosophy and Dantean poetry that Purgatory is a physical place, *Purgatory* depicts an adventure "that's west of the Pecos . . . and south of Eternity."[20]

That physical setting, the town of Refuge, is the center of this Bangsian Western.[21] Sonny, on his path to redemption, takes the role of Dante journeying through the afterlife, meeting some of his heroes. Just as the entire *Divine Comedy* is built on a series of extended encounters with the four Latin poets Virgil, Statius, Lucan, and Ovid—all heroes to Dante—*Purgatory* is built on Sonny's extended encounters with the four gunslingers who inspire him. Just as the poets provide "metonymic representations" of their own texts and "are used to comment on them, either implicitly or explicitly," so, too, do these gunslingers offer similar representations of their own legends, providing commentary on their legacies.[22] The gunmen, like the poets, are presented in the afterlife as figures with reputations and personas that precede them, and *Purgatory* is a meditation on how these men interact with and deal with their legacies; *Purgatorio* is likewise, in part, a meditation on

Dante's *Purgatorio*, engraving by Gustave Doré.

the legacies of these poets. Sonny, like Dante, encounters his idols and must reconcile his expectations of them with the reality of meeting them.

While Dante claims a textual model for *Purgatorio* through the use of *The Aeneid* (although its role as a literal model ends with the conclusion of *Inferno*), Sonny's collection of dime novels provides a guide for Sonny's path to heroism and redemption as he emulates the models he has so voraciously read. *Purgatorio* posits that man is born with an intense desire and natural thirst for knowledge, and Sonny's interest in his heroes' stories reveals his humanity.[23] Jesse/Brooks tries to steer Sonny away from dime novels, recommending "the classics," as he ironically pushes for reading that might not evoke his own memory, but Sonny remains focused on reading about his heroes. Dante finds his pattern through "recuperative reading" of Virgil; Sonny has redemptive reading about the gunfighters who populate his heroic pantheon.[24]

The redemptive story of *Purgatory* is also noteworthy for its use of this stage of the afterlife. By evoking this intermediate state, one that exists for the purgation of the soul, this fantasy Western allows for the salvation of its characters, many of whom are the iconic heroes of the West and the Western genre itself. While all Westerns are about redemption, *Purgatory*, with its supernatural setting and effects, is redemption made manifest. Most undead Westerns feature unnatural creatures such as vampires or zombies returning to and interacting with the world of the living. Those times the Western ventures into more spiritual (as opposed to simply supernatural) realms, the emphasis is primarily on hell and never on Purgatory, ignoring more potentially redemptive stories. Clint Eastwood's character in *Pale Rider* (1985), for example, serves as an avenging angel or demon, seeking to enact revenge on corrupt townspeople, but, despite his (seemingly clerical) collar and the fact that the people call him Preacher, he never offers absolution.

Purgatory suggests that even the seemingly unsalvageable characters—gamblers like Hickok and Holliday, outlaws like Billy the Kid and Jesse James—may find absolution. While, from a religious standpoint, those in Purgatory suffer intensely through "privation of God," their liminal status provides an opportunity for atonement prior to receiving eternal reward, and thus they assume eventual absolution and salvation.[25] The fact that the souls of the "marginally good," as Doc labels them, are *in* Purgatory means that they "died in a state of grace."[26] The town of Refuge is defined as a transitional stage for the undead, with Edel's film offering that these legends of the West will and can find their final reward. Like the afterlife of C. S. Lewis's *The Great Divorce*, the opportunity for absolution exists through "a stripping-away of comforting spiritual baggage like selfishness or sexual desire."[27] The rules of Refuge are strict, but they act as a tool to strip away that baggage. Those who can abide by the rules—leaving their earthly weaknesses behind, as Jesse and Billy do their wrathfulness, Doc his thirst for whiskey, and Hickok his pride—can find salvation. Those who cannot—like Lefty Slade, who loses everything in a fatal moment of weakness—have only themselves (not the Creator) to blame.

Just as the souls in Dante's *Purgatorio* desire "to be remembered in the prayers" of those left behind, the souls in Edel's *Purgatory* desire to be remembered through their legends and legacies.[28] These souls seek happiness and freedom, breaking free of the temptations that once plagued them in the mortal coil, and these souls "remain *in via*, as needy of guidance and instruction as those who still live on earth."[29] The heroes of Refuge believe they are on a path to redemption because they are following its well-defined rules, but the arrival of Blackjack's gang forces them to reach beyond the certainties of those rules and trust themselves to do the right thing as they take charge of their own fate. Guided by Sonny's words and actions, they finally reach their heavenly goal, uniting in one final gunfight as they embrace their legacies as legends of the gun—not for selfish reasons, but for the greater good. If "reunion is one of *Purgatorio*'s great themes," it also drives *Purgatory*.[30] Forrest, Glen, Woods, and Brooks wish to be restored to their loved ones in eternity and to find immortality in heaven as part of a celestial reunion. In the streets of Refuge, they come together as men on a mission, uniting as defenders of the common good. Hatcher notes that Dante's poem reveals "the purgatorial process as a quest for personal justice," and these men complete their quests with one last, combined effort for justice and glory.[31]

Throughout the story, Refuge is defined by community. Betty/Rose introduces Dolly/Ivy to the rest of Refuge and helps orient her to the town's ways/rules; Wild Bill/Forrest repeatedly watches out for Billy/Glen and stops him from committing violence; the townspeople show compassion and empathy for the fallen Lefty/Lamb. When the church bell tolls, calling the townspeople to their daily communion within, they urge one another toward the doors, knowing they must be inside before the last peal of the bell sounds. Even the outlaws—strangers with rough manners and suspect stories of hardship—are offered hospitality befitting long-lost friends, without hesitation. Sonny, though still living, proves himself a worthy citizen of Refuge by offering help to its citizens without ever being asked. His instinctive understanding of community is proof that he is fundamentally good. Just as Rachel Jacoff finds *Purgatorio*'s "most moving human encounters" to come in "its images of friendship," Edel's *Purgatory* powerfully presents moments of friendship among Refuge's townsfolk.[32]

The citizens of Refuge may have all died, but their undead lives continue, as they prepare for eternity. Heroes of the mortal world, they are immortal legends of the West. Through their tale of redemption and salvation, they extend their legacies and enhance their own legends. The story of the killer of Liberty Valance is a legend that, as the newspaperman understands, needs to be in print. The stories of the gunfighters who stop Blackjack Britton's gang in *Purgatory*, begun in dime novels and continued through the annals of print, film, and television Westerns, continue to be told and retold. *Purgatory* simultaneously recalls their figurative immortality in culture and popular memory and reveals their literal immortality in the afterlife. Forrest, Glen, Woods, and Brooks, along with Sonny, claim their places in eternity through their fantastic purification to a state of grace. Having lived their mortal lives as legends of the gun, their immortal lives come from their sacrifice in the name of others' lives. They are willing to die—potentially sacrificing eternal paradise—to stop evil, and therein they claim their true immortality.

Notes

1. While being pursued, Blackjack goads his men to escape, saying, "Any man who can keep up with me, I'll see you in Chihuahua. The rest of you, I'll see you in Hell."

2. Slade and McCullough, like Dolly Sloan, are fictional characters, but, as citizens of Refuge, they represent legendary figures of the Wild West, immortalized in the popular fiction Sonny reads and collects.

3. While Lefty Slade is fictional, he may be based on Jack Slade, a lawman known for a violent feud with Jules Reni. Slade, who is featured in Mark Twain's *Roughing It*, was reputedly quite sadistic, befitting the violent murder Lamb commits in this film. See John Whalen, "Slade: Six-Gun Sadist," in *The Big Book of the Weird Wild West* (New York: Paradox Press, 1998), 52–53.

4. The ten-year rule might be more a suggestion or a round number than a set rule. Forrest says that he has been sheriff for "the better part of ten years," but Hickok died in 1876, eleven years before Doc Holliday's death, so, for the two to be in Refuge together, Hickok would have to have been dead for more than ten years. However, Dolly Sloan does die a few days before her stage arrives in the town, so time may pass mysteriously in this plane.

5. The short, squarely built Wahlberg's rounded face more closely approximates the historical Billy than such leading men as Johnny Mack Brown, Robert Taylor, Paul Newman, Kris Kristofferson, and Val Kilmer.

6. Ironically, Quaid's brother Dennis played Holliday in *Wyatt Earp* (1994), contributing to the lineage.

7. Jacoff suggests that Dante's *Purgatorio* is deeply resonant in its exploration of the human imagination. Rachel Jacoff, "*The Divine Comedy*: Texts and Contexts," in *Approaches to Teaching Dante's* Divine Comedy, ed. Carole Slade (New York: MLA, 2001), 81.

8. One direct connection *Purgatory* makes to the cinematic West comes through the casting of R. G. Armstrong as the Coachman. Armstrong, who makes one of his final screen appearances in Edel's film, often appeared in Westerns during his long film career, including several of Sam Peckinpah's films that were considerations on the end of the Wild West. In several of his roles, Armstrong played religious figures, just as in *Purgatory* the Coachman serves as a representative of the Creator/God.

9. As noted above, Sonny also represents the archetype of The Kid in this film.

10. Woods, who serves as the physician, not simply the dentist, of Refuge also evokes Doc Boone (Thomas Mitchell) in *Stagecoach* (1939), another iconic and archetypal Western film character, the hard-drinking doctor.

11. The film does not explain why the town then has a saloon, nor does it explain why the General Store stocks bullets in a town in which the residents do not carry guns and should not be shooting them.

12. Jeffrey T. Schnapp, "Introduction to *Purgatorio*," in *The Cambridge Companion to Dante*, ed. Rachel Jacoff (Cambridge: Cambridge University Press, 2001), 192.

13. Gaetano Cipolla, "An Introduction to Dante's *Divine Comedy*," in *Approaches to Teaching Dante's* Divine Comedy, ed. Carole Slade (New York: MLA, 2001), 92.

14. Schnapp, "Introduction to *Purgatorio*," 193.

15. Schnapp, "Introduction to *Purgatorio*," 193.

16. Archibald T. MacAllister, introduction to *Purgatorio*, by Dante Alighieri (New York: Signet, 2001), xiv.

17. Kevin Brownlee, "Dante and the Classical Poets," in *The Cambridge Companion to Dante*, ed. Rachel Jacoff (Cambridge: Cambridge University Press, 2001), 104.

18. MacAllister, introduction, xv.

19. Dante Aligheri, *The Purgatorio*, trans. John Ciardi (New York: Signet, 2001), 257.

20. Text from the back cover of the *Purgatory* DVD case.

21. Also called a posthumous or afterlife fantasy, a Bangsian fantasy, named after John Kendrick Bangs, is "a fantasy of the afterlife in which the ghosts of various famous men and women come together" for adventures. Jess Nevins, *Heroes & Monsters: The Unofficial Companion to the* League of Extraordinary Gentlemen (Austin, TX: Monkeybrain Books, 2003), 179.

22. Brownlee, "Dante and the Classical Poets," 100.

23. Giovanni Cecchetti, "An Introduction to Dante's *Divine Comedy*," in *Approaches to Teaching Dante's* Divine Comedy, ed. Carole Slade (New York: MLA, 2001), 48.

24. Brownlee, "Dante and the Classical Poets," 105.

25. George Brantl, ed., *Catholicism* (New York: George Braziller, 1962), 232.

26. Robert C. Broderick, *The Catholic Encyclopedia* (Nashville: Thomas Nelson, 1986), 502.

27. David Langford, "Purgatory," in *Encyclopedia of Fantasy*, ed. John Clute and John Grant (New York: St. Martin's Press, 1999), 792.

28. Schnapp, "Introduction to *Purgatorio*," 197.

29. Peter S. Hawkins, "Dante and the Bible," in *The Cambridge Companion to Dante*, ed. Rachel Jacoff (Cambridge: Cambridge University Press, 2001), 125.

30. Schnapp, "Introduction to *Purgatorio*," 197.

31. Elizabeth R. Hatcher, "The *Purgatorio* as a Unit in a Medieval Literature Course," in *Approaches to Teaching Dante's* Divine Comedy, ed. Carole Slade (New York: MLA, 2001), 118.

32. Jacoff, "*The Divine Comedy*: Texts and Contexts," 81.

Bibliography

Alighieri, Dante. *The Purgatorio*. Translated by John Ciardi. New York: Signet, 2001.

Brantl, George, ed. *Catholicism*. Great Religions of Modern Man Series, Richard A. Gard, general editor. New York: George Braziller, 1962.

Broderick, Robert C. *The Catholic Encyclopedia, revised and updated edition*. Nashville: Thomas Nelson, 1986.

Brownlee, Kevin. "Dante and the Classical Poets." In *The Cambridge Companion to Dante*, edited by Rachel Jacoff, 100–19. Cambridge: Cambridge University Press, 2001.

Cecchetti, Giovanni. "An Introduction to Dante's *Divine Comedy*." In *Approaches to Teaching Dante's* Divine Comedy, edited by Carole Slade, 38–54. New York: MLA, 2001.

Cipolla, Gaetano. "An Archetypal Approach to Teaching the *Divine Comedy*." In *Approaches to Teaching Dante's* Divine Comedy, edited by Carole Slade, 87–93. New York: MLA, 2001.

Hatcher, Elizabeth R. "The *Purgatorio* as a Unit in a Medieval Literature Course." In *Approaches to Teaching Dante's* Divine Comedy, edited by Carole Slade, 115–21. New York: MLA, 2001.

Hawkins, Peter S. "Dante and the Bible." In *The Cambridge Companion to Dante*, edited by Rachel Jacoff, 120–35. Cambridge: Cambridge University Press, 2001.

Jacoff, Rachel. "*The Divine Comedy*: Texts and Contexts." In *Approaches to Teaching Dante's* Divine Comedy, edited by Carole Slade, 79–86. New York: MLA, 2001.

Langford, David. "Purgatory." In *Encyclopedia of Fantasy*, edited by John Clute and John Grant, 792. New York: St. Martin's Press, 1999.

MacAllister, Archibald T. Introduction to *Purgatorio*, by Dante Alighieri, translated by John Ciardi, ix–xxiii. New York: Signet, 2001.

Nevins, Jess. *Heroes & Monsters: The Unofficial Companion to* The League of Extraordinary Gentlemen. Austin, TX: Monkeybrain Books, 2003.

Purgatory. Directed by Uli Edel. 1999. Los Angeles, CA: Warner Home Video, 2005. DVD.

Schnapp, Jeffrey T. "Introduction to *Purgatorio*." In *The Cambridge Companion to Dante*, edited by Rachel Jacoff, 192–207. Cambridge: Cambridge University Press, 2001.
Whalen, John. "Six-Gun Sadist." In *The Big Book of the Weird Wild West*. New York: Paradox Press, 1998.

CHAPTER FIFTEEN

"You Nasty Thing from Beyond the Dead"

Elvis and JFK versus The Mummy in Bubba Ho-Tep

Hannah Thompson

"How does an ancient Egyptian wind up in an East Texas rest home, and why is he writing on the shit-house walls, man?" an elderly Elvis Presley—*the* Elvis Presley—asks while coming to terms with the reality of an animated Egyptian mummy stalking the nursing home in which he is living. His friend, Jack, a black man who believes himself to be John F. Kennedy (played by Ossie Davis), nonchalantly replies that the mummy likely got bored in the bathroom and began doodling. "He probably wrote on pyramid walls centuries ago," he states by way of explanation. This exchange between Elvis (Bruce Campbell), and Jack serves to underline the contradiction in *Bubba Ho-Tep* (2002) between the East, in the form of the mummy, and the Western setting and characters. The film mashes the genres of mummy film and Western, drawing its major plot outlines from the horror-adventure tradition and its characterizations from tales of the frontier. The blending works to undermine both genres, destabilizing the sexual identities that define the traditional Western and dislocating the typical physical site of the mummy film.

The film weaves a story of camaraderie, conquest, and redemption as it portrays Elvis and Jack's heroic battle against the undead predator that is killing their fellow residents. Initially distracted by his own problems—disease, loneliness, and his inability to convince anyone of his real identity—Elvis does not realize that something is terribly wrong in the Shady Rest nursing home. He is oblivious to the death of a fellow resident at the hands of the mummy and to her pleas for help while being dragged down the hall. When another resident, who dresses like the Lone Ranger and calls himself "Kemosabe,"

Elvis and Jack recover their lost masculinity, and discover a sense of purpose, when they join forces to defend their East Texas nursing home against an undead Egyptian mummy in *Bubba Ho-Tep*.

cryptically warns of the mummy's presence—"Under the bridge. I saw him under the bridge!"—Elvis dismisses him as delusional. Only after Kemosabe dies mysteriously and he himself is attacked by a palm-sized scarab beetle—a bug "the size of a peanut butter and banana sandwich"—does he begin his journey from passive observer to hero. Fighting off the scarab with the cutlery

"Kemosabe" is among the first to warn of the mummy's presence, and among its first victims, but his iconic mask helps to provide the "mucho mojo" that protects Elvis during the final battle.

left on his dinner tray, he emerges with a new sense of purpose. Jack, his only remaining friend, uses his knowledge of hieroglyphics and his personal experience with the mummy to identify their enemy: "What we have here at Shady Rest is an Egyptian soul-sucker of some sort. You know, a mummy hiding out, coming in here, feeding on the sleeping."

A hallway encounter with the mummy cures Elvis of any lingering doubts, and it fills in some of the creature's backstory. A few seconds of eye contact with the mummy transmits flashbacks between the pair, allowing Elvis to "see" both the mummy's demise in ancient Egypt and circumstances that delivered him, reanimated, to the rest home. Unable to convince the nursing home administrators of the danger to the residents, Elvis and Jack join forces to defeat the mummy, a battle of wits that results in a final moonlight showdown. Their plan goes awry, and Jack dies of a heart attack, but Elvis—though mortally injured—destroys the mummy (dousing it with gasoline and setting it on fire) before succumbing to his own wounds. A celestial sign assures him that "All Is Well"—his own soul is safe, those of the mummy's victims are released—and, muttering, "thank you; thank you very much," he, too, dies.

Bubba Ho-Tep follows the general plot lines of earlier mummy films, going back to the genre-defining *The Mummy* (1932), which in turn recapitulated themes already developed in Victorian literature focused on mummies and ancient Egyptian curses.[1] At the beginning of the film, a black-and-white clip of a royal mummy being removed from his tomb conveys the initial defilement of the mummy who later imperils Elvis, Jack, and their fellow residents. Such defilements are routinely cited in mummy films as the triggers of curses, and evidence of the arrogance of archaeologists who do not, despite explicit warnings, believe in their power. The use of this plot motif establishes a tension between scientific/rational understandings of the world and the mysterious/magical realm invoked by ancient Egyptian practice, whether real or created for a Western audience.

At the same time, the film's outward markings establish it as a Western, fitting with the relocation of its action from the usual Egypt/London axis to Texas. The mummy—"some kind of Bubba Ho-Tep," Elvis says after coming face-to-face with him—is overtly Westernized, wearing cowboy boots, spurs, and a Stetson hat. Bubba Ho-Tep's unorthodox methods of soul removal from the elderly in the rest home highlight the challenge he presents to the hypermasculinity typically found in the Western cowboy film: a horror of homosexuality in a homosocial environment. Mummies, according to Jack, can consume souls through any orifice on the body. However, this particular mummy prefers to suck them from the anus, to Elvis and Jack's horror. Elvis begins the movie emasculated, impotent, and questioning his own identity, but he regains his masculinity in the face of the threat of the soul-devouring mummy in time to defeat it and die a tragic, heroic death with his soul (and anus) intact, thus avoiding any suspicion of homosexuality.

Historical Mummy Narratives

The long tradition of mummy tales to which *Bubba Ho-Tep* (partly) belongs has its roots in nineteenth-century Europe's growing interest in the culture of ancient Egypt, rooted both in Egypt's sheer antiquity and in the exotic unfamiliarity of its culture. Mummies, more than any other portable arti-fact, exemplified the exoticism and spectacle of Egyptian culture. Victorian Britain—a society with its own elaborate burial rituals and culture of death and mourning—viewed them with particular fascination, but also with trepi-dation. The lines dividing archaeology from art collecting were vague, and frequently crossed: museums and private collectors alike freely plundered Egypt for antiquities, or paid others to do it for them. Mummies, however, were different. Unique among Egyptian artifacts, and indeed among virtu-ally *all* ancient artifacts, they had once been alive. That, alone, complicated their status and made attitudes toward them a complex mingling of delight and dread.

The stories Europeans told about mummies reflected those complex at-titudes. These tales were popularized in the late nineteenth century as a reaction to the increase in contact between European cultures, particularly Victorian Britain, and Egyptian monuments, artifacts, and mummies.[2] They also reflected contemporaneous tensions between the scientific, Christian, and spiritualist communities by emphasizing the possibility of the contin-ued existence of souls.[3] The Victorian fictions featured motifs that modern readers can easily recognize from popular movies, such as deadly curses and ambulatory mummies, but there was—broadly speaking—one major differ-ence: the mummies of many of these early stories were sympathetic, such as the "poor little mummy" referred to in Louisa May Alcott's tale.[4] A mummy described in Jane Austin's "After Three Thousand Years" had "a rare loveli-ness of the days gone" as she lay naked on the ground after her wrappings were slit open "from neck to heel" and "turn[ed] . . . back like the covers of a box."[5] The reader was meant to identify, in these stories, with the mummy, whose eternal rest was disturbed and whose body was defiled, rather than with the modern victims of ancient curses.

Popular interest in Egyptian archaeology emerged in parallel with Euro-pean imperialism in the Middle East, and both reached a peak in the decades after World War I.[6] As a result, imperialist and scientific thought gradually overrode concerns over the treatment of the dead, particularly the ancient dead buried in imperial colonies. When archaeologist Howard Carter discovered the undisturbed tomb of the pharaoh Tutankhamun in 1922, there was no question that the tomb would be opened, the contents removed, and the mummy removed from its sarcophagi, and closely studied. When several members of the expedition—including its patron, Lord Carnarvon—died under mysterious circumstances, however, rumors of a "curse" quickly spread. The supposed "curse of Tutankhamun," however, was not a tangible thing that could be stopped by battling it or otherwise destroying it; it had to run its course, claiming the lives of all those responsible for desecrating the tomb. Ambulatory mummies were another matter, and over the next few decades, mummy films used the creatures as undead manifestations of ancient curses, fully completing the transformation of mummies from passive victims to menacing creatures that had to be physically destroyed in order to be stopped. Mummies came to be treated as aggressive and violent anachronisms. Jasmine Day notes that by attacking contemporary figures, the mummies hindered the progress of science and the collection of knowledge: "As archaeology became desirable, mummies' antagonism towards the living was no longer accepted. The dead were sacred, but ancient Egyptians were only pagans and impeded the treasure hunt."[7]

This transplantation of ancient Egyptian artifacts and mummies from their burial places to the global West—typically to London—is common in many mummy fictions, from nineteenth-century literature to 1930s and 1940s film. In both Alcott's and Austin's tales, the mechanism of the curse (ancient seeds and a stolen necklace, respectively) is transported from the tomb to London.[8] In mummy films, modern explorers or scientists disrespect the wishes of the ancient deceased to leave their burial place unmolested, activating the curse or otherwise setting events into motion to awaken the mummy. The violent events in The Mummy and its quasi-remake The Mummy's Hand (1940), for example, are the result of archaeologists violating a sealed tomb. The deaths in The Mummy's Tomb (1942) and subsequent American sequels are triggered by the removal of a mummy and associated artifacts to the United States, and those in Hammer Studios' The Mummy (1959) and its sequels by their removal to England. The discovery and opening of the tomb frequently occupies a significant portion of these films and explains the source of the mummy's ire; in The Mummy's Hand, for example, the mummy Kharis, kept alive throughout the centuries to protect the tomb of Ananka, is awakened when it is violated by archaeologists. Subsequent films in the Universal Pictures mummy series centered around Kharis—The Mummy's Tomb, The Mummy's Ghost (1944), and *The Mummy's Curse* (1944)—and use flashbacks to the tomb discovery in *Hand* to reiterate the disrespect for the burial places of the ancient Egyptians.

Western fascination with ancient Egypt was rekindled in the late 1970s and again three decades later by the touring exhibitions that brought artifacts from Tutankhamun's tomb to museums in the United States. Renewed popular interest led to a fresh round of fiction and film about ancient Egyptian curses and marauding mummies, proof of the tale's enduring power.

Ancient Egypt Meets Eastern Texas

Bubba Ho-Tep carefully adapts the conventions of its cinematic predecessors to its East Texas setting. As in earlier films, flashbacks reveal the desecration of an ancient Egyptian tomb that sets the stage for the mummy attacks, showing Bubba Ho-Tep carted from museum to museum, put on display for the general public, and eventually loaded into the baggage compartment of a bus that skids off a rain-slicked road and crashes into a creek near the Shady Rest nursing home, breaking open the sarcophagus and releasing him. Elvis, JFK, and the home's other residents are not, themselves, at fault, having played no role in the desecration of the tomb or the removal of the mummy. They were attacked simply because they happened to be nearby when the mummy awoke, hungry for souls. They are—in effect—punished for the transgressions of those who plundered the sacred spaces of ancient Egypt and turned the sanctified dead into objects of curiosity to be gawked at. According to Jasmine Day, these "sins" are not limited to simple physical violation of the tombs, but they derive from an overarching cultural arrogance: "claims to authority, blind faith in logic and the treatment of mummies as objects."[9] Bubba Ho-Tep, the flashbacks reveal, was clearly treated as an object—treatment that symbolizes the arrogance and pride of the global West. The nursing home administration shows a similar imperiousness in action: first in their rejection of Elvis and Jack's identities, and then in their dismissal of Elvis's story about the scarab beetle that attacked him. The administrators' blinkered devotion to Western-style "rationality" and disbelief of the fantastic—particularly Egyptian mythology—serve as a contemporary stand-in for the skepticism of Western authority figures in early mummy tales.

The protagonists of classic mummy movies are frequently warned of the danger associated with entering a tomb and disturbing the eternal sleep of the mummy within. When they dismiss such warnings, they are further cautioned that continued disbelief will be disastrous. Only after he fights off the scarab beetle—a fantastic creature completely outside his experience—does Elvis begin to reconsider what reason tells him, and only after he confronts the mummy face-to-face is he fully convinced. As in other mummy films, the hero's dismissal of the presence of danger is necessary to create tension and further illustrate the foolhardiness of not acknowledging the possibility that mummies really can rise from the dead.[10]

Mummy-film convention requires a learned person to inform the protagonists that an ancient Egyptian mummy can indeed walk among the living and to convince them to abandon commonly accepted reason and logic in order to defeat the mummy. In *The Mummy's Tomb*, it takes the methodical application of contemporary science to convince the protagonist, John Banning (John Hubbard), that a strip of linen left behind by the mummy Kharis (Lon Chaney Jr.) had its origins three thousand years before in Egypt. A similar moment of acceptance of the supernatural as a valid explanation for Imhotep's activities comes in *The Mummy* (1932) after Dr. Muller (Edward Van Sloan) explains to Frank Whemple (David Manners) that Imhotep threatens the well-being of Helen Grosvenor (Zita Johann), the woman both Frank and Imhotep desire. In *Bubba Ho-Tep* the learned figure is clearly Jack, but the process is complicated by Elvis's conviction that Jack is "certifiable," as well as by his skepticism about the mummy and Egyptian magic. In order for him to believe anything Jack says, Elvis must first find him trustworthy. "Jack, uh, no offense but President Kennedy was a white man," Elvis points out, but Jack has a counterargument: "That's how clever they are! They dyed me this color all over!" Elvis's expression suggests his continuing disbelief, but as Jack is his only friend, he suspends his disbelief at least enough to humor Jack, and certainly enough to set the stage for the next step of the suspension of logic: the belief in the ambulatory undead.

Jack then comes into his own as a learned guide, leading Elvis into the visitor's bathroom and showing him the scrawled hieroglyphic graffiti on the walls, which he "looked . . . up in my books and wrote it all down." His books, which apparently include such obscure texts as a hieroglyphic dictionary, give him the knowledge necessary to translate the graffiti and discover that the mummy is after their souls. Conveniently, Jack even has a book on soul-sucking creatures: *The Everyday Man or Woman's Book of the Soul*. This clearly references the ancient Egyptian *Book of the Dead*, which contains spells to assist the soul in reaching the afterlife and surviving there. While Elvis reads his book, Jack explains what a small soul is ("those who don't have much fire for life") and why the souls of the elderly are the easiest to access and the least likely to be missed, making the rest home a veritable smorgasbord for a soul sucker.

Just as it seems Jack has convinced him that the mummy is real, Elvis displays further disbelief. When Jack warns him not to go into the hall, he retorts: "There ain't no mummy from Egypt!" This recurrent disbelief, even in the face of evidence suggesting otherwise, is a familiar element of mummy films, and it highlights an aspect of curse narratives discussed by Day: "Curses demand deference, not just recognition; the ignorant, dismissive, and defiant are not humble."[11] Moments later, however, the issue is decisively resolved. Elvis pokes his head out of Jack's room and comes face to face with Bubba Ho-Tep, thus erasing any further doubts as to the mummy's existence and completely validating Jack's role as learned guide.

The mummy's backstory, revealed to Elvis in the encounter, further extends *Bubba Ho-Tep*'s appropriation of classic mummy-film tropes. Like Imhotep in *The Mummy* (both the original 1932 and the more recent 1999 version) and Kharis in the 1940s Universal films, Bubba Ho-Tep was mummified alive. The image of an Egyptian woman in the flashback suggests that the cause for the live burial was also similar: love for an unsuitable, high-ranking Egyptian woman. How exactly Bubba Ho-Tep came back to life is mostly left to the imagination, although Elvis, reading from Jack's book on soul suckers, gives a nod to the sequels, which featured tana leaves brewed into a potion to keep Kharis in suspended life: "It says here that you can bury some dude and if he gets the right tana leaves and spells said over him and such bullshit, that he can come back to life thousands of years later, man." Later, Jack and Elvis come to the conclusion that the bus crash broke Bubba Ho-Tep from his sarcophagus, but the mummy has neither a specific magical cause for his reanimation nor any real purpose to his undead wandering, aside from eating souls to survive. In this he differs from both Imhotep and Kharis; the latter desires to protect Ananka's tomb, wreak vengeance on those who defiled it, and later to capture the reincarnation of Ananka, while the former wishes to regain his lost love, reborn in contemporary form.

The final battle in *Bubba Ho-Tep* echoes—in the mummy's destruction by fire—the Kharis films *The Mummy's Hand* and *The Mummy*. The central narrative of the battle, however, departs markedly from mummy-film tradition by depriving the heroes of outside assistance. In the 1932 *The Mummy*, Imhotep is only defeated due to the goddess Isis's intervention, while in the 1999 version, Imhotep just gives up after being scorned by the woman for whom he died. Kharis is regularly stymied in his efforts to protect Ananka and by the actions of the high priest who directs him. The priest, a different man in each movie, falls in love with the main female figure in each film and directs Kharis to kidnap the women for his own benefit. The destruction of Bubba Ho-Tep and the release of the souls he has consumed involves neither godly intervention nor a fortuitous event. Elvis and Jack—aged, flawed, decidedly mortal heroes—have only one another to rely on.

Taken from his Egyptian tomb and removed to America, "Bubba Ho-Tep" retains his ability to suck souls from his victims but adopts Western dress: cowboy boots, spurs, a vest, and a black Stetson hat.

Connections to the West

The staging of the final showdown illustrates that, although *Bubba Ho-Tep* takes its basic plot structure from mummy movies, the influence of the traditional Western overlays the film visually and in terms of its archetypal characters, informing the behaviors of Elvis, Jack, Bubba Ho-Tep, and Kemosabe. The setting of the movie may be a dingy rest home, rather than the sprawling frontier of the Western, but as Lee Clark Mitchell points out: "The West in the Western matters less as verifiable topography than as space removed from cultural coercion."[12] The rest home is visited more often by the employees of the funeral home than by friends and family members of the residents, cutting it off from external influences and contact. Separated from the flow of everyday life, it serves as a "last frontier" for its residents. The isolation of the physical space highlights the isolation of the hero figure and his companion in their quest, whether that is to rid the West of outlaws or defeat a soul-sucking ancient Egyptian.

Elvis, the eventual hero of this desolate landscape, must regain his masculinity in order to save the rest home and the elderly who live there. His introduction shows him laying in his bed, impotent both physically and sexually. His deceased roommate's young and pretty daughter, wearing a low-cut top with her midriff bared, flippantly answers his questions, then bends over in front of him in a short skirt to retrieve her father's Purple Heart from the trash: "She saw me as so physically and sexually nonthreatening she didn't mind if I got a birds-eye view of her love nest." Not only did she see him as nonthreatening, he reacted as such, neither commenting nor even getting an erection. At the same time, his attempts to regain his identity as Elvis, which he traded for that of an Elvis impersonator named Sebastian Haff, are met with derision by the nurse: "Now, Mr. Haff! I don't mind calling you Elvis, but you're a little confused." Ridiculed by both women, Elvis seems to have resigned himself to dying in this forgotten rest home, and it is only when he begins to fight supernatural forces that he regains his masculinity, defiantly asserting his true identity as Elvis and assuming the additional role of hero.

After Elvis does battle with the scarab and emerges triumphant, holding a skewer of barbecued beetle, he becomes more physically active in the film, and, most obviously, experiencing an erection while the nurse is administering medicine to the growth on his penis. As he lies in bed, allowing the nurse to "do that little thing," as she calls it, he begins thinking of other things, including the scarab's attack. The erection is tied to the death of the scarab in a split-second cut scene, linking the triumph over the scarab to his rediscovered sexual ability: "What gave here? Then I realized what gave. I was thinking about something that interested me. . . . I'd been given a dose of life again." Elvis's newfound confidence then allows him to regain some of the dignity previously lost to the nurse. She comes outside to tell him it is time for his nap as if he was a toddler, and that it is time to medicate the bump on his penis. He responds angrily: "I'll lube my own crankshaft from now on! You treat me like a baby again and I'll wrap this goddamn walker right around your head!" The nurse retreats, and Elvis cantankerously goes in the opposite direction to investigate the creek near the rest home where the mummy's bus crashed.

Bubba Ho-Tep also represents a threat to Elvis's renewed masculinity, a threat that originates from Bubba Ho-Tep's preferred method of soul removal. As Jack describes: "He had me on the floor and had his mouth over my asshole . . . he was after my soul!" By preferring the anus, Bubba Ho-Tep invokes the idea of homosexuality, to which both Elvis and Jack react with horror: "If he comes in here tonight, I don't want him slappin' his lips on my asshole," Elvis exclaims. His revulsion is tied not to the possible loss of his soul but to the unwanted sexually tinged contact with the mummy.

Elvis and Jack connect over the shared danger of the mummy and the scarab's attack. Soon after Elvis dispatches the scarab, Jack visits Elvis's room: "Listen. I know you're Elvis." By accepting Elvis as who he says is, Jack gains Elvis's trust, reaffirms his identity, and reinforces the bond between them. This bond is apparent when they are later questioned by the rest home administration about Kemosabe's death: "Neither of us told the truth. I mean, who was going to believe a couple of nuts? Elvis and Jack Kennedy explaining that Kemosabe was gunning for a mummy in cowboy duds? . . . So what we did was, we lied." Knowing they would not be believed, they resolve to deal with the mummy on their own.

Traditional Western films are strongly homosocial, with male partnerships demonstrating stronger bonds than those found in heterosexual relationships. As Judith Halberstam points out: "Women are seen as extraneous to the hardscrabble lifestyle of riding the range, fighting Indians, and marking territory. . . . Loneliness is almost always resolved for the cowboy . . . by another cowboy and not a woman."[13] When overt homosexual tensions are present, as in Ang Lee's *Brokeback Mountain* (2005), they collide with the traditionally hypermasculine roles of the strikingly tough cowboy, even though latent homoeroticism is a common theme in Western fictions.[14] As Alex Hunt notes, "Despite the decodable homoerotic subtext of cowboy narratives, it seems overwhelmingly evident that on most levels Americans do not want to imagine their masculine heroes having sex with other men."[15] It is this aversion to homoeroticism that helps to goad Elvis and Jack into action.

Elvis fully reclaims his masculinity in the face of Bubba Ho-Tep's questionable sexuality and the threat he poses, physically and sexually. With his decision to confront the mummy and protect the rest home rather than do nothing, Elvis steps into the role of the hero:

Elvis: "Mr. Kennedy. Ask not what your rest home can do for you. Ask what you can do for your rest home."

Jack: "Hey, you're copying my best lines."

Elvis: "Then let me paraphrase one of my own: Let's take care of business . . . We're gonna kill us a mummy."

Here, Elvis has fully accepted Jack's claim to the presidency despite any earlier misgivings, even to the point of later asking how Marilyn Monroe was in bed ("That is classified information! Top secret!"). His enthusiasm and battle readiness contrasts sharply with his initial appearance in the film. While still constrained by the limits of his aging body, Elvis is actively engaged with his surroundings, is protective of his home, and no longer lies in bed apathetically waiting to die. He brings to battle a medicine bag filled with "mucho mojo": his deceased roommate's Purple Heart and Kemosabe's mask, both symbols of identity and remembrance that Elvis has rescued from the disrespect of being cast aside as worthless and forgotten. Elvis uses these symbols of battle and honorable action to attract sympathetic magic and to assist in his own battle with Bubba Ho-Tep.

Buddies, Sidekicks, Defenders of Aging Souls

Elvis and Jack's relationship draws on the timeless cinematic traditions of "buddies" and "sidekicks" used to create affectionate homosocial pairings across genres, from comic horror films such as *King of the Zombies* (1941) and *Abbott and Costello Meet the Mummy* (1955) to classic Western tales ranging from *Hopalong Cassidy* (1935) to *Butch Cassidy and the Sundance Kid* (1969). The pair's collaboration—with all its tensions and humor—thus invokes a template familiar to audiences of both genres.

As partners in the battle between the living and the undead, Jack and Elvis alternately comment on and fulfill their classic "buddy" roles, with Elvis cast as the passionate warrior-hero and Jack as his creative and cerebral counterpart. Their relationship, in many ways, echoes that of traditional frontier heroes whose success depends on the knowledge of supporting characters around them: scouts, trappers, and prospectors possess intimate knowledge of the landscape that facilitates the heroes' pursuit of evildoers; Indian trackers, with their sharp eyes and encyclopedic knowledge of nature, point out signs that white men overlook; colorful "old timers" trade gossip at the saloon or livery stable and carry history in their heads—and share it at the drop of a hat—providing clues to mysteries and motivations through tales of old grudges and rivalries that divide the town.

The presence of Elvis and Jack's ill-fated companion, Kemosabe, also engages with a classic narrative that reaffirms the film's ties to the Western—the *Lone Ranger* series, popularized on American television from 1949 to 1957. As Tonto tells the Lone Ranger early in the series, "Kemo Sabe" means "trusty scout," and so, rest home resident Kemosabe "scouts ahead," providing one of the film's earliest warnings about Bubba Ho-Tep. When his hero's mask is literally and metaphorically stripped from him by the rest-home administration, his sacrifice inspires Elvis to pick up the mask and the mantle of responsibilities it implies.

Taking on the essence of this new persona draws Elvis—and Jack with him—in to an even more complex, and racially coded, classic Western relationship. According to the tales of the Lone Ranger, Tonto is rescued as a youth by the white man who eventually becomes the celebrated "masked man," and he returns the favor once they have reached adulthood. The Lone Ranger and Tonto then join forces to bring lawbreakers to justice, with the Ranger vowing: "Tonto, from this day on I am going to devote my life to establishing law and order."[16] Elvis, in the role of the metaphorical Lone Ranger, saves Jack by coming into his room immediately after the mummy has attempted to suck Jack's soul; Jack later goes into Elvis's room at night, wakes him, and convinces him that something supernatural is going on, thus saving him from possible death at the hands—or lips—of the nocturnal mummy. These ties of mutual assistance, mirroring those binding the Lone Ranger and Tonto, lead Elvis and Jack to form an unspoken pact against their territory's ineffective law enforcement—the rest-home administration that ignores and patronizes them—and their lawbreaker, Bubba Ho-Tep.

Elvis echoes the Ranger's vow "to make the West a decent place to live," as he decides to do battle with the mummy that threatens his personal Western landscape, the rest home. He rails: "It ain't much of a home, but it's all I got. . . . I'll be damned if I let some foreign graffiti-writing, soul-sucking son-of-a-bitch in an oversize cowboy hat and boots take my friend's souls and shit 'em down the visitor's toilet!" When Elvis clothes himself for the final battle with the mummy in a white rhinestone-studded jumpsuit and cape, with his partner Jack—on a trusty wheelchair steed—by his side, the pair take their place among the buddies, heroes, and sidekicks who have vanquished monsters, outwitted bandits, and thwarted evil across genres for generations.

Elvis enters into battle with the mummy knowing that his chances for survival are slim: "Bubba Ho-Tep comes out of that creek-bed, he's gonna come out hungry and pissed. When I try and stop him, he's gonna jam this paint-can up my ass, and jam me and that wheelchair up Jack's ass." Jack, used as a decoy in his motorized wheelchair, is knocked from the chair by the mummy,

Dressed to reflect their "real" identities, Elvis and Jack go forth to do battle with the undead intruder.

who holds him down and prepares to feed on his soul. Elvis catches Jack's run-away steed and, using it, rescues his mortally wounded friend, who declares: "The President is soon dead. So now it's up to you, Elvis. You've got to get him. You've got to take care of business." With Jack's death, Elvis is solely responsible for defeating Bubba Ho-Tep and restoring peace to the rest home.

Bubba Ho-Tep's death by fire at the hands of Elvis comes at the price of Elvis's own life: "I was going down for the last count, and I knew it. But I still have my soul. It's still mine." The mummy's defeat fulfills the final require-ment of the mummy narrative—the triumph of the modern hero over the an-cient danger—and negates the threat that homosexuality poses to the West-ern characters. In accordance with the Western narrative, it also removes the lawbreaker and the threat of lawlessness from the town, or in this case, the rest home. The residents of Shady Rest are still elderly and close to death, but they will live with their souls unthreatened and die with them intact.

The climax of the film thus satisfies the conventions of the mummy film by decisively ending the threat to the living posed by the undead. The deaths of Elvis and Jack also remove the only eyewitnesses to Bubba Ho-Tep's at-tacks and his destruction, allowing the Western world's status quo—one where ancient curses and ambulatory, soul-sucking mummies cannot even exist, much less menace elderly Texans—to reassert itself. Throughout the film, only the viewer, having been forced to exercise the same suspension of disbelief that the protagonist does, is left knowing that the curse, the mummy, and the threat were real. The disappearance of Elvis and Jack also serves the genre conventions of the Western, however, by removing the two loner-heroes from the scene as soon as the safety of those they protected is assured. Like the cowboy who, having saved the town, rides away into the sunset because he knows the town holds no place for him, Jack and (espe-cially) Elvis—having saved both their friends and their manhood—no longer belong in the world they helped to save. Regardless of whether Elvis and Jack are actually an aged—and in Jack's case dyed—Elvis Presley and President Kennedy, the mixing of mummy narrative with Western tropes serves to underscore important aspects of each genre, bringing the undead of ancient Egypt face to face with the heroes of the American West.

Notes

1. Jasmine Day, *The Mummy's Curse: Mummymania in the English-Speaking World* (London and New York: Routledge, 2006), 47.

2. While British interests in Egypt dated from long before the late nineteenth century, the 1880s saw a marked increase in the access to Egyptian artifacts and knowledge. In 1882, Britain became the sole colonial ruler over Egypt, while in the same year the Egypt Exploration Fund (now the Egypt Exploration Society) was

founded to facilitate British archaeological interests. Flinders Petrie, in 1884, led the first major excavation funded by them at Tanis. This and other excavations served to bring ancient Egypt into the lives of British museum goers and collectors.

3. Hannah Thompson, "'Your Filthy Egyptian Tricks Won't Answer in England': Occultism, Egyptian Mysteries, and the Mummy's Curse in Victorian Britain" (Presentation at the Phi Alpha Theta Biennial Convention, Orlando, Florida, January 4, 2012).

4. Louisa May Alcott, "Lost in a Pyramid, or the Mummy's Curse," *KMT: A Modern Journal of Ancient Egypt* 9 (1998): 75. Originally published 1869.

5. Jane Austin, "After Three Thousand Years," *Putnam's Monthly Magazine of American Literature, Science, and Art* 12.7 (1868): 40.

6. Donald Malcolm Reid, *Whose Pharaohs?: Archaeology, Museums, and Egyptian National Identity from Napoleon to World War I* (Berkeley and Los Angeles: University of California Press, 2003); Elliott Colla, *Conflicted Antiquities: Egyptology, Egyptomania, Egyptian Modernity* (Durham, NC: Duke University Press, 2008). On European involvement in the post–World War I Middle East, see David Fromkin, *A Peace to End All Peace: The Fall of the Ottoman Empire and the Creation of the Modern Middle East* (New York: Holt, 1989).

7. Day, *The Mummy's Curse*, 54.

8. Alcott, "Lost in a Pyramid," 1; Austin, "After Three Thousand Years," 38.

9. Day, *The Mummy's Curse*, 74.

10. Day, *The Mummy's Curse*, 75–76.

11. Day, *The Mummy's Curse*, 75.

12. Lee Clark Mitchell, *Westerns: Making the Man in Fiction and Film* (Chicago and London: University of Chicago Press, 1996), 4.

13. Judith Halberstam, "Not So Lonesome Cowboys: The Queer Western," in *The Brokeback Book: From Story to Cultural Phenomenon*, ed. William R. Handley (Nebraska: The University of Nebraska Press, 2011), 191.

14. For further discussion of homosexuality in Western narratives see Halberstam, "Not So Lonesome Cowboys"; Chris Packard, *Queer Cowboys: And Other Erotic Male Friendships in Nineteenth-Century American Literature* (New York: Palgrave Macmillan, 2005).

15. Alex Hunt, "West of the Closet, Fear on the Range," in *The Brokeback Book: From Story to Cultural Phenomenon*, ed. William R. Handley (Nebraska: The University of Nebraska Press, 2011), 140.

16. George B. Seitz Jr., Fran Striker, and George W. Trendle, "Enter the Lone Ranger," *The Lone Ranger*, Netflix, WMV file, directed by George B. Seitz Jr. (San Francisco, CA: Apex Film Corp., 1949). http://www.netflix.com/ (accessed January 17, 2012).

Bibliography

Alcott, Louisa May. "Lost in a Pyramid, or the Mummy's Curse." In "Louisa May Alcott and the Mummy's Curse." [1869] *KMT: A Modern Journal of Ancient Egypt* 9.2 (1998): 72–75, 83–85.

Austin, Jane. "After Three Thousand Years." *Putnam's Monthly Magazine of American Literature, Science, and Art* 12.7 (1868): 38–45.

Bubba Ho-Tep. Directed by Don Coscarelli. 2002. Santa Monica, CA: MGM/UA Home Entertainment, 2004. DVD.

Colla, Elliott. *Conflicted Antiquities: Egyptology, Egyptomania, Egyptian Modernity.* Durham, NC: Duke University Press, 2008.

Day, Jasmine. *The Mummy's Curse: Mummymania in the English-Speaking World.* London and New York: Routledge, 2006.

Fromkin, David. *A Peace to End All Peace: The Fall of the Ottoman Empire and the Creation of the Modern Middle East.* New York: Holt, 1989.

Halberstam, Judith. "Not So Lonesome Cowboys: The Queer Western." In *The Brokeback Book: From Story to Cultural Phenomenon,* edited by William R. Handley, 190–201. Nebraska: The University of Nebraska Press, 2011.

Hunt, Alex. "West of the Closet, Fear on the Range." In *The Brokeback Book: From Story to Cultural Phenomenon,* edited by William R. Handley, 137–49. Nebraska: The University of Nebraska Press, 2011.

The Mummy. Directed by Karl Freund. 1932. Universal City, CA: Universal Home Entertainment, 2004. DVD.

The Mummy. Directed by Stephen Sommers. 1999. Universal City, CA: Universal Home Entertainment, 2008. DVD.

The Mummy's Curse. Directed by Leslie Goodwins. 1944. Universal City, CA: Universal Home Entertainment, 2004. DVD.

The Mummy's Ghost. Directed by Reginald Le Borg. 1944. Universal City, CA: Universal Home Entertainment, 2004. DVD.

The Mummy's Hand. Directed by Christy Cabanne. 1940. Universal City, CA: Universal Home Entertainment, 2003. DVD.

The Mummy's Tomb. Directed by Harold Young. 1942. Universal City, CA: Universal Home Entertainment, 2004. DVD.

Mitchell, Lee Clark. *Westerns: Making the Man in Fiction and Film.* Chicago and London: University of Chicago Press, 1996.

Packard, Chris. *Queer Cowboys: And Other Erotic Male Friendships in Nineteenth-Century American Literature.* New York: Palgrave Macmillan, 2005.

Reid, Donald Malcolm. *Whose Pharaohs?: Archaeology, Museums, and Egyptian National Identity from Napoleon to World War I.* Berkeley and Los Angeles: University of California Press, 2003.

Thompson, Hannah. "'Your Filthy Egyptian Tricks Won't Answer in England': Occultism, Egyptian Mysteries, and the Mummy's Curse in Victorian Britain." Presentation at the Phi Alpha Theta Biennial Convention, Orlando, Florida, January 4, 2012.

CHAPTER SIXTEEN

The Subversive *Jonah Hex*

Jimmy Hayward's Revision and Reconfiguration of a Genre

Michael C. Reiff

In the late nineteenth century, the United States was at a political, tech-nological, and spiritual crossroads. Using this historic moment of national transformation as context, director Jimmy Hayward's film *Jonah Hex* (2010) presents an undead hero, a figure capable of pushing the Western genre toward its own twenty-first-century crossroads. By working within the genre of the Western and adding elements from other subgenres—including the supernatural and steampunk—Hayward's film acts as a proving ground for new interpretations and considerations of the Western. In doing so *Jonah Hex* subverts and reenvisions numerous themes common to the Western. Specifically, this chapter will examine how Hayward, using an undead West-ern hero as a focal point and engine of genre reconfiguration, continues a tradition of Western heroic revisionism, as well as further complicating the identity of the Western genre itself to create new cinematic structures for contemporary audiences.

The cinematic Jonah Hex is a crucial case study in understanding the direction of not only continuing revisionism of the Western hero but also the role of non-Western genre tropes as they become more prevalent in con-temporary Western films. Since Hex's identity in the film is drawn from re-visionist Western heroes as well as non-Western elements, his connection to previous Western works and his impact on the genre are particularly complex. However, three main elements of Hex's character are important to his compo-sition and his achievements in the film's narrative. For one, Jonah Hex (Josh Brolin) is an undead hero due to his mystical resurrection by Native Americans. Reflecting the origins of some previous Western protagonists,[1] his heroic identity is also formed partially by Native Americans. Hex's undead and supernatural status and abilities, and many of the film's non-Western elements, stem from the Native American characters as well. In fact, the success of the hero, and his continued existence, are based on both native intervention and supernatural elements. Second, while *Jonah Hex* exhibits elements of steampunk narratives, the hero's actual interaction with the out-of-time technology is complicated—even somewhat oppositional—when compared to previous Western/steampunk narratives. This aspect of Hex calls into question the Western hero's ability to properly use advancing technology and his need for antiheroic tactics. While Hex uses steampunk-type weaponry throughout the film, he doesn't vanquish a technologically advanced nemesis by harnessing his own weapons. Instead, Hex relies on the supernatural, establishing a subgenre clash within the confines of the Western. Finally, Hex's identity as a hero with acute knowledge of both the physical and spiritual realms provides an additional avenue for *Jonah Hex* to pursue and better understand the moral and ethical implications of the Western hero.

For a thematically and generically subversive Western, Hayward's *Jonah Hex* doesn't deviate substantially from the classic Western narrative structure. Mirroring the initial plot of Clint Eastwood's 1976 film *The Outlaw Josey Wales*, *Jonah Hex* begins with the hero's family being slaughtered, and it follows the hero's quest for revenge. Hex's family is murdered by former Confederate army general Quentin Turnbull (John Malkovich), a character who reflects the post–Civil War Confederate mind-set of Ethan Edwards (John Wayne) in *The Searchers* (1956), acting antagonistically toward the Union. Turnbull's hatred for the North, however, leads him to steal not money, but a steampunkesque city-leveling weapon that he directs toward Washington, D.C., on Independence Day. As previous genre films would predict, Hex thwarts this apocalyptic plan. Turnbull is defeated, Hex is recognized by the U.S. government as a righteous rebel, and he even acquires a female companion (Megan Fox). But while Hex's conventionally assured victory is present, the hero's methods complicate the genre. Hex resurrects the dead, derives direction in his quest from the underworld, and is at his most effective when experiencing the world filtered through an internal undead realm. Additionally, throughout the film Hayward provides brazenly direct indications that the hero's actions are not merely the acts of a flawed savior, as in previous revisionist Westerns, but of a man doomed for hell. Fully locating and organizing *Hex*'s genre-defying aspects and heroic reconfiguration is therefore a complicated matter, which demands a partial review of the evolution of the Western and its progressive shifts and additions.

The Revisionist Road to *Hex*

Hayward's *Jonah Hex* participates in the Western genre with an eye toward preceeding decades of revisionist films and critiques. While some consider John Ford's 1956 film *The Searchers* to be a protorevisionist Western,[2] acting as a traditional genre film that both reaffirms a genre while instigating early revisionist questions concerning its hero, the genre underwent considerable upheaval in both production and criticism in the 1960s and 1970s. As Richard Slotkin notes in *Gunfighter Nation*, multiple waves of revisionist Westerns attempted to reexamine, reinterpret, and reform the genre. Slotkin notes that, broadly, Westerns in these decades exhibit revisionist phases including formalist, neorealist, and countercultural.[3] Specific to the formalist phase is a more pronounced sense that the Western filmmakers acted and created films that expressed a "problematic . . . relationship to the history of the Western genre as a whole."[4] Additionally, Westerns such as *Hud* (1963) and especially *Hombre* (1967) attempted to deconstruct the Western, with the later openly expressing a mood of "futility" toward Western heroics, specifically the individual's "attempt to enter the 'civilized' world [that leads] only to death."[5] As Hayward demonstrates, a formalist revision of the genre, mixed with a deconstructive mind-set of looming heroic "futility," can be integrated and expressed in the narrative of *Jonah Hex* and by using non-Western genre elements.

Further foundations are laid for *Jonah Hex* with the resurgence of Western genre filmmaking in the 1990s that focus on heroic revisionism and the advancement of cross-genre filmmaking. Specifically in Clint Eastwood's *Unforgiven* (1992), the Western is returned to conventional narrative forms and aesthetics while still defying tradition by portraying, as Joseph Kupfer writes, heroic action as "violence as lacking in flair, virtuosity, and nobility" and attempting to "debunk the [internal] myths" of the Western.[6] And while Eastwood and others closely examined problematic narratives in previous Westerns, the 1990s also provide filmic versions of Western steampunk narratives, which interject anachronistic elements into the Western generic space, using the presence of improbable mechanical inventions to further shake the perceptions and presumptions of the genre. These steampunk Westerns, notably *Wild Wild West* (1999), act less as metatextual examinations and more as reimaginings of the Western cinematic space. Indeed, as Nader Elhefnawy views steampunk in general, the subgenre lends new fictions a "fresher perspective, a lost sense of surprise, wonder, novelty, and even hope."[7] Embracing those concepts of "surprise" and "wonder" as a component of Western reinterpretation, Hayward uses non-Western elements, such as those found in steampunk narratives, in an attempt to further dislodge the genre from its traditional moorings, confronting the viewer with a far more complex interpretation of the hero, and the genre itself.

Participating in Tradition

At its core *Jonah Hex* acts as a further revision of the themes and ideas discussed above. Under the umbrella of formalist revisionism, *Jonah Hex* focuses on integrating the heroic revisionism initiated in the 1960s and later in the 1990s with non-Western genre elements, including those found in steampunk texts, further questioning what the Western narrative, and Western hero, can resemble. Indeed, acting as a formalist revisionist Western, *Jonah Hex* exhibits what Richard Slotkin indicates are major aspects of this type of genre shift, including "fairy-tale-like plots, gun-fighter protagonists who ignore the normative [morally salutary] motives of Western heroes, and landscapes devoid of historical association."[8] *Jonah Hex*, with its combination of supernatural and macabre elements, produces a dark fairy tale. The hero is not primarily fighting to save a society as in previous Westerns, but to get revenge, a motive that he himself recognizes as not "morally salutary." Equally as important, by embracing at various moments strikingly non-Western and anachronistic elements, *Jonah Hex* provocatively and continuously provides situations "devoid" of connections to both historical record and previous realist Westerns as well.

Additionally, *Jonah Hex* exhibits the revisionist impulse toward confronting the underlying mythology, what Barry Langford describes as the "generic models"[9] that stitch together the Western, especially focusing on the protagonist or "hero," particularly his actions and overall perception of gun-fighting bravado. As Joseph H. Kupfer notes in his reading of *Unforgiven*, as a narrative about narrative, Clint Eastwood's film "is subversive in that it aims to demythologize the false picture that the tradition of Westerns has created."[10] *Unforgiven* uses the recurrent motif of false myths and legends to scrutinize the true role and impact of the "hero" in Westerns, and in doing so specifically, "debunk[s] particular elements of the Western such as the noble motives of the hero."[11] Hayward embraces this purpose of revisionism as well; while metaexamination of the Western myth isn't a core element of *Jonah Hex*, the demythologizing of the hero and his motives is. Throughout the film Hex is presented, through his self-assessment and the judgment of those in the underworld, as a flawed, morally compromised, and ultimately doomed character, much as Will Munny is deeply aware of his own flawed natured in *Unforgiven*.

Gabriel Miller's deconstructionist reading of the Westerns *Hud* and *Hombre* also provides important precedents to *Jonah Hex*'s own subversive elements. Miller notes that a key component of those film's critiques of the Western involve depicting the hero, and his actions, as respectively "amoral" and "meaningless."[12] As evidenced in *Jonah Hex*, the hero's violent and antiheroic style can be read as "amoral," and while Hex's actions can't be considered "meaningless" per se (his acts, while even he acknowledges them to be unethical, do save a nation) a sense of the aforementioned "futility" is expressed throughout the film as Hex's soul is considered eternally damned. Finally, the overall ambition of the two films Miller examines—which either reconfigure the temporality or the ethnic foundations of the hero—finds a continuation in Hex. Like the hero in *Hud*, Hex's chronological placement is differentiated, not by a wholesale shift of setting, but by the steampunk elements in the film. Like the hero in *Hombre*, Hex's identity is existentially an amalgamation of influences, from Western and native populations as well as the supernatural and the macabre.

Finally, the best place to consider Hex's orientation within the evolving genre may be through contemporary attempts to further reconfigure the genre as a wholesale form rather than merely using it as a vehicle to further explore historical myths and contexts. Considering the status of the contemporary Western, both commercially and thematically, Langford notes that "the precipitate decline in Westerns output since the late 1970s . . . seemed to have vacated the center-stage position in the American social imaginary allegedly occupied until then by the Western in favor of newer generic models," and he notes that these new models are "not only more popular but perhaps less fraught and conflicted articulations of American identity."[13] *Jonah Hex* follows this path by participating in the creation of "newer generic models" by integrating a wide range of other generic forms and elements, expressing this multiplicity of genres through the titular hero of the film. While the "popularity" of this model, or at least this specific articulation of it, may be called into question when considering the commercial performance of *Jonah Hex*, the film itself still remains a forward-looking and heterodox example of what Langford notes to be a continuing "rupture with tradition."[14]

Undead Departures and Complications

Jonah Hex begins with two montages establishing the hero's identity by deconstructing and then reconstructing the man, establishing a complex array of aspects that drive and empower the figure from the outset. Hex is first established as a Civil War soldier plagued with guilt for his grisly wartime deeds,[15] but he rapidly becomes something far more complicated. After watching his wife and child burned to death in his home, and being branded by the sociopathic Turnbull, a man he once served under, Hex lurches into the wilds of the United States barely alive. Native Americans resuscitate him through mystical means, and leave him, as Hex intones, between the world of the living and the dead, with supernatural abilities, a horrific appearance, and knowledge of both realms. This opening provides some striking contrasts to previous Westerns.

From the outset of the film, the hero is presented as considerably less than noble, in both his Civil War and undead identity, placing him in contrast to traditional heroic entrances. Unlike the methodical and regal entrances of the heroes in *Shane* (1953) and *The Searchers*, among other Westerns, Hex's entrance as hero into both the plot of the film and the Western generic space is far more complicated. Instead of providing a sense of rugged nobility, Hex's initial presentation indicates a man who has already fallen from moral grace. Adding to this sense of revisionism, the hero's origins are well understood from the outset, his brooding guilt and self-exile are already established before the film's conflict begins in earnest. This explicit introduction of a hero is reminiscent of the prologue to *Unforgiven*, which exhibits and explains its hero's past and current moral state in exposition. Hayward therefore acts within a formal revisionism process while engaging in some radical shifts of the hero's structure.

The second expositional montage, which establishes Hex's supernatural identity, is animated, and in using this technique, his origins are further differentiated from previous iterations of the Western hero. The stylized comic-book opening not only links the hero's narrative to a different media lineage (graphic image over moving image) but also emphasizes the further genre complications to come in the film. In the same way that *Hombre* initially establishes its protagonist's identity by juxtaposing images of native culture and images of a horse with the hero, Hex begins by explicitly tying the continued existence of the hero to Native American culture, supernatural events, and a heightened and artificial aesthetic. By concurrently pushing both the foundation of the hero and genre structure into stranger and nongeneric territory, Hex's identity as existing in both natural and supernatural spaces—as much at home in a George A. Romero zombie film as a John Ford Western—is established to further differentiate this Western from previous works.

Inextricably linked to his undead nature and identity is Hex's relationship to the Native Americans in the film. While Western films from the 1940s to the 1960s often present Native Americans as antagonistic to settlers, as early as *Hombre* natives play a role in cultivating and empowering the hero, a trend that later comes to further fruition in films such as

The animated opening sequence of *Jonah Hex* establishes the scarred bounty hunter's supernatural powers, including his ability to (briefly) reanimate, and communicate with, the dead.

Dances with Wolves (1990). Hex moves this element of Native American heroic empowerment in a far more explicit and genre-complicating direction through inclusion of supernatural elements. During the animated montage, Hex indicates his debt to the Native Americans for granting him his new identity and abilities, saying, "I hung on that cross for days—those medicine men did what they could to bring me back, but somehow they just couldn't get me all the way out—didn't make me immortal, just left me with the curse of knowing the other side." The natives resurrect the hero, empower him with knowledge and abilities, and in doing so create a hero that further revises the classic mold.

From this opening, *Jonah Hex* blurs the traditional power structures between Westerner and native and the realism of previous Western films through the consistent usage of supernatural elements. By deeply rooting Hex's new undead identity within the spiritual and supernatural realm, the film shifts the hero's power center away from previously well-established realms, such as the societal and technological. Hex must rely, throughout the film, on the aid of natives to save his life, and by extension his ability to save his nation. Additionally, when on screen, Native Americans are used not only to link the hero to the supernatural but also their entire culture is represented as consistently engaged with natural and nontechnological structures. This distinction further heightens Hex's ambivalent place between the societal and individualistic, the supernatural and mechanical. The use of steampunk-influenced high technology within the final urban settings of the film—technology that Hex must defeat by supernatural means—solidifies these distinctions.

Additionally, the Native Americans and the supernatural elements do not simply augment the hero but are a foundational requisite for his success. In *Jonah Hex*, the entire narrative of heroic victory is imperiled from the outset without the intervention of the supernatural and the Native Americans. Without these elements, as evidenced later in the film when Hex's supernatural abilities are decisive against Turnbull's mechanical might, the United States would lie in rubble by the end of the film. Whereas in other genre-bending films (such as *Wild Wild West*) where heroes use their technological savvy against their enemies, here, the Western hero is pushed to use brute force (as in *The Searchers*) and supernatural abilities. Therefore, while there is no indication that the Native Americans deliberately save the hero from death to initiate the defeat of Turnbull, Hayward does draw an undeniable link between heroic abilities and the necessity of the supernatural powers by the end of his narrative.

The inclusion of steampunk elements, and their early integration into the film, seems at first to contradict or problematize the role of the supernatural in *Jonah Hex*, but it actually further embeds the dominance of the supernatural in the film and in Hayward's vision of the Western itself. After the animated montage, Hayward continues to establish a heightened sense of revisionism and genre hybridization in the film's first set piece, which integrates elements of steampunk into Hex's heroic identity and ability. As Hex arrives in a desolate village in search of a bounty, with vagabonds and leering men lurking in the shadows, Hayward quickly indicates the makings of a traditional Western shootout. But instead of using the totemic revolver or Winchester, Hex removes a tarp from his horse, revealing large, gleaming, futuristic Gatling guns, and he easily dispatches his enemies. Later in the film, Hex visits a (rare) friend, the aptly named Smith, who appears to specialize in making the anachronistic weapons one would expect in a steampunk narrative—weapons that both resemble the aesthetics of the period (gleaming metal, a regal artistry) and possess futuristic abilities that are strikingly out of place. To wit, Hex purchases miniature crossbow guns capable of launching rocket-propelled explosives. And to fully establish Hex's place in the steampunk lineage, it is not only Hex who has access to the trinkets of the future. Quentin Turnbull acquires a city-leveling gun, whose bowels contain grinding gears and literal clouds of billowing steam. Just as the end of *Wild Wild West* features anachronistic technology no longer aiding the hero and society but becoming its ultimate nemesis, Hayward firmly places Hex in the traditional trajectory of a steampunk narrative by pitting the hero against the machinations of not only an individual but also his machine.

And yet, through these specific steampunk genre intrusions, important destructive aspects of this specific Western hero are made clear. Hex's inability to embrace futuristic force, his reliance on traditionally brutish and villainous acts, and his overall need to rely once more on his core identity and abilities as a supernatural and undead individual reinforce the Western image Hayward is creating. Whereas Hex's usage of advanced weaponry at first acts as an allusion to previous steampunk films, as well as traditional Westerns, the hero is quickly shown to be more of a brutish antihero and less of a dexterous gunfighter. Whereas Tom Doniphon (John Wayne) in *The Man Who Shot Liberty Valance* (1962) is able to dispatch his enemies precisely with a single shot, Hex is reckless and wanton with his ammunition, causing destruction beyond what is necessary to defeat his enemies. And whereas the Western shootout rarely results in widespread destruction beyond what is wrought upon the villains, or possibly the hero, Hex causes massive collateral damage, at one point riddling a mining town with bullets and later demolishing a munitions factory. Even more important, Hex is also unable to harness his weapons for precise advantage. As though Hex could not be all things for all subgenres, he evidences an inability to use his Western weapons against his nemesis with any precision or, in the case of defeating his nemesis Turnbull, any success.

Highlighting Hex's otherness and his ambivalence toward previous heroes, his antiheroic methods, involving both steampunk and supernatural elements, are as evident as his scarred features and undead status. At the beginning of the film, Hex kills a man in a bar with a concealed anachronistic gun, and in the middle of the film he flings an informant into a pit containing a vicious half-man, half-snake creature as a bloodthirsty rabble cheers. These acts seem to not only indicate a level of antiheroics but also foreshadow an overall antithetical way of achieving victory. When Hex is finally able to face Turnbull, he does not defeat his enemy through a classic Western duel. Instead, reflecting the far more brutal and problematic ending to *Unforgiven*, Hex beats Turnbull with his bare hands. Hex in the end is not an undead hero so much as an undead brute, reminiscent of the horror genre's zombie, and he distances himself even from revisionist heroes like those in *Unforgiven*, who, while still inflicting a gruesome toll on their victims, use civilized weapons. In the face of not only technology but also steampunk elements, the hero in *Jonah Hex* turns away from progress and civility.

This oppositional direction—away from technological adventurism and toward the supernatural—reinforces not only the added genre influence of the film but also a reductionist and deconstructionist vision of the hero. Specifically, in the climax of the film, Hex's blunt victory is achieved not through gunfire, but through Hex's navigation of a spiritual, undead dreamscape, which he begins to experience concurrently with Turnbull's reality. Establishing a key juxtaposition, Hayward begins the climax by positioning Hex and Turnbull on the steampunk-style warship, and he quickly moves the conflict between hero and villain into the belly of the machine. And yet, beyond the engine room a final stage is established—the world of the undead as it exists in Hex's mind. Both settings are alien to conventional Westerns. The gears and engines of the ship's boiler room are a far cry from a vacant frontier street, and the lurid phantasmagorical realm of Hex's imaginings—replete with blood-red sand, ominous lightning storms, and an ever-present coffin—reflect icons of the West, but twisted to lurid and ghoulish extremes. It's in this dreamscape that Hex defeats the villain and further skews the genre of the film toward the macabre and supernatural.

In presenting Turnbull's defeat through Hex's undead realm-of-the-mind, the film further revises the forms and rules of the Western climax. As Hayward cuts between the physical realm and the undead realm in Hex's final battle, certain aspects of the Western are emphasized or omitted, in contrast to previous resolutions in both traditional and revisionist Westerns. As noted, in the undead realm, Hex is still without any of the weaponry common in Westerns' climaxes—steampunk or otherwise. From *Stagecoach* (1939) to *3:10 to Yuma* (1957, 2007), this lack of heroic gunslinging is a striking omission. But in *Jonah Hex*, the supernatural space *is* the weapon, and in that space his macabre fury defeats his nemesis. Second, Hex's physical fighting abilities are still as imprecise as they are throughout the film when he uses technological weapons. Hex is brutal and violent in defeating Turnbull, and while he is able to leverage supernatural abilities to leverage his victory, his most potent force remains physical and personal.

Jonah Hex meets, and defeats, his archenemy Quentin Turnbull by entering a surreal, supernatural realm filled with barren red dirt and symbols of death.

Finally, the specific locality of this event—in an actual undead realm, or at least in Hex's conception of one—is the most startling shift in both Western climactic form and previous conceptions of technology's role in victory. Hex achieves victory only by harnessing his spiritual force and locality, actions that are only possible through his undead status and the specific narrative structures of the film, and not through a conventional Western hero's technological and locational means. Only by embracing and using the truly novel aspects borne of his undead status—his spiritual connection to the Native Americans, his weaponized supernatural abilities, and the nether region between the living and dead—is Hex successful. It is Hex's departures from the heroic assets of the classic Western—not his adherences—that allow him to be victorious.

With the climax complete, Hayward turns to a final problematic element, and he establishes a cinematic bookend that mirrors the thematic thrust of the film's first scene: primarily, the role of guilt in the hero's self-perception and an explicit indication of where violent heroic deeds lead. While in the beginning of the film Hex's moral circumspection is based on his grisly deeds during the Civil War, now, with Turnbull behind him, Hex reminds himself, and the viewer, that "they say a man with vengeance in his heart is supposed to dig two graves: one for his enemy and one for himself. Well, I guess mine will just have to wait." This acknowledgement, that it is his actions that bring about his eventual self-destruction, is an important shift in the hero's acknowledgement of his culpability and moral direction. And perhaps an even more striking indictment of heroic deeds occurs when Hex engages once again with the supernatural. When Hex revives and speaks to the deceased gunslinger Adleman Lusk (Wes Bentley) to learn the whereabouts of Turnbull, the important information isn't the location of his nemesis, but of Hex's soul. Lusk, himself a denizen of the underworld, promises that—as a result of his past sins—hell is the final resting place for Hex, and his torment will be especially severe.[16]

This explicit heroic introspection and acknowledgment of the protagonist's inherent problematic essence is a further jolt to the conception of the Western hero, and it continues a critical examination of the figure prior to *Jonah Hex*. As J. David Alvis and John E. Alvis establish in their reading of *The Searchers*, the issue of heroic savagery has been a problematic aspect to the genre as a whole.[17] As Alvis and Alvis note in the context of Ethan Edwards in *The Searchers*, as long as the hero is driven by a righteous sense of revenge, or the purported cause of upholding Western civilized mores, it is seemingly excusable, and even laudable within the film's fictional community, to continuously act violently.[18] With Hex, however, the hero himself punctures this myth of violence glossed over by virtue gained through acceptable motives and purported righteousness. Because of his supernatural knowledge and his explicit personal introspection Hex takes his own guilt to clear and explicit expressions and ends.

Additionally, the aesthetics and iconography of Hex's personal undead realm—the film's climactic location of "good" vanquishing "evil"—is also indicative of the hero's own troubled conception of his place in a hellish afterlife. In an earlier sequence illustrating this space, Hayward presents Hex rising out of red earth, reminiscent of the reawakening corpses in a Romero film. Hayward focuses on lurid red sand, as though Hex is rising out of the bloodied earth he himself soaked during the Civil War. And Hex's original location in this space—beneath it—reinforce the hero's conception of himself as forsaken. As both an undead hero, but also as an individual who has done terrible deeds in the past, Hex views himself, in his own supernatural space, not as a beacon of moralistic power, but as a dusty, disentombed entity, begrudgingly rising to defeat another evil. It is therefore with these key elements—supernatural abilities, individuals, and spaces—that Hayward mixes horror, supernatural, and Western genre concepts to present a starkly different future, and conception, of the morality of the Western hero. In doing so, Hayward also further subverts the foundational elements of the Western genre itself.

Paths Forward

Jonah Hex is neither a fully traditionalist Western nor a strictly revisionist one. While the film can most readily be described as a formalist revision

Scarred both physically and mentally, haunted by past deeds he cannot atone for, and shadowed by his incomplete return from the realm of the dead, Hex is far from a conventional Western hero.

of the genre, the myriad nongeneric elements propel it past the earlier conceptions of the term. The primary shifts in the heroic identity—from his heterodox origins to his methods to his moral self-perception—are so inextricably linked to the undead and supernatural elements of the film that merely revising earlier generic elements would not have produced this film. This predominance of non-Western elements points as well to the inherent struggles of a genre that continues a fight for survival. Langford notes that "it is the understanding of the work that genres do, or the need for them to be doing it, that is in crisis,"[19] a crisis that remains acute for the Western genre today. Genre works, like Westerns, can still elicit allegorical truths or allusionary histories, both of which could clarify or answer contemporary societal ills. But today genre films are largely relegated to the summer multiplex, their tropes used to fuel ever-faster blockbuster storytelling and ever-greater money making. Hayward both responds to and further problematizes the numerous genres and subgenres that cling to originality—and existence—today. By melding the Western with elements of horror, supernatural, and steampunk, *Jonah Hex* is a film that at times exists as all four, while concurrently continuing the erosion of the Western's generic consistency, meaning, and effect. At its core, however, *Jonah Hex* is still examining central themes that exist in the earliest John Ford films—the tensions between men in both civilized and uncivilized realms, the use of dangerous weapons that imperil American society, and the moral and ethical quandary of attaining peace and stability through vengeance and violence.

Notes

1. Martin Ritt's film *Hombre*, especially, establishes the hero's identity as intertwined and developed by Native American culture. Hombre's ultimately doomed hero, John Russell, is also a thematic forbearer to Hayward's specific iteration of Jonah Hex.

2. In his essay on *The Searchers*, Christopher Sharret notes that while viewed as a "quintessential masterpiece" of the Western genre, that film also provides the viewer with a "morally outrageous" protagonist that begins to revise the Western hero. Christopher Sharrett, "Through a Door Darkly: A Reappraisal of John Ford's *The Searchers*," *Cineaste* 31.4 (2006): 4–8.

3. "Three types of alternate Westerns were produced during the 1969–72 period, which might be called the formalist, the neorealist, and the countercultural (or 'New Cult of the Indian') Western." Richard Slotkin, *Gunfighter Nation: The Myth of the Frontier in Twentieth-Century America* (New York: Atheneum, 1992), 628.

4. William McClain notes that Sergio Leone's films also were problematic for their "cynical violence" and lack of "realism," all of which could also apply to Hayward's

Jonah Hex. William McClain, "Western, Go Home! Sergio Leone and the 'Death of the Western' in American Film Criticism," *Journal of Film and Video* 62.1–2 (2010): 52.

5. Gabriel Miller notes that this sense of "futility" rightly comes at the end of *Hombre* when the hero, John Russell, is killed while saving questionably moral individuals. Hex, while successful in defeating an enemy, evinces his own "futility" in the full knowledge that nothing he does as a hero will save him from hell. Gabriel Miller, "The Death of the Western Hero: Martin Ritt's *Hud* and *Hombre*," *Journal of Popular Film & Television* 2.2 (1973): 48.

6. Joseph H. Kupfer, "The Seductive and Subversive Meta-Narrative of *Unforgiven*," *Journal of Film and Video* 60.3–4 (2008): 110.

7. Nader Elhefnawy, "Of Alternate Nineteenth Centuries: The Enduring Appeal of Steampunk," *Internet Review of Science Fiction* (2009). http://www.irosf.com/q/zine/article/10562

8. Slotkin, *Gunfighter Nation*, 628–29.

9. While Langford focuses his assessment of revisionist Westerns on films focused on historical myths, his conception of the "unsustainability of traditional generic models" in the Western can equally apply to the mythologized hero in the genre as well. Barry Langford, "Revising the 'Revisionist' Western," *Film and History* 33.2 (2003): 26.

10. Kupfer, "Seductive and Subversive," 103.

11. Kupfer, "Seductive and Subversive," 104.

12. Miller, "Death of the Western Hero," 35.

13. Langford, "Revising the 'Revisionist' Western," 26.

14. Langford, "Revising the 'Revisionist' Western," 27.

15. Jonah Hex (Josh Brolin): "War and me took to each other real well. Felt like it had meaning. The feeling of doing what you thought was right. Well, it wasn't. Folks can believe what they like but eventually a man's got to decide if he's going to do what's right. That choice cost me more than I bargained for."

16. Adelman Lusk (Wes Bentley): "Listen to me—they talk about you down here. You do yourself a favor. You stay ahead of death as long as you can, you hear? Because they got plans for you."

17. "Ford chooses for the movie's central figure Ethan Edwards, a man whose heroic qualities are matched by his savagery." J. David Alvis and John E. Alvis, "Heroic Virtue and the Limits of Democracy in John Ford's *The Searchers*," *Perspective on Political Science* 38.2 (2009): 69.

18. "The settlers in *The Searchers* epitomize the kind of awful virtues from which we in civil society are happy to be free." Alvis and Alvis, "Heroic Virtue," 70.

19. Langford, "Revising the 'Revisionist' Western," 28.

Bibliography

Alvis, J. David, and John E. Alvis. "Heroic Virtue and the Limits of Democracy in John Ford's *The Searchers*." *Perspective on Political Science* 38.2 (2009): 69–78.

Elhefnawy, Nader. "Of Alternate Nineteenth Centuries: The Enduring Appeal of Steampunk." *Internet Review of Science Fiction* (2009). http://www.irosf.com/q/zine/article/10562

Jonah Hex. Directed by Jimmy Hayward. Burbank, CA: Warner Home Video, 2010. DVD.

Kupfer, Joseph H. "The Seductive and Subversive Meta-Narrative of *Unforgiven*." *Journal of Film and Video* 60.3–4 (2008): 103–14.

Langford, Barry. "Revising the 'Revisionist' Western." *Film and History* 33.2 (2003): 26–35.

McClain, William. "Western, Go Home! Sergio Leone and the 'Death of the Western' in American Film Criticism." *Journal of Film and Video* 62.1–2 (2010): 52–66.

Miller, Gabriel. "The Death of the Western Hero: Martin Ritt's *Hud* and *Hombre*." *Journal of Popular Film & Television* 2.2 (1973): 34–51.

Sharrett, Christopher. "Through a Door Darkly: A Reappraisal of John Ford's *The Searchers*." *Cineaste* 31.4 (2006): 4–8.

Slotkin, Richard. *Gunfighter Nation: The Myth of the Frontier in Twentieth-Century America.* New York: Atheneum, 1992.

CHAPTER SEVENTEEN

Queer Justice

Supernatural Strangers and Different Conceptions of Law and Punishment in Two Horror Westerns

Fernando Gabriel Pagnoni Berns

The arrival of the quintessential "outsider" in the mythical frontier town of Western film is one of the genre's most iconic images. The lone, rugged stranger brings justice into the midst of lawlessness, corruption, and coward-ice, provoking a "tension between justice and law" and creating a dislocation in the narrative arc of "life already in progress."[1] This confrontation makes the Western genre especially suitable for inquiry into the differences between justice as an abstract notion and its expression in the laws of men.

If the arrival of the outsider is central to the genre, however, what happens when the Western hybridizes with another genre, such as horror? How does the traditional plotline change when the stranger is a supernatural being? The dislocation that the outsider brings is enhanced when he displays char-acteristics that alienate him from society—more so, when he is one of the undead. This chapter will explore the ways in which supernatural Westerns both highlight and complicate notions of "justice" when it transcends the human condition, looking at two such Westerns, where the understandings and enactments of justice seem at once complementary and contradictory.

In Edward Dein's *Curse of the Undead* (1959), vampire gunslinger Drake Robey (Michael Pate) brings with him a past that only God's divine justice can forgive or condemn. His presence reveals the artificiality of human laws, while critiquing the limited binary opposition of traditional Western heroes and villains—demonstrating that "good" characters are not always good and "bad" characters not wholly bad. The outsider in Giulio Questi's *Se sei vivo spara* (aka *Django Kill . . . If You Live, Shoot!*, 1967), on the other hand, is a "resuscitated" murder victim who, because of his own condition, can see beyond conventional sociocultural boundaries to find a real empathy toward human beings, especially the weak and exploited. The film contains a homo-erotic subtext animated by a hero whose queer gaze "haunts heterosexuality"[2] and the binary oppositions its norms enforce. He, like Drake Robey, can see beyond naturalized concepts such as justice/injustice, good/bad, straight/queer, and insist on their reexamination. Vengeance and justice—whether communal, individual, or divine—collide with one another in these films, collectively embodied in the supernatural strangers.

The Stranger as Vampire

Curse of the Undead, the "first vampire Western,"[3] takes place in a California town plagued by a strange and fatal illness that strikes young women. At the same time, a rich landowner in the area, Buffer (Bruce Gordon), has illegally dammed the river where the Carter family's livestock drinks, placing the family in a desperate situation. The first minutes of the film economically establish these two main themes and the film genres to which each belongs. The first scene evokes the imagery of the vampire film when one victim dies with two small holes in her neck. The narration then establishes the conflict between Buffer, the bully of the town, and the honest Carter family, evoking a familiar theme from Western films: the struggle over water rights. Both topics and genres become connected when the patriarch of the Carter family, Doc (John Hoyt), goes to town to speak with Buffer and, on his way, is attacked by Drake Robey, the vampire who is the cause of the "plague." When the horses bring back Doc's dead body to the Carter ranch, his two sons mistakenly accuse Buffer of causing their father's death.

As a greedy land baron, Buffer is a quintessential "Western villain," but his role here is more complex than many of the other traditional villains of the genre. While guilty of much, he is accused of a crime that he did not, in fact, commit. When confronted by Doc's youngest son, Tim (Jimmy Murphy), who seeks vengeance for his father's murder, Buffer attempts to avoid a gunfight, killing Tim only when the young man calls him a coward. Tim's sister, Dolores (Kathleen Crowley), the heroine of the film, continues the family's search for vengeance—the third approach to justice that the film presents—by seeking a gunslinger to avenge her brother's and father's deaths.

The film highlights the complex relationship between vengeance and justice. The two are commonly considered to be in distinct opposition, with one dominated by emotion, and the other, grounded in reason.[4] Vengeance is the product of impulse and passion, its retaliation measured by outrage and anger, while justice is meted out by retribution that is fair and morally right.[5] But in the world of the film—and indeed, more generally, as the narrative demonstrates—this is not necessarily the case. The arrival of the vampire-stranger in the troubled frontier town of *Curse of the Undead* illustrates just how deeply interconnected the two concepts are, highlighting the ways in which codified law responds to both and is, in fact, implicated in their construction. Drake, as a quintessential outsider—not only to the community but also to the human race—serves as the agent of critique and catalyst for change, setting in motion a series of events that permanently alter the town, yet leave him unchanged.

The stranger transforms the town's idea of justice through his status as one of the living dead—beings which, by their nature, "threaten the natural order of things"[6] and blur the boundaries that define the world of the living. He is both the outlaw who has committed a crime and the avenger hired to repair it, embodying both justice and its antithesis, vengeance, and serving to illustrate Robert Solomon's notion that the former may in fact be seen as "derivative" of the latter, since both are based on the idea of retribution.[7] Just as Drake serves to merge these concepts, it is Preacher Dan (Eric Fleming), his apparent ideological opposite, who tries to point out their differences, attempting to dissuade Dolores from pursuing her personal mission of vengeance.

Dolores seeks out a gunman because she assumes that finding justice under the law will be impossible. Her assessment proves correct: the sheriff refuses action, and even the high price she places on Buffer's head is not enough to tempt any of her fellow townspeople into action. Their lax notions of justice, which encourage a certain acceptance of corruption, are bound up in the town's social inequalities—Buffer holds economic power, so the community forgives him his faults in order to maintain social stability. It closes ranks and continues its day-to-day existence, satisfied with justice "based on political not moral considerations."[8] The townspeople make this choice because, as Solomon states, the vengeance that Dolores seeks "is not the product, the responsibility, nor possibly even the concern of the law or of the larger society."[9] Revenge is individual, while codified law impels communities.

Buffer seeks the protection of this law—embodied in the figure of the sheriff—when he finds out that Dolores has hired Drake to exact her vengeance. His concern is justified; he sees the stranger's skill with a gun when Drake kills one of his men. The sheriff takes responsibility for Buffer's protection—an action that results, as Markesinis says, in "watering down"[10] the rights of the innocent. Yet even this notion is more complicated than it might seem, with the sheriff opting for "law" over "justice," and Dolores, the innocent, equating the ideal of justice with personal vengeance.

It is the preacher who finally clarifies the differences between the two notions of justice and who does his part toward delivering justice purged of any vindictiveness that might tarnish its claim to rationality. First, he convinces Dolores to dispense with the gunman and to forget her plans of vengeance. Second, he devises a complex form of restitution for the terrified Buffer: a plan that will ruin him financially if any further misfortune befalls the Carter ranch. This is a classic example of retributive justice. Buffer is compelled to ensure the ranch's safety and to begin to integrate himself into the community like a citizen, rather than exploit those around him like a man free to make his own laws.

The idea that the film presents through Dan is, in fact, a leap from the concept of retributive justice—a citizen who breaks the law and must pay "an eye for an eye"—toward the contemporary idea of *restorative justice*. "Restorative justice is a philosophical framework that focuses on crime as an act against another individual rather than against the state and focuses on the harm done and how that harm might be repaired."[11] Its acceptance signals the transition from punitive justice to justice as repair or restitution, even though the "offenders may experience restorative sanctions as painful and unpleasant."[12] Buffer dislikes the solution proposed by Dan, but he accepts it as an option preferable to death at Drake's hands.

This notion of restorative justice involves a noticeable return of justice to a personal level. Restitution, like revenge, involves restoring a state of stability that existed prior to the damage done to the victim by the offender. Otherwise, as Solomon notes, the fabric of society is in peril, because "wherever justice is at issue, the lingering shadow of vengeance is not far behind."[13] The opening half of the film, then, goes through several varieties of "justice," paralleling the evolution of the concept.

Each of these forms is embodied by one of the film's main characters. Just as Dolores stands as the pursuer of vengeance, the sovereignty of human law finds its voice in the sheriff. Following John Austin's classic "imperative theory of law," the sheriff establishes himself as the one who must be obeyed by all, but he offers his own obedience to none.[14] His word defines the law: "I have two options: arrest you or shoot you," he says at one point, illustrating his power to manipulate the boundaries of the law according to his will. Dolores disregards his dictates of law in her quest for vengeance, and she only surrenders them when Preacher Dan, who represents the final stage in the evolution of justice, convinces her of the immorality of her act and proposes instead a more civilized resolution. Dan replaces her passionate, primitive form of justice with a recompensing justice directed not toward the community but directly to the injured party—in this case, Dolores—and thus introduces restorative justice.

The town's equilibrium is reestablished because the threat of vengeance has been expelled and replaced by a more civilized ideal, but a problem remains—the vampire decides to remain in town when Dolores breaks her contract with him. Just as his arrival upset the balance of the community (bringing death and destruction into its midst), his continued presence extends his negative impact on those around him.

As a threat of supernatural origin, Drake is subject to justice that is not of this world. Dan discovers the stranger's true nature and, after Drake kills the sheriff, meets him in a final showdown: a duel between the supernatural entity and the representative of God. Drake's undead status gives him an advantage, but it does not make him invincible. He is finally felled by a single bullet, bearing a tiny crucifix on its tip—the undead, destroyed by the power of the Cross. This final showdown cannot, however, provide restitution to the town for the deaths caused by the vampire in the way that Dolores received restitution for the offences committed by Buffer, highlighting the disconnect between human justice and that of the Divine.

The Stranger, Resurrected

Like *Curse of the Undead*, *Se sei vivo spara* begins as a traditional Western, but it gradually reveals a fantastic texture closer to that of the horror genre. Cited as one of the most graphically violent films in the "spaghetti Western" subgenre, it begins with an anonymous *mestizo* (Tomas Milian) helping to steal a quantity of gold from an army convoy, only to be betrayed by the boss of the operation, Oaks (Piero Lulli), who shoots him along with the Mexican members of the band. An Indian couple finds the stranger's body and decide to perform a ritual ceremony that will return him to the world of the living, hoping that he can then describe the afterlife to them. The *mestizo*, once resurrected, promises to do so in return for their assistance.

Oaks and his band, meanwhile, arrive in a town isolated on the edge of the desert. The town's horrors are revealed in very brief cutaway scenes displaying unexplained hints at the violence perpetrated there, interspersed with the bandits' gaze: naked women, abused children, a piece of cloth making its way across the floor barely hiding the terrorized figure crawling underneath. The townspeople gives the bandits a dry welcome, then hang them in the square. Only the boss, Oaks, is able to escape, but the undead *mestizo* stranger kills him, using bullets cast from melted-down gold. Rewarded by the townspeople for killing the bandit leader, the *mestizo* decides to take the money and leave, but he changes his mind when the town is threatened by another group of gunslingers, led by Mr. Sorrow (Roberto Camardiel). Sorrow knows that the hanged bandits were carrying a wealth of gold and now intends to find it, but the preacher, Hagerman (Francisco Sanz), has hidden the gold with the town's barman, Bill Templer (Milo Quesada). When the bandits arrive, the Stranger stays on in order to protect two of the town's most vulnerable characters: Templer's son Evan (Ray Lovelock), and Hagerman's sister, Elizabeth (Patrizia Valturri).

Giulio Questi's film is a cynical Western, in a way that *Curse of the Undead*—even with its blending of genres—is not. It is typical of the type of Westerns that emerged during the progressive decline of the genre after its golden age in Hollywood: what Christopher Le Coney and Zoe Trodd call "counterculture Westerns,"[15] in which the myth of the West is revised and deconstructed to exhibit the genre's conventionalities. The dichotomy of "civilization/barbarism" progressively loses the characteristics that define both notions, disintegration especially embodied in a cynical hero who

The immaculate dress of bandit leader Mr. Sorrow and two of his henchmen belies the ruthlessness of their search for the stolen gold and the lengths to which they are willing to go to obtain it. *Courtesy Filmoteca Española*

disbelieves his own heroic mission and the moral supremacy of the white race. If, in the traditional Western, the Indians were the villains, here they offer an alternative to the corrupt and overcontrolled lifestyle of cities (thus, counterculture Westerns are also called "cult-of-the-Indians-Westerns").[16] The sheriff is no longer a figure of righteous justice, but rather a man who embodies law favoring economic power. As naive borders "where good and evil were seen as clear as the color of one's hat"[17] become elastic, counterculture Westerns present an opportunity to call into question the "naturalness" of human justice. *Se sei vivo spara* is an excellent example of the foregoing: the film is not about the conflict between civilization and barbarism, but about how immorality corrupts both sides.

The film begins with the Stranger's hand emerging from a shallow grave, beginning a hallucinatory flashback that tells of his betrayal. He seeks revenge against those who betrayed him, following them to the town, but that place proves to be even more terrible than his treacherous partners. The inhabitants of the town, pursuing their own idea of justice, nearly steal the hero's vengeance by executing the thieves themselves. There is no trial, no legal authority, and ultimately, no law. In their zeal to punish the thieves, they leave only Oaks as a target for the Stranger's wrath.

Having carried out his vengeance, the *mestizo* decides to spend the night, and so encounters the queerest characters in a film full of them, beginning with Evan, the barman's son. Fragile, effeminate, and emotionally fragmented, he is infuriated by displays of passion between his father and beautiful stepmother, Lori (Marilù Tolo), and in a fit of rage, he shreds the woman's dresses with a razor. Desperate for connection, he immediately attempts to establish intimacy with the Stranger, first by furtive glances and then by asking if they can leave the town together, a request the Stranger denies. On the following day he leaves the town, but when he sees Evan kidnapped by the men of Sorrow's gang, he goes to the youth's rescue. The relationship between the Stranger and Evan is clearly inscribed with a queer texture. Seeing the Stranger's concern for the boy's security, Sorrow interrogates him about how much interest he had in Evan, to which the Stranger responds "as much as you in the gold." Sorrow's already established obsession with the precious metal speaks volumes here.

Blonde with clear blue eyes, Evan is the perfect virgin boy to be desired by older men—making him the perfect sexualized prey for Sorrow's men, who are coded by the camera's continual close-ups as handsome, predatory homosexuals. In fact, it is suggested that Sorrow's drunken men sexually abuse the boy when he is held prisoner in their lair.

Sorrow kidnaps Evan with the intention of holding him captive and demanding the gold his father had hidden; however, when Evan commits suicide the morning after being raped, the plan must change. The Stranger is the one in charge of taking the youth's dead body to his father, with the threat that more blood will run if he continues hiding the booty. He agrees to carry the body, but his motivations are quite different than Sorrow's: to condemn the barman for valuing the gold over his own son's life. Even dead, Evan is diminished by his parents' greed—his coffin is used as a hiding place for the very bags of gold that brought about his death.

Once back in town, the Stranger's attentions turn to Elizabeth Hagerman, who has been imprisoned by her brother, the preacher. The preacher, fearful of Sorrow's men, invites the *mestizo* into his house and tries to convince him to stay on as protection. He tries to seduce the Stranger, and he offers to take care of all his needs if he will stay. When the undead *mestizo* refuses, Hagerman releases Elizabeth from her confinement (literally, letting his feminine part out of the closet) and intends to give her to the Stranger. Realizing that he cannot take the place of a woman, he frees the real woman of the house so that she can seduce the gunslinger as he, as a man, was not able to. Ultimately, however, the stranger cannot save Elizabeth's life, just as he could not save Evan's. Everyone pure or good is destroyed by the ambition and greed of the inhabitants of the town.

In *Curse of the Undead*, the arrival of the vampire short-circuits the various notions of justice accepted by the community. The Stranger's case, however, is different. As a resuscitated being, able to see beyond what the eyes of the living can, his concept of justice is no longer actively bound by human laws, be those judicial or individualistic. Although the Stranger goes after the men who betrayed him and ends up killing Oaks, his coldness has none of the passion that characterizes personal vengeance. Furthermore, against the wishes of the townspeople, the Stranger decides to take down the bodies of Oaks' men and give them a Christian burial. This action provokes his rejection by the town, in retaliation for his questioning of their methods of justice.

What the Stranger has gleaned from his foray into the realm of the dead is a new perspective on justice that extends beyond the interpretive limits of human law. The *mestizo* tries to carry on with his former lifestyle but now cannot avoid a strong empathic connection with the weak and victimized—those who need a higher order of justice. The young and feminine Evan and the poor and mistreated Elizabeth reach out to the Stranger, who intercedes for them against the powerful. He acts not to restore a lost order but to restore the alienated and oppressed, who now speak to his newfound

Contrary to the impression given in posters, The Stranger—the nameless hero of *Se sei vivo spara*—is a contemplative, justice-seeking figure rather than a conventional Western hero who solves problems with his fists and guns. *Courtesy Filmoteca Española*

heroic virtue. The laws that should ensure this fail because they are created, promulgated, and implemented by fallible human beings. The Stranger is no longer human and so, he can place himself in the Other's shoes and attempt to help them find justice.

In *Monsters in the Closet* (1997), Harry Benshoff recaptures Robin Wood's idea that the horror film consists of three elements: normality, the Other, and the relationship between the two.[18] For Benshoff, this formula is an ideal tool to explore queerness in the horror film, since "queerness disrupts narrative equilibrium and sets in motion a questioning of the status quo."[19] In *Se sei vivo spara*, a horrific genre hybrid, it is also a useful formula, as it draws attention not only to the Stranger and the nightmarish status quo of the town but also to the ways in which the outsider circumvents both law and patriarchy, engaging intimately with its weakest and most exploited members and blurring the boundaries between male and female. The Stranger merges both genders and genres not only to function as the quintessential lone Western outsider but also, as Benshoff observes, as an illustration of the "monstrous."

The queer gaze continues with the exhibition of the hero's body when he is captured and undressed by Sorrow. Crucified in his cell, his sweaty, gleaming body clad only in a loincloth, the Stranger is exhibited physically in ways that only the bodies of women are usually exhibited. If "one of the recurring motifs of Italian horror films, especially, is of helpless heroines being victimized and tortured"[20] by sadists, then this scene closes a queer circuit that begins, not with the first looks between Evan and the outsider, but with the Stranger's very condition, which is disruptive and critical due to his status as a *mestizo*—one who blurs the boundaries of insider and outsider, male and female, living and dead.

When Oaks betrays the Stranger, it is because he has no intention of sharing his fortune with a *mestizo*: a bastard of lower race who, through his mixed ancestry and queer coding, embodies an uncomfortable ambiguity.[21] But the Stranger, because of his undead status, has already lost those limits that would make him, among other things, a citizen.

As an outsider in the world of the living, the Stranger's presence is a visible critique of its idea of reality, which he shows to be purely a social construct rather than an unalterable fact. Human ideas on law are also deconstructed by the undead Stranger's presence, as he tries to promote a higher-order notion of existence, stripped of human boundaries, hierarchies, and injustices—a notion of universal "justice" found, not in the laws of Western fiction, but in the classics of philosophy.

Sociologist Georg Simmel describes the qualities of the "stranger." Two are of interest for this work and can form a brief conclusion. The stranger, says Sim-

The Stranger's identity—as a *mestizo* and as a man returned from the grave—makes him doubly a stranger in the world through which he moves. *Courtesy Filmoteca Española*

mel, does not arrive in a community simply to leave immediately after. In order for his presence to be significant beyond that of a passerby, he must remain long enough to make his influence felt in the community. In *Curse of the Undead*, Drake does not leave town when he loses his work as bounty hunter, and he requests Dolores's permission to remain, in order to pursue his own interests and to continue feeding on the community members. Although the Stranger of *Se sei vivo spara* receives money for Oaks's death, he also does not leave the town as he is requested, and when he finally does depart, he returns again and again to engage with the community on an intimate and altering level.

Simmel notes that this more sustained objective presence is critical to the stranger's ability to dislocate norms and redefine community. The Stranger possesses a totally new gaze, which decontextualizes, highlights, and reevaluates ongoing roles and practices in the town, and then acts to aggressively alter them. In *Curse of the Undead*, the arrival of the Other causes a collision of divergent notions of good and evil, right and wrong, and it produces an uncertainty in the community.

Despite these complexities, both films do show clear constructions of good and bad, right and wrong. Those dichotomies are presented, as in any traditional Western, by cues ranging from settings (saloon versus church, wilderness versus town) to the morally coded colors worn by the characters—villains in black and heroes in white.[22] But if both films give an account of the existence of good and evil, they also question the ways in which humanity copes with these notions and the ways in which communities attempt to address the plights of those whom evil has deprived or damaged. The person best able to interrogate these notions must necessarily be a stranger—an "outsider"—in this case, one of the undead.

If "it is true that a number of the 'antiheroes' of many more contemporary Western films (. . .) blur the distinction between good and bad,"[23] the outsiders of these two films bring to bear—from their own positions at the margins of society (as in traditional Westerns) and undead (unlike traditional Westerns)—a queer gaze that, in turn, produces a "shifting process that [multiplies] meanings and identities."[24] This gaze, in both the films considered here, allows the undead stranger to trouble the other characters' assumptions about how and where justice can be found—and, indeed, whether justice is even possible in their violent frontier world.

Notes

1. R. Philip Loy, *Westerns and American Culture 1930–1955* (Jefferson, NC: McFarland, 2001), 73.

2. Ken Gelder, *The Horror Reader* (New York: Routledge, 2000), 187.

3. Herb Fagen, *The Encyclopedia of Westerns* (New York: Facts on File, 2003), 112.

4. Robert George and Christopher Wolfe, "Natural Law and Public Reason," in *Natural Law and Public Reason*, ed. Robert George and Christopher Wolfe (Washington: Georgetown University Press, 2000), 51–74; Raymond Wacks, *Philosophy of Law: A Very Short Introduction* (New York: Oxford University Press, 2006).

5. Robert Solomon et al., *Morality and Social Justice: Point/Counterpoint* (Lanham, MD: Rowman & Littlefield, 1995), 254.

6. Mary Hallab, *Vampire God: The Allure of the Undead in Western Culture* (Albany: State University of New York Press, 2009), 36.

7. Solomon et al., *Morality and Social Justice*, 253.

8. Basil Markesinis, *Good and Evil in Art and Law* (New York: Springer, 2007), 19.

9. Solomon et al., *Morality and Social Justice*, 254.

10. Markesinis, *Good and Evil*, 99.

11. Kären Matison Hess and Christine Hess Orthmann, *Introduction to Law Enforcement and Criminal Justice, tenth edition* (New York: Delmar, 2012), 67.

12. Margarita Zernova, *Restorative Justice: Ideals and Realities* (Farnham, UK: Ashgate, 2007), 38.

13. Solomon et al., *Morality and Social Justice*, 256.

14. Kenneth E. Himma, ed., *Law, Morality, and Legal Positivism* (Stuttgart: Franz Steiner Verlag, 2004), 51.

15. Christopher Le Coney and Zoe Trodd, "Straight Shooters, Stainless-Steel Stories, and Cowboy Codes: The Queer Frontier and American Identity in a Post-Western World," in *Queer Popular Culture: Literature, Media, Film, and Television*, ed. Thomas Peele (New York: Palgrave Macmillan, 2007), 169.

16. Paul Varner, *The A to Z of Westerns in Cinema* (Plymouth, UK: Scarecrow Press, 2008), 5.

17. Brent Strang, "'I Am Not the Fine Man You Take Me For': The Postmortem Western from *Unforgiven* to *No Country for Old Men*," masters thesis, University of Alberta, 2010, 129.

18. Harry Benshoff, *Monsters in the Closet: Homosexuality and the Horror Film* (New York: Manchester University Press, 1997), 4.

19. Benshoff, *Monsters in the Closet*, 5.

20. James Chapman, *Cinemas of the World* (London: Reaktion Books, 2003), 301.

21. Julia Kristeva, *Powers of Horror: An Essay on Abjection* (New York: Columbia University Press, 1982).

22. Philip Skerry and Brenda Berstler, "You Are What You Wear: The Role of Western Costume in Film," in *Beyond the Stars: Studies in American Popular Film, volume 3*, ed. Paul Loukides and Linda Fuller (Bowling Green, KY: Bowling Green University Popular Press, 1993), 77–86.

23. Douglas Den Uyl, "Civilization and Its Discontents: The Self-Sufficient Western Hero," in *The Philosophy of the Western*, ed. Jennifer McMahon and Steve Csaki (Lexington: University Press of Kentucky, 2010), 38.

24. Nikki Sullivan, *A Critical Introduction to Queer Theory* (Edinburgh: Edinburgh University Press, 2003), 199.

Bibliography

Benshoff, Harry. *Monsters in the Closet: Homosexuality and the Horror Film*. New York: Manchester University Press, 1997.

Chapman, James. *Cinemas of the World*. London: Reaktion Books, 2003.

Den Uyl, Douglas. "Civilization and Its Discontents: The Self-Sufficient Western Hero." In *The Philosophy of the Western*, ed. Jennifer McMahon and Steve Csaki, 31–53. Lexington: The University Press of Kentucky, 2010.

Fagen, Herb. *The Encyclopedia of Westerns*. New York: Facts on File, Inc., 2003.

Gelder, Ken. *The Horror Reader*. New York: Routledge, 2000.

George, Robert, and Christopher Wolfe. "Natural Law and Public Reason." In *Natural Law and Public Reason*, edited by Robert George and Christopher Wolfe, 51–74. Washington: Georgetown University Press, 2000.

Hallab, Mary. *Vampire God: The Allure of the Undead in Western Culture*. Albany: State University of New York Press, 2009.

Hess, Kären Matison, and Christine Hess Orthmann. *Introduction to Law Enforcement and Criminal Justice, tenth edition.* New York: Delmar, 2012.

Himma, Kenneth E., ed. *Law, Morality, and Legal Positivism.* Stuttgart: Franz Steiner Verlag, 2004.

Kristeva, Julia. *Powers of Horror: An Essay on Abjection.* New York: Columbia University Press, 1982.

Le Coney, Christopher, and Zoe Trodd. "Straight Shooters, Stainless-Steel Stories, and Cowboy Codes: The Queer Frontier and American Identity in a Post-Western World." *Queer Popular Culture: Literature, Media, Film, and Television,* edited by Thomas Peele, 151–67. New York: Palgrave Macmillan. 2007.

Loy, Philip R. *Westerns and American Culture 1930–1955.* Jefferson, NC: McFarland, 2001.

Markesinis, Basil. *Good and Evil in Art and Law.* New York: Springer, 2007.

Simmel, Georg. "The Stranger." In *On Individuality and Social Forms: Selected Writings,* edited by Donald N. Levine, 143–49. Chicago: University of Chicago Press, 1971.

Skerry, Philip, and Brenda Berstler. "You Are What You Wear: The Role of Western Costume in Film." In *Beyond the Stars: Studies in American Popular Film, volume 3,* edited by Paul Loukides and Linda Fuller, 77–86. Bowling Green, KY: Bowling Green University Popular Press, 1993.

Solomon, Robert, et al. *Morality and Social Justice: Point and Counterpoint.* Lanham, MD: Rowman & Littlefield Publishers, 1995.

Strang, Brent. "'I Am Not the Fine Man You Take Me For': The Postmortem Western from *Unforgiven* to *No Country for Old Men.*" Masters Thesis, University of Alberta, 2010.

Sullivan, Nikki. *A Critical Introduction to Queer Theory.* Edinburgh: Edinburgh University Press, 2003.

Varner, Paul. *The A to Z of Westerns in Cinema.* Plymouth, UK: Scarecrow Press, 2008.

Wacks, Raymond. *Philosophy of Law: A Very Short Introduction.* New York: Oxford University Press, 2006.

Zernova, Margarita. *Restorative Justice: Ideals and Realities.* Farnham, UK: Ashgate, 2007.

A Selected Filmography

Robert G. Weiner, Susan Hidalgo,
A. Bowdoin Van Riper, and Cynthia J. Miller

7 Mummies (2006)—A group of escaped prisoners make their way to a ghost town that is rumored to have gold. The town, however, is filled with the un-dead, and the titular seven mummies protect the gold. Features Billy Drago and Danny Trejo. USA. Directed by Nick Quested.

Billy the Kid vs. Dracula (1966)—Dracula pits his wits against gunslinger Billy the Kid in order to make a beautiful, young ranch owner his bride. Fea-tures John Carradine. USA. Directed by William Beaudine.

BloodRayne II: Deliverance (2007)—Born half-human and half-vampire, Rayne (Natassia Malthe) joins forces with Pat Garrett (Michael Paré) to stop Billy the Kid, a vampire, from taking over the town of Deliverance. Canada/ Germany. Directed by Uwe Boll.

Bubba Ho-Tep (2002)—Based on a short story by Joe Lansdale. Two elderly nursing home residents who believe they are Elvis Presley and John F. Ken-nedy fight an ancient Egyptian mummy seeking to suck the souls from their fellow residents. Features Bruce Campbell and Ossie Davis. USA. Directed by Don Coscarelli.

Cowboys & Vampires [aka ***Dead West***] (2010)—A Western actor working in a film studio and theme park discovers what the new management is plan-ning for opening night. USA. Directed by Douglas Myers.

Curse of the Forty-Niner [aka ***Miner's Massacre***] (2002)—A group of friends finds treasure in an abandoned mine, but it is cursed, and it is protected by the spirit/zombie of a dead miner. Features Karen Black and John Phillip Law. USA. Directed by John Carl Buechler.

Curse of the Undead (1959)—Gunslinger-for-hire Drake Robey is really a vampire who preys on the town's women, even as he exacts revenge for the ranch family that hires him. The first Western with a vampire gunslinger. USA. Directed by Edward Dein.

The Dead and the Damned [aka **Cowboys and Zombies**] (2011)—After discovering a mysterious rock, miners crack it, releasing spores that change the townspeople into zombies and forcing a trio of the still living to fight for their lives. USA. Directed by Rene Perez.

Dead Noon (2007)—An outlaw is raised from the dead and takes revenge on the current citizens of a Western town, with all the powers of hell at his disposal. Features Kane Hodder. USA. Directed by Andrew Wiest.

Dead Walkers (short) (2009)—A bounty hunter and a gunslinger come across an old Western town filled with zombies. USA. Directed by Spencer Estabrooks.

Death Valley: The Revenge of Bloody Bill (2004)—A group of kidnapped young people are taken to an old Western ghost town infested with zombies led by Confederate soldier Bloody Bill. Features Gregory Bastien. USA. Directed by Byron Werner.

Devil Rider (1989)—A cowboy fugitive from hell, who has been riding the plains for a century, returns to stalk those who have turned the land he once owned into a vacation resort. USA. Directed by Victor Alexander.

Devil's Crossing (2011)—Centuries after the world is destroyed by nuclear war, a man who sold his soul to the devil fights the undead to save a town and reclaim his soul. USA. Directed by James Ryan Gary.

Django the Bastard (1969)—A Union soldier comes back from the dead to take revenge on officers who betrayed his unit. Italy. Directed by Sergio Garrone.

Fistful of Brains (2008)—Set in the late nineteenth century, a small town in the North Carolina mountains is caught between two warring brothers, each marshaling an army of the undead. The sheriff's daughter, Lily, is the only person who can save the townspeople of Shadow Hawk from the zombies. USA. Directed by Christine Parker.

The Forsaken: Desert Vampires (2001)—A young man discovers that the hitchhiker he picked up is a vampire hunter, and he reluctantly becomes entangled in a hunt for the vampire leader. USA. Directed by J. S. Cardone.

From Dusk Till Dawn (1996)—Two bank robbers and their abductees seek safety in a Mexican saloon filled with vampires. Features George Clooney, Harvey Keitel, and Salma Hayek. USA. Directed by Robert Rodriguez.

From Dusk Till Dawn 2: Texas Blood Money (1999)—As suspected by the sheriff, a bank robber proceeds with another bank heist, which is hampered when members of his gang become vampires. Features Robert Patrick, Bo Hopkins, and Duane Whitaker. USA. Directed by Scott Spiegel.

From Dusk Till Dawn 3: The Hangman's Daughter (1999)—After escaping his hanging in turn-of-the-century Mexico, an outlaw kidnaps the hangman's daughter, who is the vampire princess. Features Marco Leonardi, Michael Parks, and Rebecca Gayheart. USA. Directed by P. J. Pesce.

Gallowwalker (2010)—A gunman lives with a strange curse that causes his victims to come back to life as zombies and to seek retribution. He must kill them a second time. Features Wesley Snipes. USA/UK. Directed by Andrew Goth.

Ghost Rider (2007)—Motorcycle stunt-rider Johnny Blaze, having sold his soul to the devil, battles the forces of darkness with the original Ghost Rider, ex–Texas Ranger Carter Slade (Sam Elliot). Also features Nicolas Cage and Peter Fonda. USA/Australia. Directed by Mark Steven Johnson.

Ghost Riders (1987)—A band of outlaws, hanged for their crimes, come back from the dead seeking revenge on the descendants of those who wronged them. USA. Directed by Alan L. Stewart.

Ghost Town (1988)—A sheriff's deputy traces a kidnapped girl to an abandoned ghost town populated by outlaw spirits. USA. Directed by Richard Governor.

Ghost Town (2009)—A group of teenagers come upon a cursed town filled with the evil spirits of nineteenth-century outlaws. Features Billy Drago and Jessica Rose. USA. Directed by Todor Chapkanov.

Grim Prairie Tales (1990)—Two men exchange "ghost" stories around a campfire on an Indian burial ground. Harkens back to the old anthology films. Features Brad Dourif and James Earl Jones. USA. Directed by Wayne Coe.

Haunted Gold (1932)—John Wayne attempts to claim his share of a gold mine and bring an outlaw to justice, but first he must contend with the phantom that haunts the mine. USA. Directed by Mack V. Wright.

Haunted Ranch (1943)—Heroes and villains alike search for the stolen gold bullion hidden on a ranch. Outlaws pretend to be spirits to keep prying eyes away from the treasure until they can find it. USA. Directed by Robert Emmett Tansey.

Haunted Range (1926)—Silent Western featuring Ken Maynard, who must solve the mystery of Haunted Ranch or lose his inheritance. The haunting is a ruse, but the film provides one of the earliest examples of ghosts on the frontier. USA. Directed by Paul Hurst.

High Plains Drifter (1973)—A gunfighter known as "The Stranger" is hired to protect the people of a small mining town from a group of outlaws. Features Clint Eastwood and Verna Bloom. USA. Directed by Clint Eastwood.

House II: The Second Story (1987)—A sequel to the 1986 film *House*, with an undead Western twist. The new owner of the cursed house hunts for ancient Aztec gold and is plagued by spirits. The characters jump through a portal into the Old West for the film's climax. USA. Directed by Ethan Wiley.

It Came from the West (short) (2007)—Puppet zombies invade the West in this short comedy. A tribe of Native Americans perform the "forbidden rituals" to bring the dead to life in order to stop the "Dark Butcher" who has been abusing them. Denmark. Directed by Tor Fruergaard.

Jesse James Meets Frankenstein's Daughter (1966)—Frankenstein's granddaughter makes her own version of her grandfather's monstrous creation, all the while trying to entice outlaw Jesse James. USA. Directed by William Beaudine.

Jonah Hex (2010)—Based on the DC comic, a disfigured bounty hunter who can communicate with dead spirits is asked by President Grant to stop an ex-Confederate general's plot to cripple the Union. Features Josh Brolin, John Malkovich, and Megan Fox. USA. Directed by Jimmy Haywood.

Land of the Dead (2005)—After the zombie apocalypse, residents of a fortified city struggle to preserve their way of life amid a zombie-filled wilderness. Features Dennis Hopper, Simon Baker, and John Leguizamo. Canada/France/USA. Directed by George A. Romero.

Left for Dead (2007)—An isolated Mexican ghost town is inhabited by spirits, who terrorize a group that stumbles upon them, including a band of female gunslingers. Argentina/USA. Directed by Albert Pyun.

Legend of the Phantom Rider (2002)—A mystifying man comes to set right the evils perpetuated by a corrupt sheriff and his cronies who have taken over a town. Features Denise Crosby and Angus Scrimm. USA. Directed by Alex Erkiletian.

Living Coffin (1959)—A lawman visits a *hacienda* that is haunted by the screaming apparition of a woman whose children died in the nearby swamps, and he investigates the mysterious occurrences. Mexico. Directed by Fernando Méndez.

Near Dark (1987)—A young man from the Midwest gets involved with family of roaming vampires after trying to seduce the daughter and getting bitten by her. He must then protect his family from her predatory instincts. Features Lance Henriksen. USA. Directed by Kathryn Bigelow.

Once Upon a Time in the West (1968)—Epic film about a harmonica-playing mystery man who connects with a renegade to protect a widow against a cold-blooded assassin. All-star cast featuring Henry Fonda, Charles Bronson, and Jack Elam. Italy/USA. Directed by Sergio Leone.

Pale Rider (1985)—In answer to a young girl's prayer, a preacher comes to a small mining community to save the townspeople from a ruthless owner of a mining company and his thugs. Features Clint Eastwood, Michael Moriarty, and Carrie Snodgrass. USA. Directed by Clint Eastwood.

Planet Terror (2007)—Citizens of a small Texas town confront hordes of zombies created by a military bioweapon program gone wrong. Features Rose McGowan, Josh Brolin, and Bruce Willis. USA. Directed by Robert Rodriguez.

Priest (2011)—In a postapocalyptic dystopian West, a warrior-priest's niece is kidnapped by vampires, and he breaks his vows to go after them. A loose remake of John Ford's *The Searchers*. Features Paul Bettany, Christopher Plummer, and Karl Urban. USA. Directed by Scott Charles Stewart.

The Promised Land (2009)—Two brothers and their friend venture out of the city to kill zombies for sport. They must fight for their lives after killing the undead wife and daughter of a madman wanting revenge. USA. Directed by Phillip D. Williams.

Purgatory (1999)—After robbing a bank, an outlaw gang finds itself in the small town of Refuge, whose newly dead residents attempt to mend their ways while awaiting judgment on their eternal fate. Features Eric Roberts, Sam Shepard, and Randy Quaid. USA. Directed by Uli Edel.

Quick and the Undead, The (2006)—After a virus changes most of the world's population into zombies, bounty hunters race to collect government-issued bounties. USA. Directed by Gerald Nott.

Rango (2011)—Rango, a pet chameleon stranded in the desert and needing water, journeys to the town of Dirt, encounters the Spirit of the West, and unexpectedly becomes sheriff. Features the voices of Johnny Depp, Isla Fisher, and Timothy Olyphant. USA. Directed by Gore Verbinski.

Ravenous (1999)—A group of soldiers at Fort Spencer are taken in by tales of great strength and stamina that becoming a cannibal can bring through the spirit of the wendigo. Features Robert Carlyle and Guy Pearce. Czech Republic/UK/USA. Directed by Antonia Bird.

Riders of the Whistling Skull (1937)—The Three Mesquiteers join an archeological expedition searching for the lost golden city of Lukachuke. They encounter an Indian cult and mummies. Features Ray "Crash" Corrigan. USA. Directed by Mack V. Wright.

Shadow of Chikara (1977)—Confederate veterans seek hidden treasure and are followed by a mysterious hunter linked to Native American spirits. Features Joe Don Baker. USA. Directed by Earl Smith.

Stageghost (2000)—A group of stagecoach travelers are besieged by skeletal rider "spirits," but things are not what they seem. Features Christopher Atkins, Dana Barron, and Terry Moore. USA. Directed by Stephen Furst.

Sundown: The Vampire in Retreat (1990)—Vampires inhabit a small Western town and want to be left alone in this vampire comedy. Features David Carradine and Bruce Campbell. USA. Directed by Anthony Hickox.

Undead or Alive: A Zombedy (2007)—A zombie Western comedy about a pair of misfits—one a Union soldier on the run, the other, a broken-hearted cowboy—who must survive a zombie plague with the help of Geronimo's niece. USA. Directed by Glasgow Phillips.

Vampires (1998)—A Vatican-sponsored vampire hunter and his group of slayers battle vampires seeking a holy relic that would enable them to exist in sunlight. Features James Woods, Daniel Baldwin, and Sheryl Lee. USA. Directed by John Carpenter.

Vampires: Los Muertos (2002)—A vampire bounty hunter and his band of slayers join forces with a priest to fight vampires in Mexico intent on invading the United States. The master vampire seeks to hold the ritual that will make her invincible. In-name-only sequel to John Carpenter's *Vampires*. Features Jon Bon Jovi, Natasha Gregson Wagner. USA. Directed by Tommy Lee Wallace.

Voodoo Cowboys (2010)—After Hurricane Katrina unleashes a plague of the undead, three itinerant hoodoo practitioners roam Louisiana, killing zombies and seeking a magical blues song with the power to set things right. USA. Directed by Sean-Michael Argo.

Index

260; improvised, 59, 101–102, 105; knives, 5, 26, 30, 36, 73, 90, 101, 108, 154, 185, 222; pikes, 120; stakes, 99, 101–102, 120–121. *See also* guns

Weathers, Stephen, 84, 94

Weiner, Robert G., xx, 45–90, 283–288

Wendigo spirit, xxii, 182–202, 288

Werner, Byron, 180, 284

West: and American values, xi–xiii, xx, 49, 81, 134, 137–138, 140–142, 169, 173, 182; as American heartland, xi–xii, xv, 71; landscape of, xii, 34, 38, 75–76, 81–82, 86, 97, 117, 163, 178, 193, 198, 207, 209, 216, 218n1, 245, 248–249; as meeting point of civilization and savagery, xi–xiii, xix-xxi, xxiv, 7–8, 16, 20, 25, 43, 68, 91, 137–138, 140, 142, 144–146, 166, 179n1, 189, 207–208, 273–274; mythology of, xvn16, xxvi, 19–20, 25–26, 31n5n8, 65, 69, 78–79, 111n8, 112, 133, 146, 148n18, 178, 197, 256; and national identity, xi–xiii, xxiii, 20, 137, 158, 179n2, 180; passing of, 67, 208; taming of, xii–xiii, xxiv, 5, 22, 42, 59, 97, 193, 198–199, 208

Western (genre): anti-Fordian, 209; classic, xii–xiii, xvii–xxiii, 4, 9–10, 20, 24–25, 30, 67, 81–82–97, 101, 103, 105, 110, 145–146, 168, 170, 178, 193, 248, 254, 261, 263; conventions of, 39, 41–43, 46, 66, 69, 84, 100, 106, 111n13, 112, 116, 123, 126, 133, 136, 169, 183, 207, 209, 221, 255, 262, 273, 276; counterculture, 273–274; "cult-of-the-Indians-Westerns," 274; "Golden Age" of, xii–xiii, 12, 22, 34, 59, 212, 273; and national identity, xi–xiii, xxiii, 20, 137, 158, 179n2, 180; revisionist, xiii, xv, xvii, 4,

15, 22, 24, 34, 49, 77, 97, 104, 110, 168, 173, 177, 254–256, 261–262, 264, 266n9, 267; spaghetti, xxiii, 49, 65, 69, 74–76, 219n9, 272; transformation of, 13, 176, 253; "weird," 167

Western Zombie (film, 2006), xi

Weston, Lucy (character), 39

"What Lies Ahead" (episode of *The Walking Dead*), 86

Whemple, Frank (character), 243

Whitaker, Duane, 103, 285

"White Man's Curse," 177–178

whores. *See* prostitutes

"Why Do Cowboys Wear Hats in the Bath? Style Politics for the Older Man," 69, 78–79

Widmark, Richard, 34

Wiest, Andrew, 284

wiitiko spirit. *See* wendigo spirit

wild, the, xi, xiii, xvi, xix, xxiii, 4–6, 11, 29, 42, 69, 105, 138, 142–143

Wild Bunch, The (1969, film), xiii, 29, 34, 49, 103–104, 110, 111n10

Wild, Wild West (1999, film), 255, 260

Wild, Wild West, The (1965–1969, television series), 10–11. *See also* "Night of the Undead"

Wild West shows, 21

Wilde, Oscar, "don't shoot the piano player" quotation, 5

Wiley, Ethan, 286

Wilkinson, Andrew A., 49

Williams, Hank, 73

Williams, Linda, 40, 44n13, 147n5, 149

Williams, Phillip D., 287

Williamson, Fred, 99

Willis, Bruce, 287

Winchester, Dean (character), 19–20, 23–27, 30

Winchester, John (character), 24

Winchester, Mary (character), 24

About the Contributors

Lindsay Krishna Coleman resides in Melbourne, Australia, where he works as a private tutor and intercultural consultant. In the final stretch of his doctorate he is working on a thesis exploring the influence of Marcel Proust, Henri Bergson, and Joseph Campbell on HBO programming of the past decade. He is currently editing an anthology titled *Storytelling and Sex in Contemporary Cinema: Performance and Cinematic Technique*, which will be released by IB Tauris in 2014. He is also working on a companion anthology that explores the intersection between pornography and philosophy. Coleman will soon have chapters appearing in *Bloodlust and Dust*, an anthology on the HBO series *Carnivale*, and *Doctor Who in Time and Space*, an anthology on the famous British science fiction series. He has also written on the series *24*, *Gilmore Girls*, and *South Park*, and on the documentary film *Born into Brothels* and the mockumentary films *The Magician* and *Man Bites Dog*.

Hugh H. Davis holds a BA in English, University of North Carolina at Chapel Hill, and an MA in English, University of Tennessee. He has served on the residential faculty and as an instructor of English at Saint Mary's School in Raleigh, North Carolina, since 2004. Devoted to the study of popular culture and its use in the classroom, his scholarship is varied, often focusing on movies, television, and other literary adaptations (particularly of Shakespeare). Regularly presenting papers at the annual conference of the Popular Culture Association in the South, he has served on its executive council and is a past president. He has also presented at conferences on film and literature and has published articles in *Studies in Popular Culture*, *Literature/Film Quarterly*, *Journal of American Culture*, *Slayage*, and *Edgar Allan Poe Review*, as well as chapters in *Supernatural Youth* (2011), *Kermit Culture* (2009), *Past Watchful Dragons* (2007), and *Shakespeare into Film* (2002).

Christopher Gonzalez is assistant professor of English at Texas A&M University-Commerce, where he teaches twentieth- and twenty-first-century literatures of the United States. The managing editor of *Philip Roth Studies*, he has recently authored essays on the author Edward P. Jones, the comic artist Jaime Hernandez, and filmmaker Alex Rivera. His research uses cognitive narratology and neuroscience to better understand Latino/a literary and cultural production. His current book project, *Hospitable Imaginations: Contemporary Latino/a Literature and the Creation of a Readership*, traces the arc of Latino/a literature in the United States by investigating the relationship between authorial decisions related to the creation of narrative story worlds and reader expectations that enable or constrain such authorial decisions.

Outi J. Hakola completed her doctoral dissertation, "Rhetoric of Death and Generic Addressing of Viewers in American Living Dead Films," in 2011. Her background is in media studies, but she is also interested in American studies and cultural studies. She is currently working at the Helsinki Collegium for Advanced Studies (University of Helsinki, Finland), where she works at the project on Human Mortality, which discusses death, dying, and mortality in an interdisciplinary network. Her expertise includes Hollywood cinema production, American television studies, genre studies, postclassical narratology, mediated images on death and dying, and theories on art criticism. She is editor-in-chief of the Finnish scholarly publication *Wider Screen*, which concentrates on audiovisual culture. She is also the chair of the Finnish Society for Cinema Studies.

James Hewitson teaches in the department of English at the University of Tennessee. He completed his PhD at the University of Toronto and is currently finishing *Sentimental Apocalypticism: Technology, Hawthorne and the Civil War*, a book-length examination the intersections of sentimental and apocalyptic discourse in nineteenth-century American literature. He has published articles on Jonathan Edwards, Nathaniel Hawthorne, documentary photography and popular film, and his work has appeared in journals such as *ESQ*, *The Nathaniel Hawthorne Review*, and *Interdisciplinary Humanity*, as well as a number of collections.

Susan Hidalgo is an associate librarian and head of Access Services at the Texas Tech University Libraries in Lubbock, Texas. Her department comprises the public services of document delivery, circulation, and stacks maintenance. She works very closely with the Texas Library Association and has been published in the *Journal of Pan-African Studies*. She teaches Introduction to Library Research, a course focusing on teaching today's students how to do research properly and effectively.

Michael J. Klein received his PhD in science and technology studies from Virginia Tech. His dissertation examined the use of science fiction literature and cinema as rhetorical tropes during policy debates on human cloning. Prior to his doctoral work, he received master's degrees in technical and scientific communication from Rensselaer and rhetoric and composition from the University of Arizona. For the past five years he has served as assistant professor of writing, rhetoric, and technical communication at James Madison University. He has taught undergraduate and graduate courses, including scientific rhetoric, medical and science writing, document design, and science fiction literature. His research examines the use of experiential learning in technical communication, the transmission of technical information from expert to lay audiences, and the depiction of science and technology in popular media.

Sue Matheson is an associate professor of humanities at the University College of the North in The Pas in Manitoba—Canada's newest university. Her areas of interest include Western film (with special emphasis on the work of John Ford) and American popular culture. Currently working in the area of frontier narrative, she is the editor of two collections of articles on the subject: *The Fictional North: Ten Discussions of Icons and Stereotypes above the 53rd Parallel* (2012) and *Love in Western Film and Television: Happy Trails and Lonely Hearts* (2013). Fascinated by the subject of Western cultural failure, she also teaches and researches in the areas of indigenous literature, children's literature, and Canadian prairie literature. The founder and a coeditor of *The Quint: An Interdisciplinary Quarterly from the North*, Sue encourages and supports the ongoing conversation of new and established scholars, writers, poets, and visual artists from all disciplines and methodologies.

Rachel E. Page is a graduate student at Texas Tech University working toward her master's degree in mass communications. Her research interests include television, film, and popular culture theory, as well as online user communication and interaction. She has an undergraduate degree in mass communications from Texas Tech and has attended Ursuline Academy of Dallas. She is currently working on a collaborative study focusing on popular culture songs in animated blockbuster films. She has presented at the Southwestern Popular Culture Association (on Dr. Horrible) and is very interested in studying the work of Joss Whedon. She lives in Lubbock with Oscar, her hyperactive Boston terrier.

Fernando Gabriel Pagnoni Berns currently works at Universidad de Buenos Aires (UBA)—Facultad de Filosofía y Letras (Argentina), as graduate teaching assistant of Estética del Cine y Teorías Cinematográficas. He is a member of the research groups Investea (theater) and Kiné (cinema) and has published articles on Argentinian and international cinema and drama in the following publications: *Imagofagia, Cinedocumental, Telondefondo .org, Stichomythia, Ol3media, Anagnórisis-Theatrical Research Magazine*, and *UpStage Journal*. He has published an article in the book *Cine de terror Latinoamericano y Caribeño*, edited by Isla Negra (currently in press).

Thomas Prasch is professor and chair of the Department of History, Washburn University. He served as film review editor for the *American Historical Review* from 1995 to 2004, and since 2001 he has edited a biannual selection of film reviews for *Kansas History*. Recent publications include "Behind the Veil: Forms of Transgression in Ken Russell's *Salome's Last Dance*," in Kevin M. Flanagan, ed., *Ken Russell: Re-Viewing England's Last Mannerist* (2009); "Eating the World: London in 1851" in *Victorian Literature and Culture* 36 (2008); Entries on London 1862, Calcutta 1883–84, and London 1886 in John Findling and Kimberley Pelle, *Encyclopedia of World Fairs and Exhibitions* (2008); and "Mirror Images: John Thomson's Photographs of East Asia," in Douglas Kerr and Julia Kuehn, eds., *Century of Travels in China: Critical Essays on Travel Writing from the 1840s to the 1940s* (2007).

Shelley S. Rees is an associate professor of English at the University of Science and Arts of Oklahoma. She received her PhD in English from University of North Texas, specializing in nineteenth-century British romanticism, with further research interests in popular culture, gender studies, speculative fiction, skepticism, and humanism. She serves as area chair of Literature for the Southwest/Texas Popular and American Culture Society Conference, and cochair of Communications for the Whedon Studies Association. On campus, Dr. Rees serves as faculty sponsor for the USAO Secular Student Alliance, The Guild, and the Science Fiction and Fantasy Club. She lives in Edmond with her husband, Mike; their teenage son; a large, fluffy cat;

a small, frightened cat; and a pseudo-Yorkie named Dash. Dr. Rees hereby thanks her indulgent son, Vaughn, for watching *The Walking Dead* with her and then listening as she babbled about literary theory and *katabasis* and basically took all the fun out of the zombie apocalypse.

Michael C. Reiff has taught media studies at University at Buffalo, film at Oracle Charter School, and currently teaches English at Onondaga Community College. He is also a board member of the Theodore Case Film Festival in Auburn, New York. He is currently engaged in research and writing on graphic novels and sequential art, contemporary Chinese cinema, and genre literature. Michael lives in Auburn, New York, with his wife and his cat, Phineas.

Robert A. Saunders is an associate professor in the department of History, Economics, and Politics at Farmingdale State College-SUNY, where he teaches courses on world religions, international affairs, and global history. He holds a PhD in global affairs from Rutgers University. His research explores the impact of mass media on national identity, geopolitics, and international relations. Dr. Saunders's articles have appeared in *Nationalism and Ethnic Politics*, *Geopolitics*, *Slavic Review*, *Identities*, and *Nations and Nationalism*, as well as other journals. He is an associate editor of the *Globality Studies* journal. His books include *The Many Faces of Sacha Baron Cohen: Politics, Parody, and the Battle over Borat* (2008), *Ethnopolitics in Cyberspace: The Internet, Minority Nationalism, and the Web of Identity* (2010), and the *Historical Dictionary of the Russian Federation* (2010).

Kristi L. Shackelford received her undergraduate degree in English and communications from James Madison University. After working in the publishing industry for five years, she returned to JMU and earned her master of arts in technical and scientific communication. Originally hired to edit the 2002 JMU Reaccreditation Report and university catalogs, she has gone on to participate in the development and editing of a variety of university reports at JMU, as well as overseeing the curriculum and instruction process for the university. She acts as the faculty adviser to *The Bluestone*, JMU's award-winning yearbook, and is also an adjunct faculty member in the school of Writing, Rhetoric and Technical Communication, where she teaches courses including publication management, user documentation, and professional editing.

Matthias Stork is an MA student in the Cinema and Media Studies program at University of California-Los Angeles. He obtained a masters in foreign language education (English and French) at Goethe University, Frankfurt, Germany. His research interests include the synergies between films and video games, the aesthetics of contemporary action films, the portrayal of intercultural conflict in film, and the study and production of video essays as a new form of scholarship and criticism. In 2011, he produced a three-part video essay series titled "Chaos Cinema," examining the drastic stylistic changes in modern action blockbusters. His video essay work can be found on the Indiewire blog *Press Play*.

Hannah Thompson is a graduate student at Texas Tech University's Museum Science program. Fascinated by ancient Egyptian history, she explores ancient Egypt and modern perceptions of it in much of her scholarly work. She has presented at conferences on a range of subjects incorporating ancient Egypt, from eighteenth-century protoarchaeologists to Victorian travel writers to Nazi apologists. She began her graduate studies in the Liberal Studies program at Washburn University, during which time she received an award from the Kansas Association of Historians for a paper on post-Amarna-period iconoclasm. Her current interests include Victorian mummy's curse narratives and their articulation with contemporary events, particularly the Spiritualist movement.

Robert G. Weiner is associate humanities librarian at Texas Tech University, where he serves as the liaison for the College of Visual Arts and for Film Studies. He is the coeditor of *From the Arthouse to the Grindhouse* (2010), *James Bond in World and Popular Culture* (2010), *Cinema Inferno* (2010), and *In the Peanut Gallery with Mystery Science Theater 3000* (2011). His writing has appeared in *The Landscape of the Hollywood Western* (2006), *The Gospel According to Superheroes* (2006), *Gotham City: 14 Miles* (2010), and *Routledge History of the Holocaust* (2011). He is the editor of *Perspectives on the Grateful Dead* (1999), *Captain America and the Struggle of the Superhero* (2009), and *Graphic Novels in Libraries and Archives* (2010). He also serves on the editorial board for the *Journal of Graphic Novels and Comics*. He lives in Lubbock with a group of magical creatures known as prairie dogs.

About the Editors

Cynthia J. Miller is a cultural anthropologist, specializing in popular culture and visual media. Her writing has appeared in a wide range of journals and anthologies across the disciplines, most recently: *Télévision: Le moment expérimental* (in French, 2011); *Science Fiction Film, Television, and Adaptation: Across the Screens* (2011); *Race, Oppression, and the Zombie: Cross-Cultural Appropriations of the Caribbean Tradition* (2011); *The Gothic Imagination: Conversations on Fantasy, Science Fiction, and Horror* (2011); and *Westerns: The Essential Journal of Popular Film and Television Collection* (2012). She is the editor of *Too Bold for the Box Office: The Mockumentary, From Big Screen to Small* (2012), and coeditor, with A. Bowdoin Van Riper, of *Televised "Rocketman" Series of the 1950s and Their Fans: Cadets, Rangers, and Junior Space Men* (2012). Cynthia is also film review editor for the journal *Film & History* and series editor for Scarecrow Press's *Film and History* book series.

A. Bowdoin Van Riper is a historian who specializes in depictions of science and technology in popular culture. His publications include *Science in Popular Culture: A Reference Guide* (2002); *Imagining Flight: Aviation and the Popular Culture* (2003); *Rockets and Missiles: The Life Story of a Technology* (2007); and *A Biographical Encyclopedia of Scientists and Inventors in American*

Film and Television (2011). He was guest editor, with Cynthia J. Miller, of a special two-issue themed volume (Spring/Fall 2010) of *Film & History* ("Images of Science and Technology in Film") and the editor of *Learning from Mickey, Donald, and Walt: Essays on Disney's Edutainment Films* (2011). He is also coeditor, with Cynthia J. Miller, of *Televised "Rocketman" Series of the 1950s and Their Fans: Cadets, Rangers, and Junior Space Men* (2012).